CARING FOR JUSTICE

Caring
FOR
JUSTICE

ROBIN WEST

NEW YORK UNIVERSITY PRESS
New York and London

NEW YORK UNIVERSITY PRESS
New York and London

Library of Congress Cataloging-in-Publication Data
West, Robin, 1954–
Caring for justice / Robin West.
p. cm.
Includes bibliographical references and index.
Contents : Introduction : losing the connections—Caring for
justice—The concept of harm—Law, literature, and feminism—
Invisible victims—Postmodernism, feminism and law.
ISBN 0-8147-9291-X (cloth : acid-free paper)
1. Sociological jurisprudence. 2. Feminist jurisprudence. 3. Law
and literature. 4. Women—Legal status, laws, etc.—United States.
I. Title.
K370.W47   1997   96-51252
340'.115—dc21   CIP

New York University Press books are printed on acid-free paper,
and their binding materials are chosen for strength and durability.

Manufactured in the United States of America
10 9 8 7 6 5 4 3 2 1

For Molly, Nicholas, and Benjamin

Contents

Acknowledgments

Many friends and colleagues have provided comments and criticisms for drafts of these chapters. I would like to thank in particular Robert Green, Carrie Menkel-Meadow, Lynne Henderson, Mark Tushnet, Mari Matsuda, Judith Areen, Sivan Baron, and Milton Regan for their support of the project throughout.

Parts of chapter 1 were published in *St. John's Law Review* (1996) under the title *Justice and Care*. Parts of chapter 3 were published in *Pacific Law Review* under the title *The Literary Lawyer*. Chapter 4 was published in its entirety in *Cardozo Journal of Law and Literature* (1996). A slightly different version of chapter 5 appeared in the 1989 volume of the *Chicago Legal Forum* under the title *Feminism, Critical Social Theory and Law*.

Introduction:
Losing the Connections

Children and their parents, different as they are, share one powerful emotion: they are terrified at the prospect of losing each other. Many of us are, were, or will be parents, and all of us were once children. Throughout our lives, most of us fear the loss of our connections to our parents, and when and if we become parents ourselves we fear even more the loss of our children. Most of us, once we are grown to maturity, fear the loss of other social connections as well: of our husbands and wives, of our lovers and partners, of our extended families, of our various communities. We know, in part from the irreducibility and intensity of this fear, but from other feelings within us as well, that these connections to others and to our social worlds are important, and even central, to our identity. We know as children that they are central to our survival, and we know as adults that they are central to the richness and the meaning of our lives. Connections to others give us pleasure, they give our lives content, direction, and structure, and more than any other experience we share, they inform and constitute our "moral sense." As children our moral codes are conveyed to us within them, so that the content of that code is first determined and later colored by the quality of those connections. As adults, the connections we form with others are a large part—perhaps the overwhelming part—of "what we value," and hence either partly or totally predetermine our moral judgments. The experience of our self, of others, and of the world that emerges from those relational

[1]

connections informs our moral judgments in many—and perhaps all—of the corners of our lives.

As valuable, as pleasurable, as life-sustaining, and as central to our moral lives as most of these connections with others obviously are, however, some of the connections that characterize intimate and private life carry tremendous potential for harm. The connection to the other that is at the core of a traditional, heterosexual marriage, for example, might in most cases be central to moral life in many of the ways suggested above: for each member, learning to care for one's spouse may indeed be the experiential basis for an expansive capacity to care for others. Nevertheless, the connection between the partners in a violent or abusive marital relationship is typically the vehicle not for an enlarged moral capacity, but for profoundly damaging assaults on the abused partner's—usually the wife's—autonomy, sense of self-hood and self-regard, competencies, and privacy, to say nothing of her safety and physical integrity. When it is, such a marriage censors a woman's moral voice, as well as her self-regarding one. The inter-course, both social and sexual, which in a good marriage constitutes so much of the experience of intimacy, can be, in an abusive one, in essence, a rape—dominating and injurious rather than ethical and caring. The "connection" to the other that a bad marriage symbolizes and constructs does indeed give life a moral meaning—but the mean-ing it gives is the deeply immoral one that one's purpose in life is to fulfill the ends of others, and to do so not out of a selfless or altruistic love of service, but from a stark fear of the lethal consequences should one choose otherwise. Obviously, while some of the "connections" that tie us to others are life-affirming, others are invasive and over-powering. They diminish rather than enlarge the individuals who participate in them.

What is the relation of law, of legal institutions, and of public culture more broadly, to these connections with others, both those which enrich their members and those which diminish them? It is one of the more general claims of a good bit of feminist and communi-tarian legal scholarship since the mid-1970s that our legal institutions and common law rules have failed us on both scores: the *good* connec-tions—such as the sustaining and nurturing connections in a healthy parent-child relationship—are not sufficiently protected, and at times are actually threatened, by our public and legal institutions, while the bad connections—the connections with others that are themselves damaging, such as those in abusive marriages—are too often protected. Let me take these two points in order. Of course some threats to our most treasured connections with others are timeless and universal: we can lose the connections to those we hold dear, such as our children, through disease, accidental death, or natural disaster. But that is obviously not true of all of them. Many of the modern threats to our most sustaining connections that we most fear are neither universal nor timeless: they are the culturally specific consequences of particular and contingent political forces, and of legal and not-so-legal destructive powers, *none* of which is necessary—none of which is a part of the natural order of things. Technological innovation constitutes one such threat: our connections to our children and of our children to us are threatened, for example, by the surrogate parental authority of both television and the internet. Politics is another: the connections of poor and single mothers to their children, and of poor children to their mothers, are threatened in the United States today by a social conservative movement against state assistance to such families, in turn fueled by a punitive and racist insistence that such women are not "worthy" of motherhood and that their children would be better served in institutionalized care. The economic culture of the workplace is a third: the connection of professional and working-class women to their children is threatened by a workplace culture that equates working life with individual productivity, views the worker as individuated and disconnected from family, and persistently refuses to reevaluate and redefine the nature of work so as to accommodate the needs of familial life. The connections of the children of professionals and wage earners to their parents, correlatively and more bluntly, are threatened by too much day care and not enough parenting, and a society largely indifferent to that fact. These threats are in turn all underscored by a legal system and a political culture which refuses to provide assistance or even encouragement to parents, and material aid to children in need or crisis.

While contemptuously and dangerously neglectful of the need to sustain and nurture healthy connections between children and their parents, our legal culture is even more adamantly blind and deaf to the serious harms sometimes inflicted within some familial and intimate relationships. A social, legal, and constitutional veil of privacy, for example, continues to "protect" the marital relationship against any real possibility of community intervention on behalf of the safety or well-being of the sometimes abused woman living within that private sovereign sphere. Rape within marriage is criminal in name only, and even then generally to a lesser degree than rape outside marriage. Assaults and batteries in the home continue to go largely unpunished. The criminal statutory rapes that often precede teen pregnancies are for the most part ignored. The pressing economic needs of divorced and widowed women who have lived their lives with and given their uncompensated household and child-raising labor to men on whom they have been completely dependent, go unmet. We have not fashioned ways to protect vulnerable and weak members of damaging marital or intimate relationships from the sadism, dominance, or simple ill-regard of their stronger mates, largely because we have not fathomed the logic of the case for the need to do so.

The failure of our political and legal institutions to *either* protect and nurture the connections that sustain and enlarge us, or to intervene in those private and intimate "connections" that damage and injure us, is reflected in and amplified by—and partly explained by— the ideologies of contemporary intellectual life, both in law and legal studies, and in other disciplines as well. The "connected individual"— whether she be sustained or damaged, enlarged or diminished, by those connections—is simply not the subject of modern political and legal thought any more than she is the subject of political and legal protection. As scores, perhaps hundreds, of critics from a wide range of political perspectives have now argued, mainstream liberal theory, as well as the liberal legalism which is its outgrowth in the legal academy, is premised upon an individual who prides himself on his autonomy and on his self-chosen life projects, including, of course, his voluntary, willful decisions to interact, on a limited basis and toward self-defined ends, with others. It is that profoundly disconnected individual which liberal societies, liberal politics, and liberal ideologies, including legal ones, are designed to protect. Economic legalism—the dominant ideology of the "law and economics movement" quickly claiming the center of American legal thought—simply takes these liberal premises to their logical endpoint, positing as the subject of liberal society an individual in whom every remotely "connected" impulse, whether the product of a damaging acquiescence to power or a genuinely altruistic motive, has been thoroughly reduced to a frankly morbid self-interest, and a society and state the raison d'être of which is the satisfaction of the interests, preferences, wishes, desires, and whims of such atomized individuals. As their feminist, communitarian, and conservative critics have insisted, both intellectual movements unquestionably celebrate in the name of individualism a liberal subject who is at best a sociopathic caricature of the "individual" celebrated by classical liberals: Adam Smith, to take one example, viewed our capacity for sympathetic connection to others as at least as central to our identity as our capacity for the rational pursuit of self-interest, and John Stewart Mill, to take another, clearly understood that the subjection of women in patriarchal marriage utterly undermined their capacity for individualistic subjectivity in a free and capitalist democracy. The individual celebrated by modern liberalism, in stark contrast to the individual observed by the classical liberals, is both liberated from all hierarchic impediments to his freely chosen life projects, and pathologically disconnected from all moral entanglements with others.

It is, however, neither economic nor liberal legalism (associated generally with the political middle and the right), but rather the various ideologies which surround what we might call the "postmodern turn" in the legal academy (and which is generally associated with the political *left*), which constitute the greatest contemporary ideological threat to any conception of selfhood that asserts *either* the moral importance of the self's connections with others, *or* the seriousness of the harms those connections sometimes occasion. The reason is simply this: both economic and liberal legalism, whatever their individualistic faults and excesses, rest on a contingent, tentative, empirically grounded, and therefore *changeable* conception of the individual. The radically individuated and unconnected individual at the heart of their jurisprudential perspective is radically individuated because that is how these theorists see him as being: they are asserting a descriptive and empirical—and hence falsifiable—claim, not a metaphysical or transcendent one. Should that tentative description of human nature turn out to be wrong, there is nothing in either the logic or the politics of economic or liberal legalism that forecloses either from shifting ground. Indeed, at least partly in response to communitarian and feminist critique, prominent liberal legalists (if not economic legalists) are beginning to do precisely that.

The same cannot be said, however, of the purportedly fractured, unstable, disconnected, and inessential self, or lack of self, at the heart of the new postmodern legal scholarship. According to the new postmodernists, not just the individuated and disconnected self of liberalism, but the self however conceived and whatever its connections and attributes, is, quite simply, *inessential: all* its connections, as well as all other attributes it may be thought to possess, are accidental, contingent, or random, and furthermore, they are so *essentially.* This is not an empirical, descriptive, tentative claim about our modern nature, it is a transcendental claim about the nature of nature: that everything is up for grabs is itself, most emphatically, not up for grabs. While the economic individual who has taken such a beating from communitarian and feminist and other critics of liberalism forms or doesn't form connections based on nothing better or worse than a dreary self-interest, the postmodern self so dear to the heart of postmodern theorists is formed and reformed and unformed and disformed through connections either to others or to something or to nothing at all which are either utterly random or politically predetermined, but in any event as changing, unstable, and unpredictable as the wind. Those connections cannot be said to define the self, or nurture the self, or damage or injure the self, for there simply is no sufficiently stable self that could be so defined, nurtured, damaged, or injured: the self connects, disconnects, and reconnects at various points of intersection on a social matrix itself the product of random acts of historical convergence. To repeat, that inessential self is as deeply and utterly essential as could possibly be imagined: it is not a hypothetical description, subject to modification or amendment as new evidence presents itself. It is a metaphysically transcendent truth.

Against the weight of these liberal, economic, and postmodern denials of the connected self, it has been, uniquely, feminism and feminist theory of the past twenty years (since the mid-1970s) that has even made it possible for us to *see* the importance of our connections to our moral lives, as well as the dangers those connections pose to our individual well-being. Thus, during that time, "relational feminists" in a number of disciplines, but most importantly moral psychology and moral philosophy, have focused attention on the possibility that an "ethic of care" embedded in the female labor of attending to intimate relations is a principled moral stance, rather than an affective emotional response, and therefore might express a moral "point of view" of importance in all areas of life, and not just the familial. On the other hand, a sizable number of "radical feminists" over roughly the same time period and again in a number of disci-

[6]

plines, but most importantly in law, have focused on the profound damage some of the connecting relationships in our lives, such as abusive marriages, inflict, and on the perverse refusal of the state to even condemn them, much less try to deter them or compensate the victims when they occur. What this work jointly suggests, minimally, is that the failure of both our legal institutions and our political theory to attend to *either* the moral centrality *or* the potential for harm that are inherent in our connected, relational lives, is all a function of our sorry history of sexist exclusion: we have excluded women's perspectives and voices from our intellectual history, and thus have unsurprisingly failed to account for the ways in which our moral judgments reflect our human connections. And we have excluded women's interests and voices from our political and legal history, and thus have unsurprisingly failed to protect women from the harms they disproportionately suffer within damaging relations of connection. Relational and radical feminisms have attemptedto address and redress both injustices.

This book argues for the importance of both the moral perspective and the potential for harm that inhere in our connecting relationships with others, and more specifically for the importance of both to our public law no less than to our intimate and private lives. Correlatively, it is critical of modern jurisprudence, and modern legal scholarship more generally, for their overall neglect of both the moral potential and the potential for harm embedded in our "connected selves." Throughout the book, I invoke and combine two specific insights of modern feminist theory, each of which was briefly alluded to above. As both are controversial, I will spell them out in some detail here. First, I rely heavily on an important claim, popularized in 1982 by Carol Gilligan in her seminal work *In A Different Voice,* but which has since been made by a number of relational feminists, and from a number of disciplines: that the work, disproportionately done by women, of caring for the relationships that sustain us, is *moral* work, rather than emotional affect, and as such, that that work both rests on and expresses a defensible moral "perspective," or, as it is more often put, a particular *ethic,* usually called an "ethic of care." Second, I rely heavily on—and generally assume rather than argue for—a claim central to the work of most radical feminists: that women, as a group, have been *subordinated* in this culture, rather than simply "discriminated against" by the state. One (but not the only) consequence of

[7]

that subordination, is that *all* women's work, distinctive attributes, experiences, and sensibilities have been undervalued: such attributes, experiences, perspectives, and sensibilities must be, in order to sustain the moral justification for women's lesser status and lesser lives.

If both these insights have some truth to them, as I think they do, then they point toward a powerful critique of contemporary liberal theory as well as of contemporary legal institutions. If, as relational feminists have argued, an ethic of care has at its core a central mandate to care for the relationships that sustain life, and if this ethic both grounds and is expressive of the caregiving work women distinctively perform, and if it is true, as radical feminists urge, that the moral sensibility along with much else that is associated with women's work, will be undervalued simply by virtue of that fact, then it should come as no surprise whatsoever that dominant philosophical theories of morality will give such an ethic short shrift. More to the point for these purposes, it will similarly come as no surprise that such an ethic will not figure into the moral criteria by which we evaluate and then reform existing law, nor will it fit into the calculus by which we create new law or legal regimes, and nor will it figure into the criteria by which we judge the justice of a particular judicial decision.

Similarly, if, as radical feminists have argued, women's interests and ambitions have been undervalued, it should come as no surprise as well that the injuries and harms they distinctively or disproportionately sustain will go unheeded, and that, even in this era of relative formal equality, the legal rights and entitlements women and men equally share are rights and entitlements to be free of harms largely suffered by men. All this, as various relational and radical feminists have argued, constitutes a massive injustice to women. In this book, I hope to assess some heretofore unexplored dimensions of the damage that has been done, not only to women and not even particularly to women, but *to our law, our understanding of the nature of harm and sense of justice,* by these pervasive exclusions of women's interests and moral voice. Correcting those exclusions, I hope to show, might point us toward a better understanding of the fundamental philosophical cornerstones of our law, as well as a better understanding of how we might improve upon it.

Let me quickly summarize the gist of the chapters that follow, and then respond to one type of objection which might be made to the premises that underlie all of them. The first two chapters, the first entitled *Caring for Justice,* and the second *The Concept of Harm,* present the book's core jurisprudential arguments. In the first chapter, I argue for a reconceptualization of both the moral ideal of the "legal justice" which we generally hope and intend that courts will dispense, and for the largely personal or private ideals and virtues associated with what has come to be called an ethic of care. I argue, generally, that if it is true, as relational feminists claim, that the act of caring for others to whom we are connected in some way is central to our moral lives, then our capacity for care should be at the center of our understanding of our public and legal, as well as private and personal, virtues, and specifically that it should be central to the meaning of legal justice. For most of our history, however, our capacity to care has not been regarded as necessary to the capacity to do justice (indeed, it is more typically regarded as antithetical to it) and the result has been a deformation of *both* the private ethic of care *and* the very public ethic of legal justice. Our ideals as well as our practices, of justice have been uncaring, and our ideals as well as practices, of care have been unjust, and the consequence has been a deflation of *both* virtues. Our justice is not just when it is not caring, and care is not caring when it is not just. Again, both are deformed when polarized from the other, and it is a deformation which has proven to be tremendously harmful.

The second chapter, on *The Concept of Harm,* argues that the harms, minimization of which is largely assumed to be in some way the "point" of law, have for most of our history not included the harms suffered distinctively or disproportionately by women, and that most of those harms are inflicted within intimate relationships of close and damaging connection. Although the formal exclusion of women from law's protective domain has ended, law continues to bear the mark of its exclusionary and misogynist past: in this modern era of formal equality women are protected against harm to the same degree and in the same way as men, but the "harms" we are all equally protected from (or compensated for) are, largely, those harms which men suffer. The harms suffered disproportionately or only by women are rarely even acknowledged as such, much less deterred or compensated. Rather, the relation of "law's domain" to those harms is complicated: sometimes, of course, they are recognized, although when they are it is typically begrudgingly, but more often they are ignored, trivialized, legitimated, or even celebrated. The burden of the second chapter is to describe what these harms are, and to illustrate the ways in which law has failed to address them.

The remainder of the book takes up related issues in two subdisciplines within the modern legal academy. In chapters 3 and 4, I examine the "law and literature" movement, again from a feminist perspective, and again with the general goal of attending to the various ways in which the major practitioners of that movement have or have not incorporated these two central insights of modern feminism: to wit, that our connections to others are *both* central to our moral sense *and* potentially harmful in ways ill-heeded by the modern state. In chapter 5, I examine some of the premises of the modern critical legal studies movement, particularly as that movement has come to be defined by the postmodern sensibilities of many of its practitioners. In these chapters I try to show that the two movements in question are wanting—each has failed to come to grips with either the moral significance of our connections to others or the potential for harm that connectedness implies. Both the critical legal studies and the law and literature movements, however, are important to feminism: the concerns, methods, and central insights of all three of these "marginal" movements overlap. My aim in these chapters is in part simply to map out these sometimes complex relations.

To this overall project, of course, a number of objections might be lodged, many of which I discuss in the text. What I want to do in the remainder of this introduction is to highlight one *class* of objection, made more often than not by feminists, and which goes not so much to the thesis of the book as to the two particular feminist claims that underlie it: first, that the work of caregiving is moral work expressive of and premised on a moral ethic of care, and second, that women as a class are culturally and socially subordinated, as well as legally discriminated against. The objection, most frequently raised by feminists, is that both claims unduly essentialize women and women's nature. They both seek to express something generally true of all women and hence of each woman; they seek to give content, both political and moral, to the category "woman," and they try to do so by making universal and timeless claims about a female essence: women, if we combine the claims, are "essentially" caring, and "essentially" subordinated. The attempt to essentialize women's nature in this way, this objection proceeds, is misguided, and for at least four reasons.

First, both claims, if they are understood as "generalities," are simply false, as would be any attempted refinement. Essentially *nothing* true can be said about women's essential nature, whether or not women have one, because the task is just too complicated. The categories thereby created will inevitably be both over- and underinclusive—some men are caring, some women aren't; some men are subordinated, some women aren't—or, put differently, there are simply too many counterexamples to sustain the value of the generality. We might call this the objection from individual liberalism: the very existence of a "group attribute" is belied by the infinite variety and indescribable essence of individuals, and that is true of attributes connected with sex and gender (as well as the attribute *of* sex and gender) no less than attributes connected with other group-defining characteristics, such as race, class, or sexual orientation.

The second reason that either the radical or relational essentializing of women's difference—whether the morally different voice of care, or the politically salient difference of subordination—runs aground is both strategic and theoretic. We might call this second objection the "postmodern objection." Whether or not women "have" these attributes, according to the postmodernist, is an incoherent question—women, like any group, don't essentially "have" either these attributes or any other. Rather, these attributes are "ascribed on" or attributed to women by some contingent intersection of political forces—either for good or ill, and whether benignly or malignantly. That women "have" attributes, in other words, is a *political outcome* of a political struggle, not a fact of nature or even a fact of social life. (That *any* thing has any attribute, it should be emphasized, is similarly a political outcome. There is no distinctive claim being made about women's inessentiality—all things are inessential in just this way.) Consequently, whether women have these attributes should be understood *exclusively* as raising *strategic,* not descriptive, questions. Is it strategically wise to assert, at this time in our history, women's difference or women's subordination? If yes, then we should scream from the rooftops that women are different or subordinated; if not, then we should not. Whether or not women turn out to have these attributes, then, will depend upon the political power of the speaker or group to have its will become not just law but fact.

The answer given, overwhelmingly, by postmodernists is that it is strategically unwise to underscore harmful stereotypes of women's nature, even if the purpose is to valorize, rather than denigrate, those attributes. Again, it is important to emphasize the shift of ground from descriptive truth to political strategy upon which this judgment rests: for postmodernists, the existence of attributes connected with sex or gender is itself the result of a political act, as would be their reinforcement or reshuffling. The only question of relevance, then, is the strategic question of whether reinforcement or reshuffling of those attributes traditionally associated with women's lives will further us toward the desired political goal. Once put this way, the question answers itself. Reflecting their anti-essentialist metaphysics, the desired goal for virtually all postmodern feminists is neither the end of women's subordination nor respect for women's difference, but rather *liberation*—and specifically liberation from the straitjacket of the constraints of essences or stereotypes. Obviously, if the harm is understood to be the constraint of stereotypes, one does not attack such harm by ascribing essences to women's nature. Rather, the way to the promised land of inessentiality is by attacking, not revaluing, the gender and sex polarities.

The third argument behind this sort of objection is to my mind the most pressing, and is most assuredly the most purely political. The argument is simply that to the extent that this argument, as well as relational and radical feminist arguments on which it draws, attends to the subordination of *women as women,* it runs the risk of downplaying, ignoring, or denying the subordination of some women that cannot be so neatly defined, or so cleanly attributed to the subordination of women. Black women, for example, are subordinated in this culture not "as women" but as *black women,* and not "as blacks" but as black *women.* Lesbians are subordinated not just as women or as gays, but as *lesbians: as gay women.* A feminism that does not attend to the multiple, intersectional nature of the subordination of women of color, of lesbians, and of countless others runs the serious risk of underscoring, and feeding, the still rampant and still poisonous unconscious racism and institutional heterosexism that continue to destroy our hopes in this country of interracial civic engagement, or even civic peace. Whatever gains may be had by furthering the shared interests of all women, if *that* is the cost, it may not be worth it: the flame of women's advancement, to switch metaphors, may simply not be worth the candle of progress of racial justice.

The last reason is purely strategic, and might be the most widely shared motivation, among feminists, for the postmodern-feminist alliance. Postmodern and anti-essentialist feminists from all disciplines, but most notably from law, might be worried above all else that an acknowledgment—even a tentative acknowledgment—of the existence of nontrivial biological differences between men and women suggests, among much else, the existence of biological foundations for sexist *attitudes* and misogynist *practices.* And if *that* is granted, then it must also be conceded that such practices are beyond legal and political redress, and that the attitudes are well beyond the powers of rational dissuasion. If the "different" moral voice is rooted in biological differences, then so might be the "differential" inclination toward rape. And if that's the case, then we might as well give up: if nature ordained it, we can hardly change it. Similarly, if the different moral voice, or if women's political subordination, is rooted in biology, then so might be the perception of women's inferiority. Neither behavior nor attitude, if biologically grounded, can be significantly altered.

I will attend to some of these objections at different points in the text, but let me make some preliminary comments here regarding all four, and in reverse order. First, on the imperviousness of biologically caused behavior to social pressure: the fear is misplaced. It simply doesn't follow, from the existence of a biological difference between men and women, that a behavior associated with that difference or attribute is impervious to social or legal pressure. Rather, the existence of a biological root of an undesirable behavior counsels the *need,* indeed the imperative, for legal or social intervention; it hardly counsels the futility of it. Thomas Hobbes, to take an obvious example, clearly believed that natural life was brutal, nasty, and short, but he concluded from that observation *not* that it could never therefore be otherwise, but rather that by constructing a legal leviathan it could quite dramatically and drastically be improved. To the extent that the state fails to protect women against violence, whether or not biologically rooted, many women continue to enjoy, at most, only such nasty, brutal, and short lives. If there are demonstrable biological causes for that brutality, that strengthens rather than weakens the case for state intervention.

Feminists of *all* stripes in recent years have been led to the simple logical error of assuming otherwise: we have all been too quick to assume that if a behavior has a biological root or cause, it is therefore *inevitable:* that the biological actor, mad-dog-style, is beyond the reach not only of moral persuasion but of legal and political control (and that it is therefore, by definition, the job of feminism to disprove any such causal link). Catharine MacKinnon, for example, while recently *defending* herself against the charge of essentialism, cites as examples of the kind of pernicious essentialism from which she wishes to distinguish herself both Susan Brownmiller's early argument that rape has some sociobiological cause, and Simone de Beauvoir's claim that women's reproductive capacities are at the heart of our "otherness" in the male mind.[1] MacKinnon claims, correctly, that these are indeed "essentialist" arguments. She then goes on, however, to fault them because of it, and she does so on the clear and I think clearly mistaken assumption that because Brownmiller and de Beauvoir have identified a biological cause of an undesirable behavior and attitude (respectively), they have for that reason unwittingly conceded that there is no possibility of changing it. But this is surely untenable. Whether or not rape is in part or in whole or not at all grounded in biological urges, it is clearly deterrable behavior. That it has a biological root (if it has one) only makes *more* compelling the case for legal intervention; it hardly obviates it. That we don't have natural wings hasn't prevented us from inventing airplanes; nature being the mother of invention, that lack partly inspired it. Similarly with our moral orientations and beliefs, as well as our political status. We need to think hard, and critically, and openly, about the relationships between our natural and biological needs, our learned and natural capacity for empathy, our familial and parental roles, obligations and instincts, and our politically subordinate role. We can hardly do so by simply ruling out of bounds and by fiat the existence and relevance of the natural world, both around and within us, *in toto.*

Second, on race, essentialism, and intersectionality. The complexity of the intersection of race and sex, raises, in my view, the most challenging set of problems facing feminism, and for this reason: it is surely *true* that race and racism pose nearly intractable problems of social justice, and it is also true that unacknowledged white racism is one of the most, and possibly the most, formidable obstacle toward a racially and economically just and equitable community. It is also true, as scores of black feminists have now shown, that black women are injured and subordinated in this culture in ways that simply *are not shared* by white women or black men. They will *therefore* have experiences of subordination and interests in its eradication that are not reflected in either the theories or practices of organized feminism or the civil rights community, so long as the former is dominated by white women and the latter by black men. It is also true that *because of that omission,* the problems of unacknowledged racism in the white community, and unacknowledged misogyny in the civil rights community, are *exacerbated* rather than alleviated by a feminism or a civil rights movement that centralizes the norms and experiences of white women and black men, respectively. Feminist gains may, of course, and hopefully will, indirectly address and even redress the misogyny in the civil rights community, and civil rights gains may address and even redress the racism within feminism, but the elision within feminism of the experiences and interests of black women, like the elision within the civil rights movement of the experiences of women, entrenches rather than addresses racism and sexism respectively. It is for that reason that black feminists are distrustful of white feminism: it not only fails to address race, it threatens to *worsen* white racism, and hence worsen the lives of African Americans (and others) who bear the brunt of it. It is for that reason that the flame really might consume the candle. The same point can and should be made, of course, with respect to the relation between feminism and the gay rights community.

Again, this is without question the greatest political and theoretical challenge facing feminism—it has also, without question, been the root of the most vital recent scholarship within it. We should be clear, though, that the problem it highlights is *racism,* and specifically white racism, not essentialism. The problem of racism, both within and outside feminism, to borrow from a liberal classic, is "political, not metaphysical." *None* of the many difficulties inherent in the monumental task of addressing the multiple and intersectional nature of the subordination of black women suggest the anti-essentialist conclusion or premise which these difficulties often invoke. It doesn't follow from the complexity, multiplicity, or intersectionality of many women's subordination that any *one* of the intersecting axes on which men or women might be subordinated doesn't *exist.* Less metaphorically, it doesn't follow from the differentiating experiences and interests of black women or lesbian women from white women or heterosexual women, that *all* women don't share some experiences or interests. All women in this society, to take just one example, are vulnerable to rape and to a higher risk of serious injury from domestic violence than are men—this is not rendered *less true* by virtue of the also undeniable fact that black women's experience of rape and domestic violence has been and is different in important ways from white women's experiences, and that their needs regarding it differ as well. Similarly, that women experience the subordinating axis of race differently from men, and experience it differently because of gender and sex, does not imply that African Americans don't exist as a group, or that racism is a figment of everyone's imagination. It is real, and complicated, and more specifically complicated by its intersection, in the lives of some, with subordination based on sex. Similarly, subordination based on sex and gender is real, and immensely complicated by its intersection, in the lives of many, with the often overwhelming damage occasioned by the simple work of trying to live one's life in a racist society that fundamentally denies one's central worth.

Third, on postmodernism. I will devote a chapter to this in the text, but here let me make only the limited suggestion that the seductive postmodern claim that gender roles and attributes bear only an incidental, contingent, or socially constructed connection to sex, and that what we should therefore do is shake things up and "play" with the disconnections so as all the better to shatter the stereotypical pedestal, is a claim of which feminists should be distinctively wary, and for two reasons. First, it consigns feminism to an anti-scientific and anti-naturalist worldview that resembles nothing in the modern academy so much as it resembles the worldview of anti-evolutionary creationists. Whereas creationists view us as divinely created in our modern complexity, with no relation to nature or to our naturalist ancestors down the evolutionary ladder, so postmodern feminists and fellow travelers view us as "societally" created, or constructed, in our modern complexity, with no relation—no metanarrative connection—to a presocial natural history, or indeed to any internal or external natural world. The creationist views us as divinely created and the postmodernist views us as socially constructed, but both deny that we are the product of a natural, evolutionary history of which our social history is but a part. They both accordingly adamantly deny the relevance of our nature—biological as well as otherwise—to our ideals and mores. The postmodernist, no less than the creationist, is constitutively anti-Darwinian, anti-naturalist and anti-scientific. This is a family resemblance that ought to give feminists pause.

Second, the postmodern "playful" dismantling of the connections between sex and gender both rests on, and resembles, the postmodern dismantling of the connection between word and meaning, or signifier and signified. That dismantling, in turn, might be liberating, or it might just be destructive, but what it undoubtedly is, is capitalist. The dismantling of the connection between text and meaning and between author and text reflects among much else the ugly truth that the meaning of words, texts, songs, or documents, whether or not up for grabs in postmodern society, is certainly up for sale. Put differently, the postmodern dismantling of the connections of meaning upon which we must rely to communicate, reflects in part simply the advances of the forces of commodification: we have alienated meaning from texts because we have so thoroughly commodified both texts and meanings, and we have done so smugly aware that by so doing we have dislodged meaning from text and text from author. To take just one example, a recent television commercial for a *luxury car* plays against the background of a fully orchestrated version of the radically anti-materialist ode to simplicity, the Shaker hymnal *Tis A Gift to be Simple.* One version of this series of ads visually presents the Statue of Liberty welcoming, with an attitude of "playful" postmodern reverence, a steamer loaded with luxury car imports rather than poor immigrants. We can rage against this dismantling of the meaning of the Shaker hymn, to say nothing of the symbolic meaning of the Statue of Liberty, but such rage is truly for naught: no *author* did this, an agency did and did it with full playful knowledge of the destruction of meaning and language incidental upon the deconstruction of the representations of simplicity and compassion that had once been, but are no longer, essentially embedded within the Shaker hymnal and the national symbol. Nevertheless, while rage at a commercial may be for naught, that we feel it at all constitutes, or should constitute, a warning. Like the parent's foundational and utterly healthy fear of losing her children, our outrage at these assaults on meaning is premised on an understanding of the importance of connections to our inner lives: in this case, the connection between text and meaning. The disconnecting, dismantling impulse behind the postmodern sensibility, whether directed toward our nature or toward our meanings, is at bottom inhuman. If our postmodern glee at the liberating freedom from the constraints of meaning comes to overwhelm our love of and appreciation for the connections to others which our command of language facilitates, it will surely diminish us.

Lastly, on liberalism and individualism. There is indeed no ironclad correspondence between women and "an orientation toward an ethic of care"—there are caring men and uncaring women—just as there is no ironclad correspondence between the class of "women" and the class of "politically subordinated persons," or even, for that matter, between "women" and "persons subordinated along an axis of sex or gender." Feminine men are also subordinated along gender lines. Nor is there an ironclad correspondence between the class of "men" and the class of "persons oriented toward an ethic of justice," or between "men" and "politically powerful people." Five minutes spent people watching in a city park or any other public space will drive the point home. Of course, no one claims there is such an ironclad correspondence, so the countless admonitions in the critiques of relational feminism to ponder the counterexamples of Margaret Thatcher or Mahatma Gandhi do little but attack a straw person. Whether or not there is some lesser but still interesting correspondence is an exceedingly difficult empirical question on which the jury is still out, and will be out for a good while yet—very likely longer than our lifetimes. How we should come down on this question in the meantime, I think, is a function of two things. First, it is a question of who has the burden of proof. Second, it is a question of pragmatics: should we assume difference or should we not?

My own view on the first question—who should bear the burden— is that Carol Gilligan was right, in her response to critics in 1993,[2] to note that the burden might rightfully belong on the claims of those who assert the "no difference" hypothesis. It truly would be extremely odd, as she argued, if it turned out that the vastly greater amount of child raising and homekeeping, the world over and throughout history, in which women engage—a fact apparently conceded by all—has *no impact whatsoever* on the moral orientations of the two sexes. Similarly it really would be extremely odd if it turned out that our shared experience as infants and children under the protection and tutelage and love of *women*—our shared experiences derived from the fact that we are all *to woman* born—also has *no* differentiating effect or impact on the way the two sexes view relational ethics. It would be odd if it turned out that the experiences of pregnancy and childbirth, shared by the majority of all women everywhere, have no effect, and lend to women's perspectives no unifying and distinguishing threads.

[18]

The null hypothesis, if we are questioning sameness or difference, might more defensibly be identified as the claim of difference, rather than the claim of sameness, in the face of these quite different early experiences of the world.

On the second issue—the pragmatics of asserting difference, and especially a moral difference—it is important to stress that the most oft-cited potential negative effect—that women will be harmed by the apparent "stereotyping" of such claims—albeit real, is not the only negative effect we should be concerned with. There are at least two pragmatic reasons to resist—or at least remain uncommitted toward—the seductive anti-essentialist premise that there are no necessary attributes which women share, and hence no "essence" that can inform either our political strategy or our moral discourse. The first is purely political: if one is concerned about furthering women's well-being, it won't do to deny the existence of women. The second, though, has less to do with the politics of women's equality and more to do with the quality of our public conversations. There is a real danger of cutting off fruitful inquiry if we cut off inquiry into sex and gender differences solely out of worries over stereotyping. If an ethic of care adds an important dimension to political and legal discourse, and it is a dimension that has heretofore been lacking, we should contribute it.

Of course, it might be possible to do this, as at least Joan Tronto would have us do,[3] in a way that disavows any connection to issues of gender: if an ethic of care is something we should contribute, then we should do so whether or not it is an ethic peculiar to women. Obviously, whether or not an ethic of care is closer to the core of women's than men's experience of morality and whether or not it is more closely associated with women's work than men's, is a separate question entirely from the question of whether such an ethic is defensible. It is the premise of this book, of course, that the answer to that second question is yes: an ethic of care is a vital moral perspective that has been undervalued both in moral philosophy and in public political life, and our moral philosophy, our public life, and our politics are all the worse for it. Given that, it is certainly fair to ask—as Tronto does—why connecting such an ethic with a complicated and controversial claim about gender differences is either necessary or wise.

It seems to me that there are two reasons why it might be necessary, whether or not wise. Tronto is surely right that if an ethic of care is a defensible moral perspective, it is so regardless of where it comes from or who harbors it. Nevertheless, if it is defensible, it is so in part because of the importance and value of the experiences that inform it. And if those experiences are largely the experiences of women, then we need to know that: the experiences go to not only the "value" but also the content of the ethic they ground. Second, if an ethic of care has been undervalued, we need to know *why,* if for no other reason than to dispel the presumption that it has been assigned a low value because it is of little value. If it has been undervalued because of the unjustified subordination of the women whose lives it has structured and informed, then it obviously behooves us to know that as well. In short, we can't either understand the content, or evaluate the worth, of an ethic of care if we dissassociate it too radically from the female labor that has given it meaning.

Surely Tronto is right, though, to point us toward universalistic defenses of such an ethic, as well as toward universalistic applications. But this universalizing ambition does not require us to ignore the genesis of the ethic in women's lives. To put it in a nutshell, it might be true that the experiences that inform an ethic of care are largely the caregiving experiences of women, and that such an ethic has been undervalued because of the subordination of women—and it might *also* be true that men as well as women can and should employ such an ethic, and that women no less than men can and should employ an ethic of justice as well. It is the thesis of this book that the two ethics must be regarded as necessary conditions of the other, if either is to be regarded as an even remotely defensible ideal of private and public life, and it is clearly a precondition of such an ambition that all of us are capable of employing both these overly polarized moral voices. But this universalistic ambition—no less than Tronto's defense of the ethic of care—*depends* upon an understanding—not a celebration but also, certainly, not a denial—of the extent to which an ethic of care is animated by women's voices, as well as, it should be noted, women's silences, and women's labor, and women's longings, and women's dreams. We will not understand either what such an ethic means or demands, or why this ethic has been so universally under- valued, without understanding its roots in women's lives. We should not be deterred from examining either the roots of such an ethic, or the critical and reconstructive possibilities inherent in it, by the liberating truth that, whatever has been true of the past, an ethic of care can and should be a part of our shared discourses—not only our discourses for and about the private sphere, and not only our discourses touching on issues of clear pertinence to women—but on all issues, and in all aspects of our shared and public life.

CHAPTER ONE

C Caring for Justice

Among much else, jurisprudence demands an analysis of the aim, or point, or purpose of adjudication.[1] What are judges aiming to do when they decide cases? The traditional answer, of course, is that the point of judging is and ought to be to do justice, and any jurisprudential theory—any theory aiming to supply an analysis of the point of judging—thus immediately demands a theory of legal justice. Contemporary answers as well, although at first blush seemingly to the contrary, typically assume that the point of adjudication is justice, and that the difficult jurisprudential inquiry therefore demands an analysis of the nature of justice. Thus, legal economists argue that judges should aim for efficiency, liberal legalists argue that judges should aim to enforce rights, and legal humanists argue that judges should aim for narrative or aesthetic integrity, to take just three examples. But all these modern jurisprudential accounts are premised on the explicit or implicit assumption that the point of legal justice simply *is* efficiency[2] or enforcement of rights[3] or aesthetic integrity.[4] Therefore, *because* efficiency, rights, or aesthetic integrity is the point of justice it ought to be the point of judging as well. What all these quite different modern jurisprudential approaches share, with each other and with more traditional jurisprudential approaches, is a for the most part *unargued* (and therefore somewhat hidden) assumption that the goal of judging is justice. Where they diverge, and where their arguments begin, is over the nature or theory of legal justice.

In this chapter, I propose to set aside the vexed philosophical question of what legal justice is, and return to the more traditional jurisprudential premise, generally begged by modern theory, and ask whether and to what extent legal justice ought to be the goal, aim, or point of adjudication. I will begin this critical inquiry by first contrasting the virtue of legal justice—which most assuredly is felt by many and perhaps most *judges* to be the point of adjudication—with a seemingly different virtue judges might pursue, but for the most part don't—that of compassion, or care, for the litigants before them. At least since the publication of Carol Gilligan's groundbreaking study, *In a Different Voice,*[5] a sizable number of relational or "difference" feminists from various academic disciplines have argued that we should think of caregiving as an ethical activity, rather than as a strictly emotional—and hence morally arbitrary—response.[6] If they are right to so argue, and I think they are, then it becomes relevant to ask whether judges should feel constrained by an "ethic of care" when deciding the fate of the litigants before them, as they surely do feel constrained by an "ethic of justice." I will ultimately argue that while they for the most part don't, they could and should—and that they should do so for reasons stemming from the demands of an ethic of justice no less than for reasons stemming from the demands of an ethic of care.

My argument will have three major steps. In the first part of this chapter, using what might be called an "imagistic" approach, I will contrast recurrent, and I think deeply familiar, images of legal justice with equally familiar images of care, asking in each case what sorts of qualities the various images suggest are demanded of the purveyor of justice or care. This imagistic approach, I trust, will make clear rather quickly that the virtues of care and justice are typically understood, by traditional theoreticians of justice, by relational feminists themselves, and more generally by our culture, as oppositional, contradictory, or, at best, complementary in a sort of yin/yang fashion: while "justice" is typically associated with universal rules, consistency, reason, rights, the public sphere, and masculine virtues, "care" is typically associated with particularity, context, affect, relationship, the private sphere, and femininity. While the work of judges is replete with evidence of their respect for the constraints of the ethic of justice, they rarely exhibit any sign that they feel constrained by an ethic of care. Indeed, where "care" does make a difference in a case, it is more often associated with a sort of emotionalism or sentimentality—often on the part of the jury—that is assumed to be anathema to the workings of justice, and hence felt to be the work of the judge to ban.[7]

In the second and third parts of this chapter, I will then argue that both the widely held view, at least within the judiciary and presumably much of the public as well, of the "oppositional" relationship between these two virtues, as well as the softer "complementary" relationship espoused by a number of relational feminists, are deeply mistaken: the "ethic of justice" and the "ethic of care" are in fact much more interrelated and interdependent than this widely accepted dualism suggests. Indeed "justice," as it is generally understood, and "care," as it is widely practiced, are each *necessary conditions of the other.* The pursuit of justice, when successful, *must* also be caring, and the activity of caring, when successful, must be mindful of the demands of justice. Put negatively, the zealous pursuit of justice, if neglectful of the ethic of care, will fail not just as a matter of overall virtue, but more specifically, it will fail *as a matter of justice.* Similarly, the pursuit of care, if neglectful of the demands of justice, will turn out to be, in the long run, not very caring. In a phrase, the conclusion for which I will argue is that "justice must be caring if it is to be just, and that caring must be just if it is to be caring."

The relevance of this result to jurisprudence is twofold. First, most obviously, I will argue that *if* adjudication is to be just, then the goal of good judging must be both justice *and* care. Judges should indeed aim for justice when they decide cases. But if they zealously pursue justice *to the exclusion* of the constraints of an ethic of care, they will fail: the results will be not only uncaring, but unjust as well. If this is right, then the most fundamental premise of both traditional and contemporary jurisprudential thought needs to be reexamined. Judges should aim for justice, but if they hope to achieve it, then they must *also* aim for care. An uncaring decision will *for that very reason* be unjust.

But there is a second implication for jurisprudence that may be less obvious than the first, but may also be of greater import. If the basic relation and interconnection between justice and care for which I will argue is correct, then to the extent that we want the public, private, and intimate relationships that collectively compose our social lives to be genuinely caring, they must also be just. Indeed, it is true of *any* relationship—whether intimate, familial, social, or political—that if it is to be genuinely caring, it must be genuinely just. Although *care itself* is only rarely, if ever, regarded as the ethical "point of adjudication," nevertheless, the rules judges articulate quite often have an impact—sometimes a deep and lasting impact—on the quality of our social, intimate, and familial life, and hence on the quality of the relationships of care that make up the substance of our lives. Thus, judges do often aim, in the rules they forge, to create, protect, reinforce, or delimit a social, familial, or intimate "relationship of care," not only in family law, but in many other areas of law as well. If I am correct to claim that a caring relationship must be a just relationship if it is to be genuinely caring, then where judges create such relationships, the relationships of care so protected, created, or delimited must, then, be just if they are to be genuinely caring. Where judges create rules which in turn structure or legitimate relationships of care that are lacking in justice, that judicial act becomes *itself* an unjust— as well as a patently uncaring—act. Some of our most horrendous judicial decisions—decisions easily now recognized as both unjust and uncaring—are so precisely because they fail to respect, in the social relationships they envision, protect, or delimit, the interdependency of these two virtues.

THREE IMAGES OF JUSTICE AND THREE IMAGES OF CARE

It seems quite clear—indeed, it seems incontrovertible—from the language of judges themselves that the virtue of justice operates as a normative constraint upon, and guide to, adjudication. Judges, no less than most legal theoreticians, do seem to regard legal justice as the ethical "point" of adjudication. What, then, is required of judges by legal justice?

In a recent and thoughtful essay on legal education and social justice, Father William J. Byron, a Jesuit priest and president of Catholic University,[8] suggests that legal justice requires of the purveyor of justice three distinct virtues, each of which has been represented in our cultural history by a particular image. Consider first, Father Byron suggests, the biblical image of the *plumb line* as a visual metaphor for justice. Father Byron perceptively comments on this image:

> The philosopher tends to deal with justice as a concept; the prophet treats justice as a command. The nation will be inspected. It will be measured for its uprightness, its integrity. Just as a wall that is "out of plumb" will collapse, so a society that is unjust is going to topple. . . . Do our dealings pass the plumbline test? Are they on the "up and up," or "on the level," or "fair and square?" The plumb bob falls toward the exact center of the earth. The line between hand and bob is therefore "upright," an image of justice.[9]

Second, Father Byron suggests, consider the image of justice employed by Thomas More or the legend of Thomas More, as dramatized in Robert Bolt's play *A Man for All Seasons*.[10] Bolt's Thomas More suggests yet another demand of justice—that justice is a matter of "personal integrity":

> When a man takes an oath, Meg, he's holding his own self in his own hands. Like water. And if he opens his fingers *then*—he needn't hope to find himself again.[11]

After reviewing this image, Father Byron goes on to comment:

> I suggest that the cupped hands image the internalization of the water of justice. By opening the fingers in falsehood or infidelity, something of the self is lost. It is a matter of personal integrity.[12]

Lastly, Father Byron enjoins his readers to consider the trays in balance on a scale, held by a blindfolded judge:

> the "familiar trays in balance on a scale [held by a blindfolded judge] provide us the best image of justice. . . . An imbalance is an injustice when one's side's advantage has been taken at the expense of the other side. . . . If the advantaged down-tray represents a passive benefit derived from an injury inflicted on another—even by impersonal social forces—the question of relatedness must be traced with care. The closer the relatedness, the larger the obligation to work to bring the trays into balance.[13]

Although Father Byron has culled these images of justice from our cultural history toward the end of guiding legal education, there can be no doubt that all three images described by Father Byron guide judges at all levels of decision making, and powerfully, toward the end of justice. First, and most fundamentally, it is hard to think of a case, a court, or a judge that does *not* strive to meet the "plumb-line test"— which we might recharacterize in less visual terms as the test of internal, institutional consistency. Respect for precedent, the virtues associated with the "rule of law," indeed, the Rule of Law itself all seek to assure that judges "aim to" produce justice according to the plumb-line test of institutional consistency. Various versions of the plumb-line test are also extensively elaborated in our constitutional jurisprudence: as I will argue in some detail below, the ideal of consistency—similar treatment of groups similarly situated—under at least one interpretation, is the goal of the equal protection clause of the fourteenth amendment. Consistency is similarly at the heart of Dworkin's famous liberal jurisprudential claim that the essence of judging is the achievement of legal "integrity." [14] In short, the plumb-line test is at the very heart of our concept of legal justice; it is not an unfair recapitulation of a good deal of jurisprudence to simply equate the two.

The plumb-line test is the image of legal justice that motivates much of our criticism of legal doctrine as well. When a case or a line of cases fails the plumb-line test, it invites criticism, and criticism of a certain sort: such cases are not simply unwise, they are fundamentally *unjust.* When we criticize the Supreme Court—or any court—for its failure to administer the death penalty evenhandedly between black and white offenders, or for its failure to administer the protections of the criminal justice system evenhandedly between rich and poor or male and female citizens, we are criticizing it for failing the plumb-line test. Again, the clear implication of such criticism is that these failures are moral failures of justice, not simply failures of policy or lapses in judicial craft. "The Nation *will be* inspected." The plumb-line test is neither rule, nor standard, nor principle. It is, rather, a moral imperative; it is an ethical *command.*

Indeed, it's fair to say that the plumb-line test is so central to our conception of legal justice that glaring examples of judicial failure to meet it become not just examples of "bad cases," but more revealingly, the stuff of folk legend. Twenty-five years ago, Bob Dylan, to take just one example, immortalized in a folk song a Maryland Eastern Shore millionaire named William Zanzinger, who killed a black maid named

Hattie Carrol, "at a Baltimore Hotel society gathering," by hitting her with his cane in a fit of pique. The subject of Dylan's song about the incident, however, was not the grotesqueness of the crime, but rather, the grotesqueness of the *sentence* Zanzinger received—six months' jail time. The real villain of the song was not Zanzinger but the unnamed sentencing judge, as well as the societal acceptance of the outcome. The import of Dylan's treatment of the incident is that while the crime itself was ugly, the *sentence* exposed an even deeper villainy, because it violated the plumb-line test: it evidenced the dual standards of criminal sentencing applied to perpetrators of crimes against black and white victims, and between rich and poor defendants. The crime was horrendous, but the sentence—the measure of the uprightness of the legal system—was *unjust.* Thus, only in the last verse, when Dylan relates the *sentence,* not the crime itself, does he admonish his listeners: "Bury the rag deep in your face/For *now* is the time for your tears."

More recently, in 1994, to cite just one further example of Maryland injustice, a criminal defendant in a Maryland courtroom received a sentence of *eighteen months* in a work release/home detention program for intentionally killing his wife, a full three hours after he discovered her in the act of adultery.[15] The sentencing was accompanied by comments by the sentencing judge revealing his deep sympathy for and identification with the defendant, and the judge's belief that indeed no man, including the judge himself, would be able to walk away from the scene he had encountered without "inflicting corporal punishment."[16] The judge ended his sentencing soliloquy expressing his belief that the defendant before him was not truly a criminal and that he, the judge, was accordingly profoundly reluctant to sentence at all.[17] Like Dylan's reaction to the Zanzinger case, the public outcry that followed this incident was triggered not by the horrific individual crime, but by the judicial failure of the plumb-line test. While the crime was deplored, it was the grotesque lack of consistency in sentencing that rankled the collective sense of injustice, triggering scores of editorials and national television coverage of what would otherwise have been an ordinary case of lethal domestic violence.[18]

The second image Father Byron develops—the idea of justice as "personal integrity," or simply of holding true to one's word—although widely applicable in nonjudicial situations, also clearly moti-

vates judges and constrains their decision making, albeit in a somewhat different way. The oath of office,[19] as well as the judicial code of
ethics,[20] are institutional recognitions that justice demands personal
integrity as well as institutional and national consistency—thus the
"internalization" of the waters of justice, to use Father Byron's apt
phrase. When a judge takes the oath of office, she *vows* to use her
powers to further the ends of law, or to uphold the constitution. The
import of the oath is that by taking it the judge takes on these ends *as
her own* ends; they become, by virtue of the oath, *personal obligations.* When she fails to do so, the result is not only institutional
inconsistency—the failure of the plumb-line test—but a failure of
personal integrity as well; a breaking of the vow; a slippage of the
waters of justice. The fissures to the social fabric caused by such
injustice rarely become the stuff of legend or folk song. They do,
however, in extreme cases, become the stuff of judicial reprimand,
and in extreme instances, of impeachment.

The third image of justice Father Byron employs—the scales of
balance held by a blindfolded judge—is perhaps the image we most
often associate with legal justice, and more generally with the working
of courts. This third image, distinctively, finds expression not only in
the jurisprudential and ethical aspirations of judges, but also in our
substantive private law. The law of torts, and particularly the limiting
doctrine of causation, and the expansive abandonment of the constraint of the requirement of "duty," are directly linked to this notion
of impartial compensatory justice: not *every* imbalance of resources
brought on by a negligent act must be righted, only those where the
causal connection between wrongdoer and victim is clear.[21] But of
those where the causal connection is clear, *all* must be righted, not
only those which also breach an independently established duty.[22]
The ideal judge in a torts case must weigh carefully the "upside
disadvantage" and the "downside advantage," and must judge the
degree of causal connection between the two, but she must be blind
to all other differentiating factors. Indeed, one might plausibly argue
that the animating purpose of almost all our private law (and much of
our public law as well) is to provide remedies for societal relations
that exhibit the causally connected "imbalance of harms and benefits"
which this third image of justice so neatly captures, and to do so in a
rigorously impartial way.[23]

The blindfolded judge must be, as the image reveals, both impartial and universal. She must be blind to the individuating circumstances of the individual litigant *so that she might be attentive to*—focused upon—only the imbalance that stands in need of correction. Another way to put this is that *only* the fact of the imbalance is relevant, and it is relevant universally—every imbalance, causally connected in this way, is unjust, and it is unjust regardless of any other individuating circumstances. She can weigh the imbalance, and correct it, but her judgment that there is indeed an imbalance must not be swayed by other factors, to which she must of necessity be blind.

These three images of legal justice—the plumb line, the cupped hands, and the blindfolded judge holding the scales of justice—are all, then, in different ways, central to the "point" of judging: they all operate as normative constraints on the enterprise. They suggest, respectively, that legal justice demands of judges institutional consistency (Rule of Law virtues and respect for precedent); personal integrity (ethical uprightness), and impartial universality (the unbiased dispensation of compensation for proven wrongs). These values, and the virtue of justice which they collectively compose, are repeatedly echoed in the language and self-reflections of judges on the aim, or point, of judging. They also each find elaborate explication in theoretical writings on the nature of justice and the task of judging.[24]

These images are not only "central" to our understanding of the requirements of justice, if our practice is any guide they are also "archimedian." We employ these images or images of this sort when we wish to criticize not just particular decisions, but entire nations, empires, and eras. Furthermore, we use them when we are trying to convey both an imperative for change and an ethical urgency: "The Nation *will be* inspected"; these are the wrongs that *must* be righted. For all these reasons, I think it is fair to say that these three images— the plumb line, the cupped hands, the blindfolded judge and the scales of justice, as well as the values of consistency, integrity, and impartiality that they represent—do indeed constitute foundational elements of what James Boyd White calls our "legal imagination."[25]

Let me now contrast these images of justice with images of care. These images, I think, should also be deeply familiar, but decidedly not from philosophical, judicial, or literary ruminations on the nature of justice or the task of judging. Rather, these images, I suggest, reflect our sense of the demands of an ethic of care in the private, nonjudicial, familial, or intimate boundaries of private relational living. At least at first blush, they contrast, and sharply, with the images of justice delineated above.

First, think of the familiar image of the mother's protective and nurturant embrace of the newborn—the Madonna, if you wish. Her posture is curved, not upright. To nurture and protect, she makes of herself an "O," not a plumb line. As the tree provides shade not with its erect trunk but with its gracefully curved branches, the mother provides care, protection, warmth, comfort, and love through the interwoven, interdependent strength of the circle of care, not through the independent linearity of the erect, principled, morally upright pillar of strength.

Second, and in jarring contrast to the image of More holding the waters of justice in his cupped hands, consider this powerful image of caring, which comes from a recent news photograph: a Catholic Sister weeping over the beautiful but limp bodies of six little boys—toddlers—lined up side by side on the ground, and all killed, inexplicably, in war. The Sister is reaching out to them, her long fingers extended, spread wide. Her hands are not cupped but open, and her tears are not "internalized," but are spilling out freely. She is quite literally giving herself to these weak ones. She does not "cup" her hands, or her tears, or her self. In the act of caring, whatever may be the case of the act of justice, she neither holds herself in nor her tears back. The waters of care, one might say, unlike the waters of justice, flow freely.

The third image of care I want to consider comes from the movie *Aliens*—the second of the *Aliens* trilogy.[26] The scene to which I refer comes at the very end, after the aliens have been bested, the good fight finally won, and Sigourney Weaver, as commander and hero, is in the spaceship returning to earth, only one of two survivors. The second survivor is a small child. In this last scene, the camera focuses in on the two of them, exhausted from battle but finally at peace—first on the child, prematurely aged by the brutality of the battle, but finally able to sleep peacefully during the ride back to earth. The camera then turns to Sigourney, whom we expect to see similarly asleep. Instead, in a surprising sequence, we see that although she is lying down she is wide awake. Her wide opened eyes are focused intently on the sleeping child. She will not shift her gaze. She will protect this child, and fiercely, until she reaches safety. She will not allow this child to leave her sight. She is anything but blindfolded— again, she refuses to even shut her eyes. She is anything but impartial.

[31]

She is focused, absolutely, on the child. She is not only not impartial, she is committed, without reservation, to the child's side.

As I said, these images of care—the round, circular embrace, the flowing tears of compassion, and the focused, protective gaze—do indeed appear to be oppositional to the images of justice, to the plumb line, the cupped hands, and the blindfold. The qualities they seemingly demand of caregivers—that the caregiver be nurturant, like the mother, and that she be compassionate, like the Sister, and that she be committed to those in her charge, like the protectress—are not only *different from* but are seemingly incompatible with the consistency, integrity, and universality or impartiality demanded of the conveyor of justice. Given this apparent polarity, it is not surprising that we do not typically associate these images of *care* with the work of judges, or the virtue of justice with the pursuit of care. We do not typically demand of our judges that they be nurturant, or compassionate, or committed; nor do we typically demand of caregivers that they be impartial, universal, consistent, or possessed of integrity. For whatever the reason, and by whatever route, we have for most of our history come to see justice and care as incompatible opposites: while justice has been typically viewed as simply irrelevant to the work of caregiving, the work of caregiving has been viewed as not only "out of place" in the pursuit of justice, but as incompatible with justice and with the pursuit of justice: as peculiarly feminine impulses that must be squelched if the work of justice is to proceed.

In literature, this oppositional relation between justice and care is perhaps best articulated by Captain Vere, the central character, advocate, and acting judge in Melville's masterful study of the nature of justice, *Billy Budd, Sailor.* [27] In the pivotal scene of that novella, Captain Vere gives a lengthy statement to his drumhead court on the nature of the justice which it is their duty to dispense. The case before them concerns the striking of a superior officer by the morally innocent, but in Vere's view technically guilty, Billy Budd.[28] In the course of advocating the need for the harshest penalty—death by hanging, with no possibility of appeal—Vere argues quite explicitly that all compassion must be banished, that, in essence, the ethic of justice precludes all considerations that might follow from the ethic of care:

> Our vowed responsibility is in this: That however pitilessly that law may
> operate in any instances, we nevertheless adhere to it and administer

it. . . . But the exceptional in the matter moves the hearts within you. Even so too is mine moved. But let not warm hearts betray heads that should be cool. Ashore in a criminal case, will an upright judge allow himself off the bench to be waylaid by some tender kinswoman of the accused seeking to touch him with her tearful plea? Well, the heart here, sometimes the feminine in man, is as that piteous woman, and hard though it be, she must here be ruled out.[29]

Vere's comments received an eerie echo in Justice Rehnquist's complaint from his days as a clerk, that in death penalty litigation the overly cautious approach of his colleagues on the then-liberal Court, and their relative unwillingness to permit executions to go forward, reminded him of the mutterings of "old women." [30] As Joan Howarth has wryly noted, it is clear from the context that Rehnquist was not complimenting his colleagues for their mature and compassionate wisdom.[31] The readiness with which we all recognize Rehnquist's comment as biting, sarcastic criticism is simply the measure of the degree to which we have culturally internalized Vere's dictum: compassion is antithetical to good judging; the "feminine in man . . . must here be ruled out."

As is by now fairly well known, since the late 1970s relational feminists from a number of academic disciplines have mounted a significant challenge to this culturally accepted hierarchical relationship of justice and care. Although their emphases and methods obviously differ considerably, reflecting their different disciplines, what they share is simply the conviction that care, no less than justice, is a moral activity, reflective of ethical qualities, and should be so understood, rather than a purely emotional response and hence outside the realm of moral reasoning.[32] In a moment I will argue that this claim—which I will sometimes refer to as the "minimalist" relational-feminist claim—is "too minimal," that it does not go far enough. Caregiving is not simply "another" moral activity, or indicative of another moral virtue, but rather, caregiving and the dispensation of justice are mutually dependent activities. Before so arguing, however, let me quickly note how profoundly revolutionary even the "minimalist" relational-feminist claim—that caregiving is moral work, and not just emotional affect—is. If even this minimal claim is right, then the repercussions for both academic thought and political life are truly paradigm shifting.

First, if the dispensation of care, no less than the dispensation of justice, is moral activity, then the most fundamental assumptions in a number of disciplines, from moral psychology to moral philosophy, economics, and political theory, must be rethought. To insist as much has been the common labor of a good deal of relational-feminist thought across a range of disciplines. Within the confines of developmental moral psychology, as Carol Gilligan has argued, we must rethink and reconstruct, if not abandon, the Kohlbergian claim that principled, deductive, or simply reasoned moral decision making represents the pinnacle of moral maturity.[33] Caregiving, in important ways, is not, even in idealized fashion, principled, deductive, or reasoned, and if it is moral work, then the Kohlbergian conception of moral maturity must be significantly refashioned. In moral philosophy, as Virginia Held,[34] Martha Nussbaum,[35] Annette Baier[36] and a number of others have now argued, we must rethink or abandon the Kantian claim that reason, rather than "affect" or "inclination" is the linchpin of moral action.[37] Caregiving is importantly tied to affect and inclination, and again, if that activity is moral activity, then the Kantian distinction between principled morality and sentient inclination must be reexamined. In economics, as Julie Nelson[38] and others have recently argued, we must rethink or abandon the axiomatic microeconomic claim that a moral actor cannot "compare interpersonal utilities" —meaning, in jargon-free language, that such actors are incapable of empathically assessing the relative intensities of pains inflicted upon persons by particular actions.[39] Caregiving draws upon our ability to do precisely that. In political theory we must rethink or abandon the axiomatic claim that the sphere of public morality must be ruled by the dictates of impartiality and generality[40]—caregiving, as I shall argue subsequently, is importantly partial and particular. *All* these suppositions, most of them relatively axiomatic to their discipline, must be reexamined, and either substantially reconstituted or discarded, if the feminist reclamation of *care* as a moral activity is justified. The basic relational-feminist claim that caregiving is moral work, if taken seriously, should occasion a broad-based reexamination of virtually every field of humanistic inquiry, including the very notion of the "humanities" itself.

Second, the implications for political life and practice should be equally momentous. If caregiving is moral work, there is no reason to restrict its domain to family life. If the caring response *is* the moral response, then our public life and public decision making should obviously be caring as well. By the same token, if we regard the caregiving in the home as moral work rather than as simply the end result of an affective and irrational bond, then there is also no reason not to accord domestic caregiving equal standing *as work* with other forms of work—the giving of care in the home should be appreciated and compensated as a valuable form of labor. Any number of political practices, from the devaluation of housework and child care, to the quite general privatization of the practice of raising children, to the disdain in public life for "caregiving" services from housework to social work to even health care, should be revealed as premised on false assumptions, injurious not just to the women most directly hurt but to the political life of the community as a whole. Relational feminists in public life, paralleling the work done by relational feminists in academic life, have labored to transform our political structures to achieve a world in which the moral dimensions of caregiving are reflected in our political and economic lives and choices. All that labor is at bottom justified by the straightforward claim that caregiving is a practice with a moral point, purpose, and focus, and not simply an affect, inclination, or irrational bond, with no meaningful connection to our moral lives.

It *also* follows from the minimalist relational-feminist claim, however, that all this could be accomplished *without touching* the work of judges, for the simple reason that care, even as understood by relational feminists as moral activity rather than an emotional disposition, is nevertheless understood as moral work quite different from that of the work of justice. Thus, even the valorization of the voice of care at the heart of much of this feminist work leaves the *oppositional* nature of these two virtues intact, and it is that oppositional quality which I want to address and call into question here. Care is understood by relational feminists as a moral activity rather than an emotional disposition, but it is nevertheless understood as moral work quite different from the work of justice. Indeed much of the academic feminist work premised on the claim that the caring voice is a moral voice insists upon this point: the ethic of care is for the most part *contrasted* with the ethic of justice in Gilligan's early work;[41] it is even more starkly contrasted with masculine conceptions of justice in Nel Noddings's influential study, *Caring,*[42] and in Sara Ruddick's equally influential study on maternal ethics.[43] A good bit of the feminist work in both philosophy and moral and educational psychology that followed these early works continues in the same tradition.[44]

To a considerable degree, the insistence in feminist writing that care and justice are oppositional virtues is simply an accurate recapitulation of the theoretical and political reality noted above: the vast majority of our traditional, canonical theoreticians of justice have sharply separated care and justice, and our public life and law reflect the same polarity. The difference, of course, in the feminist analysis, is that care is given equal standing: to Gilligan, Nodding, and others, care must be understood as a moral act or quality, albeit different from the act or quality of justice. As noted above, this is quite a difference indeed. But nevertheless, the *contrast* between justice and care is as central to the feminist valorization of care as it is to the traditionalist's persistent denigration.

I want to endorse—wholeheartedly—the relational-feminist valorization of the ethic of care, and at the same time argue against the continuation of the traditional segregation of these two virtues on which much of this work is premised. In this limited sense, my argument will be as much with relational feminists as with traditionalists. Before proceeding, however, let me mention a related and more commonly heard critique of the relational-feminist project, simply to distinguish it from my own, decidedly more friendly, criticism.

A number of liberal, radical, and postmodern feminists (and some nonfeminists) have noted the critical point made here, to wit, that the cultural feminist valorization of the ethic of care leaves us with a moral world in which care and justice, although no longer viewed hierarchically, are instead viewed as complementary checks on each other, albeit checks originating from different spheres: one public and one private; one masculine, one feminine; one governing the relations of citizens, the other governing the relations of friends or intimates. They then go on, however, to make the *political,* or strategic, objection that the political *benefits* of this valorization, for women, will be minimal, and indeed may be outweighed by the costs. The work women perform, even if acknowledged as morally significant, will continue to be undercompensated and undervalued as it remains exclusively or predominantly female. Furthermore, the valorization of the ethic of care runs the risk of further stereotyping women as the "caring sex," and the attendant political risk of continuing the "gilded cage" phenomenon.[45] In essence, the critics claim, all the injurious consequences, and particularly for women, of the traditional opposition between these two virtues will remain, even assuming that the hierarchy traditionally established between them vanishes. The identification of caring with a stereotypical conception of women's work, the critics complain, will be underscored, not challenged, by the valorization of care. The "kinswoman" disdainfully dismissed by Vere as irrelevant to the proceedings of justice would no longer be excluded so rudely. Rather, her sentimentality would be recharacterized, and better understood, as moral engagement. But she would still be excluded from the proceedings. And her exclusion would still carry with it the mark of her political subordination, even if not her moral inferiority.

I think this objection to the relational-feminist project—which, again, has come for the most part from other feminists—albeit an important one, is misguided. Rather, *if the relational-feminist project is successful,* the societal valuation of care as moral work which would follow the philosophical and political work summarized above, would have real-world consequences that would help alleviate, rather than aggravate, women's subordination. If we, societally, truly valued caring work, that value would be *evidenced* in a wide array of social and political transformations, ranging from reforms in family law, social security law, and employment law, to more "macro" changes in the structures of family, wage labor, and market life. Should those transformations occur, it really wouldn't be as important as it seems to be now whether or not women are more "naturally" suited for these tasks. If there were not such a heavy economic and social penalty attached to their performance, presumably both women and men would be more inclined to engage in them. But more importantly, if we "valued" care the way we value justice, we would value, and compensate, to say nothing of ritualistically "honoring," the work of mothering equally with the work of judging. If we did so, it would matter less than it does now whether women or men tended to do the bulk of the mothering work.

Whether that's right or not, however, I want to call attention to a different problem with the "minimalist" relational-feminist claim. The objection I want to raise is that the posited relationship—disentangled but equal, a relationship, so to speak, of mutual respect—*isn't right*. It leaves us with an impoverished account of both justice and care. Thus, the widespread tendency to segregate these virtues, whether accompanied by the feminist insistence that we valorize care or not, is wrongheaded. The quality of justice we *aim* to dispense, to say nothing of the quality of justice actually dispensed, has suffered from the traditional distinction between justice and care, and the quality of caregiving has suffered as well. Consistency, integrity, and impartiality, although necessary to good judging, are not in the end sufficient to ensure it: without more, they will ensure neither public virtue nor good judging. Rather, the zealous and tunnel-visioned pursuit of these qualities, albeit in the name of justice, will result in a perversion of that virtue more often than in its fulfillment. By the same token when caregivers neglect the demand of justice, the care they give is in the end not very caring. Care is a necessary component of justice, and justice is a necessary component of care.

The interconnected relationship between care and justice for which I want to argue can perhaps best be represented by a Venn diagram. If we imagine the *pursuit* of justice, and the *pursuit* of care, as circles, then the traditional account places the circle of justice hierarchically "over," and perhaps obliterating and at best overshadowing, the circle of care. The relational-feminist account places the circles on an equal, nonhierarchical level, but still, generally, not touching each other. Imagine instead that the circles of care and justice are *overlapping*— not concentric, not independent, and not hierarchically positioned, but overlapping. My contention is that *only in the area of overlap* will one find *either* true justice *or* true care. Another way to put it is simply that each is a necessary condition of the other. In the nonoverlapping areas of the circles, one finds, respectively, only a self-righteous smugness where one would hope to find justice, and a tribal or animalistic partiality where one would hope to find care.

The next two sections argue for this result indirectly, by critically examining the nonoverlapping areas of each circle. Thus, I will first examine the quality of justice when unconstrained by an ethic of care, and then the quality of caregiving when unconstrained by justice. In the conclusion I will very summarily describe what a reconstructed and integrated theory of "caring justice" and "just caring" might require.

<font />[38]

The Uncaring Pursuit of Justice

The plumb line, the cupped hands, and the scales of justice, I have suggested, are apt visual metaphors for, respectively, consistency, personal integrity, and impartiality—all of which are undoubtedly central components of legal justice. But what are consistency, integrity, and impartiality without care? What is the worth of the quest for legal justice when it is untempered by the constraints of an ethic of care?

Let me break down the inquiry even further, by questioning each opposition imagistically suggested above individually: personal integrity *versus* compassion, consistency *versus* nurturance, and impartiality *versus* particular commitment. First, what is the value of personal integrity—the cupped hands holding the internalized waters of justice—when unaccompanied by the virtue of compassion—the overflowing "milk of kindness," or the tears and outstretched hands alluded to above?

INTEGRITY WITHOUT COMPASSION

A dramatic, and telling, example of integrity untempered by natural compassion in the nonjudicial sphere is related in an early biography of Mahatma Gandhi, entitled *The Life of Mahatma Gandhi.* [46] In that work, we learn that the private Gandhi, no less than the public Gandhi, was above all else a *just* man in precisely the sense meant by Thomas More: Gandhi took vows—the internalization of justice in the cupped hands of selfhood—and he took them deadly seriously. Indeed, eerily echoing the pivotal event in Thomas More's life, Gandhi once brought himself to the brink of death rather than drink cow's milk, which he had vowed never to ingest. In doing so, like More, he steeled himself against the pleading of his wife, the mother of his children, to not sacrifice himself, and by extension the family who depended upon him, for the sake of the vow. Gandhi viewed this challenge as a conflict between his personal integrity—evidenced through fidelity to the vow—and the earthly, contingent pull of familial compassion.[47] Like More's, Gandhi's moral duty, in his mind, went clearly to the former; the latter, at best, was a mere distraction.[48]

In the same biography we also learn that this privately as well as publicly upright man never warmed to his own sons, eventually explicitly refusing them assistance with the costs of their graduate education.[49] His biographer concludes that this indifference was not simply neglect, but was calculated: Gandhi was morally drawn to other young men who had shown signs of greater moral courage than his own sons had ever exhibited. Because they compared unfavorably, Gandhi denied them not only their graduate education, but more fundamentally, their father's affectionate *presence*. [50] He did so, according to his own statements, not only without shame or guilt, but because his own sense of moral duty demanded it of him. Like Thomas More, and echoing Abraham's willingness to sacrifice Isaac, if need be, to prove his fidelity to his God, Gandhi insisted that if moral duty so required, then the merely sentient pull of family loyalty must give way—must even be obliterated. For all three, any conflict between moral obligation and the pull of the flesh—whether one's own, one's wife's, or one's sons—must be resolved in favor of the former whatever the costs to family.

Although this story can be told, and has been told by Gandhi's biographers, as sympathetically as the bare facts might permit, nevertheless, and even if our admiration of the public Gandhi remains undiminished, Gandhi's cold, reserved distance from his own family seems morally repugnant. And it seems repugnant not only because it was lacking in compassion, which of course it was, but also because— *by virtue of the lack of compassion it reveals*—it seems to be fundamentally immoral. Indeed, it's fair to say that it seems immoral precisely *because* it lacked compassion. To deny one's sympathetic inclination to nurture one's own young, and to do it *solely* because of a personal ethical commitment, does not seem to be the essence of a heroic commitment to personal integrity. Precisely because the pull of compassion is so resolutely denied, it seems quite the contrary.

There is, of course, a distinguished lineage of argument urging a relationship between moral integrity and felt compassion directly opposite to that urged here. Gandhi's dilemma is hardly confined to the intricacies of Hindu theology. In spite of numerous critiques to the contrary, it is still something of a mainstay of Western moral philosophy that personal integrity—the individual pursuit of moral obligation—is only evidence of moral worth precisely when it is *not* motivated by care, or sentiment, or sympathy, or compassion, or most broadly perhaps, by inclination, but rather, when it is motivated exclusively by *duty*. As the political and moral philosopher Wai Chee Dimock reminds us in her book on justice,[51]

> [In] obsessively repetitive pages in the *Groundwork of the Metaphysics of Morals*, Kant insists, over and over again, that "the highest and unconditioned good can alone be found" in those instances when one acts "not from inclination, but from duty." Kant concedes that there might be those who actually "take delight in the contentment of others as their own work," but, "an action of this kind, however right and however amiable it may be, has still no genuinely moral worth." Indeed, for him, the only genuinely moral person, is someone who does good not because he likes to, but because he dislikes it, someone who is
>
>> cold in temperament and indifferent to the sufferings of others— perhaps because, being endowed with the special gift of patience and robust endurance in his own sufferings, he assumed the like in others or even demanded it. . . . It is precisely in this that the worth of character begins to show—a moral worth and beyond all comparison the highest—namely, that he does good, not from inclination, but from duty.
>
> Kant's moral agent, then, confronts a world he does not love, but which, for just that reason, he is bent on fulfilling his duty toward. To the extent that Kant remains the central figure in Western moral and political philosophy, the language of justice is thus centrally premised on the opposition between "duty" and "inclination": the former acquiring the status of ethical sufficiency, the latter suffering the fate of ethical dismissibility.[52]

One does not need to look hard in our case law to find echoes of this Kantian, Gandhian distinction between duty and inclination. Indeed, it is precisely because of the depth and breadth of the commitment, in the legal imagination, to the proposition that the judge's vow to uphold the law precludes, or bars, personal compassion that an explicit *expression* of compassion in the course of a judicial opinion sounds so dramatic, so out of character, so injudicious, and to many legal readers, no doubt so off-putting: think of Justice Blackmun's "Poor Joshua!" exclamation in *DeShaney*.[53] Similarly, it is only because of the depth, and breadth, of our commitment to the Kantian distinction that it could, with only whispers of dissent, become a *part of our fundamental, constitutional* law that the nature of the juror's personal vow to do justice in a death penalty case is such that a state might constitutionally *preclude,* or forbid, an instruction inviting the juror to sympathetically or compassionately engage the defendant's life story.[54] The insistence that the juror's obligation to do justice is fundamentally inconsistent with her potential for compassionately understanding the capital defendant's circumstances rests, at root, on the Kantian distinction, still central, albeit increasingly discredited in moral philosophy, between affect and reason, between sympathy and justice, between inclination and duty.

The distinction has also affected, and profoundly, our substantive private law. To take just one example of what is a fairly constant staple of legal thought, Holmes's famous argument against strict liability, which surely continues to influence as well as resonate with modern sensibilities, echoes the Kantian distinction. Not only is it unwise, for policy reasons, to seek to compensate every suffering victim for any and all mishaps through the simple expediency of picking the deep pocket, but, Holmes argues, of even greater consequence—*it would be unjust* (and this from a man who chastised lawyers for invoking the ethereal concept of justice in legal argument).[55] One can hear in Holmes's words the Kantian (or George Willian) disdain for those who confuse compassion for suffering with justice and the true dictates of duty:

> The state might conceivably make itself a mutual insurance company against accidents, and distribute the burden of its citizens' mishaps among all its members. There might be a pension for paralytics, and state aid for those who suffered in person or estate from tempest or wild beasts. As between individuals it might adopt the mutual insurance principle pro tanto, and divide damages when both were in fault, as in the rusticum judicium of the admirality, or it might throw all loss upon the actor irrespective of fault. The state does none of these things, however, and the prevailing view is that its cumbrous and expensive machinery ought not to be set in motion unless some clear benefit is to be derived from disturbing the status quo. State interference is an evil, where it cannot be shown to be a good. Universal insurance, if desired, can be better and more cheaply accomplished by private enterprise. The undertaking to redistribute losses simply on the ground that they resulted from the defendant's act would not only be open to these objections, but . . . *to the still graver one of offending the sense of justice. Unless my act is of a nature to threaten others, unless under the circumstances a prudent man would have foreseen the possibility of harm, it is no more justifiable to make me indemnify my neighbor against the consequences, than to make me do the same thing if I*

had fallen upon him in a fit, or to compel me to insure him against lightning. [56]

What should we make of this noncaring, duty-bound man of justice? What to make, ultimately, of the modern Supreme Court's insistence that the moral juror, when judging whether or not to impose the death penalty, might constitutionally be instructed that she must specifically *not* sympathetically engage the life story of the defendant before her, because to do so would be emotional, hence not rational, hence not just? What to make of Holmes's clear assumption—and his equally clear assumption that it is one widely shared—that it would be a sure sign of character weakness were one to confuse compassion with either sound policy or justice, even to the point that one might think that the man struck by lightning, simply by virtue of his suffering, deserves some communitarian compensatory response? Of what moral worth *is* this conception of personal integrity—whether the juror's or the judge's—when it is so radically divorced from compassion, from our inclination to care, or from our sympathetic ability to take comfort in the comfort of others and to suffer with them their pains?

Whatever may be the assessment of Western moral philosophy, Western literature has been almost relentlessly harsh on this Kantian man of duty, to put it lightly. When not downright villainous, he is an object of caricature, ridicule, or contempt. Indeed, one can quite readily find scores, probably hundreds, of examples, drawn from canonical literature, of the moral pitfalls of this anti-sentient, Kantian pursuit of justice. What I want to emphasize here is that in much of this narrative literature, if not all, the moral failing exhibited by the a-little-too-upright "man of justice" is not only a failure of care, it is also a failure of *justice*. More precisely, like the story about Gandhi noted above, what a good deal of this narrative literature tells us is that *because* the man of justice steels himself so steadfastly against the pull of natural compassion, the justice he achieves is cramped, often dishonest, fundamentally false, and oftentimes lethal.

The clearest example, in canonical literature, may be the Melville novella already referenced: Melville's Captain Vere, by steadfastly and at least arguably pathologically silencing, in both himself and in his jurors, any compassionate "sentiment" for the morally innocent Budd, winds up dictating what was not only an uncaring but also a fundamentally unjust sentence of death.[57] Because he silenced compassion, Vere misread the law: the law did not require, as he claimed it did, a nonappealable, immediate sentence of death for a provoked and unpremeditated striking of a superior officer. The law was, in point of fact, far more generous and forgiving than the upright Vere was inclined to be. Because he misread the law, he broke his vow to apply it, and he accordingly convicted unjustly.[58] Because he was, quite literally, *obsessed* with the need to banish compassion—to obliterate the "feminine in man," as he put it—he acted unjustly; perhaps more unjustly than any legal figure in canonical literature to date.

I will return to Vere, and some of his real-world counterparts, in a moment. Before leaving literature, however, it's first worth noting that nonlegalistic narratives make the point even more starkly: whether or not it perverts our reading of *law,* when we root out natural compassion *in order to do the right thing,* the result is not only uncaring, but unjust. One of the most haunting examples from American literature of this more general lesson can be found in Flannery O'Connor's story, "The Lame Shall Enter First."[59] In that story, the reader learns of a Southern minister, who, following the death of his wife, takes into his own home, out of an overdeveloped sense of moral duty, a young, troubled, delinquent adolescent boy. The minister then becomes so absorbed in the moral reconstruction of this youth's character that he neglects to notice that his own son has become dangerously depressed with unresolved mourning over the death of his mother. The delinquent adolescent, living in the household, is not so oblivious, and eventually manages to manipulate and twist the son's grief, ultimately causing the young boy's suicide. The son's suicide plunges the father—the moral and religious man of duty—into still-uncomprehending despair. O'Connor surely has one thing right. That is that the *story* of this man of duty who resisted the pull of sentient feeling, as exalted by Kant—whatever may be true of the theory of justice or morality which he represents—is too often a tragic one. And it is tragic, in short, because this man of duty failed not only to act compassionately, but because he breached his highest duty of filial loyalty to his own son. And because he breached that natural duty, grounded not in a vow but in connection, he acted unjustly, albeit toward the end of justice.

For a less tragic rendition, one need look no further in American literature than *Huckleberry Finn.* [60] When confronted with the question from the slavehunter, "Is your man white or black?" and hence with the duty of turning in the escaped slave Jim, whom he has befriended, Huck responds:

> I didn't answer up prompt. I tried to, but the words wouldn't come. I tried, for a second or two, to brace up and out with it, but I warn't man enough—hadn't the spunk of a rabbit. I see I was weakening; so I just give up trying, an up and says—
> "He's white."
>
> They went off, and I got aboard the raft, feeling bad and low, because I knowed very well I had done wrong, and I see it warn't no use for me to try to learn to do right; a body that don't get *started* right when he's little, ain't got no show—when the pinch comes there ain't nothing to back him up and keep him to his work, and so he gets beat. Then I thought a minute and says to myself, hold on,—s'pose you'd a done right and give Jim up; would you felt better than what you do now? No, says I, I'd feel bad—I'd feel just the same way I do now. Well, then, says I, what's the use you learning to do right, when it's troublesome to do right and ain't no trouble to do wrong, and the wages is just the same? I was stuck. I couldn't answer that. So I reckoned I wouldn't bother no more about it, but after this always do whichever come handiest at the time. [61]

As is obvious to every teenage reader of *Finn* over the last hundred years, Finn chooses friendship, compassion, and even the guide of sentient experience over his own perception of the requirements of principle, duty, and moral dictate. As such, he nicely exemplifies the actor, scorned by Kant, who does the right thing for no better reason than that he "finds contentment" in the contentment of others, and whose act, for that very reason, has no "genuine moral worth." Huck, as well as the reader, knows all this. Huck, in fact, would agree with Kant's assessment of his act.

But surely, the *reader* would not. The reader, if not Finn, knows that Finn has in fact acted not just compassionately, but justly as well. It's just not right, whatever Finn's (or Kant's) beliefs to the contrary, to say that Finn chooses compassion, with sentient experience as his guide, *over* the dictates of justice. Rather, Finn chooses compassionately, and *for that reason,* chooses justice over injustice. The reader of *Finn,* contra Kant and contra Finn himself, sees intuitively and quickly not only who is compassionate and who is not, but also who is just and who is unjust in this passage. What Finn teaches is the *in*justice—not the justice—of divorcing the pursuit of justice from natural inclination, from the sentient, felt bonds of friendship, and from the moral dictates incident to the pull of fellow feeling.[62]

Let me return to law, and the judicial vow to apply it. Does the judicial vow to apply the law preclude—or does it require—the exercise of compassion? Must we root out compassion to achieve legal justice, or by so doing do we risk Vere's error: an uncaring *and wrong* understanding of the law, and hence an unjust, rather than just, result? The *argument* for the conventional view—that whatever might have been true for Finn or for Vere in real life, these virtues must be disentangled—is easy enough to see. What judges are supposed to aim for is legal justice, and legal justice is in turn the *result* of ascertaining, and then fairly and accurately applying, the law. The vow to apply the law, to put the same point differently, requires that the judge fairly and accurately ascertain it, and to do so requires a state of mental clarity unclouded by emotion or affect. Compassion must be ruled out to ascertain and apply the law. Only when a judge does so can he or she achieve legal justice. Whether the law itself is good, bad, just, unjust, wise, or foolish, of course, is another question entirely, but it is not the judge's question, and regardless, the quality of the legal justice the judge dispenses is in no way affected by the quality of the law applied.

Imaginative literature, as suggested above, gives us reason to doubt this argument. Of perhaps greater import here, however, is that history does so as well, or at least the work of a number of modern legal historians suggests as much. Some of the most searing moments of judicial and legal complicity in monumental acts of injustice are precisely those moments during which judges rooted out their instincts for compassion, so as to be all the more faithful to their duty to accurately apply "the law." Let me cite three modern examples. First, in his important and eloquent new study on the French bar and judiciary during the Vichy era in Nazi-dominated France,[63] Richard Weisberg argues convincingly that French constitutional lawyers and judges, otherwise legally creative, morally serious, and inventive people, but operating under an anti-Semitic hermeneutic, consistently "interpreted" both the French Constitution and the anti-Jewish race laws in a way that was *unnecessarily* brutal: both the Constitution and the anti-Jewish laws themselves would have been susceptible to liberal interpretations that could have resulted in either the total voidance of the latter as unconstitutional, or a far more constricted reach than they were in fact given. Instead, the bar and bench read the Constitution in an unduly cramped and literal way, while *at the same time* reading the race laws themselves in an unduly broad and overreaching way. The result was all too clear: first the harassment, then the persecution, the exclusion, and ultimately the annihilation of thousands of Jewish French citizens. The result of this ruling out of compassion so as to give effect to what Weisberg identifies as an "anti-Semitic" hermeneutic of legal interpretation was not just hateful, but obviously unjust.

Closer to home, Robert Cover, in his famous treatment of the judicial treatment of the Fugitive Slave Act, shows that even liberal judges harboring abolitionist political sentiments prior to the Civil War, read the Fugitive Slave Act—again unnecessarily—in such a way as to vindicate the rights of slaveholders, and in so doing were either willfully or unintentionally blind to possible interpretations which would have been far more generous and liberating.[64] Less momentously, John Noonan showed in 1976, in *Persons and Masks of the Law*, that Judge Cardozo likewise willfully or unintentionally blinded himself to more generous, and hence more just, interpretations of law, both in *Palsgraf* and in less famous cases.[65]

There are, no doubt, profound differences between these three examples of judicial injustice: according to Weisberg, the Vichy judges and lawyers were or felt themselves to be constrained in their interpretive choices by an anti-Semitic hermeneutic of interpretation. According to Cover, the abolitionist judges were or felt themselves to be constrained by a prevailing positivist ethic of judicial responsibility. And according to Noonan, Cardozo was constrained by the felt imperative to don a mask of impartiality, thus distancing himself from the plight of the litigants before him. But all three share one striking feature. In all three cases, the judges in question "rooted out compassion" in order to apply the law, and in all three cases, the result was an at least arguable misinterpretation, or misapplication, of law, and an inarguable miscarriage of justice. What we might negatively infer from these exemplars of injustice is that the conventional understanding, cited above, of the relation between felt compassion, justice, and the duty to obey law—to wit, that legal justice is the *result* of the

[47]

correct application of the law, which in turn requires a silencing of the voice of compassion—is badly and tragically mistaken. Justice is not the *result* of the accurate application of law, the ascertainment of which requires the censoring of compassion. Rather, justice must *inform* our ascertainment, and hence our application of law: to determine what the law is, we must *exercise* our capacity for and sense of justice. And the capacity for justice we must exercise, if we are to ascertain and apply the law well, must in turn be informed by our capacity for compassion. At least that is the overwhelming lesson, not only of our canonical literary classics but of our modern legal history as well.

It may well be the case, of course, that some thoroughly unjust laws permit of no just or compassionate interpretation, and when that occurs, the just and compassionate judge is most assuredly faced with a crisis of professional responsibility. But it is also striking how very many instances of glaring injustice are not of that sort: how often the injustice could have and should have been avoided through a better, more sensitive, and in a word more compassionate reading of the applicable law. In those instances, at least, which may be more numerous than conventionally believed, legal justice is not achieved by rooting out compassion; quite the contrary. Rather, they are examples of injustice which are unjust precisely *because* they were uncaring. They are examples of the vow to uphold the law being broken, not honored, at the moment compassion was rooted out. Again, what these examples show is that at least oftentimes the traditional or conventional formulation of these virtues is simply wrong: legal justice is not the result of a fair application of law, which has in turn been ascertained through a rigorously rational mental process from which the compassionate impulse has been rooted out. That is a recipe for injustice, not justice. To avoid injustice, the sense of justice must inform the attempt to ascertain the law, and the sense of justice in turn must be informed by—not segregated from—our capacity to compassionately care for others.

If that is right, then it follows that Justice Blackmun was quite right, in *DeShaney,* to implicitly insist, in his dissent, that the just outcome in that case must be grounded in a compassionate response to Joshua's plight. Just as surely, it follows that the modern Court is quite wrong, as a matter of justice, no less than as a matter of compas-

sion, to insist that the juror's personal moral obligation in death
penalty cases is to render decisions untouched by sympathy for the
defendant's life circumstance.[66] The Court's failure in *DeShaney*, like
the Court's insistence that the just juror can constitutionally be instructed to shed her inclination to sympathize in order to fulfill her
duty to do justice, results in a failure of justice, albeit in the pursuit of
justice, for precisely the reason so readily intuited by Huck and his
young readers: justice, divorced from compassion, is lethal. To return
to, and mix, Father Byron's metaphors, the "cupped hands" that hold
back the self who is constrained by a vow, do nothing but isolate us in
sociopathic self-delusion, where the content of the vow, as well as its
application, is not informed by our involvement and engagement in
the processes and values of life. Similarly, on an institutional level,
the "plumb line" of justice is the flat, horizontal line of death when
divorced from the compassion that otherwise animates it.

The work of doing legal justice—of remaining true to a judicial
oath, of applying the law, of treating like cases alike, of insisting on
institutional consistency, and so on—must be in the service of values
which are life-affirming, if the result is to be justice, and a just society
worthy of the name. Justice ought to be an interactive human value,
and an ideal of human communities. If so, it can no more be analogized to a cup holding and isolating each of our upright selves from
others than to a geometric relation between points in space, or to an
arithmetic relation between weights on a scale. The rigorously consistent application of laws, or rules, that do *not* themselves aim toward
the affirmance of life will result in injustice. The unbending application of the slave codes of the prewar South, of South African apartheid
laws, or the "race laws" of midcentury Germany, were strikingly unjust acts, made all the more so by the fact that they were not necessary: generous interpretation, informed by a compassionate and inclusive sense of the human community, rather than a cramped and
hateful hermeneutic, could have pointed the judge toward a fair but
radically more generous understanding. Because of that, these were
not unsavory acts necessitated by the vow to do legal justice—they
were acts which themselves violated the vow. They were not uncaring
deeds required by duty; they were themselves a breach of duty. They
were not otherwise just applications of bad law which happened to be
lacking in compassion. They were interpretations and applications of

law which, because uninformed by compassion, resulted in injustice. The judicial vow, and the virtue of integrity which it serves, were compromised, not upheld in these judicial acts.

More generally, the ethical mandate to "apply the law," like the precedential mandate to "treat likes alike," both of which are, in some sense, the essence of "pure" legal justice, are morally sterile as well as conceptually empty commands. To know which case is like which and what law is to be applied, one must *exercise* a sense of justice, and the sense of justice so exercised must itself be one which is respectful of life. To do justice in a manner which is life-affirming is to require of the judge that she distinguish "like cases," and ascertain the law, and then uphold her oath to apply it by attending to the life-affirming characteristics of the human situation. And to do that is to require her to develop a "feel" for the living, moving, changing, ever-trans-formative essence of a biological and spiritual *process.* In order to do that well, she must act, and judge, compassionately. When we shut off compassion, we do it badly, and when we do it badly, the result is not only a set of rigid, unbending, mindlessly consistent, sterile, and life-less legal results, but it is injustice as well.

IMPARTIALITY WITHOUT RELATIONSHIP

What of the second opposition suggested above—that between unbi-ased universality, or impartiality, and a highly partial, committed sensitivity to contextualized relations? What should we make of the judge's claim that the virtue of justice lies in his judicious balance, his impartiality, his impulse for universality, when those qualities are untempered by the particularizing gaze of the discriminating protec-tor? Put imagistically, I want to question the value of the blindfold when worn by the unbiased judge holding the scales of justice. What do we lose when we don the blindfold to take up the scales of justice?

Here again, the legal imagination is so unequivocally committed to the virtue of the blindfold that it is hard to discern any dissident tradition.[67] But once again, literature has not been so uncritical of the excesses that can be committed in the name of the virtue of impartial-ity, when untempered by the partiality of loyalty, friendship, and relational bonds. To take one example from among many possible ones, an early story by Kurt Vonnegut entitled "All the King's Horses"[68] gives us a nightmarish vision of impartiality, admittedly under nonadjudicative conditions that no judge will ever have to face. But the story is nevertheless instructive. Vonnegut's protagonist finds himself and a party in his charge on the proverbial desert island in the clutches of a mad tyrant, who insists on a chess game in which the chessmen are the live persons in our hero's party. Each captured chess piece is then killed, and the hero is given to understand that should he lose, all his players, including himself, will be killed as well. He suddenly sees a move that will win him the game—but it requires sacrificing a knight who happens to be his son. If he does not make this move, he sees with equal clarity that he will lose, and all, including his son of course, will die. The reader suffers with the hero, who finally drags himself to the tortuously reluctant conclusion that he must sacrifice his son to save the lives of the remainder. His wife, who is one of the chessmen, also sees the move and the logic of it, and eventually sees as well her husband's intention to go through with the sacrifice. She yells at him not to do it and throws herself protectively on her boy. Eventually, they all somehow escape.

What is missing from the chess player's decision? Why does it seem so repugnant; why does the wife's intervention in the story seem to have greater moral worth than her husband's decision, which would, of course, have saved lives? Unlike Abraham's decision to sacrifice a son for the sake of a higher command, or Gandhi's or O'Connor's fictional minister's neglect of their sons for the sake of a higher moral principle, the chess player's decision cannot be faulted on the simple, anti-Kantian ground that it lacks compassion; that he has fetishized duty over fellow feeling. The chess player's decision, again, would have *saved* lives, and his son would clearly have died in any event, given the situation as he understood it. But all four decision makers do have something in common and that is their zealous and misplaced insistence on impartiality: their refusal to see and respond to the *particular* situation and relationship they find themselves in; the particular claims upon them *as parents* to heed the needs and lives of their own children; to distinguish and prioritize the claims of those to whom they are bound by parental obligation; to honor those claims above conflicting commands of God, or claims of utility, or of consistency, or of duty, or of personal integrity; to honor those claims, in short, above the impartial pursuit of justice.

I think one can see the chess player's dilemma played out again and again in the act of judging. And I think we can rightly fault the pursuit of impartiality and universality when it is untempered by a judicial recognition of the particular claims of the particular litigants on the court's legal and moral imagination and resources, just as we can rightly fault the pursuit of utility by the chess player, of personal integrity by Gandhi, or loyalty to God in O'Connor's minister, when that pursuit is untempered by a recognition of the particularizing claims of their children. The judge is not, of course, in a relationship with litigants that even approaches the emotional and moral complexity and depth of a parent's connection to her children. But nevertheless, there are shared characteristics. The judge is in a relationship—a judicial rather than parental relationship, but a relationship nonetheless—with *these* litigants, not with the "public" at large, and not even with the class of similarly situated individuals the litigant may in some ways resemble, just as a parent is in a relationship with her children, not with children at large. Particular litigants come before a particular judge seeking justice which only this judge can grant, given the existence of the relationship between them, just as particular children present their parents with particular needs which only their parents can fulfill, given the existence of their relationship. A judge who decides issues affecting the litigants before her, no less than a parent deciding issues affecting her children, as though such a relationship did not exist surely exhibits a breach of the ethic of care. For that very reason, however, such a judge or parent also breaches an ethic of justice.

Let me give just a few examples. First, let me reexamine in this light two doctrinally related cases from the legal canon familiar to every first year contracts student: *Hawkins v. McGee*[69] and *Peevyhouse v. Garland Coal and Mining Co.*[70] In *Hawkins v. McGee*, a patient sued his doctor for what the Court eventually characterized as a breach of promise: the doctor had promised to rid the patient of an unsightly and somewhat uncomfortable scar on his hand. Instead the doctor's botched surgery had made the scar significantly worse, the hand more painful, and the injury considerably more disabling as well. In a much quoted segment of the opinion, the Court decided to treat the conflict between the parties as a breach of promise—and hence a contracts case—rather than a case of personal injury—and hence a torts case. The shift from tort to contract had a direct impact on the rule of damages applied: the Court insisted upon a "warranty-based" rule of damages—the standard rule in a contract action—requesting the jury to subtract from the "value of the promise" the value of what was delivered, rather than an "injury-based" rule of damages—the standard in a tort case—which would have required the fact finder to more simply compensate the patient for the injury sustained.

The importance of the case to historians (as well as to law students) goes well beyond the shift in damages rules, however. *Hawkins* signaled a change in cultural and legal consciousness, away from a social world constituted of particular relationships—and therefore a social world legally governed by tort law—to one constituted instead of commodities and warranties—and therefore a social world governed legally by contract law. In the course of clarifying the relevant rule of damages, the Court famously analogized the injured hand to a broken machine part, and the doctor's liability for the breach of his promise that he would repair the hand to a seller's breach of warranty regarding a machine. The point of the analogy, as the Court made clear, was to facilitate the use of a quite general commodity-based rather than a fact-specific injury-based rule of damages. In the course of effecting that shift, the Court quite willfully "blinded" itself to precisely the aspect of the particular litigant—that he was an injured boy, not a broken machine part—to which most readers as well as most courts at the time would have been most attentive. And precisely because it did so, the case is a landmark in the radical expansion of contract law, and the legitimation of the impulse toward commodification and market behavior upon which it rests.

Peevyhouse v. Garland Coal and Mining Co.,[71] decided in 1962, represents the same impulse toward commodification and contract. In *Peevyhouse,* a farmer sued a strip mining company for the damage he sustained when the company refused to honor its promise to restore the stripped land to its original state. Refusal to do so left the land useless and the farmer without a livelihood. As in *Hawkins,* the defendant admitted liability, and the only issue for the Court to decide was how to measure the damage. The farmer requested a rule of damages that would compensate him for the full extent of his injury— his lost livelihood, in effect—and the company asked for a rule that would simply look to the difference in market value between the land in its original state—as farmland—and in its postcontract state. That difference, of course, was minimal. The Court embraced the rule requested by the company, and assessed the injury done the farmer by the wrongful mining of his farmland by the diminution thereby effected in the farm's market value rather than by the devastation of human lives.

As in *Hawkins,* the Court chose the market-based rule, in part toward the end of articulating a general, market-based rule of damages which could be implemented without reference to the particular specifics of the farmer's injury. Again, the Court blinded itself to that aspect of the litigant's situation—that this injury resulted in personal ruination, not just diminution of market value—to which most readers, and most courts of the time, would have been most attentive. And again, because it did so, this case in retrospect is an important part of the rise to prominence of twentieth-century contract law: it pointed courts in the direction of contract, and further legitimated both the impulse to commodify an injury—in this case, the impulse to equate the injury to a person's livelihood with the difference in market value between what was promised and what was delivered—and the valorization of prudent market behavior underlying that commodification.

Both cases, then, solidified the role of legally enforceable contracts in our economy, and both stabilized the rules of law governing their breach. Both are often heralded as foundational contract cases for that very reason. But both cases also strike large numbers of readers—even today—as fundamentally unjust, and even bizarre misapplications of contract doctrine. Why? In both cases, one might argue, the judge sought to commodify what perhaps should not be commodified—personal injuries in the first case, a way of life in the second—and this no doubt accounts for some of the unease. There may, though, be another (and related) reason these cases strike so many readers as unjust, and that is that in both cases the deciding judge sought to "universalize"—to don the blindfold, and ignore individuating circumstances—in a particularly objectionable and inappropriate way. Indeed, the universalizing impulse revealed in these cases seems, at least to some readers, to be their Achilles' heel rather than their strength.

In both *Hawkins* and *Peevyhouse,* the outcome of the case represented not only an undue enthusiasm for commodifying injuries, but also an unduly enthusiastic refusal to acknowledge the particular, human *relationship* between court and litigant. It is one thing to note the similarities between a doctor's promised performance to a patient, and a seller's warranty of quality to a buyer of machine parts. It is quite another thing, however, for a judge to tell a particular litigant who appears before him that his lifelong disfigurement and handicap are in essence most like a faulty machine part, and should be evaluated as such. Similarly, it is one thing to note that the damage done to a farm—and hence a livelihood—ruined by wrongful strip mining might be reflected in the difference in market value of the property before and after the wrongful act. It is another thing entirely, though, for a judge to face the ruined farmer and reduce the damage done to livelihood, family, peace of mind, and security by virtue of that ruination to such a measure. In both cases, the latter is not just an instance of inappropriate commodification. It is also, and perhaps more fundamentally, a failure of a relational ethic of care.

Thus, in both cases, the judge has treated the litigant as, essentially, a "stand-in," or representative, of a large class of cases—contractors injured monetarily by the nonperformance of their cocontractors. In terms of the virtue of justice, we might then applaud each judge for donning the blindfold. Each judge, blindfold fashion, refused to consider any circumstances but the extent of the monetary imbalance caused by the breaching party. But interestingly, even for many modern readers, the nagging doubt remains that in each case the judge wrongly overgeneralized, and *because he did so,* the result was not only an uncaring but also an unjust decision. The judge in each case essentially compared apples and oranges—treated unlikes as though they were likes—and thus breached the ethic of justice no less than the ethic of care. Both judges refused to acknowledge the nature of the claims made upon them by virtue of the particular circumstances of the litigant before them—circumstances of which they should have been aware. By ignoring particularity, both judges breached the ethic of care incident to the judge-litigant relationship thereby created, but they also, by virtue of the same willful blindness, breached the ethic of justice. The impulse toward universality, generality, and impartiality—no less than the market commodification of the injury—in those two cases, at least to many readers, frustrates rather than furthers the pursuit of justice.

One sees the same urge toward impartiality—and the same danger of injustice—in contract cases brought by would-be contract-parents for strict performance of surrogacy contracts breached by the biological, or surrogate mother, who, after bearing and giving birth to the baby, seeks to avoid performance of her contractual obligation.[72] When a biological mother seeks to void a surrogacy contract she has entered, so that she might keep the baby she has carried and borne, she will typically find herself urging a court to either strike the contract in its entirety, on the grounds that the contract is contrary to "social policy," or alternatively, to "read into" the contract an implied term allowing her a "grace period" within which to change her mind and keep the baby (thus rendering such contracts comparable to adoptions), or lastly, perhaps, limiting the contractual parents to the standard remedy of money damages—requiring her to pay damages but allowing her to keep the baby. *Whichever* strategy she employs, it is central to her claim to establish the *uniqueness* of the damage that would be done to her were her baby taken from her. For the judge to strike the contract in its entirety, typically on the legal ground that such a contract is contrary to "social policy," the judge must first find that the damage done this sort of contract breacher by the imposition of any judicial remedy for the breach is simply weightier than the damage done other sorts of breaching parties, and that partly for that reason, it is unjust to enforce such contracts. Similarly, for the court to imply a grace period, it must first find that the potential damage done the breaching party is sufficiently weighty and distinctive that such paternalistic "rewriting" of the contract is called for. To limit the nonbreaching would-be adoptive parents to monetary damages also requires a finding that the damage done the biological mother by requiring strict performance is of greater magnitude than the damage that would be done the nonbreachers by limiting their remedy to a monetary sum. To resolve this issue properly is unquestionably a tall order—it requires the judge to attend, empathically, to the wrenching pain of litigants before her who unquestionably have diametrically conflicting needs.

It is also a decision, however, and an empathic process, which a number of judges simply refuse to undertake, and they do so, as often as not, by adopting the metaphoric blindfold and analogizing the plight of the biological mother to that of "any" contractor who discovers after contract formation that performance will be more expensive and hence less profitable than initially contemplated.[73] These decisions can be criticized on any number of grounds, not the least of which is that they are fundamentally uncaring and oblivious to the particular context in which the promise in question was made and breached. My point here, however, is that again, precisely *because* they are so oblivious to context, they are *therefore* fundamentally unjust, as well as uncaring. The particular, distinguishing sort of anguish experienced by a later-regretful surrogate mother is an obvious distinction, and one of obvious legal relevance, between her situation and that of other breaching defendants who find their circumstances changed after the formation of a contract. Ignoring that distinction leads to a *mis*application—not an application—of basic contract law. The law does not *require* that a breaching surrogate mother be treated "like any other breaching contractor." As noted above, a judge could hold the breaching mother to the contract by requiring her to pay damages (on the assumption that the adoptive parents can be "made whole" if awarded enough money to begin the process anew with a new surrogate), could void the entire contract as contrary to public policy, or could read into the contract a mandatory term permitting the mother to change her mind within a short period following the birth. Any of these three solutions would be supportable under the law. To resolve the conflict over whether the contract should be struck, an implied term read in, or the nonbreaching party limited to monetary damages or granted specific performance the judge *must* take off the blindfold. If she is to correctly apply the law—and hence do justice—she must undertake the comparative empathic work of deciding which party will be most hurt by losing the winner-take-all decision regarding the child's custody.

To refuse to do this work, and to instead reach the Draconian conclusion that the birth mother must be forced to give up the baby because of the apparent similarity between the plight of such a person and any commercial contractor who discovers that the cost of performance is higher than initially presupposed, is a failure of a relational ethic of care: it is a refusal to grant the uniqueness of *this* litigant, and the moral duty of relational recognition she imposes upon *this* court and *this* judge. The judge must determine the nature of this litigant's injury should she be required to give up a baby; *that* is the constraint imposed upon the judge by virtue of the ethic of care. But again, what I want to argue here is that where the judges in surrogacy cases fail to respect that constraint of the ethic of care, that failure results in a failure of the ethic of justice as well—the resulting decision is unjust precisely because it ignores the constraint of a relational ethic of care. Justice requires that likes be treated alike, and that unlikes be treated differently, and that the law be fairly applied. The refusal to see the difference between the injury suffered by the breaching mother, should she be required to perform, and the profit loss suffered by the commercial contractor, should he be required to perform a commercial contract which has turned out to be less profitable than he initially contemplated, is a failure to treat things that are different differently, and hence a failure of legal justice. In short, the impulse, fairly widespread in surrogacy cases, to commodify the baby and treat the surrogate "impartially" as a representative of all breaching contractors who fail to turn over the commodity after contractually agreeing to do so, is a failure of care, and precisely for that reason, it is a failure of both law and justice as well.

Again, one problem with all three cases—*Hawkins, Peeveyhouse,* and the surrogacy cases—is simply a lack of compassion; a lack of compassion for the injured, nonbreaching parties in the first two cases, and for the breaching party in the third. A second problem is the tendency toward commodification which all three in different ways exemplify—there *is* something morally repugnant about reducing an injured hand, the loss of one's livelihood, and a newborn baby to the status of a commodity. But I think we can say more. As was true of Vonnegut's chess player, of Abraham, and of Mahatma Gandhi as well, the moral failing of these cases also has to do with the court's, or the judge's, refusal to differentiate the claims of these litigants before this court from the interests of a general class of "all potentially contracting parties" which these litigants might be considered to represent. The claim of these litigants is for justice from this judge, just as the claim of the chess player's son is for a particular, relational bond with his father. To fail to respect the moral demands imposed by that relationship is a failure to protect, to prioritize, to connect with these particular persons as persons within one's ambit of particularizing obligation. The judge has a special obligation to the very particular litigants before her, as the parent has a special obligation to her children. He or she must listen to the injured patient, the ruined farmer, or the despondent mother to understand the particularizing details of *their* predicament, not simply universalize each case, each injury, and each contract so as to fit it within a more general rule. The failure to do so is not only a failure of a relational ethic of care. It is also, and for that reason, a failure of law and justice—our positive law of contracts, our common law methodology, and most widely held norms of legal justice require that unique situations be treated differently.

On a more theoretical level, the insistence by normative economists that courts adopt an "ex ante" rather than "ex post" perspective
when resolving cases poses the same problem, perhaps not as compel-
lingly as Vonnegut's chess player, but the same problem nonetheless.
Economists urge courts to think not of the plight of particular litigants
before them but of the incentives for (or against) prudent market
behavior that will result from particular decisions, and to treat those
incentives as dispositive.[74] Thus, from an "ex ante" perspective, surro-
gates should be required to relinquish their babies, just as injured
hands and personal ruination should be reduced to market value for
the purpose of assessing damage, because to do so will encourage
more exacting and more careful marketing behavior by all potential
contractors.[75] Litigants in particular cases, on this view, are simply
vehicles for the articulation and enforcement of general norms of
prudent market-oriented behavior. Again, this ex ante preference
might be objectionable on any number of grounds. But surely one
reason—and perhaps the main reason—that it strikes so many as
counterintuitive *as a rule of judging* is that it denies the centrality of
the *relationship* of judge to litigant, and asserts instead the centrality
of the assessment of interests affected by a holding. But in so doing it
is mistaken—a judge is not a legislator, and there is a difference
between "doing" justice and "doing" sound economic social policy.
The difference is relational—a judge is in a relationship with litigants
that is quite different from the relationship of legislator and constit-
uent. That judge-litigant relationship imposes caring constraints on
decisions that are simply not a part of the constraints imposed on
legislators or policymakers. The judge's relationship with a litigant
simply *is* an ex post relationship. To deny that is to deny the constraint imposed upon judicial decision making by virtue of the ethic
of care.

We can see the tension between the relational constraint and the
economic constraint in Justice Skelley Wright's decision in *Williams
v. Walker Thomas Furniture Company*[76]—perhaps one of the most
honored, as well as most criticized, contracts decisions of the modern
era. In *Walker,* the Court struck down as unconscionable a contract
imposing unduly harsh repayment terms in a personal loan contract.
The decision has been applauded by scores of legal theorists for its
liberal use of the "unconscionability" doctrine to refuse enforcement
of contracts between parties of widely disparate bargaining power,

where enforcement would impose an unconscionable hardship upon the weaker party. The decision has been criticized, primarily by legal economists, for the perverse as well as intended incentives it will produce: poor people are not held to the letter of their promise, and hence have no incentive to be careful when entering contracts, and retail outlets will simply make up the loss by raising prices across the board for all goods and services—particularly those in most demand by poorer customers. What is noteworthy about the decision and the controversy surrounding it for these purposes, is simply this: Judge Wright's decision is both honored and criticized for essentially the same reason: he more or less explicitly *refused* to adopt the "ex ante" perspective.[77] He refused to universalize the plaintiff before him. He refused to see her as representative of a class—as a vehicle for the articulation of market-based norms of prudence. He refused to treat her as anything less than uniquely within his ambit of particularized obligation. That decision, as numerous economic critics have charged, may well have created perverse disincentives encouraging less than prudent market behavior among poor people. But in part because it insisted on uniqueness and particularity, it did justice between the parties. It did so, in large measure, because of the care Judge Wright bestowed upon the particular litigants before him, and the respect he accordingly showed for the constraints of an ethic of care attendant on the judge-litigant relationship.

These cases, and many like them, also shed light on the opposition discussed above, between fidelity to a vow and the pull of natural compassion. There are undoubtedly some cases in which that opposition is quite real: a judge faced with a mandatory sentencing guideline, for example, which he finds to be inexcusably harsh, may feel a very real and unresolvable tension between his inclination toward compassion for the defendant and his vow to uphold the law. But in many cases—including these contract cases—the basic judicial *vow*—the promise to faithfully apply the law—not only is not *in opposition to* a compassionate response to the particularized situation of particular litigants, but much more importantly, at least according to the best interpretation of the content of the law the judge has vowed to uphold, that vow can only be fulfilled by attending carefully and compassionately to the particularized situation of the litigants before her. At least in these cases the judge who is true to her vow, in other words, *is* the compassionate judge: contract law *requires*—

it does not preclude—the judge to distinguish carefully, and hence compassionately, between the nature of the injuries parties sustain, and the application or nonapplication of ameliorative or excusing doctrines that soften the blow of the remedy or that cushion the impact of a breach. At least the judicial vow to do justice by applying the law—whatever may have been true of Gandhi's vow, or More's, or Abraham's—and at least in many if not all cases, can only be fulfilled by attending to the sentient and particularized pull of compassion, not by ignoring it or steadfastly silencing it out of a misguided urge to don the blindfold, toward the ultimate end of a false generality.

CONSISTENCY WITHOUT NURTURANCE

And what of the most basic opposition suggested by the triad of images sketched above: what is the value of consistency—the plumb line—untempered by nurturance? I suggested above that the test of consistency—the plumb-line test—is central to our concept of legal justice: it is the metaphoric core, so to speak, of the rule of law, the rule of precedent, indeed of the concept of law itself. Yet, as countless scholars and judges from the heyday of the legal realist movement to the present have argued, the zealous pursuit of consistency in the law, particularly in the common law, can lead to injustice and even absurdity if it is not tempered by an attitude of care toward, or at least sensitivity to, contemporary circumstances, including whatever circumstances characterize the pending case. At best, the zeal for consistency will result in a wooden and irrational refusal to come to grips with the changing context and needs of modern life, and at worst it will result in patently unjust outcomes—the all too predictable result, to use Holmes's famous formulation, of a "follow-the-leader" view of law that can seek no better rule of decision other than to do today precisely what was done in the time of King George III. Precedential logic, pursued zealously without regard to context, leads not to justice but to a cramped, time-frozen, and at times absurd jurisprudence, unbendable and unbending to the changing demands of a changing and complex society. Indeed, it has become a truism that the ideal of common law judging is not blind consistency to past precedent—a consistency which Justice Holmes, Karl Llewellyn, and other realists found so easy to mock—but a sensitive, evolutionary reworking of precedential rules and decisions so as to better account for current

[61]

realities. Although it is rarely put this way, the workings of legal justice through the rule of precedent may be one area—perhaps the only area—in which the need to temper the thirst for justice—consistency—with something like a nurturant regard for the particular needs and circumstances of the present, is fairly widely acknowledged.

However, the ideal of consistency—the virtue imaged by the plumb line—finds a way into our conception of legal justice in a second, less direct, but more substantive way as well, and here the interplay of the demands of consistency and the ethic of care is not so readily acknowledged. Consistency is central not just to dominant conceptions of *legal* justice, but to most developed conceptions of *political* justice as well. Although it may be tempting, in the name of efficiency, to limit the judge's responsibilities and hence this discussion to the domain of legal justice, the line between legal justice and political justice simply cannot be maintained. The judge's legal duty—as a matter of legal justice—is to apply the substance of our law and, as Ronald Dworkin has correctly argued since 1977, the substance of our law, at least at its highest, most "constitutional" or constitutive levels, does aim to incorporate the "best" possible conception of political justice. The conclusion is inescapable that a robust conception of legal justice must incorporate some view of political justice as well.

It is obviously well beyond the scope of this chapter, or book, to look critically at every conception of political justice which has had an impact on the development of our substantive law, or even on our constitutional law. What I propose to do here instead is look in some detail at just one conception of political justice—John Rawls's conception of "justice as fairness"—which undeniably has had an impact on our constitutional arguments, and which, also undeniably, has at its core an insistence on the virtue of *consistency.* Through the use of this example, I want to suggest that the *political* ideal of consistency, as it has worked itself into our constitutional jurisprudence, and hence into our conception of the legal justice which judges are obligated to dispense, is flawed when it is not tempered by an ethic of nurturance, no less than the legal ideal of consistency is flawed when not tempered by respect for changing circumstances.

John Rawls has given us what must be the most rigorous—as well as generous and humane—liberal theory of political justice in the second half of this century, and it is surely a mark of the strength of that theory that it has profoundly influenced the way a sizable number of liberal, progressive, and egalitarian legal scholars think and argue about constitutional law. As is well known, at the center of Rawls's famous account of political justice is the claim that we should conceptualize justice as that to which each member of society has freely consented, so long as we further define "each member" as a disembodied, rational, contracting agent ready to give rational consent where it best serves his or her self-interest, but in ignorance of his or her distinguishing characteristics, and hence ignorant of what those interests might be. The substantive, political consequence of this thought experiment, Rawls argues, is a society in which individuals possess a good deal of political liberty, more or less tracking those liberties guaranteed by the Bill of Rights, but also, and more controversially, a considerably more egalitarian society than the one we currently have constructed. Stripped of the knowledge of our own genetic and material endowments, it would become clear to each of us, as rational contractors, that the product of each member's natural talents and inclinations—for which, after all, he can take little or no credit—should be regarded as in effect societal wealth.[78] So long as we do not violate the individual's liberty, what we would each ultimately agree to at the bargaining table behind the veil of ignorance is a social and political structure in which we should regard the fruits of individual talents and inclinations as a part of societal wealth subject to the demands of justice. Obviously, the overall impact of such a scheme would be to equalize fairly dramatically the material holdings of each citizen.

Both the procedural mechanism—the veil of ignorance—and the substantive outcome—liberty and significant redistribution of wealth—of Rawls's conception of political justice are no less grounded in the perceived virtue of consistency—the plumb line—than the legal justice constituted by precedent, the Rule of Law, and the idea of law itself. For Rawls (as for Kantians more generally) it is, above all else, an insistence that our moral commitments be *consistent* which demands of us that, in specifying a redistributive scheme, we envision ourselves as rational but self-ignorant contracting agents, for the simple reason that only such agents, virtually by definition, can *be* perfectly consistent in their treatment of themselves and all others. It is the vehicle of contract that allows us to treat each cocontractor as *equal,* and hence consistently, and it is the ideal of consistency that requires us to abandon particularizing and distorting attributes of personal identity so as to guard against self-bias. Substantively as well, it is consistency which forces us to acknowledge that were we so constituted, what we would consent to would be a social world in which the fruits of our accidentally acquired and inconsistently distributed talents and inclinations would be regarded as social property. It is respect for consistency, then, achieved through the mechanism of the universalized, nonparticularized contracting agent, that requires considerable redistribution of societal material wealth. The political weight and importance of Rawls's famous argument about the requirements of justice is surely that some measure of egalitarianism, no less than a healthy dose of personal liberty, is the *political* consequence of taking seriously the virtue of moral consistency, just as respect for precedent and the Rule of Law are the legal consequence.

To this argument, Nozick, as well as a number of libertarians, have famously responded that there is something in the Rawlsian "veil of ignorance" metaphor, and the redistributive scheme which is its consequence, that fails to take the differences between persons seriously:[79] people come to society fully embodied and dramatically different in endowments and entitlements, and political justice must respect and protect those differences. From the other side of the political spectrum, Michael Sandel, as well as a number of other communitarians, have famously responded that there is something in the Rawlsian procedural mechanism and redistributive scheme that fails to take the communitarian connections between persons seriously:[80] people come to society not as disembodied, rational, egoistic agents, but as connected members of community, and political justice must respect and protect those connections.

I want to make a rather different objection, albeit related to both the above. The problem with such schemes, from a relational-feminist perspective, is not so much that they fail to take either the differences between persons seriously, or that they fail to take the connections between persons seriously. The problem, in a nutshell, is that they fail to take seriously the nature of our nurturant practices, and hence fail to take seriously the particularistic values those practices reflect. The mandate of justice agreed to by rational and self-regarding but self-ignorant entities is of little relevance to a society populated by individuals who are as essentially *nurturant* as they are essentially rational, and who nurture in ways that are profoundly, and inescapably, particularized—meaning, among much else, profoundly and inescapably inconsistent.

The heart of this objection to Rawls's egalitarianism is nicely captured, I think, in yet another Vonnegut story. In a short story in his early collection *Welcome to the Monkey House* entitled "Harrison Bergeron,"[81] Vonnegut imagines a society captured by a redistributive zeal, in which it has been decided that the effects of unevenly distributed talent, so grossly disproportionate to moral worth, must be neutralized—the next best thing to being redistributed. So, dancers must wear clunky weights to make them clumsy; tall basketball players must stoop; intelligent people have buzzers inserted in their brains to interrupt complicated thoughts; musically gifted individuals wear devices in their ears that cause a diminution in their hearing. Material reward and psychic reward are thus rendered *consistent* with moral desert—but at a considerable cost, and not just to the societal pool of talent on which to draw. The insistence on consistency—consistent treatment of each member so as to reflect their equal moral worth— in the culture Vonnegut describes, renders that culture a cruel one, albeit a consistent one, and it is a cruelty the weight of which is borne by the individuals that populate it.

The danger that more or less egalitarian schemes of justice, of which Rawls's is simply the most carefully worked out, will prove to be non-nurturant, or inhuman, is well recognized when the egalitarian scheme is overtly disrespectful of individual rights—the extreme case, of course, is Stalinism. It is not so well recognized, however, that a similar danger arises when what is risked by the egalitarian mandate of justice is not individual *rights* per se, but the practices of nurturance which inform and to some degree constitute our moral life— nurturant caregiving toward and of human, or for that matter animal, life. Political conceptions of justice, including egalitarian conceptions, that rest on respect for consistency—and the social policies they seem to suggest—can be made compatible with liberal regimes of individual rights, as Rawls's own work quite spectacularly shows. It is harder, though, to render such visions compatible with the mandate of particularized, and above all else *embodied,* nurturance suggested by an ethic of care.

It is accordingly not surprising that constitutional arguments put forward by progressive and egalitarian lawyers and scholars, and which either explicitly or implicitly urge the Court to incorporate into our constitutional doctrine Rawls's famous metaphor, are also hard to square with the mandate of particularized nurturance. I will discuss two such examples. First, an entire "family" of arguments for reproductive rights stems quite generally from this Rawlsian image of justice as consistency, or of consistent treatment of individuals regardless of distinguishing characteristics. Although the Supreme Court has never endorsed the argument, it has often been urged in liberal legal scholarship that the right to an abortion follows from the mandate of justice, in part because it is necessary to render consistent, or equal, or the *same,* the burdens of reproductive life for men and women.[82] Unwanted pregnancy is a nine-month condition which no man ever endures, so to render consistent the social situation of women and men, women must be given the opportunity to opt out. More generally, abortion rights are necessary to fulfill this mandate of justice because such rights render consistent the potential for individual, autonomous, and "disconnected" social interaction available to men and women: neither men nor women, given available and legal abortion, need ever undergo *other than through their own choice* the tremendously anti-individualistic and counterautonomous experience of pregnancy and parenthood. The availability of abortion, particularly combined with the availability of contraception, renders men and women more similar, and hence their burdens more consistent, by severing the woman's tie to fetal life generated by the natural condition of pregnancy.

This argument has undeniable strengths—it echoes the Rawlsian insight that the rules we live under should be those to which we would agree unburdened by knowledge of our particular distinguishing characteristics, including gender. More bluntly, it neatly captures the widely shared and basically Rawlsian feminist intuition that "if men got pregnant, abortion would be sacrosanct." But it has pernicious consequences. One such consequence is simply that by insistently describing, and to some extent rendering, the profoundly counterindividualistic condition of voluntary and wanted pregnancy as a *chosen* condition—in part because it is one freely terminated—this argument for abortion rights thereby further *privatizes* the condition as well, thus weakening whatever lingering societal obligations the community may feel to extend aid toward the pregnant woman, the new mother, and the new life dependent upon her. If the availability of legal abortion means that we can choose to terminate a pregnancy, *or choose to carry it to term,* then, by virtue of the fact that the mother has *chosen* to carry new life and bring into the world a new human being, that new life can now be regarded by the community as simply another of her projects and pursuits—no different, conceptually, from her neighbor's decision to pursue a new career or sail around the world. It is something she has chosen to do, and therefore the burdens it imposes upon her are her burdens—there is no reason to expect the community to take responsibility for or even interest in the nurturance of that new life.

However, the argument also has a second cost. By entirely subordinating the experience, potential, and the value of extant fetal life to the abstract demand of consistency, the argument appears to run roughshod over the moral mandate of nurturance that is implied by the ethic of care. Thus, it is not only the fetus, but the value of the highly particularized nurturance the fetus (and child) needs in order to survive that is seemingly sacrificed by the justice-based mandate to render *the same* the distribution of burdens between men and women for reproductive activity. The mandate "to nurture" is the ethical imperative that renders acceptable the tremendous power imbalance between parent and child, and when that mandate is seemingly breached through abortion rights, so as to render the situation of men and women more similar, an entire ethical system, not just fetal life, appears to be sacrificed in the process.

This is a cost that should not be taken lightly, for the straightforward reason that this zealous pursuit of consistency, at the cost of the value of nurturance, will fail—and again, it will fail as a matter of justice no less than as a matter of care. It is only a superficial interpretation of the justice-based requirement for "consistency" that seems to require that women be accorded the same "right" as men to simply "walk away" from a pregnancy without incurring any costs. On a deeper level, "consistency," as it pertains to justice, requires foremost that our rights be consistent with our moral practices. This particular argument for reproductive rights assumes a moral stance toward dependent life which unnecessarily renders a decision to abort as diametrically at odds with women's and men's nurturant *practices:* women do indeed nurture fetuses, and women as well as men make huge sacrifices to nurture babies and young children. Those nurturant practices—regardless of whether or not any individual woman partakes of them—in turn play a constitutive role in the ethic of care: as

[67]

Sara Ruddick has argued, they form the experiential basis for much of the moral reasoning that is at the heart of a maternal and caring ethical outlook.[83] The characterization of the decision to end a pregnancy as necessitated by the abstract need to equalize or render consistent the ability of women and men to abandon dependent fetal life, does violence to that ethic, because it appears to be so profoundly at odds—so deeply inconsistent—with the constitutive nurturant practices on which that ethic is based. Consistency might be better served by requiring of men both sexual restraint and a greater responsibility toward the new life they have created, than by granting a right explicitly premised upon the ideal of rendering consistent our freedom from nurturant practices.

Women's own decision making regarding abortions,[84] whatever may be the case regarding liberal or liberal feminist arguments for abortion rights, rarely are premised on an abstract insistence that we render consistent the nurturant obligations of men and women. Rather, as numerous studies of women's decisions to abort make clear,[85] and as an increasing number of even liberal, as well as postmodern and radical arguments for abortion rights are beginning to acknowledge,[86] the interests and value of the fetus, as well as the woman's connection to it, must be taken into account if the decision to abort, or the decision to permit the woman the freedom to make the decision, is to be a just one. Both women's own decision-making processes as well as these recent arguments make clear what I will argue in a moment, which is that the decision to take the value of fetal life into account is by no means "fatal" to the cause of reproductive freedom. What I want to stress here is that the liberal argument for abortion rights premised on a superficial ideal of consistency between men and women is itself inconsistent—and hence unjust—in a fundamental way: it is inconsistent with the nurturant practices that is central to the experiences of at least many of the women on whose behalf the argument is cast.

The second example, and closer in spirit to both Rawls's conception of justice as fairness and the Vonnegut story that can be read as a mocking critique of it, are those arguments—again, never endorsed even by the liberal Warren Court, but often urged upon the Court in constitutional form—for any redistributive scheme—including progressive taxes, welfare entitlements, and any number of other social welfare plans—that aim to equalize the given resources of individuals, so as to maximize the degree to which differences in lived outcomes are directly reflective of nothing but differences in chosen life paths.[87] Building directly and explicitly upon Rawls's initial insights, an entire "family" of generally liberal arguments support such programs, on the justice-based grounds that only by equalizing given entitlements can we render *consistent* the degree to which differences in wealth reflect private choice rather than arbitrary allocations of resources—including "resources" of talent, character, and the like—which are morally irrelevant to individual worth. Again, these arguments have obvious strengths—they seek to render our social practices consistent not only with each other, but also with our widely shared intuition that we should not be rewarded for morally irrelevant factors such as skin color or nobility of birth. There is indeed no obvious way to differentiate on moral grounds between the degree to which we "deserve" the rewards of genetic endowments such as intelligence and talent, or family inbred traits such as initiative and ambition, from those of skin color or sex, and there is similarly no obvious way to differentiate inherited wealth from inherited title. Social programs that aim to ameliorate the sometimes drastic degrees of difference in outcomes caused by these moral "irrelevancies" do indeed seem justified by an ethic of justice that has at its core an egalitarianism stemming from a mandate of ethical consistency.[88]

But again, these arguments come at a cost, and one of the most salient is that, as is the case with the similar argument for abortion rights, they fail to respect our nurturant *practices*—and for that reason, seem at odds with the ethic of care that is in part constituted by those practices. When we nurture, we nurture particular persons, not groups, nations, or species, and when we nurture a particular person, we seek to make that person as fulfilled as possible by using— not ignoring or slighting—that person's distinguishing attributes, whether inherited or not. This particularizing characteristic of the ability and act of nurturance, and hence the role of particularity and context, is *central,* not peripheral, to an ethic of care. We can indeed learn to *care* quite broadly—even universally—as I will argue in the next section. But when we *nurture,* we nurture particular persons within the context of particular relationships. A mandate of consistency in our political ethics will inevitably be violated by our nurturant practices—we simply do not nurture consistently across persons or populations. Yet the impulse to nurture, and our nurturant practices, are in some sense the experiential heart of the "ethic" of care.[89] Social schemes, whether from the left or right, which threaten the health of those relationships, are accordingly a threat as well to an ethic of care. We cannot nurture our young, in short, if we do not regard their strengths as being as much "theirs" as we undoubtedly regard their vulnerabilities. If consistency requires us to so view our children, and if consistency is the heart of justice, then justice is indeed a threat to our nurturant practices and the caring ethic they ground.

There is accordingly not only *not* an identity, but there is a palpable tension between an ethic of care and justice-based arguments for egalitarian redistribution, and it is a tension which is just as deep, and at root grounded in the same source, as the more widely recognized tension between liberal rights discourse and an ethic of care. In fact, from the perspective of the ethic of care, and more specifically from the perspective of the constraints of particularity, concreteness, and context it imposes, liberal rights discourse and egalitarian social justice have far more in common than what divides them: they both schematize our moral relation to the distant "other" on the model of an abstract inference from principle, rather than on the model of our felt commitments to those we nurture. Both view our tendency toward particularized nurturance—the nurturance of *this* person because of *those* attributes within *this* relationship—as not only not the source of our moral abilities, but rather as deeply antagonistic toward the ends of social justice. In the long run, the ethic of care, so long as it is built upon the inclination to nurture, and so long as it accordingly incorporates a constraint of particularity, is the enemy of, not the handmaiden of, a consistency-driven mandate of social egalitarianism.

I do not mean to imply that there is an *inevitable* tension between welfare entitlements, redistributive progressive taxation, or reproductive rights on the one hand and an ethic of care on the other, nor do I mean to suggest that there are not better arguments to support these beleaguered policies. I do want to insist that the arguments for these egalitarian programs that are grounded *solely* in an ethic of justice that is itself premised on an egalitarian zeal for consistency, and that are accordingly blind to the conflicting and particularizing perspective of an ethic of care, are weak arguments. An egalitarianism—whether invoked in the service of wealth redistribution or reproductive freedom—which is in turn compelled by an impulse for consistency which denies or obliterates concrete differences between persons, not only addresses a counterfactual social world, but also is virtually forced to either ignore or suppress our tendency to empathize with, and then sacrifice for, those particular persons whom we nurture, for particularizing reasons of choice, role, or duty. That capacity, however, is itself a moral capacity, and it is very likely the root of whatever moral obligations we eventually learn to assume toward all others. A theory of justice which views our capacity to particularistically nurture as antithetical to—rather than the foundation of—the demands of social morality is at bottom simply inhuman. Furthermore, it is self-defeating: it is premised upon a desire to render consistent a set of moral intuitions which are themselves antithetical to—and accordingly inconsistent with—our nurturant practices.

And finally, that inconsistency in turn gives rise to a problem of justice. It is only transparently paradoxical, and it is nevertheless true, that an ethical requirement of consistency that is itself inconsistent with our particularizing nurturant practices—our inclination toward inconsistency—will be itself an unjust mandate. The ugliness of a totalitarian system that requires children to inform on their parents or vice versa is echoed, however slightly, in any regime which requires, in the name of consistency, an egalitarianism that flattens the differentiating features of individuals, and their differentiating pull on our affection, loyalty, and commitments. It is, in the long run, not only inhuman and self-defeating to ask us to deny this part of ourselves—it is emphatically unjust. It pits our affective ties against our moral duties in a way that requires the sacrifice of one or the other. To construct our moral duties in such a way is to insist upon an inconsistency at the core of our moral and affective lives. *That* insistence—on that inconsistency—is itself an example of injustice.

Stronger arguments for egalitarian policies such as these are available, and they all, not coincidentally, rest upon the embrace of an ethic of care no less than an ethic of justice: indeed the two are so intertwined as to be indistinguishable. A political program premised on egalitarianism might be, but it need not be, driven by a zeal for consistency. It can also be driven by a felt *and learned* sense of empathic identification with the sufferings of very particular vulnerable persons. A program motivated by such an empathic response to the suffering of others is not only not at odds with our nurturant practices, but it is deeply consistent with it: it has its human source in a healthy expansion of the desire to nurture one's own children, family, clan, or community—in an expanded "circle of care." The alternative, in other words, to an egalitarian ethic premised on an abstract and bloodless zeal for consistency is one premised on a sense of brotherhood and sisterhood. We seek to equalize, because we seek to alleviate misery (rather than achieve consistency), and we seek to alleviate the misery of strangers because we have come to regard that misery as something of *our own concern*—as a pain that we share, and hence have a direct interest in ending. Such an egalitarianism then *draws on* and expands—rather than ignores or seeks to deny— the particularistic, inconsistent, and profoundly *unequal* nurturant impulses we feel toward "our own."

Thus, arguments for the redistribution of wealth, progressive taxation, welfare programs, or subsistence rights, or other similarly progressive social programs, can be, but need not be grounded in the impulse to equate desert with moral merit, thus ameliorating or eliminating the role of undeserved and unearned attributes, whether genetically or legally inherited—the very attributes which *trigger* and *sustain* the impulse to nurture. They can alternatively rest upon a recognition and *incorporation* into one's own feelings of the anguish of impoverishment, the pain of malnutrition, the exclusionary dignitary harms of racism, the profound frustrations stemming from growth stunted by lead paint and inadequate education, and the felt rage and self-contempt of unemployment and underemployment. When those pains become my pains, then it makes sense to speak of the man who suffers them as my "brother," just as it makes sense to speak of my biological brother as my brother largely *because* I do indeed "feel his pain." With that expansion of the capacity for empathy to embrace the concerns of those outside the immediate circle of the biological family, comes a transformation and expansion of self. And from that transformation of *self,* a commitment to egalitarianism, albeit grounded in shared fellow feeling rather than in principle, is virtually inevitable. Of the two commitments—one from principle, and one from fellow feeling—it may also prove to be the more enduring.

Arguments for reproductive freedom and abortion rights, as well as for wealth redistribution or welfare entitlements, that acknowledge rather than seek to diminish the constraints of an ethic of care are also readily available, and they are also stronger, both as a matter of justice and as a matter of care, than arguments which zealously pursue the former to the neglect of the latter. These arguments all seek to retain recognition of the distinguishing differences between people, and to draw on the universal human ability in any given individual or culture, albeit perhaps latent, to empathize with the pain of such persons and to seek to fulfill needs. Thus, reproductive freedom, and the abortion rights that at least in the short term must be a part of that freedom, particularly given the continuing climate of societal hostility toward children and their caretakers that exists in this culture, is a necessary prerequisite for nurturant relationships between the pregnant woman and the fetus, as well as between the mother and child, which an ethic of care seeks to encourage. Without that freedom, the "relationship" is one of nonconsensual servitude, not nurturant, interdependent care. Reproductive freedom is as necessary to nurturance, in other words, as it is to an abstract consistency between the choices of men and women in this culture.

If this is right, then two consequences follow for our constitutional jurisprudence. First, the case for reproductive freedom ought to be cast as precisely that—the case for reproductive *freedom.* As numerous feminists have now pointed out, it should not be cast as an argument for abortion "rights" grounded in an abstract concern for sexual "privacy"—an argument which almost blithely, and indeed almost cruelly, ignores the degree to which sexual privacy has meant, for women, only that their sexual violation is shielded from public scrutiny and legal compensation by a wall of secrecy and privilege. But nor should it be grounded in an equally abstract concern for formal gender equality—which *also* blithely ignores the degree to which women's reproductive nurturant practices, including the practice of nurturing fetal life—is constitutive of the ethic of care.

Rather, and as the National Abortion Rights Action League has argued in a series of amicus briefs[90]—reproductive freedom might better be viewed, consistently with the nurturant practices at the heart of the ethic of care, as a necessary *positive* liberty to secure women's and children's well-being, and the nurturant practices and values that secure them. If we want nurturant relationships between parents and children to be a part of our social world, and hence a part of the positive liberty each individual is entitled to possess in order to participate in that social world, then we must allow women the freedom to choose to terminate or carry a pregnancy to term. The justification for this freedom, in other words, does not stem from a right to

[73]

violate or abandon fetal life consistently with men's apparent inclination to do so. It must stem, rather, from a right to create materially secure, consensual, and safe nurturant relationships.

Similarly, redistributive social policies might be sensibly viewed as constitutionally mandated, if we view the constitution as requiring the community to ensure not that each individual is accorded "consistent" equal treatment along a strict measure of moral desert—and thereby requiring compensation for morally irrelevant features of personality, such as ambition, talent, drive, and so forth—but rather, as requiring the community to ensure that each individual is accorded the liberty—again positive in nature—to live a good life: one free of threats of violence and material need, and enlivened by culture, education, public participation, and intimacy. As in the case of reproductive rights, this suggests a reorientation of constitutional argument away from abstract equality to positive liberty—and away from "equal protection" jurisprudence, or at least one version of it—and toward "liberty" jurisprudence. Elsewhere, I have argued at some length that such a reorientation—although admittedly built on a reading of the constitution which is not widely shared—is justified by both the literal language of the fourteenth amendment and our post-Reconstruction constitutional history.[91] Here, I only want to note that such a reorientation is also justified, and perhaps mandated, by respect for an ethic of care, and for the nurturant practices, particularizing instinct, and respect for context and difference which are its constitutive components.

THE PURSUIT OF CARE, UNCONSTRAINED BY THE ETHIC OF JUSTICE

Let me now address the other side of my Venn diagram. What is the value of compassion, and nurturance, and particularity, when untouched by the demands of justice—the demands of consistency, of integrity, and of impartiality?

NURTURANCE WITHOUT CONSISTENCY

Let me start with the ethical quality of the act of nurturance when it is untempered by the demands of consistency. Just as the parent's failure to pay special heed to the demands of his or her own children seems a bit "inhuman"—even when in the pursuit of justice—an excessive preference given one's *own,* particularly in the face of extreme deprivation of others, seems a bit "too human," to put it mildly. Nurturance untempered by the consistency demanded by justice shades into racism, nationalism, tribalism, or speciesism—in short, into fascism. There is, I imagine, emblazoned in the memories of those of us who lived through the civil rights era the haunting and horrific image of a white woman—a mother—protectively, compulsively, committedly, holding her daughter tight in her grasp, while yelling hateful, injurious, spirit-murdering racial epithets at small, innocent African American children attempting the heroic and commonplace act of entering a school building.[92] This is a compelling image of "particularity with a vengeance"; of nurturance untouched by consistency, and more generally, of care untempered by justice. However, it also exemplifies the hard truth that care untempered by justice fails as a matter of care no less than as a matter of justice. What could possibly be clearer than that this white mother's response is not only obviously unjust, but that because of that, it is uncaring as well?

Of course, the white mother in the above example is not a judge. Nevertheless, the quality of the care she exhibits, or the lack of quality in the care her actions exhibit, is not unrelated to the decisions of judges. Indeed, our most notorious cases in the various fields of law impacting upon race relations can be accurately recast as examples of judicial decisions that result in rules which in turn encourage, protect, or delimit, in our social world, precisely the sort of nurturance untempered by the demands of justice as exemplified by the mother's actions and posture above. *Plessey v. Ferguson,*[93] in which the Supreme Court upheld the apartheid policies of separate but equal, most obviously both *exhibits* and *extols* a white racism that demands of each individual a nurturant response toward "his own kind" in the social world without regard of consequences for others. The case in fact *turned on* the Court's embrace of an ethic of white solidarity in the face of black challenge—the Court virtually instructed its white readers to nurture their own whiteness and their white community, whatever the consequence for excluded outsiders. Even Justice Harlan's eloquent and much lauded dissent speaks approvingly of white loyalty and of white social supremacy in the social sphere, so long as the law itself remains pure.[94] *Dred Scott*[95] as well is simply a more extreme and more lethal example of the same phenomenon. The lesson of these explicitly racist cases is simply that judicial decisions which encourage or legitimate relationships of "selective nurturance"—in which we zealously pursue the virtue of care, embodied in our nurturant practices, but untempered by justice—invariably reduces the humanity of the persons outside the circle of care to the status of property.

As Patricia Williams, among others involved in critical race studies, has so eloquently argued, the impulse to ground public responsibility in an ethic of caring for the needs of others, whether the political root of that impulse be socialistic, feminist, or simply humanist, must be forever vigilant against the potential for viciousness toward those outside the protected "circle of care" which such an ethic carries.[96] The act, feeling, and value of nurturance is inevitably, invariably, and, as I have argued above, to its credit, *relational*—few if any of us have *nurturant* impulses toward humanity at large. Relationality is in turn inherently exclusionary. A public ethic of care grounded in our nurturant impulses, untempered by the demands of consistency, risks becoming a communitarian dystopia known not for its nurturant softening of a hard-edged individualistic ethic, but rather for its vicious hatred of outsiders and xenophobic intolerance of nonconforming insiders. Such a community is quite obviously unjust.

The point I want to stress here, however, is that because such communities—and the judicial decisions that reinforce and legitimize them—are unjust, they are *for that very reason* uncaring as well. One recent Pennsylvania case involving the Amish well illustrates both points.[97] The Amish have a practice of "shunning" those who have broken some aspect of the various strict codes of behavior that define as well as confine Amish life. In 1945, a Mr. Aaron S. Glick, after breaching the Amish code of simplicity by using a fuel-powered rather than animal-powered tractor, received for this transgression the harshest "shunning" penalty the Amish prescribe. Even after leaving the community and joining the more flexible Mennonite church and community nearby, he was not permitted to use Amish commercial or retail outlets to purchase needed materials for his farm and business, or to ride in a buggy with or to eat at the same table as Amishmen and women, including his own relatives. No Amish members, again including his children and parents, who remained in the Amish community, were allowed to physically touch him. When he would engage in physical labor with his grown son, a carpenter, the two would pass tools back and forth by laying them on the floor for each other to pick up. After *forty years* of this penalty, he tired of it, and brought an action in front of the Pennsylvania Human Relations Commission against the Amish retailers, basically for religious discrimination—and he won.

His victory, in a dramatic and obvious sense, represented a victory of legalistic justice over xenophobic and intolerant care—the Amish defended the practice of shunning, both in front of the Commission and in the media coverage that followed, on the grounds that this practice like any number of others strengthened the communitarian bonds so central to their continued existence. And so it did—at the cost of justice. But interestingly, the principal actors involved, including most importantly Mr. Glick himself, did not quite see the outcome in those terms. Rather, at least in the minds of Mr. Glick and a number of his Amish friends and neighbors, the action represented the victory of a *truer* ethic of care over a false caring ethic which had become poisoned by fear, intolerance, and a sort of bullying or intimidation of both outsiders and insiders. Those Amish who had somewhat secretly remained loyal to Mr. Glick, and who were openly pleased and vindicated by the judicial decision, expressed their satisfaction with the result in terms of an ethic of care, not justice: to their minds, the importance of the Human Relations Commission's decision was that it could well spell the end of the uncaring and cruel practice of shunning. Mr. Glick himself put the point most succinctly. When asked what motivated him to finally bring his legalistic challenge to the practice of shunning, he said simply, "It ain't biblical." At least in this instance, the failure of justice implicated in the practice of shunning was a failure of love, and ultimately a threat, not a handmaiden, to the creation of community as well.

Discretionary Judicial Decision Making   As noted above, judges rarely "aim for" the virtue of care in their decisions. The Glick case, *Plessey, Dred Scott,* and other racist decisions are unjust not so much because they aim for the wrong virtue, but rather because they facilitate social relationships which are themselves unjust. Nevertheless, judges do on occasion directly aim for the virtue of care in their decisions, particularly when they are explicitly directed to engage in "discretionary" decision making. And *when* they do, and when the care they exhibit is untempered by justice, the results are disastrous. The sentencing of criminal defendants (in state courts) remains one vast arena of just such discretionary decision making, and in that arena one can find numerous examples of judicial failures which stem in one way or another from the failure to constrain a nurturant impulse toward a criminal defendant with the demands of justice.[98] Modern cases extolling the need for "cultural defenses" to violent crimes committed by displaced members of other cultures in which violence—typically violence against women—is allegedly more accepted as a way of life, are one such example of judicial care untempered by the constraint of justice.[99] The nurturant judicial response to excuse or mitigate the punishment of a criminal defendant who has committed a homicide, at least in part because he was raised in a culture of permissive misogynist violence, errs on the side of inconsistency, and the result is an outcome manifestly unjust—this defendant is accorded more sympathy, and less jail time, than other defendants who have committed similar deeds. And, as in the case of the segregationist mother protecting her own progeny by hurling hatred at the children of others, the judicial decisions are strikingly uncaring as well—the nurturant response to the defendant is at the cost of a dehumanizing callousness toward the victim.

The same can be said of *Peacock v. Maryland,*[100] the recent (1994) Maryland case discussed in the first section of this chapter, Three Images of Justice, in which a criminal defendant was given an extraordinarily light sentence for killing his wife three hours after finding her in bed with another man. The sentencing judge in *Peacock* stressed his deep sympathy for the cuckolded homicidal defendant, his identification with the defendant's rage, and his sorrow at the distasteful task of having to impose any sentence at all upon an individual he viewed as essentially noncriminal. The result—a sentence of eighteen months in a work-release program—was not only unjust, it was also—and *for that reason*—manifestly uncaring. The judicial character that emerges from that sentencing transcript exemplifies callous, uncaring misogyny, not nurturant sentencing. Feminist critics of the Alternative Dispute Resolution movement—which seeks, in part, and quite consciously, to ground judicial decision making on an ethic of care rather than an ethic of justice—have voiced similar suspicions of informal or simply discretionary methods of dispute resolution.[101] To the extent that those methods rely upon the partial, biased, particularized nurturant impulse of the mediator, and downplay the demands of justice, they risk exacerbating the underlying problems of sexism and misogyny that prompted the turn to alternative fora in the first place. Judicial nurturance that does not hold itself to the test of consistency will result in injustice and viciousness from judges and decision makers, no less than from individual citizens.

COMPASSION WITHOUT INTEGRITY

Just as nurturance is not in the end very caring if it is not tempered by the justice-based demand for consistency, so compassion is more lacking than exemplary of an ethic of care if not tempered by personal integrity. Although there is much to admire in those individuals among us who are so genuinely giving and compassionate as to be in some sense "selfless," there is also good reason to be wary of a quite different kind of "selflessness," often coupled with shows of compassion. That is a selflessness rooted not in a genuinely empathic regard for the other, but rather in a harmful and injurious lack of regard for oneself: a sense of self-loathing, a lack of self-esteem or self-respect, and at root a failure to give oneself one's "due": a quite general, massive denial of the importance, equality, and dignity of oneself. The self-loathing individual often appears to be what might be called a "giving self," but she is giving for the self-denying, rather than other-affirming, reason that she defines herself by giving herself away.[102] Such a self is, quintessentially, a self that lacks integrity. Because she lacks integrity, she is also a self that cannot truly be compassionate. It is hard to "give" when one defines oneself as by nature "giving," and given.

I will comment in much more detail on the distinctive and distinctively gendered harms done to and occasioned by what I call the "giving self" in a subsequent chapter.[103] Here, let me try to quickly capture the essence of the problem I'm trying to highlight with two images. The first comes from Carol Gilligan's *In a Different Voice.* [104] In that work, Gilligan famously articulates an alternative "ethic of care," grounded loosely in nurturant relationships and compassionate impulses, and argues that this alternative ethic of care is found disproportionately in women, as contrasted with an "ethic of fairness" found more commonly in men and boys. One of the often neglected strengths of that study is the attention Gilligan bestows upon the peculiar ethical *disabilities,* or failings, to which an ethic of care leaves women peculiarly vulnerable. What she found in her studies was precisely the problem noted here: an ethic of care, if it becomes self-defining, threatens—and mightily—the sense of personal integrity, and ultimately even the sense of self, of self-regard, and self-possession that is at the core of that virtue:

> Since women, however, define their identity through relationships of intimacy and care, the moral problems that they encounter pertain to issues of a different sort. When relationships are secured by masking desire and conflict is avoided by equivocation, then confusion arises about the locus of responsibility and truth.[105]

To illustrate the point, she quotes from a diary of Mary McCarthy, in which the author remembers an early experience of untruthfulness:

> Whatever I told them was usually so blurred and glossed, in the effort to meet their approval (for, aside from anything else, I was fond of them and tried to accommodate myself to their perspective), that except when answering a direct question, I hardly knew whether what I was saying was true or false. I really tried, or so I thought, to avoid lying, but it seemed to me that they forced it on me by the difference in their vision of things, so that I was always transposing reality for them into terms they could understand. To keep matters straight with my conscience, I shrank, whenever possible, from the lie absolute, just as, from a sense of precaution, I shrank from the plain truth.[106]

Gilligan comments:

> The critical experience then becomes not intimacy but choice, creating an encounter with self that clarifies the understanding of responsibility and truth.
> Thus in the transition from adolescence to adulthood, the dilemma itself is the same for both sexes, *a conflict between integrity and care.* But approached from different perspectives, this dilemma generates the recognition of opposite truths. These different perspectives are reflected in two different moral ideologies, since separation is justiced by an ethic of rights while attachment is supported by an ethic of care.[107]

The problematic nature of the "giving self" is even more starkly, and I suppose unintentionally, revealed in a children's book entitled *The Giving Tree.* [108] *The Giving Tree* tells the story of a boy's relationship with his friend, a tree. At the beginning of the story, the tree nurtures the young boy by providing shade from the sun with its branches. Later, it provides a playground, as the boy learns to climb and jump from branch to branch. Still later in life, the tree provides wood for the young boy, now a young man, to build a house. Eventually, the tree gives the boy everything it has. At the end of the story, the boy, now an old man, approaches the tree, now nothing but a stump, and the stump offers the boy a place to sit. The tone of this modern children's classic, as far as I can tell, is entirely laudatory. The reader is supposed to admire the boy's cleverness and resourcefulness in finding ever new ways to use his friend the tree, and we are supposed to admire the tree's generosity in continually giving itself up, all the way to the point of its own exhausted extinction. Yet surely for many adult readers (and perhaps some younger readers as well), *The Giving Tree* sounds more like a parable of exploitation than of compassionate generosity. At no point is the child-reader invited to question the lack of reciprocity in the relationship—the boy gives the tree *nothing*—and at no point is the child-reader invited to question the tree's continuing acts of cheerful self-annihilation.

Relationships of care, untempered by the demands of justice, resulting in the creation of injured, harmed, exhausted, compromised, and self-loathing "giving selves," rather than in genuinely compassionate and giving individuals, are ubiquitous in this society, and it is far more often women than men who are injured by them. There are two major reasons for the disproportionate impact. The first is simply that by upbringing, girls, far more than boys, are taught through the medium of parental love—that all-powerful creator of the sense of self—that at least in the domestic realm it is self-sacrifice that will be rewarded (or will be rewarded above all else) with the bestowal of parental approval. The girl who learns that self-sacrifice in the home is rewarded with parental love, or attention, or praise, may well become a compassionate person, but the compassion is rooted in a deep need for acceptance which is itself tied to sacrifice. The result may be a good deal of "caring" for others: women, far more than men, perform the overwhelming number of utterly *un*compensated domestic tasks—from the emotional labor of maintaining adult intimate relationships to the time-consuming, repetitive, physically exhausting and emotionally demanding work involved in raising children and running a home—which are needed to keep this society functioning. And they do so, for the most part, within "relationships of care" within which their self-sacrifice is assumed both by the participants in the relationship and by the outside society as exemplary of virtue.[109] That "virtue," however, comes with a high psychic price as well as the self-evidently high economic price, and that is the damage done to the woman's own sense of personal integrity, and even sense of selfhood: the caring is for approval, and the self who seeks approval is a self who must deny her own interests, ambitions, projects, and independence. More concretely, to perform daily, time-consuming, difficult tasks for no compensation and with no recognition of the toll taken on one's own individuated life projects is to undertake work which can only be understood, much less accomplished, through a process of self-belittlement and even self-betrayal. A caring relationship that disproportionately shifts the great bulk of this work on one member but not the other is exemplary of injustice, whether or not the unjustly burdened partner views herself and her work as embodying an ethic of care.

The second reason that women, more than men, may be "giving" for less than laudatory reasons has to do with the prevalence of sexual violence directed against women, far more than against men, in this culture.[110] Because of that violence, women live with a source of fear that must somehow be *managed* if one is to navigate adulthood. And one way to manage that fear is to "give oneself" to a marriage, or a long-term relationship with a man, which the woman perceives either rightly or wrongly will stave off the danger, and hence the fear, of sexual assault by other men. Many of these relationships may no doubt be joyous, but it is not unreasonable to assume that many of them are quite the opposite: that on a very deep emotional level, they are joy-deadening pacts of protection in which the woman has traded away, in a sense, her right to bodily pleasure, full autonomy, and sensual integrity in exchange for a measure of safety. This "trade," far from rational, may be unacknowledged, and when it is so, the result will often be a giving self of the sort that concerns us here—a self who learns to give not out of an admirable compassionate impulse, but because of a fear that should she not, she will be *taken,* and perhaps in violent and life-threatening ways. One of the hidden costs of this psychic transaction, which again is a part of women's lives far more than men's, is a sacrifice of personal integrity on a very fundamental, even physical level. That sacrifice of personal integrity is a failure of

[82]

justice, and that failure of justice renders the relationships in which it occurs not only unjust, but fundamentally uncaring as well. Put imagistically, if the tree relinquishes its trunk, branches, and leaves because it knows that if it does not they will be violently and lethally taken, the act of giving is neither just nor caring. It is not just because it is lacking in integrity as its true nature goes unacknowledged, and it is not caring because it is motivated by fear and desperate self-preservation, not true friendship or compassion. The relationships in which such "caring" or "compassion" or self-sacrifice is constitutive, are hardly relationships to applaud or cherish.

More simply, the reason for women's disproportionate embrace of the giving self, and the psychic cost to personal integrity that self entails, might simply be women's political subordination to men—it would surely not be the only example of a subordinated class coming to accept its own subordination by accepting a dwindled-down self image. But whatever its causes, the giving self to which I'm referring reflects a trait of personhood—a very real human potential— which is far better characterized as an injury than as a virtue. The many women and the occasional man who define themselves as not-selves suffer a decreased sense of personal autonomy, of independence, of individuation, and of integrity. There is no reason to celebrate these stunted selves whose very existence is dramatic evidence of massive societal injustice, by misconstruing the selflessness they exemplify as the virtue of compassion.

The relationships just described, and the failure of the interlocking ethic of justice and care which they exemplify, are of course relationships between husbands and wives, domestic partners, or sexual partners, not between courts and litigants. Courts and judges, as noted above, do not enter into relationships of care. One might, then, question the relevance of this sort of internal critique of the ethic of care to jurisprudential inquiry: if caring relationships should be made more just, then so be it, but that is hardly a matter of interest to jurisprudential inquiry. But the conclusion here clearly does not follow. Courts and judges do not themselves enter into relationships of care, but they are deeply complicit in the construction of those relationships. Even more so than legislatures, courts have created, through common law adjudication, an interlocking web of family law, criminal law, tort law, and contract law[111] doctrine that in some cases reinforces and in other cases virtually mandates relationships that may or may not be "compassionate," but are demonstrably unjust. They are unjust precisely *because* they constitute one member of the relationship—typically the woman—as a giving self, incapacitating her from participation in the internalization of the waters of justice marked by the cupped hands and the sworn vow—incapacitating her from personal integrity.

Rape law in its entirely, and particularly the so-called marital rape exemption is simply the most egregious example.[112] Personal ethical integrity is bound to be a mirage when the *physical* integrity of the body is neither respected nor protected. The rape itself, of course, is the assault, and the rapist is the culprit, but the failure of the courts to criminalize and punish—to disproportionately deny this protection to women—renders the courts and the interests they represent complicit. Family law and contract law interrelate and reinforce each other in such a way as to render noncompensable the domestic and child-raising labor of women—thus insuring that the unjust relationships in which this labor is borne are insulated from the pressures that would otherwise be exerted by a free market toward compensation. This list could easily be extended, and in the next chapter I will expand upon it considerably. The point here is simply that courts, the state, and generally "Law" are all directly involved in the construction of the relationships that make up social life. To the degree that those relationships are unjust, even when compassionate, courts and judges—who aim for justice in the rules they create as well as the decisions they hand down—are involved in a massive act of injustice.

PARTICULARITY WITHOUT THE SCALES OF JUSTICE

And finally, what is the value of particularity and respect for context untempered by the scales of justice? To return again to Father Byron's imagistic approach, we should recall that the "scales of justice" actually make two demands of the adjudicator: first, that the adjudicator be impartial, as imaged by the blindfold, and second, that the adjudicator compensate wrongs—that wherever a "downside" advantage borne by one side is causally related, *"even by indirect social forces,"* to an "upside disadvantage" enjoyed by the other, the wrong must be somehow righted. I argued above that the zealous pursuit of impartiality untempered by respect for the relational values of particularity and context, could perversely lead to injustice. It is also true, however, that a zealous and highly partial respect for the particularity of the litigants before a judge, without regard for the constraint of justice, can lead to decisions both unjust and uncaring.

The most tragic example is the modern Court's affirmative action jurisprudence. From *University of California v. Bakke,* [113] the Court's first significant decision on affirmative action plans, to *Croson v. City of Richmond* [114] and *Adarand Constructors Inc v. Pena,* [115] the modern Court has steadfastly refused to carefully trace, in the demanding manner urged by Father Byron, the causal relationships between white privilege and the sufferings of people of color. In all these cases, the Court has been extremely solicitous—even caring— of the claims of the *particular* aggrieved white complainants: the white medical school applicant denied admission to University of California Medical School, allegedly because of an affirmative action program designed to increase racial and ethnic diversity in the school and in the profession, and a white subcontractor denied a city or federal contract allegedly because of a legislated set-aside program for contractors predominantly owned by racial minorities. The Court's method and decision in these cases have been respectful of the constraint of *particularity* imposed by an ethic of care. What the Court failed to do, in both cases, was to undertake the inquiry demanded by the constraint of *justice.*

To break it down somewhat, the Court's failure has been twofold. First, as just suggested, in virtually all its affirmative action jurisprudence, the Court has essentially refused to "don the blindfold"—it has attended with care to the needs, concerns, and particularly the "guiltlessness" of the (white) litigants before it. Standing alone, this departure is not fatal to the task of doing justice. Indeed, it can evidence respect for the constraint of an ethic of care. Judge Sokorow, a liberal, compassionate, fair-minded judge who is unquestionably a friend of affirmative action, once remarked that the only qualms he had about affirmative action programs stemmed from the intensely personal difficulty he had facing an essentially "blameless" white litigant, and denying that litigant his or her "place" in an apprenticeship program or applicant pool, so as to make space for a minority competitor. Thus, the only reservation about affirmative action programs, for this ardent defender of such plans, came at the moment of particularity—the moment when the blindfold is discarded and the litigants are faced in their human particularity.

What *is* fatal to the Court's attempt to do justice in the affirmative action cases, is not so much an excess of particularity—an undue regard for the dilemma of blameless whites—as its *coupling* of that particularized solicitude with its steadfast refusal to take up the *substantive* task demanded of the blinded, impartial adjudicator, which is to determine whether the "downside" advantage enjoyed by the one side is *causally related* to the "upside" disadvantage suffered by the other, or, in less imagistic terms, whether the advantages enjoyed by white subcontractors in Richmond, Virginia, or the advantages enjoyed by white applicants to medical schools in Davis, California, are causally related to the disadvantages suffered by their minority competitors. The Court has refused to ask whether, to use Father Byron's phrase, the downside advantage of white medical school applicants and white subcontractors should be attributed, in part, to the historical and ongoing subordination of African American citizens in this culture. The subtle, nuanced, and complex *substantive* inquiry which is demanded by the constraint of justice—whether the downside advantage can be attributed to the upside disadvantage, "*even by indirect social forces,*"[116]—is precisely the inquiry the Supreme Court has mandated that the courts should *not* undertake in their fourteenth amendment jurisprudence. The result is a tragic and ongoing failure of justice of monumental, national proportions.

It is also, however, and precisely for that reason, a failure of care. Recognition of the claims of justice of others is a way to acknowledge the commonality between ourselves and those "others," it is a way of forming as well as acknowledging community. Failure to rectify even the most obvious and most glaring instances of injustice between members of a community is itself a form of excommunication, a "shunning" which "ain't biblical," a refusal to care as well as a refusal to compensate. Indeed, it is a failure to care because it is a refusal to compensate. The result—at least one result—is, not surprisingly, an explosion of hate. The privileged majority must somehow come to grips with the collective refusal of the community to engage the dialogue of justice, and compensate for the injustices of our history of race relations. It must, somehow, *justify* that failure, if it is not to rectify it. The result of that attempt is, almost necessarily, the pathology of overt or covert racism—bold claims of moral or intellectual superiority of the advantaged over the disadvantaged. Thus, the particularized attention accorded the particular aggrieved white plaintiff and the refusal to engage the inquiry of justice which accompanies it results not in a victory of care over justice, but rather in a failure of both. Again, the constraints of care and justice are revealed to be intertwined and codependent, not oppositional.

The Court's affirmative action decisions, however, were not made in a conceptual vacuum. Even our most ardent *defenders* of affirmative action policies, and some of our harshest critics of the Court's dismantling of those programs, rarely seek to justify such policies on the straightforward ground that they are a necessary reparation for a massive societal and historical injustice, and tend to rely instead heavily on utilitarian and consequentialist arguments. More broadly, both the Court's refusal to engage in this inquiry as a matter of law, and its critics' refusal to engage the same inquiry as a matter of advocacy, reflect and reinforce larger cultural and social patterns of denial among the members of the privileged classes of this heavily privileged society. We rarely even ask, much less answer, the question of justice propounded by Father Byron: whether the advantages we enjoy in this First World industrialized culture are causally related to the sufferings of disadvantaged persons in other parts of the globe. Thus, precisely the same failure of justice—and resultant failure of care—is revealed by the daily denial of each of us in the First World that enjoy the fruits of this privilege to acknowledge the demands of the scales of justice, and to adjust our very private lives and public practices accordingly. Both as parents and as a society, we care deeply about, and will move heaven and earth to protect and nurture, the particular individual talents and potentials of our own and, for some of us at least, our own culture's children. We have failed utterly to balance that privilege against the suffering of the rest of the world, or to consider the causal relationship between the two. As Father Byron insists, that is indeed a failure of justice, and it is by quite a margin the greatest moral challenge of our day.

It bears emphasizing that *because* of it—because of that refusal to pick up the scales and weigh our global responsibilities—the otherwise healthy, happy, joyous, particularizing nurturance we bestow upon our children is not in the end very caring. It does not, in other words, represent a triumph of the constraint of particularized care over an oppositional constraint of justice. Rather, because of the neglect of the constraint of justice, the ethic of care is also breached. If we want to be truly caring, in short, we must widen the circle of care to embrace the demands of global, no less than social, justice. And until we do so, it should come as no surprise that both the decisions of our judges and the rhetoric of their critics in the heavily contested field of civil rights also reflect, and profoundly, those deep moral failings.

CONCLUSION: TOWARD A SYNTHESIS OF JUSTICE AND CARE

Let me briefly recapitulate. What I have argued so far is that the zealous pursuit of justice, or of some attribute of justice—be it institutional consistency, personal integrity, or impartiality—when unconstrained by the demands of an ethic of care, will fail as a matter of justice as well as a matter of care. On the other hand, the zealous pursuit of some attribute of care—nurturance, compassion, or particularity—when unconstrained by the demands of an ethic of justice, will fail as a matter of care no less than as a matter of justice. We can easily find examples of both sorts of failures in the decisions of our judges. The zealous pursuit of generality or universality revealed in the movement toward full commodification of injuries and claims that is so widespread now in private law, is at root a failure to respond in a particularized, and hence caring way, to the uniqueness of certain sorts of claims or injuries—and because of that failure, the cases themselves seem unjust. On the other hand, the zealous pursuit of caring in the form of respect for the "innocent" white victims of affirmative action policies revealed in the fourteenth amendment jurisprudence of the Supreme Court is at root a failure to examine and respond to the demands of justice. Because of that failure, the inter- as well as intraracial social relationships these cases have engendered bear the marks of hate and bigotry far more than of care and fellow feeling. A failure of justice, in short, will prove fatal to a relationship of care. A failure of care, on the other hand, proves just as fatal to the pursuit of justice.

Put affirmatively, an integrated conception of judging requires that justice be caring, and that the caring in our public and private lives—

lives to a considerable degree affected by, if not determined by, the decisions of judges—be just. Let me depart from images and illustrations, and try to say analytically why this might be so. First, legal justice, as is widely acknowledged, requires that judges treat "like cases alike." This is the legalistic definition, in a sense, of both the requirement of consistency represented in Father Byron's trilogy as the plumb line, and the related virtue of impartiality represented by the blindfold. But if judges are *to do* that—if judges are to identify "likes" and treat them "alike"—they must be able to understand the shared qualities of certain experiences which on their surface may appear to be quite different indeed. That perception—the perception of a deeply shared commonality in the face of surface differences—is a type of understanding that is *of necessity* empathic. Thus, to take an example, if justice *demands* recognition of gay and lesbian marriages, it does so because of the *similarity*—the sameness—of the yearnings for intimacy, commitment, and public recognition experienced by both gays and lesbians and heterosexuals at that poignant moment of intersection of the public world with intimate lives, which is so central to the ritual of a marriage. And if justice demands such a recognition, it demands judicial decisions that rule accordingly when faced with challenges to the constitutionality of state laws forbidding such marriages. Such a justice, however, will never be forthcoming unless and until judges involved in adjudicating claims of these sorts exercise their empathic, caring ability to understand the quite private lives of gay and lesbian citizens. That ability will in turn not be exercised, because it will not even be tapped, so long as societal perceptions or claims of "difference" are allowed to trump empathically, and caringly, acquired understandings of a deeper commonality.

By the same token, legal justice requires that judges treat situations which are truly different, differently. Again, if judges are to do so—if they are to differentiate experiences which are truly different, whatever their surface similarity, from each other and treat them differently—then they must empathically understand those differences and their import. Again, to take an example, if a judge is to justly decide upon the appropriate remedy for a breached surrogacy contract, then she must, as a matter of positive law, be able to understand the difference between the pain felt by the breaching contractor for the loss of a recently carried and delivered child and the loss of a profit caused by a changed circumstance in a more traditional commercial contract. If the former is truly *different*—if the pain felt by the loss of the child simply cannot be analogized to the pain of lost profit, and if the changed feelings engendered by a nine-month pregnancy simply cannot be analogized to the changed costs generated by a newly discovered condition on a construction site—*and if* the loss of the carried and delivered child to the biological mother is greater than the loss of the child to the contract mother who can, presumably, engage a substitute surrogate parent and begin the process anew, then the "changed circumstance" is of a sort which should trigger either the imposition of a mandatory term, such as a three-month waiting period, voidance of the contract in its entirety as contrary to public policy, or at least an insistence on the traditional (and less demanding of the breaching party) remedy of money damages over the more demanding remedy of specific performance. But here as well, unless the Court engages in the empathic work of feeling and then comparing these potential losses, the magnitude, much less the nature of these losses, cannot be appreciated. And if they are not appreciated, the law will be misapplied—a failure of justice, no less than a failure of care.

Second, consistency, in the sense of equal treatment, is a core demand of our constitutional justice. Yet here as well, the zealous quest for consistency without respect for the human practice of particularized (and inconsistent) nurturance, common to a good deal of liberal and progressive argument for both reproductive rights and redistributive welfare entitlements, will run afoul of moral intuitions premised on and constituted by those practices. If, at the heart of constitutional arguments for reproductive freedom and welfare entitlements is a zeal for consistency which is *itself* inconsistent with nurturant, particularized practices, then those arguments—generally grounded in the equal protection clause—will to that degree seem unjust. Those freedoms and entitlements might be better defended, both as a constitutional matter and morally, by appealing not to our attraction to an abstract virtue of consistency, but rather to our human ability to expand our sense of empathic understanding of and sympathy for others who are outside our immediate circle of care. If we care about others in our community, we should care about the quality of their lives. And if we care about the quality of their lives, then we should willingly accord them the positive liberty to ensure it. The "right," then, to reproductive freedom or to welfare, might be better understood as a constitutional embodiment of our expanded capacity for caring rather than a constitutional embodiment of our impulse to reduce ourselves and each other, for the sake of an abstract commitment to consistency, to that which is common, and meanest, within us. Constitutional arguments and judicial decisions which directly aim to improve the quality of life of those who are most endangered, and which do so, in essence, because an ethic of care demands it, are stronger arguments—and more just—because of it.

And third, justice demands integrity—that the adjudicator, whether judge or juror, apply the law faithfully. Yet to hold fast to a legalistic faith without regard for constraints on action demanded by an ethic of compassion rarely leads to a robust justice. Justice, one might say, requires more than legalistic or positivistic purity, as the better jurists have uniformly known and argued. It requires, at a minimum, an appreciation of each participant's human *essence,* and that in turn requires a compassionate attempt to understand his or her lived dilemma. The law itself, in its nobler moments, does and always has recognized this—from the historical interplay between "law" and "equity" to the modern insistence on "mitigation" in criminal sentencing, and even to academic and juristic movements insisting upon open interpretation of legal norms so as to insure their compliance with just and humane ends.

On the other side of the equation, our relationships of care must be just if they are to be caring, and judicial decisions which create, legitimate, or provide incentives for the construction or maintenance of such relationships must carry the burden of this requirement. To take some obvious examples, the relationship of master and slave is highly particular, concrete, and even, in a perverse sense, "total," whole, or holistic. As Mark Tushnet has argued, it is far more particular, concrete, and whole, in a number of ways, than that of employer and wage laborer.[117] But it is also manifestly unjust—it is incompatible with both the mandate of consistency and the scales of justice— and because of that it is uncaring, no matter how much the particular parties may protest to the contrary. The same is true of relationships of husband and wife where the husband has the legal entitlement to rape his wife at will. Judicial decisions which legitimate, legalize, or encourage legal regimes in which such relationships are tolerated or valorized are accordingly themselves unjust.

Somewhat less obviously, the caring relationship of parent to child is marred by the presence of injustice in the relationship between them, but it can also be marred by the presence of injustice *between the parents:* love of a child by an unjustly subordinated parent is felt as love *by someone who is herself unworthy,* and such love does little to encourage a child's sense of well-being or self-esteem. Such love is, to that degree, non-nurturant. As Susan Okin has eloquently and persuasively argued, children raised in unjust families are not taught the virtue of justice.[118] It is not clear they will ever be able to "learn" the meaning of that virtue if they have not lived it. What Okin does not make clear, however, but what seems equally important, is that such children are *also,* and for that reason, deprived of a good deal of genuine care as well, with considerable damage done to both boys and girls.

Lastly, but just as importantly, children raised in families which are in some sense internally just but which are unconstrained by the demands of justice in their relationships with outsiders, are being taught not just lessons in injustice, but are also being raised in an atmosphere of hate. The child raised in an atmosphere of bigotry matures into an adult who is not just unjust in his relationships with the vilified "other" but uncaring as well. The result is not only a mean-spirited, bigoted, and unnecessarily stunted adult, but a continuation of the societal climate of hate and lack of trust which is itself essential to societal injustice. One does not, in short, treat those one has been taught to care about in an unjust manner, and one does not treat uncaringly those one has been taught to understand as entitled to the deserts of justice.

In the societal, rather than familial context as well, a genuinely caring relationship requires a stance of justice, toward both those inside the relationship and those outside it. Racism is surely the clearest example of a complete failure of these interdependent ethics. The intentional racism espoused in hate speech, for example, is obviously both hateful and unjust: a failure of care and justice. But subconscious racism, as well as societal neglect of institutional, historical, and ongoing less visible forms of disadvantage also constitutes an injustice—a failure to rectify the imbalanced scales—and for that reason a lack of care. The ethical value of the particularized affection for one's own child is undercut, then, by a callousness toward disadvantaged children—it is again a failure of care because it is a failure of justice. The solicitude of the Supreme Court for the particular circumstances, and the particular "guiltlessness" of the white litigant, is profoundly and utterly overshadowed by the lack of care reflected in the Court's simultaneous refusal to engage in the substantive work of justice—to determine whether the advantage enjoyed even by the guiltless is causally related to the disadvantage suffered by the subordinate. Again, we don't behave unjustly toward those we care about. And of more moment, those toward whom we refuse to accord this simple justice become the objects of our hatred.

Just as judicial decisions which are themselves uncaring because unjust, or reinforce societal relationships which are themselves unjust and uncaring, judicial decisions which break these cycles of hatred represent true moments of nobility. Great judicial decisions which are exemplary of a caring justice are, perhaps unsurprisingly, far rarer than judicial decisions which pointedly fall short. I think it's fair to say, however, forty some years after the fact, that *Brown v. Board of Education,*[119] whatever its many flaws, and however much it got wrong, is such a decision. It demanded that we attend to the pain and hurt caused by societal racial relationships, and by so doing it brought into being not only a new understanding of the equal protection guaranteed by the constitution, but a new understanding of racial justice. The justice of that decision was quite explicitly premised upon the insistence that the pain caused by those social relations between the races *must be* understood, acknowledged, felt, shared, and ended. Again, whatever the decision's flaws, the fact that it was so motivated marks it as a decision both caring and just—and just *because* caring, and caring because just. Perhaps it is for that reason that *Brown v. Board of Education*[120]—one of the most criticized decisions of our history—continues to stand, for almost all of us, as exemplary of the potential for moral greatness inherent in every judicial declaration.

CHAPTER TWO

The Concept of Harm

What is the "point" of law? According to at least one prominent jurisprudential understanding, law is essentially an *instrument:* it is a human creation, designed to minimize the harms we suffer in social life.[1] If that is right, and surely to some degree it is, then it would seem that an understanding of what constitutes a *harm* would be central to jurisprudence. If it is true, as instrumentalists hold, that the primary instrumental function of law is to deter harms or compensate for them through legal means, then surely we need to know what harms us, and how much.

For the most part, however, most contemporary legal theorists — and even most contemporary instrumentalists — have neglected that question. Instrumentalists have instead typically assumed that the definitional question is straightforward, and focused on a rather different issue, namely, whether the sorts of actions we might take through law to deter harms, or to compensate for them, would turn out to be more costly in the long run than the harm itself. In fact, entire jurisprudential schools and political philosophies have their origin in attempts to systematically specify a mechanism for resolving questions of this sort: classical liberalism is grounded in the insight that the social costs of preventing harms caused by speech and thought outweigh the harms themselves,[2] and "law and economics" has its origin in the claim that the very definition of what constitutes a compensable harm depends upon the relative costs of the harm-causing event compared with the costs of preventing it.[3] By contrast, much less attention has been paid to the more fundamental issues of what a "harm" is, how, in a general way, we recognize when we have sustained one, or perhaps more importantly, how we assess the claims of others that they have sustained harm. The consequence is that while we have a good deal of jurisprudential scholarship on what might be called the "instrumental" premise of law—that law is basically an instrument for the redress of harms—we have very little understanding of what might be called the necessary "hedonic" foundations of that instrumentalism—what harm is, what harms we suffer, and how we come to know about them. We don't presently have what might be called a "hedonic analysis" of the very phenomenon harm which, at least according to most instrumental legal theorists, is the target of law.

This neglect is not really surprising, and indeed may appear to be relatively inconsequential for much of law's domain. Thus, we don't seem to need much by way of a hedonic analysis to reach a consensus that battery and homicide are harmful events, and that law might be one useful instrument for minimizing their occurrence. The only relevant issue, from an instrumentalist perspective, appears to concern the legal response: how much of our social resources should be spent deterring or punishing those actions which cause them, and compensating for the injuries they occasion? Many of the harms that law is concerned to prevent, deter, or compensate seem to be of this nature. For that reason alone, it's not surprising that the concept of harm has not necessitated a substantial literature within instrumental jurisprudence. Instrumentalism is a practice-focused, practice-minded, anti-theoretic theory—and from a practical point of view, the concept of harm appears to be relatively problem-free.

There is, of course, one (but, significantly, only one) sustained analytic inquiry into the nature of harm that can be found in contemporary instrumentalist jurisprudence, and that is that put forward by the law and economics school. As I will discuss in some detail below, however, that inquiry, far from opening up the nature of harm as a fruitful jurisprudential issue, had exactly the opposite effect. In his seminal 1960 article *The Problem of Social Cost*,[4] the legal economist Ronald Coase argued that it is at least oftentimes not clear whether the "harm" caused by a polluting industry, for example, should be characterized as the injury done to those suffering the pollution, or the cost to the industry of avoiding it, should those aggrieved by the pollution be granted a right to be free of it. The central thesis of Coase's article—which became one of the defining ideas of the law and economics movement taken as a whole—is in essence that we should *replace* the idea of harm with the much more relative and quantifiable concept of *cost*. Coase's article, rather than opening up an inquiry into the nature of harm, essentially closed it: Coase defined the discipline of law and economics in such a way as to marginalize the concept of harm, and law and economics eventually came to dominate the theoretical side of instrumentalist jurisprudence. The combined effect of the practice-driven neglect of the issue by pragmatic, noneconomic instrumentalists, and the theoretic dominance of instrumentalism by normative economics, is that instrumentalism— the only contemporary jurisprudential perspective which would logically center the concept of harm, and take up the project of a hedonic analysis of its contours—has shunned such an inquiry.

In this chapter, I want to try to show two things. First, I want to argue that the absence of a jurisprudential analysis of the concept of harm, and particularly the economist's collapse of the concept of harm with the concept of cost, far from being totally inconsequential as it may first appear to be, has had adverse consequences, and particularly for women. Because we lack a focused dialogue on the concept of *harm*—as opposed to the concept of *cost*—we make largely unthinking assumptions about what sorts of events harm us and what sorts of events don't. Those largely unthinking assumptions, in many respects, do not fit the distinctive experiences and sensibilities of women. Women suffer harms in this culture that are different from those suffered by men. And partly because they are different, they often do not "trigger" legal relief in the way that harms felt by men alone or by men and women equally do. As a result women are doubly injured: first by the harm-causing event itself, and second by the peculiarity or nonexistence of the law's response to those harms. Both the state of our feminist jurisprudence and the political and legal status of women would be improved, albeit, in both cases, perhaps only marginally, by an airing of the differences between the harms suffered by women and men, and the role the legal system plays and should play in responding to those harms. The first aim of this chapter quite generally is to provide at least the beginnings of such an account.

Second, I want to show that even a bare description of gendered harms reveals significant problems with the pragmatic instrumentalist assumptions quickly reviewed above. Law does, at times, minimize the gendered harms I will identify, as instrumentalists hold. But, as I will try to show, at times it also trivializes or ignores them, occasionally legitimates them, and indeed at times protects or celebrates the events which cause them. Instrumentalists are simply wrong to assume that law essentially seeks to minimize harms. A robust instrumentalism should illuminate—and surely should also interrogate—all the ways in which law impacts upon harm, including the various ways in which it aggravates it.

My argument will rest in part on three assumptions, which I hope are relatively uncontroversial. First, I will assume that instrumentalism does indeed express a sensible working *ideal* of law: whatever it *is,* law clearly *should be* an instrument for the redress, compensation, or deterrence of harms. In that sense, this is an entirely "internal," or friendly, critique of legal instrumentalism. Second, I will also assume what has been exhaustively demonstrated by two decades of feminist legal and historical scholarship, although rarely noted or noticed by nonfeminist instrumentalists, namely, that for almost all its history, Anglo-American law has been, at best, an imperfect "instrument" for the redress of harms suffered by *men.* Third, I will assume that in our era of relative "formal legal equality" historical "gender bias" in law is widely condemned, and I will assume that it has also been, *for the most part,* eliminated. Our modern commitment to formal legal equality between men and women *minimally* requires that women are entitled to *more or less* the same legal remedies, and for more or less the same harms, to which men are entitled.

What is not so widely acknowledged, however, is that the substantive law that defines those compensable harms, legal redress for which both women and men are equally entitled, is the product of our legal history, and consequently bears the mark of its historic gender bias. In a nutshell, this means that the rights and remedies universally available to both women and men are for *those harms,* and for the most part *only* those harms which, historically, have been suffered by, recognized by, and taken seriously by, men. Men can be killed, assaulted, battered, and threatened, and because men understand these events as harms, the law provides compensation for them, attempts to deter the behavior that causes them, and punishes those who inflict

[97]

them. Men can be the victims of theft, and because men understand these thefts as harmful, the law provides for compensation, deterrence, and punishment when thefts occur. Women too, of course, are harmed when they are robbed, assaulted, or killed, and our formally equal legal system provides women the same rights and remedies against these harms as it provides men.

But, as I will argue in the first part of this chapter, at least *some* of the harms frequently sustained by many women are quite *different* from the harms typically sustained by men: they are triggered by different events, they have different repercussions, and they cause different sorts of physical, emotional, and psychic trauma. When women sustain "gender-specific" harms, our guiding norm of "formal equality" is simply not sufficient to ensure justice.[5] In other words, even if it's true that, by virtue of our commitment to formal equality, women are entitled to whatever remedies men are entitled to, if it's also the case that, by virtue of the law's historical bias, the harms recognized by law as worthy of redress are those which men have sustained, and if it's also the case that women sustain some harms which are gender specific, then the conclusion should be obvious: the law is not adequately or indeed "equally" serving the instrumental needs of women. We might sum up the situation in this way: in an age of formal equality, women no less than men have access to the mechanisms of law to achieve some redress for harms—so long as those harms are the harms men recognize. Whenever a woman has sustained a harm *in the same way that a man might,* she has a good chance of receiving some legal relief. Where she has sustained gender-specific harms, however, the situation is far more complicated. As I will try to show in the second part of this chapter, gender-specific harms, and the women who sustain them, create anomalies in our legal system, to which the system responds in a number of different but invariably perverse ways.

There are, of course, any number of ways we might go about demonstrating that gender-specific harms are underdeterred, and that women are undercompensated for their sufferance. The "hedonic" argument I hope to put forward in this chapter—a contrast of the nature of the harms women suffer with mainstream understanding of the harms that are legally compensable—is only one such way. It does, though, have the advantage of serving two ends simultaneously. First, I hope to show through this exercise that women are indeed seriously injured by the legal system's neglect of the "harms" we suffer. The political point is simple, and of obvious consequence for feminism: women suffer harms that are different from those suffered by men, and those harms are underdeterred and undercompensated, relative to harms suffered by men, or by men and women equally, and that fact in turn imposes yet additional harms on women. But second, I also hope to show, through the same exercise, that the concept of harm, already seriously undertheorized, has been even further impoverished by the neglect of women's input: our neglect of the ways in which law compounds rather than deters gender-specific harms, has impoverished our understanding of the relationship between law and the harm it ostensibly is designed to minimize. Thus, a hedonic contrast of the harms women suffer with the nature of the "harm" largely assumed by mainstream theorists might both enrich our feminist understanding of the ways women are underserved (or worse) by law, and at the same time enrich our jurisprudential understanding of the relationship between law and harm. Taken jointly, the project might show the direction we might take to achieve an ideally reconstructed legal system—one which would aim to minimize the harms sustained by all its subjects, and not just by the dominant few.

In the first part of this chapter, I will catalog some of the harms which women, either distinctively or disproportionately, suffer. My aim here will *not* be to argue that for every harm discussed there should be a legal remedy or legal response of some sort, quite the contrary. In this first section, I only want to suggest that the internal quality of women's lives in this culture is different from men's, in part because of the difference in the nature of the harms women endure in daily life. In the second part, I will discuss the different ways in which the legal system and the legal culture have compounded the harms. Again, I will neither argue nor imply that the law "should" recognize, deter, or criminalize the events which cause gendered harms. What I want to argue is that the law and legal culture as they are presently constituted affect these harms in various ways, only *one* of which is to instrumentally minimalize them.

The third part of this chapter briefly addresses *why* it is that harm is an undertheorized concept in both jurisprudence generally, and theoretical instrumentalism more specifically. I will then argue that just as the legal neglect of the harms women suffer has disserved women, so this jurisprudential neglect of the concept of harm has also disserved women—the neglect of the concept of harm within jurisprudence is, in effect, yet another "gender-specific harm." In the conclusion, I address feminism rather than instrumentalism. I will suggest that some of the theoretical issues that currently plague feminism might look more manageable if we embraced a straightforward instrumentalist approach to legal reform—but place at the heart of it a more nuanced and feminist understanding of both the nature of harm and of the nature of law's relation to it, than that which instrumentalists typically employ.

GENDERED HARMS

Women sustain *physical, emotional, psychic,* and *political* harms in daily life—indeed, for many women, on a daily *basis*—which have no or little counterpart in men's lives. For the most part I will try to establish this conclusion by example, but the differences can also be described somewhat categorically in this way: physically, women suffer harms of *invasion* not suffered by men; emotionally, women suffer greater harms of *separation* and isolation than do men; psychically, women suffer distinctive harms to their subjectivity, or sense and reality of *selfhood* that have no correlate in men's lives; and politically, women suffer distinctive harms of patriarchal *subjection* that again have no correlate in men's lives. These harms all interrelate, and a particular harm-causing *event*—such as a rape, or an incidence of street harassment, or an act of intimate violence, or of incest—will often trigger, domino-fashion, all four sorts of harms. Nevertheless, for purposes of imposing some sort of linear order on the presentation of that which admittedly defies linearity—the quality of inner life—it makes sense, I think, to catalog these harms in a way that tracks this delineation. I begin, then, with harms of invasion, and then proceed to harms of separation and isolation, harms to selfhood, and lastly harms of political subjection.

HARMS OF INVASION

Let me start with distinctive harms of invasion occasioned upon women's physical bodies. Women's bodies, whether by nature or training, are smaller and weaker than men's, and, also unlike men's, can be vaginally penetrated in a way which gives some men sexual pleasure.

Women's bodies can also, of course, be impregnated, while men's cannot. As a consequence, both sexual assault and unwanted pregnancy are central and even defining harmful experiences for women in ways that have no correlate in men's daily lives. I will begin by looking first at the harms done to women by sexual assault, and then turn to the problem of unwanted pregnancy. In each case, I will first look at aspects of the *experience* of rape or pregnancy which are gendered, and then try to describe what I take to be the gendered harms that follow.

The centrality of rape and the fear of rape to women's lives have of course been exhaustively documented in feminist writing over the last twenty years,[6] and I won't attempt to redocument it here. It is worth pointing out, however, that much of that writing on the harm of rape has sought to render rape intelligible and worthy of serious attention, by essentially analogizing the *harm* of rape to harms that men sustain in different contexts. Thus, feminists have argued, variously and with varying degrees of success, that the *real* harm done by rape is the violence it incurs—indeed, that "rape is a crime of violence, not sex" has become something of a rallying cry for an entire generation of feminist women.[7] Alternatively, feminists have argued that the real harm done by rape is the threat to women's *autonomy,*[8] or that the real harm done is the residue of fear that the threat of rape leaves in all women, both survivors and others.[9] There is undoubtedly truth in all these propositions: rape certainly is a crime of violence, it does indeed threaten autonomy, and it unquestionably induces fear. All these harms of rape, however, are at least similar to harms men sustain in other contexts: men are victims of violence, that violence and potential violence threatens their autonomy, and burdens them with the fear of its recurrence. What these accounts omit are those aspects of the experience of rape which are, in a word, *gendered:* the aspects of the experience of rape which simply have no correlate in (most) men's lives—although they do, of course, recur in the lives of some.

There are (at least) two aspects of the experience of a rape which are deeply gendered. First, the physically invasive penetration of the woman's body by the man's penis is itself a painful part of the experience,[10] and it is one which cannot simply be "folded" into the more general attacks on autonomy or security noted above. Second, the *coupling* of painful, nonconsensual sexual penetration with further violence or the threat of further violence renders the invasion of the woman's body—which in other contexts, of course, can be a source of pleasure rather than pain—not only painful but life-threatening. The painful physical invasion becomes not just *unwanted,* but terrifying, and terrorizing. This coupling of unwanted and painful sexual penetration *with the experience of terror,* I think, is the most gender-specific aspect of the experience of rape.

The specific *coupling,* central to rape, of painful, physical, *sexual* invasion with the terror that accompanies life-threatening violence is not only gendered, it is, in a sense, archetypal: it is a depressingly dominant feature in the distinctive internal quality of the harms that recur in women's lives. The distinctiveness of marital and domestic violence, for example, lies in this coupling of invasion and terror. Men as well as women suffer violence and the threat of violence from strangers; but women far more than men suffer violence and the threat of violence from *intimates.*[11] Again, the violence itself is of course a harm, in ways well documented, but the fact that the harm is suffered because of the actions of intimates compounds it: the harm is one of *invasion* as well as violence, and of *betrayal and exposure* as well as fear.[12] When a woman suffers violence or threats of violence from an intimate she loses not only her sense of security against physical assault, but also her privacy—both the privacy of her body and the privacy of the dwelling in which the abuse occurs. When there is no safe haven—when, instead, the haven *is* the locus of danger— the body and home become not simply on occasion threatened by external danger, but *identified* with the external danger; they *become* the danger. When *invaded* with violence and the threat of it, rather than simply violated or threatened with violence, the home and the body—and specifically the sexual body—become themselves dangerous. Marital rape, domestic violence, incest, and more generally the sexual abuse of young children by intimates all trigger invasive harms of this sort: not only is the body physically invaded, but the sense of security one should garner from intimacy is shattered, and the privacy of one's body and home is extinguished.[13] Even an occasional, or once-in-a-lifetime rape of a woman by an intimate causes serious harm to her sense of psychic security in her body and home, and often over the course of a lifetime.[14]

Street harassment and sexual harassment have a similar dynamic, and although the damage is less profound, it is also more widespread.

Street hassling and sexual harassment are not merely assaultive, although they are clearly that, they are also *invasive*. And because they are invasive, the harms they cause are different from those brought on by simple assaults. The coupling of the implicit or explicit threat of force with sexual suggestion quite literally, albeit not physically, *penetrates* the body. A woman harassed on the street feels not only afraid, but also chilled, humiliated, dirty, and above all, *exposed;* she's been turned inside out.[15] The fear engendered by walking past a whispered message—"Hey cunt, hey bitch, hey YOU, come sit on my face"—is compounded by the feel of involuntarily exposed intimacy—of invasion. A part of the invasion, of course, is simply an invasion of privacy: the private space of anonymity on a public street is shattered, the complicated or serious train of thought is lost, the comfortable gait becomes awkward, the light mood is gone, the feeling of comradery and equality with cocitizens is obliterated.[16] Even more painful than the invasion of privacy, however, is the verbal and visual invasion and exposure of the sexual body—it is that invasion which renders a woman, or at least an unprepared and undefended woman, humiliated, infantilized, chilled, and exposed. The invasion renders her a sexual amusement for others—she becomes a toy. And again, that *invasion* is gender specific.

The psychic harms occasioned by these sexual assaults are also gendered, however, and perhaps for that reason also not well understood. That harm might best be captured by contrasting the individual who has sustained it with one version—more specifically, the modern "economic" version—of the liberal paradigm of individual health or well-being. Central to the liberal idea of a healthy, assertive individualism, at least according to most economic-liberal theorists, is a pair of what might be called "hedonic connections": the *desires* of the healthy individual, according to modern liberal theory, are prompted and informed by experiences of pleasure, and the *actions* of the healthy individual are prompted by desires.[17] Thus we desire what pleases us, and we act on the basis of our desires: this is largely *what it means* in this culture to be a self-possessed individual. One way to describe the distinctive psychic harm of sexual violence is that it is precisely these distinguishing hedonic connections of a liberal and individualist concept of selfhood—the internal connections between pleasure, desire, and action—which are threatened or severed by these invasions. The individual who suffers a sexual assault moves her body not in response to her own desires but rather to the desires of the attacker, and to the extent that she desires her own preservation, she desires not her own pleasures, but his. The woman who sustains these assaults repeatedly may literally redefine herself in such a way: she lives to meet the desires of and bring pleasure to the feared other. When extreme, the result is, quite literally, the death of a liberal and individualistic conception of subjectivity: there can be no sense of self-possession when the self has been invaded by the desires, pleasure, will, and actions of another, and stronger, and life-threatening, human being.

The girl or woman in whom these hedonic connections are severed[18] because of repeated or long-term sexual assault, is not going to be capable of a robust, autonomous individualism.[19] She becomes almost by definition incapable of the subjectivity that engenders the rational act—the act based on self-interest, as informed by one's own pleasures, and as mediated by one's own desires—central to that form of being-in-oneself. Similarly, she becomes incapable of the quintessentially individualistic act of positioning, asserting, or *thrusting* herself into the world, thereby changing the world with a felt presence. To be sure, any woman, or any man, may of course resist this liberal-individualist mode of being for the noblest of reasons: a woman may *choose* not to construct herself in that way, and may even, for religious or spiritual reasons, embark on a rigorous course of training to self-consciously sever those hedonic connections.[20] At least in some cases, however, the explanation of a woman's seeming passivity is not so heartening. The individualistic act of thrusting oneself into the world—like the simple survivalist act of thrusting oneself out of one's house—may be the very act which engenders life-threatening violence and, therefore, a fully rational terror.[21] When it is, the will to act on one's own pleasures, desires, or interests—to act in a way that furthers one's own security, secures one's well-being, or "maximizes" one's safety—may have quite simply been beaten out of her.

Street hassling, like more violent assaults, also severs the hedonic connections of economic-liberal individualism—although again, the harm is obviously not as severe. A girl or woman sexually harassed on the street might "ignore it," might smile, might will herself to be smaller, might walk stonily past the harasser, or might simply freeze up inside—hide and preserve her subjectivity against the assault on her sexual body—all in an attempt to make the harassment stop. All of these responses might be "rational," but they are also hedonically perverse. It's not natural to *smile* when one is afraid or insulted. It's not natural to try to make oneself small or frozen. Again, what's severed in these transactions is the quite ordinary connection between pleasure and pain, and between desire and outward act. What is taught, and learned, is an inversion of these ordinary hedonic connections: for *his* pleasure, by virtue of an imperative issuing from *his* desire, one's body must absorb and respond to sexual assaults. The body is in effect ordered to respond to the commands of his pleasure rather than one's own. One's own pleasures—and one's entitlement to act on them—are frozen or obliterated. The distinctive, gendered aspect of the experience of assaultive sex—whether rape, incest, sexual abuse, or harassment—is the coupling of fear, pain, exposure, and humiliation with sexual invasion. The distinctive gendered *harm* is the spiritual murder of the economic-liberal hedonic self.

Unwanted pregnancy constitutes a quite different, but equally gendered, invasion of women's bodies, also carrying the potential for distinctively gendered harms. First, the physical invasion of the body occasioned by a pregnancy, like the physical invasion of the body occasioned by sexual penetration, when unwanted, is itself a harm: pregnancy is at best uncomfortable, almost always at some point painful, and at worst dangerous and life-threatening.[22] But there is one aspect of the experience of an unwanted pregnancy not shared by sexual assault, which again has no obvious correlate in men's lives: such a woman finds herself in an *involuntarily nurturant* position. The discomfort, pain, and dangers of any pregnancy, wanted or unwanted, are all endured toward the end of nurturing the fetus. When the pregnancy is voluntary and wanted, this is an uncomplicated act of altruism. When the pregnancy is involuntary, unwanted, or both, however, it is something quite different. The woman who is pregnant but does not wish to be is doing nurturant work *which she does not wish to do.* Her moral, relational life is thus as fully invaded as is her physical body. She nurtures, but without the preceding act of will and commitment that would engage her moral, choosing self. She becomes a nurturant but *unchoosing* creature—a little more like the spreading chestnut tree that gives without choosing to give, and a little less like an autonomous individual whose selfhood is strengthened rather than threatened by altruistic acts.[23]

There is, consequently, a psychic dimension to the otherwise well-documented harms of unwanted pregnancy, which, perhaps because it is so deeply gendered, often goes unnoticed. Here again, the nature of this harm might best be described by contrasting the self who sustains it with our liberal understanding of what it means to be a healthy individual. The autonomous and healthy individual, according to the economic liberal invoked above, acts on the basis of pleasures, pains, and desires.[24] But for most contemporary liberals, such a conception is unduly cramped. To capture the spirit as well as the contradictions of modern liberalism more adequately, we might offer this disjunction: the truly healthy individual, at least according to what might be called "ethical" as opposed to economic, or rational, or egoistic liberalism, *often* acts on the basis of pains, pleasures, and desires, as described by the economic liberal and his utilitarian forefathers, *but at least on occasion, and perhaps often,* he acts on the basis of a freely willed moral commitment, in the Kantian, deontic, and duty-bound spirit of ethical liberalism.[25] This specific conjunction of the *moral* act with the *free* act—and the identification of that conjunction with a definition of individualism—is precisely what an unwanted pregnancy threatens. For someone with an unwanted pregnancy, the nurturant act of sustaining the fetus with one's body—what would otherwise be a quintessentially moral, altruistic act—*is* the unfree and unwanted act. The nurturant self becomes *identified* with the self that does not choose; the nurturant self *is* the self that does not engage her will with her actions. Her morality is a passive, unwilled morality—not just unaccompanied by, but *contrary to* the actively engaged, autonomous self presupposed by ethical liberalism. She is giving and nurturing life, but in the manner of inanimate objects, plants, or animals. Selfhood is thus further undermined.

Just as the distinctively invasive harms of unwanted sex—of rape, sexual abuse, domestic violence, or sexual harassment—sever the hedonic connections between pleasure and action which are central to the self presupposed by economic liberalism, so unwanted pregnancy severs the moral connections of will, choice, and moral act which are central to ethical liberalism. Thus, while unwanted sex couples sexual intimacy with physical invasion, thereby harming the "hedonic self," unwanted pregnancy couples a sort of forced nurturance—the sharing of one's body—with physical invasion, and harms what might be called the "moral self." The raped woman moves her body so as to

[106]

give pleasure to another, and the woman repeatedly raped by an intimate learns to define herself in precisely such a fashion: she lives, acts, responds, and moves her body in response to the pleasures and desires and passions not of herself, but of another. In a parallel way, the woman who is pregnant against her will or desire nurtures the fetus altruistically, but does so without having committed herself to the moral project, and if she goes on to mother, continues to do so for a good part of her adult life. She too may eventually define herself in such a fashion: she *is* a being for whom nurturance, altruism, and morality itself are severed from the Kantian will. When she is *most* giving—in pregnancy and motherhood—is precisely when she is least willful. Pregnancy thus undermines personhood.

The physical invasions of rape and pregnancy, then, in addition to being harms incurred upon and in the body, are also destructive of both the sense and reality of at least liberal conceptions of selfhood. The woman who survives a violent, aggravated rape suffers a shattering of selfhood so profound and traumatic as to echo throughout a lifetime: her sexuality, her own body, her physical existence itself, are forever objectified as that which brings on danger, injury, fear, and death. The many more women who consent to undesired sex, and who passively acquiesce in unwanted pregnancies, undergo a destruction of selfhood which is quite different: it is less shattering and more subtle, but in some ways more insidious. The self is not simply assaulted, or threatened, or endangered, but, more exhaustively, is *redefined* as a self who gives, nurtures, pleases, or acts *for others,* rather than on the basis of one's felt physical pleasures, desires, and passions, or one's freely willed altruistic or moral decisions. What is lost, then, is the self who acts on desire, and who desires that which pleases. Equally lost is the self who acts compassionately, nurturantly, or morally on the basis of a willed decision to do so; the self who *decides* to give of herself in such a way, who makes a *decision* to forge a moral bond with another. What is adopted instead is female passivity. It is not a passivity artificially imposed upon a truer but suppressed active, willing, liberal, moral, hedonist, Kantian, or Benthamic self. It is, rather, simply the way these women *are.*

The cumulative effect of these psychic harms, I believe, is a profound divergence between women's experience of selfhood, and hence of the world, and at least liberal understandings of the nature of the self, which whether or not dominant ones, are certainly contenders.

At the center of virtually all liberal understandings of selfhood is a *directness* between desire and act. "You want it? Then *take aim and fire*. Life is just that simple." From women's perspective, that liberal self, when not imperialist and threatening, is often an object of amusement—think of any of hundreds of Cathy cartoons—or an object of admiration. The ejaculatory, self-imposing, world-conquering, nature-taming, capitalistic, commodificationist, and infinitely creative masculine self described admiringly in Camille Paglia's *Sexual Personae,*[26] whether or not "masculine," is recognizably liberal in this way: the liberal individual who egoistically acts on his pleasures, in a Benthamic manner, or who morally acts on freely chosen principles, in a Kantian manner, is, perhaps quintessentially, rationally capable of and desirous of making his own imprint upon an external world.

Whether this liberal self is something to fear, abhor, laugh at, or admire, it seems to be a conception of self that, at least in this culture, is more foreign to women than to men. There are probably a number of reasons for this. Let me quickly mention—to set aside—three possibilities. In *Sexual Personae,* Camille Paglia provocatively suggests that women's biological sexuality—inner, secretive, hidden, and self-referential, rather than outward, displayed, and in-the-world[27]— may have something to do with it, and she may well be right. Second, and as many feminists have argued, young girls, by training, far more than young boys, are simply *taught,* contra Bentham,[28] to act deferentially so as to please others rather than to act on the basis of their own pleasures.[29] And third, the experience of morality most common to women—that of nurturing *even fully wanted and celebrated* fetal and newborn life—is diametrically at odds with the willed, principled, universalized rationality which for the Kantian is the necessary foundation of the moral act. It is an act which is particular, contextual, and utterly nonuniversalizable. It is a profoundly physical, rather than rational act. It is, most importantly, motivated by intense, consuming, and to some degree instinctual emotion, rather than any sense of willed duty. Each maternal act, when the fetus is in utero, is a relatively passive, largely *unwilled* and profoundly role-governed "giving over" of one's body to the creation and nurturance of another life.[30] The experience of pregnancy and of mothering young infants may render the Kantian liberal individual a more foreign prototype of selfhood for at least many women than it is for men.

There may, though, be another reason for the foreignness of this liberal conception of selfhood to women's experience of self which is less discussed in feminist literature. This is the cumulative effect of the much larger number of invasive harms women suffer, with the attendant harms to the psyche those invasions cause, as compared to the number of such harms sustained by men. The *security* and expectation of security of the self within the body is shattered by a violent rape, and the security of the body within the home is destroyed by rape or violent abuse by intimates. The hedonic connections so central to contemporary liberal conceptions of selfhood, between pleasure and desire, and desire and act, are severed by violent and sexual invasions of the body. Further, the *expectation* that pleasure and desire will in a general way be connected with one's will to act is severed by habitual violence or unwanted consensual sex. In a parallel way, the connection between choice and a principled moral act, also central to contemporary liberal conceptions of selfhood, is severed by an unchosen and unwanted pregnancy, and the connection between a principled rational commitment and a moral act is severed by an unwanted pregnancy, even when chosen.

These harms, endured by many women throughout the course of a lifetime, and endured by most women in our culture at some point in their childhood or adulthood, take their toll. Their cumulative effect in extreme cases is the death of subjectivity—one ceases to *have* pleasures, pains, desires, and passions of one's own when such sensations are never acted upon. The harm caused by invasive terror is ultimately the cessation of selfhood. The self is objectified, and when that occurs, it ceases to exist.

HARMS OF PRIVATE ALTRUISM

Women, more than men, are expected to be and to some degree are more "altruistic" than men in their private and intimate lives: women, more than men, are inclined to subordinate their own interests, desires, and pleasures to those of persons with whom they are intimate. I have suggested above that part of the reason that at least some women are more inclined than men toward intimate altruism is the disproportionate amount of intimate violence women sustain: such violence undermines the egoistic connections between pleasure, desire, and act. But it is by no means only women who are victims of sexual violence who seem to exhibit greater inclinations toward inti-

mate altruism than do men. Rather, women's relatively greater inclination toward intimate altruism is so pervasive that it is largely invisible. It is in a sense the white noise of private or family life: because it
is always around us, and around us everywhere, it is all the harder to
see.

I want to ultimately argue in this section that these acts of intimate
altruism are both harms and harmful, but first let me begin with
some examples of intimate altruism, simply to try to foreground the
phenomenon I wish to discuss. If there are four family members, and
four dinner rolls, and one roll is burned, the altruistic wife-mother will
take the burned roll—not every fourth or every other time, but every
time. If a man wants to have sex and his female partner doesn't, they
more often will than won't—because she wants to be nice, wants to
be giving, because it's expected of her, or because she doesn't want to
bother with the sullenness or fight that will ensue if she doesn't. If
someone must stay home from work with the sick child, she will, and
if someone must be mommy-tracked to nurture and raise small children or care for aging parents, she will. If someone must give up a
better job for a lesser job to accommodate a partner's career goals,
she, rather than he, will do so. If someone must sacrifice avocational
pursuits such as golf, piano, writing, or watercoloring so as to get the
laundry done, the diapers changed, and the meals cooked, she will. If
someone must absorb a man's anger and rage from an ego-bruising
day in the outer world, she will be the punching bag, and if someone
must smile while doing so to keep a level of sanity and normalcy in
the house, she will.

I have no doubt—indeed I have elsewhere argued as much—that
to some degree, and in some contexts, these large and small acts of
self-sacrifice are emblematic of a distinctive moral voice, and as such
they are expressive of a noble human longing for community, and an
important human potential for caring. It has been the burden of
"difference," "relational," or "cultural-feminist" writing, and the burden of the first chapter of this book, to urge that this moral perspective
should be enlarged, and transported, so to speak, out of the realm of
intimacy and into the public realms of market economies, politics,
government, and law. But it is also clear that that is not the entire
story. As a good deal of recent feminist writing has also gone to lengths
to demonstrate, women's inclination toward private or intimate altruism—particularly in the home—is also, many times and in many

ways, the measure of the harms such women have distinctively sustained. They originate not in an ethic of care but in self-denigration, and reflect not a moral sensibility but a battered sense of self.[31] Furthermore, these private acts of altruism are also many times not only the measure of past harms, but the cause of further harms. For both reasons, the altruistic acts women disproportionately perform in the domestic sphere are at least at times more properly called "altruistic harms."

The harms caused by private and intimate acts of consensual altruism that women perform are hard to describe, largely because they are hard to *see*. And they are hard to see, in turn, because of the pervasive effect of two widely shared and generally liberal assumptions about the nature of consensual acts. First, most of us in a liberal culture tend to assume that altruistic acts, like all consensual trades, bargains, or decisions, must *by definition* increase the personal welfare of the actor. Second, we tend to assume that, whatever may be the case definitionally, simply as an empirical matter, every individual is the best judge of his or her own well-being, and that as a consequence consensual acts, including consensual altruistic acts, are beneficial to the actor. In the case of domestic altruism, these liberal assumptions about all consensual acts are often bolstered by yet a third "anti-statist" assumption, namely, that whatever goes on in the home, so long as it steers clear of criminal violence, is and ought to be protected by a thick shield of privacy against communitarian or state intervention. For all three reasons, the harms that might be done women by virtue of their greater engagement in household tasks— their intimate altruism—are cast into a sort of definitional oblivion.

When we put aside these assumptions, it is in fact easy to see that women's disproportionate household labor, even if in some sense "consensual," is harmful to women by even the most objective measures. In the wake of Arlie Hochschild's demonstration, in her book *The Second Shift,*[32] that women do indeed do more housework and child care than men regardless of class or employment status, a number of feminist economists argued that as a consequence women are not only more exhausted and enjoy less leisure, but are more impoverished as well—women's earned wages as well as their income potential are deflated for the simple reason that their productivity in every sphere other than reproduction and domesticity suffers.[33] Other objective consequences also follow, albeit not so easily quantifiable, and hence not so often noticed. The relative silence of women in the literary and visual arts, for example, is due in large part to disproportionate household labor.[34] Harriet Beecher Stowe wrote long ago of the damage done to the quality of her writing (on the topic of slavery) by her own uncompensated duties on the second shift.[35]

Women's duties, rights, and responsibilities as citizens also suffer from "second shift" duties. Simply put, so long as there is laundry to wash, diapers to change, children to feed, and houses to clean, and so long as women more than men are disposed to do them—for *whatever reason*—there is that much less time for women to engage in public debate, run for office, form citizen or community groups, serve on juries, or even just *vote*. There is, of course, nothing new about the inverse correlation of domestic tasks and democratic or political deliberation: the ideal Athenian citizen of antiquity had women and slaves to tend to the earthly, biological demands of life, thereby freeing him for the ideal life of politics and inquiry that Aristotle envisioned. The biological necessities of life are not much different today than they were in the time of Socrates. Someone must tend to the body's very real, earthbound, and contingent needs if the mind is to be freed for transcendental and political deliberations. So long as women disproportionately tend to those earthly, bodily needs, they are that much less equipped for the duties of citizenship—as citizenship has been traditionally understood.[36]

When we embrace the welfarist, anti-paternalist and anti-statist assumptions outlined above, however, these harms simply disappear. After all, if women *prefer* housecleaning to wage earning, and if they freely *choose* such a life, there is no reason to dispute such a choice—it must by definition maximize their welfare. If Harriet Beecher Stowe *prefers* raising her children to improving her writing, there's no reason to think that any outsider should second-guess such a choice. And of course if women prefer cooking and cleaning to running the government, there is again no reason to interfere with these private choices. The individual by definition can't be made worse off by her own freely made choices; no one can decide better than the agent herself how best to live her life, and the alternative to individual determination is intolerable state oppression. Furthermore, societally, what women lose in leisure time, income, cultural productivity, and citizenship, we gain in healthy children and clean households. Both the second shift and the delegation of a disproportionate share of domestic labor to women that underlies it may be efficient, even given the harms spelled out above. Any harm done in effect disappears, if we take the assumptions on which rest the economic, liberal, and libertarian case for individual freedom as seriously as their proponents clearly intend them to be taken.

Furthermore, there is an additional reason, far removed from the definitional presumptions of liberalism, to applaud these altruistic acts, even assuming they have the negative "externalities" mentioned above. These acts are, after all, by all appearances, almost paradigmatic acts of care. And if we should celebrate care, as both communitarians[37] and relational feminists[38] argue we should, then we should certainly celebrate these acts as well. In fact, they might be worthy of respect precisely *because* they are so radically anti-individualistic: they are acts which build community, and such acts are in pitifully small supply these days. In short, they are moral choices; that they come with costs to the moral actor should come as no surprise. Indeed, it is acts of precisely this sort which render us fully human: to identify one's own well-being as continuous with that of others, and to sacrifice narrowly construed self-interest for the sake of a larger community is not to be harmed, it is to live up to potential. We should celebrate, not denigrate, these quintessentially moral acts of private altruism.

To see the harm these acts do—indeed to even see *whether* these acts do harm—we must look beyond the definitional presumptions of both liberalism and of an ethic of care, and look directly at both the motivation for and the effects those acts of altruism have on the subjective lives of the women who perform them. The case for both the efficiency and the morality of the second shift rests, in effect, on the assumption that the women who make these decisions are what might be called "self-possessed individuals"—individuals who choose, decide, and act on a solid, static core of settled preferences and desires, which are themselves grounded in either self-regarding pleasures and pains or freely chosen moral principles. But, as I will argue in a moment, the women who engage in these altruistic acts and suffer what I am calling altruistic harms are, very often, not such people (leaving aside the question whether anyone is). Because they are not, the altruistic acts in which they engage are neither the welfare-maximizing, privacy-enhancing, autonomous decisions honored by libertarians and economists or the moral decisions celebrated by communitarians and relational feminists. They do not stem from a willed decision to engage in such care, and they are destructive rather than constructive of the spirit and well-being of the actor. The altruistic decisions of what might be called the "giving self," even when uncoerced, unlike those of the self-possessed individual or of the caring moral agent, are not decisions which will necessarily promote the autonomy or well-being of the agent, or spring from a free decision to care. Because of the blanket definitional assumption that, like all uncoerced actions taken by free, adult individuals, they will, both the economic case for the rationality and efficiency of women's work in the domestic sphere, as well as the communitarian and relational-feminist celebration of its morality, ring hollow.

The hypothesis I would like to propose is that women's apparent altruism in the private sphere is a source of harm rather than either individual or communal well-being, *to the extent that* the altruistic acts women perform, unlike true altruistic acts, stem neither from self-interest nor from a caring instinct but, rather, from fear. I suspect that this covers a great deal more of such apparent altruism than might first appear. The reason is twofold.

First, women who engage in what might be called sexual altruism—consensual but unwanted sex with an intimate—are often motivated neither by self-interest properly understood nor by an ethic of care but rather, and more simply, by *fear*—not, perhaps, of their partner, but more generally, of sexual violence from other men. Let me explain why this might be true of more women than one might think. All women—not just those who have been victimized by it—must somehow come to grips with the danger of violent sexual assault. All women must somehow learn to live in a world in which what should be a source of pleasure and identity—one's own adult sexuality, whatever may be its nature—is instead, or is also, a source of very real, even lethal, danger to one's life. So long as some men will use force to "take" her sexuality from her, and so long as such acts are not successfully deterred by the state, a woman's sexuality puts her in serious harm's way.

This profound existential fact—that the most primal source of pleasure, located in one's own body, is a source of danger and constitutes a risk to one's survival—is something all women must somehow learn to live with, *and* it is something only very few men ever confront. The causal connections between pleasure, desire, and decision

[114]

which I have suggested are central to liberalism are in a sense para-
digmatically embodied, for a man, in his sexuality: his sexual pleasure
uninterruptedly prompts desires, which in turn prompt decisions and
actions. For a woman, there is no such paradigmatic connection.
Between her own recognition of her sexuality as a source of pleasure,
and her decision to act on it, lies a hostile world in which that source
of pleasure—her sexual body—is a source of profound danger. As the
adolescent girl awakens to her adult sexuality, she awakens simultaneously, and necessarily, to her vulnerability to assault, rape, violence,
and death. Rather than "learn" a connection between pleasure and
action, she "learns" instead a connection between pleasure and violence; between pleasure and danger; between pleasure and fear.

There are any number of strategies for coping with such an ugly
lesson about the world, and one's place within it, but one way to do so
is by altering one's own self-concept: if a girl or woman simply *defines
herself* as one who exists, sexually, so as to give herself to a man for
his, rather than her, pleasure, then she need not negotiate, on a
timely, daily, energy-sapping basis, the lethal conflict the world throws
at her between her own pleasures and her own survival. This is the
woman's lived reality behind the second wave feminist claim that
heterosexual marriage is basically nothing more than a rape protection racket. Thus, many women enter into and then remain in long-
term heterosexual relations with a man for whom they may feel very
little, and from whom they obtain precious little that could conceiv-
ably be called "pleasure," for the straightforward but rarely acknowledged reason that such a relationship, and such a man, can protect
her against the threat of violent sexual assault from other men. Some
women, of course, are expressly taught, as girls, to do precisely that,
by their mothers or other female caregivers. But virtually all women
"learn" that this is an at least acceptable, and at best socially approved
way of dealing with the dangerous conflict between one's own sexuality and one's own survival. Every woman in this culture, for example,
knows that even the risk of street hassling, to say nothing of rape,
diminishes dramatically—virtually to zero—when she is accompanied by a man.

One thing a woman undeniably gains when she enters a heterosexual relationship or marriage with a relatively safe, nonviolent man, is
greater protection *from other men*—*and* therefore, assuming the man
in the relationship is not himself a source of danger, a good measure

[115]

of safety. When she is with him, she can more safely walk the streets at night, eat dinner in restaurants, frequent public places, go out in the late afternoon and evening. That is no small thing. What is given up, however, is the relationship between one's own sexuality and one's own *pleasure*; sex in such a marriage or relationship is given not for one's own pleasure but for one's own *safety*. Pleasure has been sacrificed for safety so as to break the far more lethal connection between one's own sexuality and life-threatening danger. It is a simple bargain. What it requires, however, is a redefinition of self on an extremely fundamental level. The sexual self must be redefined as one who gives for the pleasure of the other—rather than for the pleasure one might take from sex oneself.

A woman in such a relationship—a relationship in which she engages regularly in sexual altruism, meaning a relationship in which she regularly has sex from which she derives no physical pleasure—is not necessarily going to, and is even not likely to, experience such a relationship as driven by fear. Fear is a terrible burden to live with on a daily basis and women will go to extraordinary lengths to shed themselves of it.[39] It is, in the long run, psychically simpler to redefine oneself as giving (rather than individualistic) than to be in a state of fear, and it is not all that surprising that that is precisely what so many women do. The woman's experience, then, is not of sex driven by fear, but of giving herself over to serve or service the pleasure of another. But we should not confuse these acts as moral altruistic acts worthy of celebration.[40] Even if on an unacknowledged level, they are fundamentally grounded in the survivalist need to protect oneself from violence, not by compassion or care.

Nor should we confuse these acts of sexual altruism with the sorts of self-regarding decisions agnostically celebrated by egoistic liberalism or libertarianism. First, they are not self-regarding. But further, this giving of the sexual self—the deep psychic decision to act on the basis of the sexual pleasures of *others* rather than oneself—is precisely the sort of psychic decision which becomes constitutive of the self in nonsexual contexts as well. A woman who has severed the connection between her sexual body and her own pleasure will eventually sever the connection between her body and her pleasure in other spheres. When she does so, she *becomes* less capable of the hedonic connections assumed by liberalism between pleasure and act. These acts of sexual altruism, in other words, are not only *not* the acts of an individualistic, self-regarding self, they are destructive of that self. Female sexuality, to the degree that it is constituted by altruistic acts driven by fear, is not only not emblematic of the liberal ideal of selfhood, it destroys it.

The second way in which fear grounds altruistic acts in the domestic sphere concerns what Camille Paglia has recently called the "nursemaid" ethos characteristic of "successful heterosexual women"—a rule of behavior by which the woman regularly puts her own interests last, or at least subordinates them to those of children and husbands, in the day-to-day running of the household.[41] From whence comes this "nursemaid" ethos? Paglia doesn't say. Feminists for the most part have focused on social construction of the role: women's greater inclination to succumb to the nursemaid ethos is simply a function of training. That is surely true. What I want to suggest here is that it may *also* be, in part, and for many more women than may be initially apparent, a function of fear.

Look again at a biological difference between men and women, but one not often noted: the biological relationship *of the mother to the newborn* is radically different from that of the father—almost as different as the relationship of mother and father to fetus. First, the mother, but not the father, is necessarily physically *there* when the baby is born. And second, the mother, but not the father, will lactate, and if she is to avoid painful engorgement of her breasts, will breast-feed. A newborn baby instinctually knows how to breast-feed and knows from which parent to do so. From the baby's birth, the mother is physically connected, and remains physically connected, to the baby in ways which are not true of the father, simply by virtue of physical proximity and her ability to lactate. Mothers are more inclined to nurture their children, perhaps, *in part* simply because they are necessarily physically proximate and universally capable of doing so from the beginning of life. If so, then that is a major and important difference between men and women: as I will argue below, for example, it has major implications for the vastly different legal responsibilities of mothers and fathers vis-à-vis newborns. However, it also has implications for a woman's self-concept.

A mother who, for reasons of either biology or training or both, *will care* for a child is differently situated vis-à-vis the brute force of necessity than a father who may or may not engage in caregiving work. If a newborn is to be breast-fed, only the mother can do it. An

[117]

older child must be not only fed, but clothed, sheltered, bathed, stimulated, entertained, and educated, and, if, for whatever reason, the father *will not* perform these tasks, the mother will. The mother feels the imperative dimension of that *must* as directed at her in a way the father does not. Necessity—whether biological or cultural—becomes, for the mother, a moral imperative. To put the point negatively, whatever the reason, most women are not going to engage in a labor strike that will endanger their children. They will not engage in such a strike so as to achieve greater leisure time for themselves, and they will not engage in such a strike so as to achieve a politically and economically more equitable world. The children will be cared for, and while fathers *may,* mothers *will* do the caring.

A woman who *will care* for a newborn is considerably more vulnerable than a man or woman who feels no such imperative, simply because she is radically less autonomous—anyone with obligations is less autonomous than someone without.[42] Care of newborns, babies, toddlers, and young children is round-the-clock work, and anyone doing it is going to require help from others to ensure survival. A woman giving birth cannot defend herself against attack—think of the depiction in the movie *Little Big Man*[43] of the Indian woman giving birth during Custer's Last Stand. A woman breast-feeding cannot engage in other remunerative labor while doing so. If either the woman or the child is to survive, the mother will have to depend on the assistance of others for the provision of food, shelter, and other necessities.

If the mother is supported by a community of adults that she fully trusts, and if they are as invested in the nurturance of new life as she, then the relationships that she forms with them will truly be a web of interdependence between equals—she needs them for support, but they are equally in need of her. Such an arrangement, designed for the support of mothers and their new life, could surely be the basis for a robust morality of care—and if it ever becomes a cornerstone of public as well as private life, it will indeed be a morality quite different from the principled morality of respect premised upon independent, autonomous adults.[44]

But at least in a patriarchically designed society, the new mother is typically not so fortunate. She is typically not *interdependent* with a community of equals. She is, instead, often if not typically, *dependent* upon, rather than interdependent with, a man who is not as involved in the nurturance of new life as she is. Because of that inequality and the unequal investment on which it rests, she rightly fears he may disappear at any point. The relationship formed around this triad of inequality, fear, and nurturance will not be the relational foundation of a robust morality of care. It will be, rather, the relational foundation of a neurotic nursemaid mentality. Such a woman is *dependent* upon a man rather than interdependent with him, precisely *because* of his willingness to leave: it is that willingness which renders her unnecessary to him, but he necessary to her. If she is relying for support on such a man, then the entirely rational emotional stance for her to take is fear. She fears his departure, and she engages in "altruistic" domestic acts to protect against it.

Just as a woman may define herself as giving rather than individualistic so as to ward off the burden of living with fear of sexual violence, so a mother may define herself as giving rather than individualistic so as to ward off the burden of living with the fear of abandonment. And again, just as a woman who defines herself as sexually giving will not experience her sexual life as fearful, so such a mother will no doubt not experience her day-to-day life, and the innumerable altruistic acts she performs in the course of that life, as driven by fear. Rather, she will more likely simply consider herself *by definition* someone who performs such tasks, and *by nature*, perhaps, someone who performs such tasks cheerfully. But these individual acts of self-abasement, and the cheerfulness which oftentimes is their accompanying affect, take a serious toll. Such a woman does what must be done to keep her man relatively content, to induce in him a state of happiness to secure his presence. That may mean serving as his literal or psychological punching bag, absorbing the anger that collects in him through his daily interactions and battles with the hostile outer world, serving and servicing his needs, moving from state to state when his work requires it, or cleaning up after him as one would a baby—again the nursemaid mentality of successful heterosexual women toward their male partners of which Camille Paglia speaks (and, apparently, speaks approvingly).[45] Whatever particular tasks are required, their collective message is clear: the connection, central to liberal understandings of the individual, between one's own pleasures, felt desires, choices, and actions is severed. When these actions become so everyday, so commonplace, so mundane, that they constitute not just the quality of a day, an afternoon, or a week, but an adult lifetime, they become constitutive as well of the individual's self-definition. They become who one is: a helpmate, a nursemaid, a wife.

These actions are, then, neither the moral, compassionate, nurturant gestures of a generous spirit celebrated by relational feminism, nor the self-regarding welfare-maximizing choices of an autonomous individual assumed by economic liberalism. Actions driven by fear are neither inherently generous in the sense applauded by the morality of care, nor genuinely self-regarding in the sense assumed by liberalism. It is indeed possible for an entire adulthood to be spent in such a state of duress. An adult life spent entirely or almost entirely in a private home in which the threat of violence or desertion is ever present, and which is accordingly reconstructed so as to ward off the risk of such a threat being acted upon, may well be such a life.

Let me turn now to the harms these altruistic acts—acts which should be understood as emanating from neither a self-regarding nor moral core—cause, rather than the harm they reflect. What I wish to propose is that the giving self constituted through duressed private altruism becomes in a literal sense *incapable* of the self-regarding acts that are constitutive of the liberal self—and that that *is* the harm that these acts occasion. They do so in three ways.

First, a woman who thinks of herself as the conduit for the pleasures of *others,* rather than as acting toward the maximization of her own, will not make decisions or choices that maximize her own welfare. Let me use an example that may be familiar to readers of this book: the decision by the dual academic couple to relocate so as to further the academic advancement of one of the members of the pair. As every appointment committee chair knows, such couples rarely make decisions regarding relocating so as to accommodate the woman's optimal career choice, where a conflict appears. One reason for this may be that the woman in the two-career couple reasons in a fashion that is at least hedonically interdependent, and often entirely altruistic: she does not want to make the choice that will inconvenience or set back her husband, *even if* that inconvenience would be more than offset by her own advancement, and even if he is willing to make the sacrifice—*either* because she simply cannot envision herself or her partner acting in such a way, *or* because her own sense of well-being is inextricably intermingled with his in a way that is not reciprocated. Either way, she will act "altruistically" and either way, the decision the couple reaches—fully voluntarily—is considerably less than optimal. Because of that the decisions reached within such a unit run contrary to the welfare-maximizing presumption at the core of economic liberalism: to wit, that freely reached cooperative decisions or exchanges will definitionally maximize the couple's collective welfare. A woman who thinks, feels, and acts in such a way repeatedly eventually simply *becomes* someone who thinks, feels, and acts in such a way. The acts are no longer altruistic, if they ever were—they are simply reflexively masochistic.

Second, a woman who routinely performs harmful altruistic acts loses the sense of *integrity* necessary to at least liberal conceptions of individualism. Integrity is largely a matter of personal consistency—a refusal to waver in the face of oppositional pressures; an ability to be truthful and consistent; commitment to one's own life projects across time. None of this is even a coherent aspiration for a damaged giving self: the self whose only self-concept is one of being *for another* will not have *personal* commitments; will not have a core of beliefs or projects with which the self is identified and to which one might hold strong across time or in the face of opposition in the name of integrity. Such a person will be more inclined to lie,[46] to abandon commitments, to realign loyalties when exigencies present themselves. There is, after all, no self being betrayed; no centrally felt conviction being dishonored.

Third, a giving self damaged by altruistic acts lacks the *self-assertiveness* that is assumed by both liberalism and libertarianism: the giving self, or given self, has no straightfoward "self"-interest to assert. The self has, rather, been insinuated, not asserted, into the well-being of others. There is no individualized, self-identified "point of view" of the world or set of interests, desires, or passions that will seek to impose itself upon the world, or that will emanate from such a fear-driven and other-defined self. For all these reasons, the giving self lacks autonomy; indeed the condition is antithetical to autonomy. A woman who views herself as essentially altruistic in the intimate sphere of domesticity or sexual life is not "free" to give or withhold that generosity: she is identified with the beneficiaries of her altruism, and will cease to exist should the occasions for altruism disappear.

It is true that the decisions within families are more "altruistic" than the decisions in more public markets, as communitarians,[47] feminists,[48] historians[49] and theorists of the family, as well as market economists,[50] insist. That fact alone, however, is nothing to celebrate: it renders the family neither the morally superior realm, nor the safe haven to which market actors can retreat at the end of the day. The family is more altruistic than the market, in large part because women behave more altruistically than men within families. But these acts of altruism disserve woman, and because they do, they don't serve the overall welfare of the family unit. They ennoble neither the giver nor the beneficiary. Altruism grounded fundamentally in fear, or in a self-concept itself defined by fear, does nothing but perpetuate destructive cycles of self-denigration on the part of the giver, and a truly deadly sense of perpetual entitlement on the part of the beneficiary.

Altruism *per se,* of course, is not necessarily harmful to the altruist, nor is the development of a sense of self committed to serving others. Again, it is those altruistic acts motivated fundamentally by fear, or by a sense of self which is itself fragmented by fears, that I have relabeled "altruistic harms" and which I claim do real although perhaps unmeasurable damage to the person who performs them. There are, of course, altruistic acts motivated by a strong sense of empathic concern for others, and I do not mean to imply here that these acts should be regarded as harmful; quite the contrary. Rather, such acts very likely constitute the experiential core of the unified sense of moral obligation toward others now popularly known as the ethic of care.[51] It is worth noting, however, that even healthy altruism is anomalous, whether or not damaging, in our highly individualized culture. Much as we admire the fierce devotion of a mother to her children, or the loyalty of a man or woman to his or her spouse or life partner, and the sacrifices these individuals might make for their loved ones, it is virtually impossible to reconcile the "virtues" these commitments represent with the "virtues" associated with other virtues of liberal or radical political culture: such loyalties are antithetical to, not consonant with, the individualism, liberty, or equality we assume or strive for in public, political life.[52] My point here, however, is more limited. When motivated by fear rather than by a sense of communal and reciprocal purpose, these acts do real harm to the person performing them, not the least of which is that their constitutive character renders the liberal, individualized, self-regarding, assertive, fully possessed self increasingly illusory. I have argued thus far that the altruism so often associated with femininity is *in part,* or oftentimes, grounded in a fully legitimate *fear* of either sexual invasion, domestic abandonment, or both, and that when it is, the altruistic acts that follow should be recognized as harmful rather than ennobling for the woman who persistently engages in them. A woman giving birth, breast-feeding an infant, or raising toddlers and children has that much less time and energy to devote to her own material support. She needs help. If she rightly fears that those to whom she turns for material support may at any time abandon her, she will for that reason alone tend to redefine herself as someone who must be there for that person, in order to insure that he remains there for her. The altruistic acts follow, with the consequences I have described above.

It does *not* follow, however, that there is an essential or fundamental component of female altruism that is necessarily connected with fear, and necessarily harmful (any more than that there is an essential component of female altruism necessarily connected with care). Rather, the fact that women are fearful of abandonment and respond with acts of seeming altruism, is entirely a function of the way we organize intimate and family life in this culture. Obviously, it both could be and should be otherwise. Fear is never healthy, and a world in which women bore, fed, and raised children in a community in which they had justified trust would be a considerably less fearful world. Such a community might consist of extended family, female friends, or a lifelong female or male companion, whether or not the father of the children, or some combination of these. Undoubtedly, some heterosexual relationships might resemble this ideal, and some present heterosexual relationships already do. But many do not, and of those that don't, a good many are marked by both an underlying fear of desertion and a constant flow of large and small altruistic feminine acts. It is those acts in turn which undermine the self-possession, integrity, self-assertiveness, and autonomy which characterize the individualistic conception of selfhood in a liberal society.

In this time, place, and culture, the inability to develop these traits of character—self-possession, integrity, self-assertiveness, and autonomy—carries with it tangible costs. Such a person will not find it easy to survive, much less thrive, in the public world. When women enter arenas in which the expectation is that they will perform as atomistic, individualistic maximizers, and they do not, they are more often than not harmed as a result. They will not anticipate, and therefore not be able to rebuke, competitive challenges to their place in the workforce as readily as men.[53] More overtly, lacking skills in *self*-defense, they will not be able to stave off attacks on their physical or sexual security. They will not bargain competently: again, they will neither anticipate nor respond appropriately to offers that do not reflect the "best" price they could obtain with forceful bargaining.[54] They will not be inclined to engage in the public work of coalition building with others who similarly need political support, as they will be disinclined to recognize the self whose interests are being neglected.[55] In short, the psychic inability to articulate, present, and extend one's self into public spaces injures women's tangible interests, whether physical, political, or economic.

This inability is sometimes characterized as, and might sometimes be, a laudable refusal to participate in market or political transactions on Hobbesian terms. Admittedly, so the argument might go, the woman who is *too* trusting, too eager to please, too "willing to compromise," too nice, will not do as well in markets or social contexts as others who are behaving not as cooperators but as egoists.[56] But rather than reflect an "inability," this may reflect a conscious moral choice: the woman who so "underperforms" in public markets might be simply willing to pay the price necessary to place social transactions on a higher moral plane.[57] You do, after all, sometimes win by losing. The inability, in other words, might be recharacterized as a sort of virtue, and more specifically, a virtue of care, which, although its exercise might hurt the woman's interests in the short run, might in the long run represent a morally and socially superior "way of being" in the social world.

Well, maybe, but maybe not. At least much of the time, the apparently "too trusting," too nice, woman whose cooperative spirit is matched by exploitation is motivated to behave inappropriately altruistically in public spheres not because of an excess of *trust,* or even niceness, but by an excess of *fear.* If one has come to fear the bargain, the trade, or the exchange in the political and economic realm because one has learned in the intimate world that potential conflict can explode into a situation in which one's security is severely threatened, then the rational response will be to bring the economic bargain or political exchange to a close on whatever terms will ward off the danger. And again, where this fear has been internalized to such a degree that the self is reconstituted as giving, these everyday exchanges will not *feel* coerced or driven by fear. Rather, the woman will experience herself in these exchanges as the party who is more in-clined than the opposing party to seek cooperation, to act on interde-pendent utilities, to behave more responsibly, to seek to improve rather than challenge the other's well-being. What grounds her behav-ior, however, is not necessarily an admirable desire to place social transactions on a higher moral plane than the Hobbesian. What may ground it instead is the utterly self-regarding judgment that if she doesn't give a little here and a little there, and a little everywhere else, then all hell will break loose and she will lose all. What grounds the inability to perform egoistically in the public sphere, in other words, may be the learned ability to behave in the private sphere in such a way as to keep "the lid on": to counter the ever-present danger of male anger, desertion, or violence with a willingness to sacrifice one's own interests for those of the other.

Whether or not there is anything biologically given about the moti-vation of private altruistic acts, there is clearly nothing socially neces-sary about the injurious consequences in the public sphere incident to the giving self. One can imagine a social world, in other words, in which self-possession, integrity, self-assertiveness, and autonomy are not as highly regarded and not as necessary for survival in public realms, and in which other traits, such as loyalty, compassion, or a communitarian ethic, are more highly regarded. In such a world altru-istic harms and the giving selves they constitute might not have such devastating economic, political, and social consequences. That the giving self, constituted by altruistic acts performed in the private sphere, performs poorly in the public sphere, in other words, is indeed a function of the way we have constructed that public sphere. Giving selves just don't do well in public worlds constructed along Hobbesian lines: where egoism is expected, the cooperator loses. Obviously, if we so choose, we can help the cooperator here by challenging the expectation of egoism in the public sphere rather than by challenging the spirit of cooperation, if we come to believe, with good reason, that the exercise of unbounded egoism in the public spheres of life is not the best way to go about organizing our social world. Were we to do so, at least some of the pernicious economic and social consequences of being a "giving self" in the public world would be mitigated.

I suspect, however, that no matter how we organize our social world, some of the psychic harms sustained by the giving self would not be so easily socially deconstructed. A life marred by self-denigration, self-abasement, and the repetitive performance of quasi-coerced "altruistic acts" is, simply, not a good life. It is, in a word, *unpleasant*. When one is constituted as a giving self, one becomes, perhaps ironically, unable to feel the intense pleasure of "losing oneself" in a large project—whether the large project be one involving a collective social effort or an individual effort—because it has become impossible to *identify* oneself with the larger project. There is, after all, no "self" to identify when the self has been given. It is impossible to live and feel *freely*— unencumbered, for an afternoon, an hour, or a weekend, by the needs of others. It is impossible to feel in control of one's own destiny. It is equally impossible to feel and act responsibly toward one's dependents. All these are pleasurable feelings, perhaps the most intensely pleasurable experiences of a lifetime. All of them are forgone when the self is given, essentially out of fear that her survival or the survival of her children will be threatened if she does not make the sacrifice.

That women are economically harmed in tangible ways by their private altruism—by the "second shift"—has been fairly well established by feminist social scientists.[58] What I want to stress here is that it also has psychic harms that go beyond the economic. Part of the problem, of course, is simply that the altruistic acts themselves are exhausting and not particularly pleasurable—menial domestic labor, and a good deal of child care as well, is repetitive, understimulating, physically demanding work. It is boring. It is also, of course, enraging to know that one is doing considerably more than one's fair share and to know that the consequence of insisting on domestic justice for oneself will very likely be child neglect and an unacceptable degree of filth. Rage, particularly impotent rage, is not carried lightly. And it is exhausting to live with the knowledge, even if buried, of dependency— that disaster is around the corner should one's life partner choose to desert. But most important, the damaged "giving self" that is constituted so as to ward off the boredom of the work, the rage at the injustice, and the fear of abandonment also sustains distinctive moral wounds—wounds to self-possession, integrity, autonomy, and self-assertiveness—which undermine both success and competency in public life and pleasure in private life. Those moral harms in particular render anomalous the liberal rejoinder to feminist critiques of the second shift—to wit, that the second shift is undertaken voluntarily, and hence not harmful. The second shift is often not "voluntary"—

not because it is invariably coerced, but simply because there is no self doing the volunteering. The self has been too utterly compromised by the fully rational fear of abandonment, and the disastrous consequences, given a social world that prizes autonomy and individuated independence above all else, which that abandonment would entail.

HARMS OF SEPARATION

All children, at some early point in their lives, physically, emotionally, and then psychically "separate" from their mothers, and all endure some degree of trauma by so doing.[59] All adults, of course, endure painful separations as well: parents and spouses die, grown children move on and move out, lovers depart, husbands and wives divorce, and friends move away. Nevertheless, girls and women undergo some separations which are distinctively different and of greater intensity than those which boys and men undergo. Some of those separations are liberating or joyful. Some are necessary for growth. Some are painful but beneficial, and some are both harmful and unnecessary.

Whatever their value, however, the pain of separation seems to be a constant, and even a universal, in the lives of girls and women. Think first of the different experiences of mothers and fathers in reproducing and raising their children. Surely the most obvious and perhaps the most significant difference between women and men is the different roles the two parents play in the biology of reproduction. The mother's biological role in reproduction minimally involves pregnancy, childbirth, and lactation, while the father's is limited to ejaculation. One consequence of that baseline difference is that women, unlike men, invest a good bit *more* of their material, physical, bodily resources in the development of fetal life. Women, unlike men, form a material, physical, bodily bond with the fetus, and women, unlike men, must endure the physical pain of breaking that material bond when the baby is born. The physical process alone may or may not be joyful, but it is always painful,[60] sometimes injurious, and until very recently often lethal.

Women who conceive, but for whatever reason lose the fetus, also experience a painful separation with little or no correlate in men's lives. Women who miscarry undergo what is sometimes a physically painful separation from the fetus, even where the emotional pain—the grief—is shouldered by both parents. Women who abort a pregnancy, for whatever reason, also undergo a physically painful separation that has no correlate in men's lives, whether or not there is emotional pain relating to the separation, and if there is, whether or not that emotional pain is felt as intensely by the father. Women who give birth and then lose the baby to adoption often, although not always, experience a loss related to the separation of a magnitude we are only now beginning to understand. This sense of loss is apparently greater than that felt by men.[61] Again, although all are painful, these separations are clearly not all *harmful:* some may, for some women produce lasting psychic or psychological harms, while others may be quite insignificant, or even give rise, for the most part, to feelings of relief.[62]

Other separations, however, are not so benign. Consider first the emotional pain of "separating" from older children in order to work in the paid labor market. Although separation from older children obviously might pain fathers as well as mothers, it seems to hurt mothers more and more often than fathers,[63] in that the *prospect* of such a separation deters mothers more than fathers from income-producing activities which would require just such a separation.[64] Whatever the cause of this difference, the result, in part, is the relative impoverishment of women vis-à-vis men, or at least of mothers vis-à-vis nonmothers. It is a difference which impacts adversely not only many women's earned income, but also their wealth at the point of divorce: it has now become such common knowledge that divorcing women are more likely than men to fear separation from their children, that the threat of losing custody has become a much used and much feared bargaining chip for men seeking to minimize alimony and child-support payments.[65] Similarly, mothers more than fathers will sacrifice schooling and work to spend more time with young children. As a consequence, mothers are more likely than men to either voluntarily accept, or be funneled into, lower-paying "mommy tracks" in professional jobs,[66] noncommissioned, local, regular-hours work in retail,[67] and greater interruptions for child care in training for virtually all spheres of labor, with the consequent difference in seniority and hence in wages and salaries vis-à-vis their male colleagues.

Even a mother able and willing to devote herself entirely to the nurturance of her children will experience more pains of separation than mothers or fathers who sacrifice the connection to facilitate work. Again, not all this suffering is harmful, or even experienced as such: women who proceed after birth to invest labor, time, and physical bodily resources in the breast-feeding of their babies, for example, will eventually wean them from the breast—a physical separation of mother from child which is physically uncomfortable and has no correlate in men's lives, but which causes no one harm. However, some of the separations in the lives of even the most "connected" mothers are not so benign. A "full-time" mother has obviously invested greater time than a working father in raising, nurturing, and preparing their children for adulthood,[68] and such a mother must then eventually endure the grown child's departure from her home as the child enters adulthood. As Carol Gilligan has noted, if she has invested more in the bond, this separation as well is likely to be felt more intensely by her than by the father.[69] What Gilligan famously concluded from this difference, of course, is that while difficulties achieving comfortably intimate relationships tend to be central moral dilemmas for grown men, difficulties *separating* the self from the other—from friends, lovers, and grown children—tend to be central moral dilemmas for adult women. If she's right, then there is a clear "moral harm" entailed by women's disproportionate work in connective labor, which, although also experienced by men, is experienced differently and less intensely.

Although not stressed by Gilligan, it nevertheless seems to be implied by the logic of what she argues that women who spend a substantial or near total part of their adult lives in heterosexual relationships or marriages—whether or not they mother—will endure a second sort of "separation harm" which again will be felt, if at all, less intensely by their male partners. If it is true, as Gilligan and others have argued, that girls do not *dissassociate* themselves from their mothers in order to forge their own separate identity, or at least do not do so as early or as completely as their brothers,[70] then it is also true that girls remain more connected, and for a longer time, to their mothers than do boys. While heterosexual relationships or marriage for a young man is in some way a *return* to a world of primary maternal attachment, for a young woman heterosexuality is not only a coming together, in union, with a man, but it is simultaneously also a separation, and often a painful one, of the girl from the maternal world. By the time such a separation occurs, she has formed a self-identity that very likely includes—and even is fundamentally grounded in—her feeling of connection with that maternal and feminine world.[71] If the Gilligan-Chodorow thesis is even partly right, then it would be reasonable to infer from it that separation from that maternal world is likely to be more stark and more uncomfortable for the young woman who abruptly departs it, than it is for the young man.

The contrast between the maternal world from which she comes and the heterosexual world of traditional marriage can be very vivid indeed. Not only the mother-daughter relationship, but the adolescent and early adulthood female friendships that are to some degree an extension of it are (at least often) intimate, warm, sentimental, affectionate, and above all *safe*. A heterosexual relationship or marriage often fails to even approach the intimacy or degree of affection—to say nothing of the safety—characteristic of the mother-daughter bond or the female friendships of adolescence and early adulthood. The heterosexual relationship, unlike the same-sex friendship, is much more likely to be—in a word—*work*. The young woman may be alarmed, and will no doubt be saddened, to realize that her husband or lover will not be as companionate as were her friends: will not talk as freely, will not be as open, will not be as giving, and will not be as affectionate. She will find herself assuming roles and duties she has not been prepared for and for which there was no correlate in her female friendships. In a not so atypical heterosexual relationship, unlike a same-sex friendship, the woman must often learn to absorb her husband's or partner's "free-floating anger," buffer his moods, and soothe his ego. These tasks are unpleasant. They are, largely, the emotional labor that makes the heterosexual relationship "work" for her, even when it is a safe haven for him.[72]

Although for women much of the trauma of heterosexual relations stems from "too much" of a connection within the relationship to the partner, a good deal of it stems from too little connection. This damage, in turn, originates in the separation from earlier relationships which the dominant heterosexual relationship displaced. The easiness and equality of the teen and preadolescent same-sex friendships are gone. Those bonds of straightforward and pure, loving affection are severed. There may or may not be compensating pleasures and joys from the adult heterosexual relationship to fill the void created by the separation from her peers. But whether or not there are such compensations, unless the young woman takes some measure to assure otherwise, the void will be there. The sense of isolation and separation a woman lives with in such a relationship may lead to only a sort of low-level sadness, or it can be truly terrible—a living death.

Although we are not accustomed to thinking of the harm done to women by ordinary, cold heterosexual relationships as involving, in part, the harm of separation from female friendship, or more generally, simply separation from intimacy that harm has been a staple of women's fiction since at least the turn of the century. The early-twentieth-century novella, *A Jury of Her Peers,* [73] for example, which I will discuss in some detail in a subsequent chapter, relates the lethal consequences of the loneliness and isolation of the wife of a silent and angry farmer who lacked *not* the proverbial room of her own, but *the company of other women.* The separation of these wives *from each other*—their utter social isolation, each with their sullen, noncommunicative, and emotionally stunted husbands—constituted, for them, an enormous, almost unspeakable, emotional harm. That harm was twofold: the harm done the woman by the lack of intimacy in the marriage itself, but just as important, the harm done the woman by her separation from her "peers" which the marriage occasioned. One message of *A Jury of Her Peers,* (among several others) is simply that the harms done by separation and isolation seem to be a more pronounced theme in women's lives than in men's.

As noted above, one quite general explanation for why this might be so is implied by the work of object psychologists. Nancy Chodorow posited in the early 1980s that boys "separate" from their mothers at a much earlier age than girls simply because they become aware of their distinctive gender, while girls retain a sense of connection with their mothers on into adolescence and adulthood.[74] If that is right, then it makes sense to think that girls and women view themselves as more connected than individualized from others, and consequently, are more harmed by separations of either a natural or cultural sort. Another reason for the difference may be cultural: girls have, after all, far more than boys, been taught to view themselves as potential mothers and caretakers, and hence as persons whose identity *requires* them to forge connections with others. As a result they may be more harmed by events which challenge that taught self-identification. Part of the reason might be biological—women's differing role in biological reproduction, after all, is at the root of the greater harms women sustain in the separating processes of giving birth.[75] But whether biological, cultural, or psychological, the pattern is persistent: women's lives are more defined by the connecting relations with others which are at their core. If that is so, then it also follows, although it is not so often noted, that women will be differentially pained by the separations from the other lives we sustain, and which sustain us. Again, some of those separations, even the painful ones, are not harmful, and might be benign, liberatory, and healthy, and many, of course, are equally shouldered by men. Some, though, are neither necessary nor benign, and of those which are not, the preponderance of the harm seems to be disproportionately borne by women.

PATRIARCHAL HARMS

Finally, women sustain harms different from those sustained by men because they live as political inferiors, or subordinates, within a patriarchal culture. By patriarchy, for the purpose of this discussion, I mean simply the social system in which men's interests trump women's wherever they conflict. Some societies are more patriarchal than others and some are *certainly* more patriarchal than this one: we do not mutilate our daughters' genitalia, burn women to death for infidelity, sell girls into slavery, or kill female infants and abort female fetuses solely because of their sex. By the same token, however, while no society is through-and-through unequivocally patriarchal—there are always countervailing humanistic or feminist tendencies—no society is utterly free of it, including this one. Thus, I use the word "patriarchy" as shorthand for the ways in which we prioritize men's interests over women's in social life and then constitute the harms women sustain (whether natural or not) as inevitable, trivial, or desirable, and for whatever reason, not eradicable.

"Patriarchy," then, includes both more and less than biased or discriminatory *law*. In many societies, patriarchy is indeed simply encoded in legal norms, breach of which will trigger serious legal sanctions. In our culture, however, patriarchy is *for the most part* enforced not through legal norms, but through a combination of two sorts of *extralegal* forces. First, it is enforced through both legal and illegal, but in any event largely unregulated, private violence—rape, domestic violence, incest, sexual harassment, street hassling, and other forms of sexual assault. Second, it is enforced through the promulgation of a distinctively patriarchal *culture,* which consists in turn of norms that determine the way we behave by influencing the ways we think of ourselves and of our fate. Although the first of these—the patriarchal violence—is still largely unregulated by the state, its existence is rarely flatly denied by the legal and larger culture, and, as I discuss in some detail below, it is increasingly recognized as a legitimate "problem" for both law enforcement and public health. Patriarchal violence, in other words, is increasingly viewed by even the mainstream culture as both illegal and undesirable. The very *existence* of a nonviolent and fully legal patriarchal culture, however, the purpose of which is to secure and prioritize men's interests wherever they conflict with women's, is often denied. It is that culture, and the damage it inflicts, that I want to examine here.

Let me begin with three examples of conflicts between men's and women's interests, and describe the ways in which patriarchal culture seeks to secure the former against the latter. First, most men, at least in this culture, need women's bodies (or think they need women's bodies) to satisfy their desire for sexual release. It is sometimes possible to attain that end without a woman's consent, and to the degree that such acts go unpunished by the state, the law is indeed a primary cornerstone of a patriarchal regime. But again, the relationship between law and patriarchy is by no means that simple—nonconsensual intercourse is, after all, in at least some circumstances a very serious crime that at least sometimes triggers a very serious penalty. It is, rather, patriarchal culture, far more than patriarchal violence coupled with legal complicity, which insures men's access to women's bodies. It is, of course, much easier to invade a woman's body for sexual release if the woman consents. It is not surprising, then, that in a patriarchal system in which men's interests are counted as of greater weight than women's, social life is organized in such a way as to provide women with enough incentives that they will consent to intercourse, *whether or not* they find it pleasurable. The many, many ways in which women, as girls, are culturally trained for passivity, and especially for sexual passivity, can easily be seen as a network of social norms designed to secure their consent to sexual invasion and intercourse which is not necessarily pleasing to them. In *this* society, in other words, culture, rather than law, is the primary mechanism by which women's consent to even unpleasant and unwanted intercourse is secured, and the severance of the connection between desire and physical action is achieved.

This aspect of patriarchal culture is ubiquitous. It is so pervasive that it borders on invisibility. Women are taught from a very early age to be and to view themselves as being physically weak: passive, defenseless, and obedient in the face of male sexual aggression. *And they are also taught* that such a stance will in the long run secure for them *at least* physical or economic security, and at best the peculiar, irresponsible pleasures of an extended, childlike dependency. A perusal of pornography will certainly drive this message home—this is, after all, the shared message of both soft-core and hard-core pornography—but it is by no means *only* pornography which contains such a message. In any Toys R Us aisle, one will find, in the pink rows, fake fingernails, high heels, Barbie dolls with feet permanently slanted to accommodate high heels, toy cosmetics, and ultrafeminine pink and yellow power rangers, all aimed at the four-year-old female consumer. From early childhood through adulthood the message is relentless: female sexual acquiescence is natural and inevitable. It is a part of one's identity.

J. C. Smith and Carla Ferstman have recently argued in a provocative study of Lacanian psychoanalytic theory that we might profitably view this aspect of patriarchal culture in purely Nietzschean terms.[76] On their analysis, patriarchy is a moral, cultural, and coercive system designed to insure that men get what women are naturally empowered to have or withhold—the means to men's sexual gratification. Patriarchal culture, they argue, fundamentally reverses a natural female empowerment: because men so badly want what women have, women are by nature the more powerful. Patriarchal culture achieves a systemic reversal of those positions: it strips women of the power to withhold their sexuality.[77] From this perspective, the cultural, moral, and physical threads of patriarchy are revealed as a seamless web with a single purpose. That women are *very* injured by rape, albeit not an unambiguous good, does have one positive side effect for men not inclined, by nature or by morality, toward violence themselves: it provides women a concrete, compelling reason to consent to sex with a nonrapist, if he offers her protection in return. Sexual harassment on the street and in the workplace similarly reinforces the message of availability, infantilization, and powerlessness. Cultural norms teach passivity, and moral systems teach availability—from the traditional-ist's admonition to restrict sex to marriage, but within marriage, to view sex as a part of one's duty, to the 1960s sloganeering admonitions to "make love, not war," and to "say yes (to sex) to boys who say no (to war)." Whether or not women receive pleasure from the sex to which they say yes is simply inconsequential. If men's interests trump, the harms women sustain from unpleasurable but consensual intercourse will not be recognized as harms, much less as harms worthy of societal concern.

Second, as sociobiologists tirelessly remind us, men need women's sexual loyalty and fidelity in order to insure their paternity of the children they raise.[78] In order to secure that *knowledge*, they must secure women's continual, uninterrupted *presence* at their side or in their home, and in order to achieve that goal they must *separate* the woman who mothers their children from other communities, includ-ing the community of female relatives and friends from which she came. The primacy of the mother-child family unit must be destroyed, as must the companionate woman-to-woman friendship, so that the husband-wife marriage and traditional family unit—both necessary to secure male knowledge of paternity—can thrive. Again, one might achieve this result simply by capture, but it is easier if the woman consents. And following Nietzsche as well as feminist critique, we might view the mystique of heterosexual romance and love as the patriarchal means by which men get what they need from women—knowledge of paternity—and the means by which the natural power women have—to grant or withhold that knowledge—is neutralized, or turned against them. In a patriarchal world in which men's interests trump women's, that women are emotionally bruised, harmed, or in some cases utterly shattered by this separation from their community is not going to be a harm worth considering. Patriarchy triumphs over matriarchy. That women are hurt by this displacement will not be a harm worth notice.

Third, men need women's domestic services in the home, and patriarchal culture is designed to insure that they get them. Girls and women, again from a very early age, are inundated with the cultural message that sacrifice in the home in order to provide comfort to its other inhabitants is central to their identity. Thus, girls are sur-rounded not only with Barbie dolls with slanted feet, but with baby dolls that pee, toy stoves, refrigerators, plates, cups and saucers on which meals can be prepared and served, toy brooms, dust pans and mops with which houses can be cleaned, and book after book of mothers servicing the needs of others in the home. The cultural message is that it is part of a woman's identity to provide such services *free of charge*—thus leaving her lacking in marketable skills and therefore dependent upon the partner she services. It is of course women's "willingness" to provide these services which in turn allows men to be the liberal individualist or the civic-minded communitarian, no less than the slave class of ancient Athens allowed citizens to enjoy their aristocratic responsibilities. That the dull, repetitive, monotonous, and time-consuming labor required of women injures their capacity for economic self-sufficiency and political citizenship, will not rank as an injury worth reckoning in a world in which men's interests trump women's.

Again, in this society, we do not allow men to simply rape women at will, to capture and hold women hostage so as to assure paternity of the children they bear, or simply draft them into domestic slavery. Not only do we not allow it, but we have laws that forbid it—a simple fact which is itself powerful evidence of the liberatory potential of the Rule of Law. Rather, the sexual availability of women, their isolation and separation into marital and heterosexual units, and their domestic service, all of which serve men's interests, are achieved in large part in this culture not through legal compulsion, but through ideological manipulation. Our prevailing culture—not our prevailing law—encodes norms of sexual availability and passivity, heterosexual normalcy, and female domestic altruism, and by doing so profoundly affects a girl's and a woman's view of what she is, and what fate holds in store for her.

The violent, terrorizing side of patriarchal control is partly legal and largely illegal, but in any event it is for the most part *hidden:* it consists of violence in the *privacy* of the home, whispered threats of coercive sexual physicality on the street, and the ever-present and unspoken possibility of rape. The ideological and cultural side of patriarchy, by contrast, is *relentlessly* public and visible. It is so visible, so routinely present, so immovably, unavoidably *there*, that it is in effect a part of us rather than noticed by us. It is inseparable from us. From the toys of early childhood, through the cheerleading squads of adolescence, the mystique and beauty of weddings, and the depictions of womanly sexuality, nurturance, and maternalism found in pornography, romance novels, and fashion, we are taught, through an endless parade of commodities and images, the monotonous tripartite patriarchal message of female sexual availability, heterosexual normalcy, and domestic altruism.

Women suffer distinctive, and distinctively different, harms from these two "faces" of patriarchal control. Obviously, and as I will discuss in greater detail in the next section, women suffer harms *by virtue of* the *unregulated* aspects of the private violence which constitutes the coercive side of a patriarchal regime. Thus, in addition to the harms occasioned by the acts themselves—the harm of rape, of incest, of harassment—women sustain harm by virtue of the knowledge that these violent acts perpetuated upon them are largely unregulated by the state. The harm occasioned by the cultural, "softer" side of patriarchal control is somewhat different: it is the harm done to our sense of our own potential, entitlements, and self-worth by virtue of a damaging set of beliefs about the necessity and justice of our fate. It is the harm done, for example, to women who believe that sexuality is not, and should not be, a source of pleasure for them by virtue of the fact that they are women, and who accordingly submit to a man's sexual demands in spite of that fact. The disorientation, the detachment, and indeed the alienation from one's body and one's sexuality occasioned by these beliefs are very real harms. It is the harm occasioned by the fact that most women in this culture have *never* contemplated for even a second the possibility of spending their adult, intimate lives with another woman instead of with a man.[79] It is the harm occasioned by the belief, widely shared among women, that it is inevitable that they work harder and longer than their husbands, male partners, or the fathers of their children.[80] It is the harm to the richness of inner life and the potentialities of public life occasioned by the belief, again widely shared, that one's nature dictates a life of relative drudgery serving the bodily needs of others.

The pain and harm occasioned by unwanted sex, unwanted abortions or pregnancies, violent and coercive rape, the second shift phenomenon, and compulsory heterosexuality are all harms done to women, by men, and in the interest of men. But the harms done by these *beliefs*—the belief that women are not sexual subjects, the belief that marriage is and should be a matter of providing nursemaid services, the belief that women are and should be passive, receptive, and sexually vulnerable—are harms of a very different sort. All these

[137]

beliefs are constitutive of identity, and the harm they cause is that they make it impossible to conceive of other ways of organizing social life. They all make it difficult or impossible to view oneself as the victim of a contingent and unjust social arrangement. They make it difficult or impossible to view oneself as sharing with other similarly situated women a common interest in creating a new social reality. They make it difficult or impossible, in short, to view oneself as an agent for social change.

LAW'S DOMAIN

As I will try to show, contrary to the pragmatic, working assumption of legal instrumentalism, law only occasionally directly targets and seeks to minimize the gender-specific harms described above. Neither is it the case, however, that law directly *causes* these harms. Rather, law stands in a complex and generally autonomous relationship from both patriarchy and the harms which are a part of it. Sometimes law does target a part of the harm—typically that part which is most like, or at least most analogous to, a harm suffered by men. This is the case, for example, of the criminal law governing rape, the civil rights laws forbidding sex discrimination, and constitutional principles governing and generally protecting abortion rights. At other times, there is simply no law regulating or even acknowledging the existence of the harm whatsoever. This is true of many of the sexual harms women suffer, from the physical and sexual harms of some forms of marital rape—still undercriminalized in most jurisdictions and underenforced in all—to the sexual and psychic harms of street harassment, all of which are still largely unregulated. At other times, the gender-specific harms women sustain may be acknowledged but are nevertheless simply not calculated in the cost-benefit analysis at the heart of various civil legal remedies. This is true, for example, of the emotional harms sustained by regretful surrogate mothers when courts rule on the enforceability of such contracts, the emotional harms felt by mothers facing the tortuous, negligently caused death of a child, and by wives seeking relief from psychologically abusive marriages, or compensation for the injuries those marriages have caused.

At other times, the law *indirectly supports* or legitimates both the harm and the events and institutions which cause it. What I have called altruistic harms are indirectly legitimated, if not caused, by a wide array of laws governing social security and other entitlements, as well as an array of employment laws. These legal regimes consistently fail to provide adequate compensation for women's domestic work, and thereby consistently insure that such work remains in the sphere of private and uncompensated "altruism." At other times, law quite directly protects the event which causes harm from legal challenge. The first amendment, for example, and its core or penumbral protections of both "privacy" and patriarchal culture aggressively protects much of the speech and conduct that harms women's conception of self and of political possibilities. And finally, the law on occasion not only protects but celebrates the harm, converting it in the public eye into virtue or public benefit. The current reactionary welfare reform movement, for example, is quite explicitly premised upon the desire to characterize the mother who is fully dependent upon her husband as the embodiment of virtue, and any departure from that "norm" as the cause of almost all social ills.

I will comment in the next few sections on each of these in turn. My purpose is *not* to provide an exhaustive survey. Rather, I want to provide enough examples to show that the instrumentalist's assumption that law seeks to rationally minimize social harms (or maximize benefits and minimize costs) is wildly inadequate to the task of accounting for the relationship between law and gender-specific harms. By the same token, however, it is clear that law is only rarely the *cause* of gender-specific harms. Law is no more an "instrument" wielded by patriarchal powers than it is an instrument poised against them. Law is indeed a relatively independent or autonomous sphere of power. Because it is autonomous, it can at times be used to destabilize that power, and to at least begin to address some of the gendered harms of daily life.

PARTIAL REGULATION OF
GENDER-SPECIFIC HARMS

First, many of the laws that do appear to target gender-specific harms do so only partially, are themselves derived from earlier legal norms which protected men's interests more than women's, and even today only target that part of the law which most resembles harms suffered by men. Thus, rape law, as numerous historians have demonstrated,

[139]

was initially intended to protect men's property interests in their wives' and daughters' chastity.[81] In modern times, of course, it is understood to protect women from harm. However, it does so only partially. The two areas of sexual assault which are most underregulated are precisely those areas which are gender-specific.

First, rape law does not touch *at all* a good deal of marital rape, and it covers only haphazardly rape by dates or intimates.[82] Thus, the rape that invades not only the integrity of the woman's body but also the integrity and safety of her intimate life, is precisely the rape that is least regulated. And second, rape law fails to cover, in many jurisdictions, nonconsensual intercourse which is not accompanied by either a weapon or at least a credible show of force by the perpetrator, as well as, in some jurisdictions, resistance by the victim.[83] In practical terms, rape law is clearest, its prosecution most vigorous, and its rationale most self-evident when the rape itself most resembles the sorts of nonsexual physical attacks men suffer and are themselves in fear of: attacks committed by strangers and accompanied by actual or threatened violence. Rapes committed by husbands upon wives, or by boyfriends upon girlfriends, or by johns on prostitutes, and rapes committed without a show of violence that goes beyond the violence of the penetration itself and the force required to accomplish it, are underregulated, or not regulated at all. To put it positively, those two aspects of the lived experience of sexual assaults that are *most gender-specific*—the *invasion* of the integrity of a woman's body and the invasion of the safety and integrity of her intimate life—are the very aspects of nonconsensual sex that are *also* most unregulated.

In modern times, rape is criminal because of the harm it does to women, but only so long as, and to the degree that, it shares in the violence of nonsexual *ungendered* assaults. The more "violent" the sex, the more criminal the act[84]—so long as the penetration *itself* does not count as a part of the violence, and so long as the violence is not perpetrated by an intimate. The gender-specific invasion of women's bodies and the gender-specific invasion of the safety of women's intimate spheres is precisely that aspect of the lived experience of sexual assault which is undercriminalized, or not criminalized at all.

Constitutional protection of women's reproductive freedom—the so-called "constitutional right to privacy"—shares some of the same general outline. While it was originally conceived as a right *of women and men,* rather than of men exclusively, it was nevertheless conceived as a right guaranteeing against that aspect of the harm of an unwanted pregnancy which is shared by men—the unwanted participation *of the state* in the *decision* to procure or not procure an abortion. The privacy of family life, like the decision to abort, and unlike, of course, the abortion or the pregnancy itself, is the aspect of reproductive freedom and privacy shared by men, and it was *that* aspect which received explicit protection from the Supreme Court in *Roe v. Wade.*[85] The *unwanted pregnancy itself*—the gender-specific aspect of the harm—was not conceived as the harm—rather, the unwarranted, genderless, intrusion upon private decision making was. Thus, the harm was reconceptualized as not involving the unwanted intrusion of women's bodies, but rather, as involving the unwanted intrusion of the contractual relationship between doctor and patient, or the familial relationship between husband and wife. *Roe v. Wade,*[86] which guaranteed the limited right to procure an abortion under certain circumstances, like *Griswold v. Connecticut*[87] before it, which guaranteed the right to procure birth control, both have at least as much to do with assuring to men and women a degree of sexual autonomy (and therefore, to men, a degree of sexual access) as with protecting women against unwanted pregnancies.[88]

While the harms done to women by the criminal law's neglect of the gendered aspects of the harms of rape have been thoroughly discussed in feminist literature, the harms done to women by the neglect of the gendered aspects of the harms of anti-abortion laws are not as well recognized. There are, I think, at least two pernicious consequences of the law's emphasis upon contractual, medical, familial, and sexual freedom, rather than upon women's physical integrity, in the area of reproductive rights. First, as Catharine MacKinnon has argued, sexual autonomy, and the contractual freedom to purchase whatever contraceptions and abortions are necessary to insure it, impacts women and men differently in a world in which men and women have such widely disparate amounts of power.[89] An extraordinarily high number of abortions, and a comparably high number of completed pregnancies, are undergone by teenage girls impregnated by older, and sometimes much older men.[90] For these men, the "constitutional right to privacy" does indeed guarantee them a degree of sexual autonomy free of the responsibilities of parenthood, while for the girls, it guarantees them little but the "right" to be invaded once again: by the abortion itself, and then to be rendered available for further sexual assault.[91] The "right" to free oneself of an unwanted fetus, albeit a blessing, is a decidedly mixed one for these girls.

A less noted but perhaps more significant consequence of framing reproductive freedom as the genderless right to enjoy a degree of contractual, sexual, and medical freedom *from the state,* is that women thereby lose the opportunity to even conceive of, much less realize, reproductive freedom as the positive freedom to make life-enhancing decisions regarding their reproductive lives, rather than simply the negative freedom to be free of state intrusion into decisions to end pregnancies. For such a positive freedom to exist in any meaningful way, two conditions would have to be met, both of which would require substantial state action. First, women and girls would have to be empowered to resist sexual assault. Many unwanted pregnancies are the results of rape, statutory and otherwise.[92] But second, women and girls, particularly poor women and girls, would have to be given opportunities for growth and self-fulfillment other than the opportunity provided by motherhood. Many unwanted but consensual pregnancies lead not to abortion, but to unwanted—even if noncoerced—motherhood, and those pregnancies are also harmful to the women who bear them. Motherhood does provide a purpose, an identity, and a *job* for young adulthood, and even when it is essentially unwanted and in no one's "best interest," if no other opportunities for adult fulfillment are presented, it will be the "chosen" career path of countless girls and women. For that matter, even wanted pregnancies are often injurious for much the same reason: they are the result of an immature quest for love, itself reflecting an emotional lack rather than strength. Mothering provides not just a job, but a chance for emotional fulfillment—an infant, baby, and child will love you back, and intensely. Many children get pregnant, in short, so that they can produce someone who will love them.[93] What "causes" these pregnancies is that the girls are themselves not sufficiently loved.

A world in which women and girls were protected against the harmful intrusions upon our bodies and lives by injurious pregnancies—whether coerced, uncoerced but unwanted, or wanted but harmful—would most decidedly *not* be a world in which the state simply "stayed out" of the private or intimate spheres. The state needs to be more, not less, involved in securing the conditions that must be met for such a world to come into being. The state needs to be more, not less, involved in the work of protecting women against criminal sexual assault. The state needs to be more, not less, involved in the work of providing women with the education and training for a public life of responsible civic engagement, and for remunerative, fulfilling work. The state needs to be more, not less, involved in the work of supporting families so as to ensure the presence, in every family, of parents who have the time required to provide not just physical necessities but love, play, companionship, and fun for their children. If women are to be genuinely freed of the consequences of coerced, unwanted, and harmful pregnancies, we need the state not "off our backs," or "out of our lives." We need the state on our side.

NONRECOGNITION OF GENDERED HARMS

The second way in which law perversely aggravates, rather than benignly regulates, harms which women distinctively suffer is simply by not recognizing their existence. The most serious consequence of nonrecognition is that by not responding *at all* to often life-threatening harms suffered by women in the private sphere, the law creates through its inaction what I have elsewhere called a "separate sovereignty." Let me briefly elaborate.

All citizens, women as well as men, must acquiesce in the sovereignty of the state. The state has the potential to inflict considerable harm on any citizen, and every citizen must adjust his or her behavior and aspirations accordingly. But to the degree that the state does not protect women against violence and other private harms, women, and only women, must *also* acquiesce in the sovereignty of the *men* whose violence they rationally fear. The significance of this separate sovereignty in terms of women's lives is twofold. First, like subjects within any state of sovereignty, women must adjust their behavior in light of the risk (or certainty) of this source of violence. But second, and possibly more seriously, where the harm or the potential for harm inflicted by one citizen upon another goes unrecognized, uncompensated, unpunished, and undeterred by the state, the violator becomes much more than simply a source of potential danger. He becomes, in essence, a political *authority* as well—his power is *legitimate,* and he thereby enjoys the normative mantle of authority as well as the prerogatives of brute force. He becomes someone with not only political control over the actions, but also with normative control over the self-image and aspirations, of his subjects.

Consider a world, for example, in which one group of citizens—say, democrats—could, without fear of prosecution, inflict violence or harm at will upon another group, say, republicans. In such a world, republicans would have to live in fear not only of the state but also of democrats, and would eventually learn to adjust their view of themselves and their world accordingly. However, just as most of us do not live *in fear* of the state, but rather adapt our behavior and self-concept to its commands so that we don't *have to* fear it, so likewise, in this hypothetical world of democratic immunity, republicans would eventually adjust not only their behavior, but also their self-concept, to the expectations of their more powerful democratic cocitizens. They would subject themselves to not one but two sovereigns, and would learn to live within the prescribed worlds of both.

This is, of course, the relationship of master to slave, virtually by definition.[94] A master in a slave society simply *is* someone whose violence perpetrated against a slave will not go punished by the state—the Slave Codes of the South made this chillingly clear. Conversely, a slave simply is someone who can be violated without consequence—and hence, from the slave's perspective, must live within the threats, prescriptions, and normative influence of both the state and the master. The sovereignty of the master over the slave can even be defined by reference to this nonrecognition by the state of the violence and threats of violence directed by the one against the other. The master's sovereignty over the slave, in other words, is a direct consequence of—indeed, equivalent to—the state's *in*action in the face of violence perpetrated by the master over the slave—violence which would be criminal, were the perpetrator and victim both cocitizens in the eyes of the law.

The explicit refusal of virtually every state, until very recently, to criminalize rape within marriage[95]—the so-called "marital rape exemption"—and the continuing refusal to enforce those laws, is directly analogous to the perpetuation of slavery through failure to criminalize the violence perpetrated and threatened by masters against slaves.[96] During the 1970s and 1980s, all states abolished the most sweeping version of the marital rape exemption, but only a few abolished it entirely—a good number of states continue to criminalize only first degree rapes within marriage or only criminalize rapes within marriage where the couple have separated.[97] And virtually all states continue to fail to enforce these statutes: the number of successful prosecutions is deminimus.[98] To the (considerable) degree that women within marriages can be raped at will with no realistic prospect of state control, they exist in a state of sovereignty: the husband-rapist becomes a political authority rather than a criminal. He is her *boss,* not her attacker, when the violence against her is legitimate.

The woman in such a relationship does not have the degree of selfhood and selfacknowledgment granted to victims of crime. She is in a literal sense reduced to the status of a thing: something to be used in whatever way he needs. The response to this assault on subjectivity is simply to self-protectively shrink subjectivity—to retreat the self into a smaller and smaller "place" of relative safety. The self is thereby protected but it is also thereby diminished. The sphere of life within which one can enjoy pleasures for oneself, make decisions on one's own behalf, is exploded, or imploded, or at any rate it disappears.

The lack of recognition by the state, and many times by the community as well, of the severity of this life-threatening harm not only renders the violence that much more lethal, but underscores the assault on selfhood. Nonrecognition by the state of intimate violence, in other words, becomes a part of the constitution of the self within intimate spheres of association. One *becomes* someone not worthy of state involvement when the harm one suffers is too trivial to be criminalized, or enforced, or prosecuted. Nonrecognition of the harm occasioned by street harassment, although not as lethal, has many of the same consequences. The state's refusal to even *attempt* to criminalize these assaultive threats underscores the degree to which women exist on public streets for the visual and verbal sexual consumption by men. A woman who is hassled on the street knows that neither the community nor the state will come to her aid. She knows, then, that she is "at the mercy" of the harasser—he can continue or cease the harassment, with no consequence to him either way. The harassment itself can be terrifying, humiliating, and scarring in any number of ways, as discussed above. But the nonrecognition by the state of the criminality of these assaults, and the abandonment of her that that nonrecognition implies, carries further harms. She is in the position of a truly helpless infant whose well-being is at the whim of sadistic parents. One does not sustain harassment as a rights-bearing cocitizen. One sustains the harassment as an object, subjected to a very real political authority.

[145]

It is extremely damaging to be raped or sexually abused, and it is extremely damaging to be assaulted, yelled at, jeered at and worse on the street. But it is made all the more so by virtue of the sure knowledge that *you have to take it:* that one is *not entitled* to redress for these harms; that one has no *rights* in the face of their occurrence. What a woman will often do in the face of this knowledge of her own nonentitlement is to reduce her*self*—thereby trivializing the harm. The state did not and will not respond; the culture does less; it must truly have been inconsequential. It "was nothing." And since it was inconsequential, I too, who nevertheless *felt* harmed, must be inconsequential. If women first learn low self-esteem in school, as a number of feminist educators now claim, there can be little doubt that that message is underscored by the nonresponsiveness of the state to the undeniable and undeniably harmful physical assaults and intrusions on her body.

Lastly, the nonregulation of these violent events "objectifies" women. If one is treated "like an object" often enough, one eventually begins to feel like an object, meaning one feels less and less. When harassed on the street, almost all women report that their first defensive response is to "freeze up" inside—to stop feeling, stop thinking.[99] Fear and rage are unpleasant, draining emotions, and one way of coping with them is to dull that which is endangered, which is one's subjectivity. To dull subjectivity is to objectify. If the message is internalized that one's subjective well-being is not valued, then subjectivity itself suffers.

We can characterize the impact of this nonrecognition in this way. As boys mature into men, they grow into a world in which they will be "equal" in spite of their physical differences in strength. They leave the playground, and the playground bully, behind them. The servility, the queasiness, the humiliation, of the physically weaker boy is a *boyhood* experience. It may leave scars, but it is nevertheless put behind him as he enters the world of adulthood. Importantly, he can make this transition largely *because* he becomes more and more protected by the state as he meets the conditions of citizenship. A boy on the schoolyard truly is vulnerable to the taunts, threats, potential and actual violence of other boys who are larger and stronger than he. As the smaller boy becomes a man, however, the state is more likely to intervene to protect him against the larger man's threats, and for most men, accordingly, those threats diminish in number and consequence. His mature sexuality becomes, in a sense, the *marker* of his equality with other men, and it is by virtue of state intervention—state protection of the weak against the threats of violence by the strong—that it is so.

Women experience precisely the *opposite* transformation. As women sexually mature, they become *more* vulnerable to violence. They become more open to taunts, threats, assaults, and actual batteries. And again, it is largely *by virtue of state nonrecognition* that this is so. While a boy entering manhood leaves behind the world of radical inequality that characterizes boyhood, and enters instead a world of state-created and law-created equality, a girl entering adulthood leaves behind the relative calm, placidity, and equality of young female companionship and enters a state-created world of sexual vulnerability and radical inequality. While a man's mature sexuality is therefore not only a marker of his relative equality with other men, but also a marker of his recognition *as an equal* by the state, so a woman's mature sexuality becomes not only a marker of her vulnerability to harm, but also of her infantilization by the state. As girls become women, they leave behind them a world of relative *equality* and enter a world of profound *inequality:* the adolescent girl's early lessons in and about her sexuality will underscore her physical vulnerability.

The consequence of this nonrecognition of violent harms is that as a girl matures, one lesson she learns from the world around her is that *as she becomes a woman* she becomes profoundly vulnerable physically—*and that* her adult sexuality *is the cause* of that frightening state. This knowledge is infantilizing—it reduces her to the status and psychic awareness of a small child. It is infantilizing to know that one is at the mercy of a man, or of any man; to know that one is "under his thumb." The state of servility which this kind of subjection engenders is, simply, childlike. One's physical survival and well-being are dependent upon the goodwill and graces of the stronger other. The state's nonintervention transforms what would otherwise be a violated right into a natural mode of being, and transforms what would otherwise be a citizen with a legitimate grievance into a dependant.

Nonrecognition by the state of harms of separation and isolation have similar repercussions. As divorce law moved increasingly toward a no-fault regime,[100] and as family law generally becomes subsumed by contract,[101] and as laws governing the placement of children are increasingly transformed to meet the rigorous demands of formal

THE CONCEPT OF HARM

equality,[102] there are fewer and fewer legal contexts in which the emotional harms of separation and isolation differentially sustained by women are even *relevant* to, much less compensated by, any form of state intervention. The emotional harms sustained by women in noncommunicative and emotionally cold marriages, for example, are at least in part, and often for the most part, a function of the separation and isolation from her larger community which the marriage has caused. As long as the marriage is intact, self-interest as well as spousal immunity laws prevent the emotional harms inflicted by the husband upon the wife from being compensable.[103] And in a no-fault regime, any award given at the point of dissolution of the marriage will by definition not be conceived as one to compensate for harms perpetrated within the marriage.[104] "No-fault," at least in the context of these emotional harms, directly implies no responsibility: harms which could in a fault regime have been compensated, after a fashion, in an alimony award, are no longer compensable at all where the amount bears no relation, either theoretical or in practice, to either harm or fault.[105] Similarly, where a contract, rather than family law, governs the terms of dissolution of the marriage, as well as, increasingly, the terms of the marriage, such harms become legally irrelevant.[106] Unless an explicit term of the contract so dictates, the award at the breakup will be limited by the contractual agreement; it will not expand to include compensation for inflicted marital harms.

Not only the pain of the marriage, but much of the pain of divorce as well, for many women, is unrecognized and uncompensated. Even a good marriage, but almost invariably a bad marriage, isolates and separates wives from communities of friends, families of origin, and companions, and if and when that marriage ends, the woman is often left not only unemployed and unemployable, but without any emotional support as well. While a support award may include compensation for the difficulties of reentering the labor market, nowhere does such an award include compensation for the difficulties of reentering or re-creating a supportive community. The severance of community life which marriage often entails and which divorce then aggravates, and the harm that severance inflicts upon women, is simply not recognized, much less compensated, by governing family law norms.

The harms mothers sustain when forced to separate from their children is also nowhere recognized, much less compensated, in family law norms. Custody disputes, for example, are now typically gov-

[148]

erned by a "best interest of the child" standard,[107] and that standard is often influenced by the antagonistic parents' comparative income. As men continue to earn more than women in the paid labor market, and as mothers continue to lose income and income potential in that market by virtue of the greater time they spend with young children, the application of this standard has resulted in more mothers losing custody in contested cases.[108] Not only, then, is the mother's greater unpaid labor investment in raising the child not recognized in the custody dispute itself, but the greater harm done her by separating her from her child is similarly uncompensated.

The pain of separating from a newborn child pursuant to a surrogacy agreement is also not well recognized, where the biological mother seeks to contest the contract after having borne the child. The emotional harm of the separation is rarely, if ever, included in a judicial calculation of the increased "costs" of performing the contract, pursuant to a determination as to whether or not full performance should be required against the will of the biological mother.[109] Contested adoptions similarly fail to consider the cost to the separating mother—whether the biological or adoptive mother—as part of the equation of interests being weighed.[110] And finally, tort actions for the wrongful death of a child routinely include in a damage award to the parents an approximation of the child's lost potential income that may have accrued to the parent, as well as an approximation of the "cost" for the child's pain and suffering, as well as, in some jurisdictions, an approximation of the emotional "cost" of witnessing the negligent action which caused the death—all, of course, being only grossly speculative approximations of intangibles. They never, however, include an approximation of what is surely the greatest "cost" when such a tragedy strikes, and that is the emotional cost of losing a child.

I do not mean to suggest that all these harms *should* be compensable. The failure to compensate for them, however, has real consequences, the most obvious of which is that in the absence of regulation by the state, women's emotional well-being is to a considerable degree hostage to the whimsical desires of men. The result is not only that these harms go undeterred as well as uncompensated, but also that the *threat* of their infliction then becomes a weapon by which other assets can be extracted. As noted above, the threat of contesting the custody of minor children, with the very real possibility that such a contest would result in a victory for the income-productive father, is now a routine weapon in contested divorces for reducing the amounts of alimony or support payments.[111] That this is a weapon now routinely employed against mothers, but almost never against fathers, simply illustrates the differential emotional impact of a forced separation from one's child. A blanket regime of formal equality imposed over such a difference does nothing but empower one side to extract concessions from the other.[112] It creates the potential for exploitation rather than real equality.

Less obviously, but just as important, the lack of recognition of the emotional harms women sustain in marriages (and elsewhere) affects the richness of emotional life itself. A woman whose emotional life is inconsequential to the state, and whose emotional injuries are not recognized as injuries by the community and the laws it recognizes, will eventually view her own emotional well-being as expendable, unimportant, and of no consequence. Eventually, it simply disappears, or dwindles. As her sexuality becomes something possessed by the other, so her emotional life as well becomes that which is sacrificed for others. A woman who nursemaids through marriage—whose emotional life consists of tending the emotional needs of others—is viewed by her husband, the state, and eventually herself as not having needs worth recognizing, or interests worth attending to. The peaks and valleys of a healthy emotional life are in a sense worn away from disuse. Intensity is forfeited in the name of peace and security. There is little laughter and few tears where one's emotional life consists of absorbing the anger and tending the ego of a man. The lack of state recognition of serious emotional harms simply underscores the man's lack of recognition, in too many traditional marriages, of his wife's emotional life. Both in tandem deaden emotional subjectivity itself.

LEGITIMATION OF GENDER-SPECIFIC HARMS

As critical legal scholars have repeatedly argued over the last two decades, one very general problem with legal instrumentalism is that instrumentalists assume not only that the primary purpose of law is minimization of harm, but also that law achieves this goal through the use of sanctions that directly influence the way we behave.[113] By imposing additional costs—fines, imprisonments, damage remedies—on certain behaviors, instrumentalists assume that, through law we can harmonize the actor's individual calculation of harms and benefits with the societal tally, thereby bringing about the optimal result. But it seems clear that this is not the only way law influences behavior. Legal *culture,* no less than legal sanctions, exerts an influence on the way we think and the way we behave. How it does so simply cannot be captured, or even glimpsed, by an exclusively positivistic or instrumentalist study of fines, imprisonments, and civil damage remedies. Both through the larger culture of which law is partly constitutive and which it in turn partly constitutes, and through a system of justificatory norms and ethics interrelated with the larger culture but also quite distinct from it, law influences our behavior and thoughts by affecting the way we think about ourselves, each other, and the larger society of which we are a part. The overall efficacy of legal culture in shaping our behavior through its impact on our self-concept, in fact, may well be far greater than that of the legal sanction itself.

Although there are any number of ways in which legal culture affects our perceptions, self-perceptions, and consequently our lives, one of the most powerful and certainly the one which has received the lion's share of attention from the critical legal studies movement, is its ability to *legitimate* some of the harms that we sustain in social interactions. To the degree that this process of legitimation is effective, the harmed party or individual loses consciousness of himself or herself *as harmed.* The consequence, then, is that for those legitimated harms, the victim not only has no legal recourse, but also comes to seriously question whether or not she has been harmed at all[114]—or, alternatively, simply never comes to see herself as harmed. Legal culture in this way serves to legitimate not only the specific harm but also the hierarchic distributions of rights and powers that facilitated its occurrence.

Thus, to take just one example, the victim of a grossly unjust contractual bargain in our market economy generally lacks any protection from or redress by the state—contract law enforces wise and unwise contracts against "losers" and winners equally.[115] Similarly, workers discharged from their jobs "at the will" of the employer are for the most part without legal remedy even if the discharge was malicious or capricious. Extremely unjust and regressive contracts, and extremely unjust employment relations, are routinely enforced against extremely vulnerable and weak people. The larger culture justifies this outcome with a sort of harsh, Emersonian, ethic of self-reliance: we have to learn to take our lumps, it's the price of freedom. *Legal* culture, however, goes one step further: the harm is not simply justified, it is *legitimated,* which means in effect that the harm disappears.

In the case of unjust bargains, the critical scholars' argument continues, this process of legitimation is mediated by a set of "belief clusters," widely if inarticulately shared by both winners and losers alike, and which have at their core what is now called the "exchange theory of value": if I exchange A for B voluntarily, then I simply must be better off after the exchange than before, having, after all, agreed to it.[116] If these exchanges *are* the source of value, then it is of course impossible to ground a *value* judgment that some voluntary exchanges are harmful. If the contract was "free" then all parties *must,* by definition, have gained. There is, in effect, no loser in a market economy, where one invariably consents to only what one wants and one only wants what will benefit one. No one's actually been harmed. To the extent that, by virtue of the force of legal culture, both the fired worker and the contract victim subscribe to this "theory of value," they too, no less than the employer and the superior contractor himself, will come to view the bad bargain and the at-will employment contract not simply as the inevitable cost of a system of free contract, but as precisely what the loser *wanted.* The fired worker and the losing contractor eventually view themselves as not only not entitled to legal relief, but as not harmed. Their acquiescence in the larger system is thereby secured.[117]

Whatever the general merits of this "story" of legitimation with respect to market-based harms, it seems clear that legal culture legitimates a number of gender-specific harms in precisely the way described by the critical theorists: by virtue of a set of commitments partly shared by the larger culture but partly unique to legal culture, some of the harms that women suffer are simply not perceived as harms at all, even by the women who sustain them. To whatever extent the harm has been legitimated by the legal culture, and to whatever degree a woman herself accepts the normative authority of law, the gender-specific harm will not be felt as harmful by the woman who sustains it. Alternatively, if she is unquestionably hurting, she will frequently rationalize the pain by simply minimizing her own importance. The logic is simple enough: if the pain *feels* severe but *is* inconsequential, it must be because the person feeling it is of relatively little importance.

More specifically, at least three interrelated legalistic commitments, or, to use the postmodern term, "constructs," tend to not just minimize, or ignore, or only partially regulate, gender-specific harms, but more aggressively, to convert them, in the legal and to a lesser degree in the popular imagination, into unequivocal *gains*. First, the exchange theory of value, or the "ethic of consent" converts not only market losses into gains, as described above, but consensual sexual harms as well. Given a system of consensual ethics, consensual sexual harms (like consensual market harms) simply disappear, or are rendered oxymoronic, where "consent" is in essence the source of value.[118] Similarly, the harms caused by consensual pregnancy, motherhood, and marriage are not harms if we by definition benefit from whatever it is to which we consent.

Second, the ethical and normative system implied by our law of anti-discrimination, and the formal equality it requires, not only permits but more aggressively legitimates the sufferance of harms which cannot be accommodated by its logic. Formal equality requires the state to treat persons similarly who are similarly situated—and affirmatively forbids as "discrimination" different treatment of persons based upon gender.[119] Where "discrimination" is understood as the core and only problem in the social relation between the sexes, and equal treatment under the law its solution, whatever harms are inflicted and cannot be understood as a product of state-based discrimination fade from view. Those harms become, in effect, not harms at all, but rather, the result of well-functioning private and cultural markets, free of pernicious and inefficient state intervention.[120] They become something to celebrate rather than worry over.

And third, the continuing commitment within legal culture to a firm distinction between the public world of government and employment, and a private world of home and domesticity, renders whatever happens in the latter sphere not only outside the proper bounds of public regulation, but by definition beneficial to all parties who live within it. The private home gives respite from the harsh competition of the public worlds of civic responsibility and work. Home life, unlike public and economic life, is soft, tender, gentle, and caring. Whatever occurs within the private sphere *must be* beneficial to those who enjoy its comforts. Again, the injustices within the home are not merely thereby construed as outside the proper bounds of state intervention, they are celebrated as transcending the need for it.[121] No rights exist within the home, in effect, not because the state cannot, for practical or prudential reasons, effectuate such a radical penetration, but because no rights are needed, wanted, or desirable. The home is the locus of rights-lessness, because it is the locus of harm-lessness.

These three commitments operate jointly within legal culture, and operate in conjunction with commitments of the larger culture, to render invisible a good number of gender specific harms. For example, the altruistic harms women sustain in the home—women's disproportionate share of uncompensated home maintenance and child care—as well as the indirect and harmful effects of the second shift in the workplace, from the lack of social security protection for unpaid domestic labor, to the deflation of wage income for "female ghetto jobs," to "mommy tracks" in high-paid professions—are all to some degree justified in the larger culture by a pervasive ethic of female self-sacrifice: women do this additional work, and should do this additional work, simply because they are better suited for it. But all these harms are *further* legitimated within legal culture and by legal culture, by the three commitments outlined above. Thus, because women *consent* to these additional burdens, they must benefit by whatever they gain in exchange for their sufferance. Because the work is consensual there must be a trade-off, even if it is not an obvious one. Women are not only not harmed, then, by the second shift, they must benefit from it.[122]

Second, the altruistic harms sustained within the home and its indirect effects on women's wages and security in the workplace are not a consequence of any inequality in treatment of women by the state. No norm of formal equality is breached by women's unequal labor in the domestic sphere. Furthermore, for the state to take into account this disproportionate labor through gender-specific relief in family law, or social security regulations, or comparable worth legislation, or the imposition of maternity leave requirements on major employers, for example, would be to engage in a pernicious form of "affirmative action" that would merely reinforce "stereotypes" of female dependency, thus further entrenching women in harm-producing domestic roles. Therefore, the uncompensated work performed disproportionately by women within the household is emblematic of her *equality,* not of her inequality.[123]

And third, these "harms" occur within the private sphere, a world which should be protected against the invasive, intrusive glare of state intervention. The state has no "business" interfering in quintessentially private decisions made by private people regarding home maintenance and child care. These are the private decisions which, so long as they are free of state intervention, are the substance of intimacy. They are what gives life texture, as well as value. These harms are not harms at all; they are simply private life. What the state should do is leave it alone. The private sphere—the place of women's injury—is the genesis of value for the community.

PROTECTION OF THE HARM

Fourth, some of the gender-specific harms discussed above are not only ignored or legitimated by law, but the events which cause them are aggressively protected against legal challenge. Until their quite recent abolition, spousal immunities against liability, although written in the language of gender neutrality, overwhelmingly protected men from suffering any legal consequences for the injuries inflicted during marriage,[124] as did, to a lesser degree, spousal privileges against testifying.[125] The marital rape exemption, again to the limited degree to which it still is a part of our positive law, explicitly protects forced marital sex and the harms it occasions from legal intervention.

Less obviously, but at this point in the development of law more debilitating, the entire panoply of what I referred to above as cultural-patriarchal harms, as well as the events which cause them—including pornography, street hassling, and sexual harassment in the school and workplace—are at least arguably protected against legal intervention by none other than the constitution itself. If we leave aside, for a moment, constitutional considerations, it is clear that at least *some* of the cultural-patriarchal harms detailed above are harms which could be and should be redressed by legal forms of action. Pornography, street hassling, and sexual harassment all injure women in concrete and cognizable ways which are different from, but are certainly no less serious than, other, and fully recognized forms of psychic harms: they occasionally provoke violence, they often instill fear and inhibit action and movement, they trigger self-loathing, and they project a massive image of female inferiority, objectivity, and passivity into public discourse. In theory, pornographers, street hasslers, and harassers could all be made liable, either through tort or civil rights causes of action, so as to compensate the victims for the most egregious (and foreseeable) of these harms, and hence deter their further occurrence.[126] In theory, law could and should be used as an instrument to minimize the harm done by these damaging demonstrations of patriarchal culture.

In the last twenty years, a number of feminists, but most notably and most persistently Catharine MacKinnon, have tried to translate this theoretical possibility into practice. Most successfully, of course, in 1986, the Supreme Court, at the urging of a number of feminist groups, held in *Meritor Savings Bank, FSB v. Vinson*[127] that sexual harassment on the job is a form of illegal discrimination, and that accordingly the Civil Rights Act does indeed include within its scope the sexual harassment of women in the workplace. Some victims of sexual harassment at work have consequently received damage awards in lawsuits, and there is no question but that the overall amount of sexual harassment on the job has dramatically dropped as a result. Considerably less successfully, MacKinnon, Andrea Dworkin, and others have pushed for the enactment of various "anti-pornography" ordinances which would create a civil right of action *for women* against pornographers, for the harms done to women by pornography.[128] According to these proposed ordinances, where a woman could show that she has been injured in some concrete way by pornography, she could seek either damages or injunctive relief against the offending vendor or manufacturer. And most recently, Cynthia Bowman has argued in the *Harvard Law Review* for the enactment of ordinances which would provide urban women with a similar "cause of action" against street hasslers.[129] Again, where a woman could show that she has been injured by street hassling, she could seek relief of a quasi-criminal nature against the hassler. Each case represents an attempt to use law in precisely the way envisioned by instrumentalists, so as to address gender-specific harm. The civil rights law, the MacKinnon-Dworkin anti-pornography ordinance, and the street hassling ordinance proposed by Cynthia Bowman all aim not only to compensate victims but also to minimize the harms women sustain, by burdening the actions which cause the harm with additional costs.

Each of these efforts to use law instrumentally so as to compensate for and minimize gendered harms, however, has been or could be met with constitutional challenge. As is now well known, the anti-pornography ordinance proposed by Catherine MacKinnon was struck by the Seventh Circuit United States Court of Appeals in *Hudnut v. Booksellers,* [130] as violative of the first amendment, and has been similarly struck by lower courts in every jurisdiction in which it has been proposed. Although the Court's decision in *Meritor Savings Bank v. Vinson* [131] defining sexual harassment on the job as actionable sex discrimination has not been subjected to constitutional challenge, the Court's more recent decision in *St. Paul,* [132] invalidating on first amendment grounds a city ordinance providing for enhanced penalties for hate crimes, suggests the possibility of a similar outcome with respect to the regulation of sexual harassment. [133] And Bowman acknowledges, in the same article in which she proposes the anti-hassling ordinance, that the logic of the Court's decision in *St. Paul* might well encompass any attempt to regulate the harms of street hassling. [134]

It is not my intent to discuss the complex issues raised by legal attempts to control pornography and the harms it causes. My point here is only that the apparent unconstitutionality of such efforts, as well as the possible unconstitutionality of efforts to control sexual harassment and street hassling, all point to the possibility that *one* function of the first amendment, albeit by no means its only function, is the protection of (rather than the dismantling of) patriarchal culture. The possibility I want to raise is that, although law surely *could* be used instrumentally to address patriarchal harms, the first amendment—which is, after all, a part of our "higher law"—exists in part to *prohibit* precisely such a challenge. The doctrinal reason is straightforward: the first amendment protects speech, and it is largely through speech that we create culture, including the culture of patriarchy which harms women in the ways discussed above. If that is right, then it's not as odd as it first sounds to think that the first amendment specifically, and to a lesser extent the constitution more generally, quite aggressively protect the culture of patriarchy against legal challenge. [135]

Furthermore, although at first blush appearances may be to the contrary, such an interpretation is also not at odds with dominant liberal or libertarian understandings of the theoretical underpinnings of the first amendment. It is often claimed by liberals and libertarians that the purpose of the first amendment, as well as, to a lesser extent, the constitution in its entirety, is to foster dissent and hence perpetuate challenges to hierarchy.[136] Because of its protection of dissent, it is further claimed, and much more widely simply assumed, that the constitution is the vehicle for, and not an obstacle to, the liberation of subordinated groups and persons.[137] Against this understanding of the first amendment, it does seem odd to suggest that the role of the first amendment is at least in part to protect patriarchal culture. But there is no real inconsistency. It is quite clear that, at least with respect to the first amendment, the challenges to hierarchy which receive constitutional aid and comfort are only those which emanate from culture itself, and not from the state. As the libertarian repeatedly urges, the "cure for bad speech is good speech"—not legal regulation—and the good speech will receive the same constitutional protection as the bad. From a libertarian's point of view, what is constitutionally prohibited is attempts to change the culture through nonlegal means. It follows that any *law* that affects the culture by censoring some speech but not others is therefore unconstitutional, and it is in that sense that the constitution protects patriarchal culture. Again, it is perfectly consistent with such a view to abhor patriarchal culture, but at the same time view attempts to regulate the harms caused by that culture as unconstitutional.

Nor is such an interpretation at odds with at least one possible nonlibertarian understanding of the deep structure, and fundamental purpose, of constitutionalism itself. The fundamental point of constitutionalism, as both Cass Sunstein[138] and Roberto Unger[139] have argued at length, may be to provide a means by which we might systematically and continuously reexamine the moral justifications for the extant distributions of power and wealth across various subsections of our society, and an extralegal structure through which those distributions could be altered. On this understanding, the point of constitutionalism is indeed to foster dissent, liberation, and in the long run substantive equality, and on this view, it is indeed peculiar to posit the protection of patriarchal culture as a function of the first amendment. It is also possible, however, to view the fundamental purpose of constitutionalism, and certainly the fundamental purpose of the first amendment, in a quite different and decidedly more conservative light. The justification for putting certain legislative options constitutionally out of bounds might be, far from encouraging rational reexamination, to *conserve* certain aspects of social life against the threat of precipitous redistributive change.[140] Property entitlements and the rights of capital, for example, have, throughout our history but most dramatically during the Lochner era,[141] benefited from constitutional protection against such change far more than they have been threatened by constitutional challenge. Far from being an anomaly, the Lochner Court's protection of property and wealth against legislative redistribution is fully in accord with at least one possible understanding of the constitution's deep structure. The "point" of the constitution might be to keep certain "spheres" of social life— economic, familial, and cultural—untouched by law. If so, to whatever extent those spheres of life embody and reflect hierarchies of power, including unjust hierarchies, the point of constitutionalism will be to protect those *hierarchies* against legislative attack.

As a number of constitutional scholars have argued, there are indeed parallels between modern courts' use of the constitution so as to invalidate legislative initiatives that target patriarchal culture (such as anti-pornography ordinances) and the Lochner Court's use of the constitution so as to invalidate legislative initiatives that targeted the privileges of capital.[142] It does not follow, however, that the former is an illegitimate or wrong understanding of the constitution. Rather, both the Lochner Court's jurisprudence and the developing modern first amendment jurisprudence may simply evidence one always present possible understanding of constitutionalism itself. It is no doubt true that the constitution can be used, and has been used from time to time, so as to challenge aspects of patriarchal culture, particularly where that culture manifests itself in formal, legal inequality. Similarly, the constitution can be used, and has been used from time to time, to challenge other unjust forms of private culture. But we should not allow that truth to blind us to what may be an even more fundamental fact about our constitutional system. The constitution can also serve, and historically has *usually* served, to protect extant culture, and the cultural norms and resulting hierarchies thereby constituted against legislative change. That it protects pornography against legislative challenge should come as no great surprise.

Pornography, furthermore, is only the tip of the iceberg. The culture of patriarchy in fact consists overwhelmingly of various "speech acts" that, like pornography and harassment, are not only immune from constitutional challenge—because they are the acts of individuals and private groups, not of states—but are also themselves *protected* by the constitution against legislative challenge—precisely because they are speech. Consider, as a further example, the feverish, violent, and virulently misogynist "speech" of students and teachers in private military academies, when those individuals are working themselves and their underlings into a frenzied state of war-preparedness. This speech—"KILL THE CUNT!", etc., uttered while thrusting a bayonet into a dummy—undoubtedly does women real harm, and puts them in real danger. It engenders in precisely those men who are most accustomed to the use of violence and force the view that women are the entirely proper receptacle of violent instincts. Yet this speech—and the similar speech of college football players and fraternity brothers—is, first, surely not *unconstitutional:* in spite of its unambiguous role in the creation and construction of inequality, it is simply not the result of state action. But it is also, arguably, constitutionally protected against legislative challenge: it is the political speech of private persons. Likewise, the "speech" that constitutes the advertisements and commercials that sexually objectify women, the reading primers, fairy tales, Batman and Ninja cartoons and (now) the Disney fables that constrict and distort girls' and women's self-images, from "Snow White" and her Prince Charming to Dick and Jane, to say nothing of the girls and women of romance novels and Melrose Place, would clearly be protected by the first amendment against legislative attack. Even the nonspeech artifacts of patriarchy are most likely immunized, by virtue of their connection to speech and the very overtness of their patriarchal, and hence political, character. "Cheerleading" squads that blatantly train women for the nursemaid role in traditional heterosexual relations, the rows of miniature false fingernails and cosmetics targeted at the four-year-old consumer in toy stores, "beauty birthday parties" marketed to preschoolers at which three- and four-year-old girls celebrate each others' birthdays with child-sized tubes of lipstick and mascara, and the hundreds of products encountered daily that diminish, in the minds of all of us, women's nature and potential, are all, by virtue of their clear ideological content, arguably protected by first amendment guarantees against legislative challenge.

There are (thankfully) two complications. First, constitutional doctrine on virtually every issue concerning individual rights and liberties is complicated, largely because of the plethora of conflicting interpretations, or understandings, one might legitimately put forward regarding the fundamental point of constitutionalism. It is possible to argue—and I have argued elsewhere—that not only is patriarchy not properly the subject of constitutional *protection,* but it should be understood as flatly illegal—as being *itself* unconstitutional. But second, and perhaps more importantly, even assuming otherwise, the protection that the constitution accords to patriarchal culture, ought in theory, and oftentimes does in practice, extend to *challenges* to that culture as well as to the culture itself. Indeed, when it demonstrably doesn't, the entire system becomes by virtue of that fact open to the charge of hypocrisy. Thus, just as the constitution arguably protects the artifacts and "speech acts" of patriarchy, so the constitution ought also protect the artifacts and speech acts of dissent from that culture. If so, even assuming the constitution protects, say, pornography, then it should also protect the speech acts that constitute gay or lesbian marriage ceremonies,[143] as well as those speech acts presently prohibited by the "don't ask, don't tell" anti-gay policies now embraced by the Clinton administration and codified in federal regulatory policy.[144] To take a simpler case, the constitution ought to, and clearly does, protect feminist, womanist publications against state censorship, no less than it protects Walt Disney and Milton Bradley against legislative challenge.

This protection of cultural dissent is of course a great virtue of our constitutional system. But what too often goes unacknowledged by the liberals and libertarians who trumpet it is that it comes at a heavy price: the constitution protects the culture dissented from no less than the dissent. Where the culture is extremely powerful, pervasive, and all-encompassing, and the forces of dissent relatively weak, what constitutionalism ensures first and foremost is that the potential powers of the state will not be allied with the forces of dissent. Nor, of course, can the powers of the state be employed against dissent—at least in theory, and at least much of the time. But whether (and when) the benefits of the promise of state neutrality—a promise as often breached as upheld in practice—outweigh the loss of the constitutionally forbidden alliance of the state with cultural dissent, is an *empiri-*

cal, although difficult, question. It is one which cannot be answered by definitional fiat, and it is simply a mistake for liberals and libertarians to assume otherwise.

MANDATING HARM

Finally, at least on occasion if not systematically, the law *mandates* certain gender-specific harms by punishing as criminal, or burdening in some other way, either individual or collective attempts by women to circumvent them. A number of what I have called "invasive harms" are further aggravated by the punitive sanctions imposed upon chosen alternatives. The clearest examples of this might be the criminalization of same-sex sexual activity,[145] the law's nonrecognition of same-gender marriage,[146] and the significant legal obstacles placed in the path of parenting by lesbians and lesbian couples.[147] Although some of the harms caused by these sexual regulatory schemes obviously fall equally on gay men and lesbians, to the extent that heterosexuality and marriage harm women more than men, women more than men are further harmed by sexual regulations that punish realistic alternatives to heterosexuality and marriage: alternatives that might provide greater intimacy and less intrusion than the dominant heterosexual model. Refusal to provide for the funding of abortions for poor women is a second example.[148]

A less obvious but arguably more fundamental instance of the law protecting the harm women suffer, rather than protecting women from harm, is the law's underscoring of the disproportionate *mandatory* parenting required of mothers. Consider for a moment a hypothetical mother who gives birth to a baby in an unregulated, nonhospital environment—in a home or on a street—and then simply walks away. This woman has committed a serious crime: she is guilty of child abandonment, and may be guilty of a homicide should the abandoned baby die. By contrast, a father who impregnates a woman and then does nothing further, will be criminally liable at most for failure to pay child support. This stark legal asymmetry reflects a natural asymmetry: a woman is inevitably *present* at the birth of her child, while a man is not. The difference in the legal consequences of abandoning that child, however, is a legal and cultural choice, not a natural inevitability. A mother, unlike a father, is required to burden the invasive harm of either giving up for adoption, or actually *raising* (as opposed to simply supporting) unwanted children.[149]

Although these criminal sanctions are real—they are hardly the figment of imagination—their impact is largely symbolic. There are, for example, no women incarcerated for having sex with other women of whom I am aware. Furthermore, lesbians who wish to confirm a lifelong commitment to each other through a private, religious, or secular but formal and public ceremony may obviously do so, and lesbians who wish to parent will find nonlegal obstacles to that pursuit of greater consequence than legal obstacles, whether they wish to do so through adoption or pregnancy. Similarly, unwanted babies no less than wanted babies are generally born in hospitals, and if abandoned by the mother are then left to the mercies of the state's foster care system, with few adverse consequences to the natural mother. The *indirect* effect of these sorts of legal regimes, however, is enormous, and twofold.

First, the occasional criminal or civil case that does arise radiates a powerful cultural message to potential nonconformists. When a lesbian mother is denied custody of her own child, *solely* on the basis of the possibility that she engages in same-sex sexual relations with another woman, and that case is upheld and the outcome broadcast as national news,[150] a powerful message is conveyed regarding the incompatibility of lesbianism with motherhood: the overwhelming cultural imperative to ground child raising in a traditional heterosexual relationship is dramatically underscored. Consequently, although lesbians do routinely parent without challenges to their custody based on their sexuality, the strength of the moral and cultural norms to the contrary which are both reflected in and created by an occasional lawsuit, is magnified, not diminished, by the rarity of the legal proceeding. To take a grim but structually similar example, parents rarely willfully hurt or abandon children, but when they do the legal consequences are different, and gendered: women injure their children much *less* often than men, and receive far harsher consequences for doing so. Again, the rarity of the occasional criminal prosecution for child endangerment underscores and reinforces, rather than diminishes, the moral and cultural norms: the media's faithful, meticulous reportage of the Susan Smith case failed to note that relative to the amounts of time spent with each, children suffer more abuse from fathers than mothers.[151] Rather than right the balance, however, the media's bias here simply reinforces and reconstitutes its underlying cause: mothering is mandatory while fathering is voluntary, as reflected by the criminal sanctions for deviance.

Second, the occasional state sanction of the deviant attempt to avoid or circumvent gender-specific harms complements the pervasive state support, through incentives and disincentives, of the cultural imperatives that require sufferance of those harms. The most notorious example, perhaps, is Congress's refusal to provide funding for abortions for poor women,[152] coupled with its willingness to fund childbirth. The societal "preference" for the decision to bear the child over the decision to terminate the pregnancy may indeed be cultural rather than legal, but that preference, in turn, is powerfully underscored by the state's willingness to subsidize the second but not the first. The state sends a complementary message, of course, through its refusal to counter the market's devaluation of female labor, both in and out of the home. Again, that devaluation may indeed be a function of market forces, but those forces, and the normative lessons they impart, are then underscored by the state's refusal to intervene. The message conveyed by this network of legal regimes is clear enough: women should marry, mother, and stay home. Intimacy outside marriage is unthinkable, mothering is inevitable, and working outside the home unprofitable. While it is private culture and markets that primarily generate these messages, the state underscores them not only by, on occasion, punishing deviance, but also and probably more importantly, by systematically providing incentives for compliance. Participation in the patriarchal norm is expected and problem-free. Deviance from it will be punished.

THE JURISPRUDENTIAL CONCEPT OF HARM

The primary obstacle to creating a legal world in which the harms women suffer are taken as seriously as the harms suffered by men is political, not jurisprudential. If women were taken as seriously as men, by citizen-voters, by legislators, and by judges, law would not so frequently, consistently, and predictably trivialize, ignore, legitimate, protect, or celebrate, rather than minimize, the harms that women and only women suffer. If we could create a world in which the fates and internal lives of women mattered as much as those of men, then instrumentalism would *be,* for women, a more recognizable jurisprudential perspective: it would more accurately capture the quality of their interactions with law. Politics, in this sense, must precede law. If, societally, we *care* about violence against women, then we will do something about it, and what we do about it will perforce involve the law. Law, however, will not take gendered harms seriously until "society" does, and society won't until women's interests are weighted equally with men's. That in turn will not occur until women are viewed as of coequal importance, and that, finally, is a political and moral, not a legal or intellectual transformation of the heart.

In addition to whatever political obstacles there may be to the achievement of a world in which gendered harms are taken as seriously as nongendered harms, however, there are also *conceptual* obstacles to even the articulation of such a project. Most importantly, the argument for the existence and importance of gendered harms is burdened by the substantial degree to which the concept of harm *itself*—both gendered and ungendered—has been marginalized by the development of instrumentalist jurisprudence. When we critique the "dominant" concept of harm as "gendered," we are, in effect, tendering a marginalized critique of a concept—harm—which has itself become marginalized within the jurisprudential perspective to which it should be central. This development has been harmful for women—women, as I will argue below, need legal reform, and instrumentalism is the jurisprudential perspective of the legal reformer. But women distinctively need an instrumentalism that centralizes rather than marginalizes the concept of harm. The marginalization of the concept of harm within instrumental jurisprudence *itself* constitutes a gendered harm. The impact of that intellectual development falls disproportionately on women, as well as other groups who could benefit from legal reform.[153]

It is worth noting that it was not always so. In the first half of this century, the "first instrumentalists"—the American legal realists and their politically and philosophically allied pragmatists—did put the concept of harm and its theoretical and descriptive exploration at the center of jurisprudential inquiry.[154] This centering of the concept of *harm* distinguished the realists and pragmatists both from their natural law colleagues, who saw in ideal, if not actual law, a manifestation of God's will or Kantian transcendental principle, and from their conservative political adversaries, who might or might not have viewed law instrumentally, but either way, saw it and used it as a tool not for the progressive minimization of harms but for the preservation and entrenchment of the "rights"—primarily property rights—of the privileged. The realists, distinctively in the history of jurisprudence, combined the positivism of their English utilitarian predecessors with American pragmatic progressivism and forged from that alchemy not only a powerful voice for reform, but also a powerful jurisprudential movement at the center of which, unequivocally, was the concept of harm.

Harm is still central to the rough instrumentalism employed by lawyers and judges, and it is still central to some forms of theoretical instrumentalism—notably, neopragmatic forms. But as a general matter, the theoretical side of instrumentalism has become less and less focused on harm as the century comes to a close. The reason for that development is not hard to discern: it is a function of the dominance, within theoretical instrumentalism, of "law and economics." As law and economics has come to dominate the theoretical development of instrumentalism, the concept of harm, as well as the idea that law is a tool for minimizing it, has steadily receded into the background, and has been eclipsed by more "quantifiable" targets of legal regulation. Economists, and the legions of legal instrumentalists who now adopt quasi-economic modes of legal analysis, almost entirely eschew the concept of harm in favor of "cost-benefit" analysis as a way to guide public policy and judicial decision making. Benefits and costs may, of course, reflect some conception of harm, and some notion of the good in some rough way. Whether or not they do, however, is not as important to the economist as that they undoubtedly *do* correlate with something which can be observed, measured, and verified, and that is our revealed *preferences*—preferences objectively manifested in market choices, and reflective of our subjective desires, attractions, and revulsions, whether or not reflective of our ideals, and whether or not reflective of that which actually causes us harm.

In part, this law-and-economics driven movement away from the concept of harm to the twin concepts of preference satisfaction and cost and benefit analysis, is simply a function of the felt need to secure legal reform and legal study in as quantifiable a foundation as possible: preferences, costs, and benefits are observable, measurable, and quantifiable, while harms, like "pains" and "pleasures," are precisely the opposite. The movement toward cost and benefit analysis, then, is in part a reflection of the economist's disciplinary desire to render instrumentalism precise and scientific. The spirit of the economist's preference for the scientific and the quantifiable, and his consequent preference for the concept of preferences, market choices, and costs, over the more illusive concepts of well-being, harms, pleasures, and pains, is nicely captured in Richard Posner's denunciation of Jeremy Bentham's instrumentalist "hedonic calculus" for legal reform, on precisely those grounds.[155]

As important as the disciplinary drive for precision may be, however, the shift within instrumentalism from harm to cost is not only a function of the need for quantification. At least four other assumptions within normative law and economics, largely about the nature of the individual and hence of individual decision making, taken jointly, render this transition virtually inevitable. Because all four of these assumptions may be in tension with women's experiences, they are worth examining in some detail.

First, legal economists widely assume that individuals for the most part make decisions egoistically—this is what it means to behave "rationally," and for the most part, economists argue, people do so.[156] The assumption of rationality in turn rests on two more basic (albeit implicit) claims about human competency and motivation: first, it assumes that people are *capable* of ascertaining what choices from the possible pool will maximize their own subjective well-being, and second, that people are *motivated* to do so. If both these assumptions are fair, then it is also safe to assume that the decisions and choices we make accurately maximize our own subjective well-being, and minimize to whatever extent is possible our subjectively felt pains. Even if the ultimate target of law or of legal reform, then, is the minimization or elimination of harms, economists argue that legalists can best achieve this goal by maximizing each individual's *preferences,* as those preferences are expressed or manifested in market choices. Given both the cognitive and motivational assumptions— that each individual can and wants to maximize his or her own subjective well-being through choices—the legislator or judge can simply use preferences as a proxy for well-being. Rather than aim for the minimization of harms *directly,* we can do so indirectly by minimizing those costs and maximizing those benefits registered in the preferences expressed in free markets.

[167]

Second, normative economists assume that the individual is what I have elsewhere called "empathically impotent": [157] he or she is incapable of *assessing* the subjective well-being of others, and comparing it to his own so as to determine the "all-around" best course of action. To use technical jargon, he is incapable of making "interpersonal comparisons of utility": he is assumed to be incapable of deciding whether the subjective pain you might feel from a proposed course of action is greater or less than the subjective pleasure another individual might feel, and then acting on that knowledge.[158] This incapacity is partly a function of the severely idiosyncratic nature of pains and pleasures—we are each so utterly different, there simply is no way these comparisons can sensibly be made—but it is also partly a function of the empathic limits of the deciding individual: this is just a form of knowledge of which we are incapable.[159] But whatever the reason, the consequence is clear enough: since we can't in any meaningful way "know" the subjective hedonic lives of others, we *must,* if we wish to maximize their subjective well-being, rely on objectively knowable proxies. And since each affected individual is presumed to be both motivationally and cognitively rational—both capable of pursuing his or her own interest and motivationally in-clined to do so—there is no loss in terms of welfare in not attempting the impossible task of ascertaining and then maximizing subjective well-being. We may as well, in other words, stick with what's doable— satisfying preferences and minimizing costs—rather than seek to di-rectly minimize harms.

Third, the undermining of the concept of harm within economic interpretations of instrumentalism is underscored by a quite indepen-dent, albeit congruent, libertarian assumption regarding the dangers of a paternalistic state.[160] Even if we do not simply *define* value as that which is wanted, or that which is gained through exchange, we may nevertheless believe as a matter of contingent fact that each individual is better able to ascertain his or her own best self-interest than some objectively embodied, distant "state." If so, we have rea-sons quite independent of normative economics, but entirely consis-tent with instrumentalism, for distrusting state action and valorizing individual decision making. We might accordingly decide, on contin-gent rather than definitional grounds, that each individual's desire is the best evidence of what either harms or enhances that person's well-being.

[168]

Fourth, and most importantly, at least since the publication of Coase's famous essay, *The Problem of Social Cost,*[161] it has become routine for economists and economic-minded lawyers to assume or argue that the goal of law should be the promotion of *efficiency* rather than the minimization of harm, for a quite different reason: the substitution of the goal of efficiency as the ideal of law, rather than the minimization of harm, is viewed as a concession to *brute necessity.* What the Coase theorem famously "proved" is that, assuming no transaction costs, liability rules will have no direct impact on the "amount" of harms done in the world, although they may indeed affect the distribution of wealth. Whether polluters are or aren't liable for the harms caused by pollution, they will bargain (if they can do so costlessly) with the affected parties so as to achieve the least costly outcome: if the cost of pollution is less than the cost of preventing it, the polluter will pay damages to the "polluted" parties rather than stop polluting if there is a liability, and will obviously continue to pollute if there is no such rule. Whether or not there is a "rule," then, has no effect on the amount of pollution in the air.[162] Likewise, if the cost of pollution is greater than the cost of preventing it, the polluted parties will pay the polluters to stop polluting if there is no liability rule, and the polluter will stop polluting if there is such a rule—the cost of doing so being less than the amount of damages he would be required to pay to continue polluting. Again, the rule unquestionably affects who has how much wealth, but it has no effect one way or the other on the amount of pollution in the air. If the "harm" we are seeking to minimize through law is polluted air, then the "law" is simply irrelevant: the parties will bargain around it and toward the efficient outcome whatever the content of the law. Assuming no transaction costs, the "harm," then, of polluted air seems utterly impervious to the legal regime.

Although the law can't affect the harm, it can promote the goal of efficiency. In the real world, of course, unlike the hypothetical one described above, transactions are often expensive and sometimes impossible at any price. In this world, then, it is often impossible or prohibitively expensive for parties to bargain toward the "best"—meaning, most desired—result, whatever the rule of liability might be. Legal rules, should serve, at most, the more modest but at least *doable* goal of mimicking the result the parties would most likely bargain for were there no obstacles to cost-free bargaining. Thus, *if* the pollution could be stopped for less than the amount of damage sustained by the polluted parties, then the law should impose a rule of liability. But we should be clear: the law is serving to promote the goal of efficiency, not clean air. It is helping us achieve the world we would bargain for were there no impediments to bargaining, not a "harm-free" world of clean air.

The Coase theorem, then, provides powerful support for the economist's assumption that the law should only aim to maximize efficiency rather than aim to minimize social harms: *if* the theorem is valid, and if ought implies can, then that's really all it can do, given assumptions of individual rationality. The most important consequence of the Coase theorem in terms of our intellectual history has been to crystallize the suspected incoherence of the concept of harm as well as the related or complementary ideal of a "good" or "flourishing" human life. The only harm the law ought to address—because, after all, it is the only harm that it *can* address—is the "harm" of transaction costs: the obstacles, whatever they may be, to the ideal world in which we seamlessly bargain without friction to achieve maximal exchange value—the perfectly bargained-out world.

By undermining the concept of legally cognizable harm, the Coase theorem thus simultaneously undermines the preeconomic, instrumentalist *ideal* of a harm-free, good, or flourishing, social world. The instrumentalists' ideal, in other words, from the economic perspective, should be a world of satisfied bargained *exchanges* rather than a world free of harm. It is a world, to take some examples, in which we have achieved the closest approximation to the level of clean air that we want to live with that is compatible with our other desires, as those desires are revealed by our expressed preferences and market choices, rather than a world with the level of clean air requisite for healthy living.[163] It is a world in which we have achieved the closest approximation to the level of freedom from crime, or from injurious consumer products, or of a well-informed citizenry, that is compatible with other competing desires for civil rights against a too-intrusive government, for a panoply of low-priced but dangerous consumer goods, or for entertainment, rather than a world with the level of safety from crime or injury or engaged democratic dialogue that is essential for a decent life in a republican democracy. It is a world, more generally, in which the ideal of satiated desires, as revealed by market preferences, whatever those desires or preferences may be and from whatever source they may be derived, is the goal of law and the goal of social life, rather than a world of meaningful work, clean air, safe streets, high culture, or an educated citizenry. Corelatively, it is a world in which the frustration of desire imposed by obstacles to trade, rather than violence, pollution, poverty, or crime, becomes the only social harm, or ill, addressed or addressable by law. It is a world, in short, in which the notion of an objective harm has been scuttled as a meaningful target of law, to be replaced by the notion of subjective frustration.

The larger significance of the Coase theorem is that it represents a turning point not only in the development of instrumentalism but in jurisprudential and political thought quite generally.[164] From a *non*economic instrumentalist perspective, the law is a tool toward achieving an ideal world in which the content of the "ideal" can either be understood positively—as a world possessed of moral value—or negatively—as a world free of harm. But either way, it is an ideal which is in turn defined by our understanding of some objective conception of the good life, not by reference to presently constituted desires. The harms we aim to be free of are harmful *regardless* of our desires, wishes, or trades to the contrary, and the value toward which we ought to strive is of value regardless of our contrary inclinations. Some level of clean air, safe streets, civil liberties, education, high culture, and meaningful work constitutes "the good life," and some level of pollution, crime, civil restraint, ignorance, aesthetic dullness and underpaid and meaningless work constitutes "harms," and it is the business of law, where possible, to move us toward a world in which the good life is enjoyed and harms avoided. The content of the good life, and the content of harm are, must be, and should be, of course, highly contested, but they are nevertheless understood as the goal and target of law.[165] From an economic-instrumentalist conception, these twin concepts of value and harm are simply meaningless.[166] Rather than aim for the good life or the avoidance of harm, the goal of law is simply the satisfaction of desires through voluntary exchanges.

The importance of this transformation cannot be overstated. The scuttling of the twin notions of harm and objective value, and their replacement with the twin concepts of market preferences and transaction costs, is largely responsible for the transformation of instrumentalism from a progressive conception of law to a conservative and libertarian one. So long as harm and the content of the good are understood idealistically—as dependent on an ideal of healthy living, meaningful work, and safe intimacy—there is a goal toward which law ought to strive and toward which society can be understood to progress. Where satisfaction of desire and the removal of obstacles to the creation and enjoyment of exchange value are understood as the goal, by contrast, the law becomes, even in its idealized form, at best a morally static mirror reflection of our present desires. Those desires, in turn, are at least in part a product of extant social and political institutions. Law becomes an "instrument," in this instrumentalist view, not for any progressive movement toward a world free of harm and enjoyed by healthy, engaged, and productive citizens, but rather for the satisfaction of presently dominant desires.[167] It becomes an instrument, in short, for the perpetuation of the status quo.

But furthermore, the assumptions about social living which undergird this legal-economic view, whatever may be the case with regard to men's lives, are radically discontinuous with women's experiences. First, as argued above, the egoistic, self-regarding individual assumed by economic instrumentalism is at odds with many women's experience of selfhood. Many women, much of the time, engage in private and public altruistic acts which are at the same time extremely self-destructive; indeed many women eventually come to define themselves (and are often defined by others) as the antithesis of the egoistic individual assumed by economic instrumentalism.[168] Second, and as scores of relational feminists have argued, the capacity for sympathy and for the empathic understanding of the subjective well-being of others which undergirds it—a capacity routinely denied by economic instrumentalists—is at the heart of many women's understanding of moral reasoning and indeed of moral life.[169] And third, the core assumption of the libertarian political outlook that so often complements normative economic instrumentalism—that whatever harms may be visited upon women in the private sphere are simply outweighed by the harm, both potential and actual, suffered by citizens because of state interventions—is simply belied by women's experiences.[170] Women are better off in a world in which a restraining order, an arrest, a conviction, and incarceration are all realistic options in dealing with abusive intimates, than one in which there is no state involvement, even given the degree of cumbersome state intrusion, the possibility of error, and the invasion of privacy that that involvement necessarily entails.

[172]

But most importantly, the economist's definitional collapse of the ideal of the good life with the satiation of presently constituted desires, and of harm with the transaction costs that frustrate those desires, is utterly at odds with contemporary women's experiences of growth and liberation within feminism. Central to contemporary feminism has been (and continues to be) the experience of what is sometimes called "consciousness-raising" but which is more widely called *growth:* the constant reexaminion of presently constituted desires so as to reclaim deeper desires for a truer and better life. Contrary, perhaps, to popular caricature, this has not involved or required the suppression of desire for the sake of a politically correct or ideologically dictated ideal, or the stoic denial of desire so as to accord with doctrinal truth. Quite the contrary, consciousness-raising within feminism has pointed to the *reclamation* of desire, as what is realized more than any other truth is that one's own desires have been blunted and negated by patriarchy. The individual and collective experience of consciousness-raising has also, though, alerted women to the truth that the notion of the good life toward which we ought to strive, and the harms we ought to avoid, can never in any facile way be simply equated with that which is presently desired, or represented as desired, by dominant or even subordinate groups. While what is reclaimed is, in a sense, subjectivity, what is discarded is a false, extremely limited, and indeed self-denigrating and self-denying conception of one's own "role."

It would be a mistake, however, to assume from this noncongruence of contemporary economic instrumentalism and women's lives that women would be better served by noninstrumental conceptions of law. The ahistoric "principles" underlying liberal legalism, whether they are themselves grounded in purportedly universal truths of human nature or deontic truths of moral logic are peculiarly (or not so peculiarly) unhinged from women's experiences,[171] while the all-too-historic "traditions" jealously guarded by conservative legalists are not just irrelevant to, but often directly hostile to, women's interests.[172] Indeed, in spite of its flaws, neither liberal nor conservative legalism holds out a credible alternative to instrumentalism for women. The distinctive virtues of both economic and noneconomic instrumentalism—its insistence on flexibility and pragmatism, its nondogmatic, anti-ideologic structure, and its responsiveness to the lived human condition—make instrumentalism the natural jurisprudential perspective for feminism as well as for any other liberation movement. Instrumentalism *is* the jurisprudence of reform—indeed, it always has been—and feminism is and must be centrally concerned with legal reform. The neglect of the concept of harm within instrumentalism has undoubtedly disserved women. But it is a disservice to which we should respond by filling in the missing gaps, not by discarding instrumentalism altogether.

INSTRUMENTAL FEMINISM

I want to conclude this chapter by suggesting that instrumentalism, particularly if informed by feminism, would illuminate some of the major theoretical conundrums within which feminist legal theory is presently entangled. Let me mention three quickly, and then focus more closely on a fourth.

First, a feminist instrumentalism would provide a language with which to address the ways in which strict formal equality—equal treatment by the state—can disserve women's interests. Where "equal treatment" is nothing but a vehicle for the perpetuation, through "equal neglect," of gender-specific harms, it does not further women's "equality" to insist upon it. No-fault divorce and gender-blind child custody "reforms" are obvious examples: simply treating men and women as "the same" at the point of divorce, where men and women are in fact in drastically different economic circumstances and often have drastically different levels of emotional attachment to their children, runs the real danger of jeopardizing women's well-being for the sake of a dubious ideal.[173] Within feminism, attempts to resolve or address these problems through arguments over the relative merits of "special treatment," asymmetrical approaches to equality, the harms of stereotyping, and meanings of equality have stalemated. A focus on the gender-specific harms women sustain at the point of divorce, for example, would highlight the need for family law reforms to attend to those rather drastic differences.

Second, a feminist instrumentalism would provide a language with which to address problems of false consciousness. Feminists need to explore and expose the ways in which the institutions to which women tender consent harm us. Participation in the creation and distribution of pornography, in surrogacy contracts, or in prostitution, may all be extremely harmful to the involved women even though fully consensual, and the harm may be of a sufficient magnitude as to justify "paternalistic" state regulation of these institutions. Whether or not the harms done by these markets exceeds the risks of benign or not so benign state intervention is not a question which can be answered by simply assuming that the institution is harmless because consensual, or that state intervention is unwarranted and unwise because paternalist. Rather, what is needed is a detailed examination of the harms these consensual institutions sometimes cause, and the risks and dangers brought on by state intervention into these markets. The liberal-feminist insistence that these institutions are problem-free because consensual does little but assume away a set of harms, and the radical feminist insistence that because these institutions are harmful they must therefore be subtly coercive, even where seemingly consensual, does little but give offense to the women and their advocates whose competency is thereby challenged.[174] A focus on the harms caused by these institutions would focus critical attention on the harms and the institutions, rather than on the competency or supposed freedom of the affected women.

Third, and relatedly, an instrumental feminism would provide us a language with which to address problems of legitimation. We need to be able to discuss the harms done to women which are most likely beyond legal redress, but which are undoubtedly legitimated, and therefore aggravated, by legal structures. Without a language of harms, we have no way of even discussing, much less redressing, those aspects of our culture which are and should be beyond legal reform, but which nevertheless badly injure women's lives.

The most pressing reason, however, for feminists to attend to and reinvigorate instrumentalism is simply that instrumentalism continues to be the language of legal reform, and legal reform continues to be the motivating impulse of feminist legal scholarship. It is worth noting, I think, that this abiding faith in the efficacy of legal reform distinguishes feminist legal scholarship from *both* feminist scholarship from other disciplines, and a good deal of critical legal scholarship, all of which tends to be far more skeptical of the value of legal reform.[175] For the most part, feminist legal scholars do not share this skepticism, and for one simple reason: women have undeniably benefited by legal reforms of the last few decades. Laws prohibiting sex discrimination in employment, constitutional protection of reproductive rights, the reform of rape laws, and the prohibition of sexual harassment on the job have all improved the quality of women's lives. There have indeed been costs, and of precisely the sort noted by critical scholars: the protection of reproductive rights has legitimated the insularity of the private sphere within which women suffer life-endangering violence, the prohibition of "unequal pay for equal work" has in some ways burdened the much larger and possibly more urgent task of achieving higher pay for women working in the pink collar ghetto by legitimating the larger labor markets within which equal pay laws apply; rape reform, by relying so heavily upon the liberal constructs of consent, autonomy, and exchange value, arguably burdens the task of articulating the harms of consensual heterosexual transactions. But there is simply no question but that the gains women have garnered through laws prohibiting sex discrimination in employment, mandating equal pay for equal work, expanding the scope of the prohibition against rape, and protecting reproductive freedom, outweigh these admittedly quite real risks of legitimation. Women have tremendously benefited from law reform, and still have more to gain than to fear from further legal protection.

What feminists need to do is to reinvigorate traditional instrumentalism by reexamining its basic building blocks from the ground up, beginning with a detailed examination of the concept of harm. In contrast to the strategic assumptions of economic instrumentalism, we need to give substantive *content* to the concept of harm: we need to articulate what harms us, and how, and by how much, and what the law could do to minimize those harms. Without a robust, substantive, and feminist analysis of harm, instrumentalism will fall back on either the economist's quite willful and definitional obliteration of the concept, or the more common but equally damaging assumptions about what harms us and what doesn't. Those "assumptions" are as untrue to women's experiences of harm as the more explicitly articulated definitional assumptions of the economist. The sensible response to both is not to turn our backs on either instrumentalism or legalism, but to push both in a feminist direction.

A reinvigorated inquiry into the concept of harm, whether motivated by feminist or some other political or moral impulse, should find fertile ground within instrumentalism itself. The neglect of the concept of harm within academic instrumentalism is a feature of modern, economics-dominated instrumentalism; it is not in any sense central or necessary to instrumentalism more generally construed. The prominence of economic modes of analysis within the law schools notwith-standing, it is still true that of the many lawyers and appellate judges who are instrumentalists, most continue to view law as an instrument for the minimization of social harms, and of those, many—perhaps most—continue to instinctively or intuitively understand the concept of harm (as well as the concept of value) as to some degree independent of felt desires. Many instrumentalists, to return to the above examples, resist the full equation of the harm of polluted air, or the value of safe streets, with a dollar amount to be traded against other goods. Many resist the equation of the political and legal issues surrounding the regulation of natural resources as a conflict between the desires of some people to hike and the desires of others to make things to sell. The resistance to the commodification of these harms no doubt has many sources. But part of that resistance, I think, is grounded in an instinctual sense that the harms of pollution, crime, or accidents, have some objective reality: they are harmful because they interfere with our capacity for good, healthy, productive, and valuable lives. To whatever degree we sacrifice these ideals because we want other things, those wants are harmful as well.

A noneconomic instrumentalism does indeed carry with it the dangers of unbridled paternalism: when the concept of harm is severed from the definitional restraints of presently constituted preferences, it runs the danger of privileging dogma over human interest.[176] The definitional collapse of harm and value with "that which is desired," however, is also dangerous.[177] Obviously, what would best serve us is a *balance* between objective and subjective conceptions of harm, objective and subjective understandings of what we do and should value; objective and subjective conceptions of the good life. We need to check our desires against our rational understandings of our best interest, and we need to continually check our rational understandings of our best interest against our present desires, and we need to use each "check" as a skeptical harness on the other. But we cannot provide those checks by definitional fiat.

What I hope I have shown in this chapter is that instrumentalists of all stripes need to attend to feminist scholarship, because that scholarship illuminates serious shortcomings in our dominant understandings of the harm that is the ostensible goal of legal prohibition. What I want to emphasize in closing is the political corollary of that admonition: feminists need to attend to and revitalize instrumentalism. Feminists, perhaps surprisingly, share with instrumentalists a relatively *benign* view of the overall impact of law on the quality of life: law can and often does improve (rather than simply reify or legitimate) a prelegal status quo. It is this faith in the potential of law to improve upon a Hobbesian and decidedly misogynist state of nature that unites feminists with both instrumentalists and liberals, and distinguishes their jurisprudential commitments from critical legal scholars. But unlike instrumentalists, feminists are acutely sensitive to the alarming degree to which law disserves women's interests, and often aggravates rather than either deters or compensates gendered harms. Feminists are aware of the pitfalls of law and law reform, but are nevertheless still committed to the potential of law as a vehicle for the improvement of women's lives. The creation of a robust instrumentalism which would reflect both the skepticism and the faith might constitute the beginnings of a distinctively feminist reconstruction of that still vital jurisprudential movement.

CHAPTER THREE
Law, Literature, and Feminism

Humanistic interest in the various connections between the fields of "law" and "literature" was rekindled in the law schools in the mid-1970s, eventually coalescing in a modern "law and literature" interdisciplinary "movement," or enterprise. In the last twenty years, that movement's growing number of practitioners have focused their attention on a number of distinct but loosely connected projects, including the initial, and to some degree still-defining exploration of both canonical and noncanonical literature for its insights into the nature of law, comparative analysis of the nature of legal and literary interpretation, investigation of the use of narrative in legal scholarship and in adversarial legal argument, and the relationship between the legal "subject" and the various sorts of "discourses" that arguably constitute it, including not only the legal and literary, but also the economic and historical. Taken collectively the work produced by "law and literature" scholars puts forward not just a set of questions but also a "family" of tentative answers: conceptions of law, of lawyering, of judging, and of justice which bear some vague resemblance to each other, and which constitute a significant departure from the various "families" of views of law and justice that dominate mainstream legal scholarship. For this reason alone, it now makes some sense to speak of the law and literature movement as a recognizable discipline, or subspecialty with its own set of defining questions and tentative lines of analysis within the legal academy.

Almost from the outset of this law and literature renaissance, feminist scholars working in law schools realized they had much to learn from and much to contribute to the developing law and literature movement. It is by this point clear to law and literature scholars and to feminist legal scholars that the two groups have common concerns that go well beyond their shared status as interdisciplinary and marginalized movements in the legal academy. Feminists are an important presence in the law and literature movement, while law and literature is becoming a major subdivision of feminist legal theory. In this chapter, I will simply try to map the strands, and tensions, of this developing relationship.

Each of the first four parts below examines, sequentially, feminist participation in each of four major projects within the law and literature movement, looking both at feminist *contributions* to the law-literature project, and feminist *critiques* of that project. The conclusion then looks at more general points of intersection of the law and literature movement and feminist legal theory.

The Construction of the Literary Lawyer

Enthusiasm for the law and literature renaissance we are presently experiencing must be tempered: surely by any objective standard, law and literature is a marginal movement, which, although healthy, is viewed by everyone but its practitioners as voicing peripheral concerns to the overall pedagogical and scholarly missions of the legal academy. A quick contrast with its interdisciplinary cousin, the law and economics movement, should bring the point into focus. It is often—perhaps routinely—claimed that the contemporary lawyer must have at least minimal exposure to, if not competency in, the interdisciplinary tools and accomplishments of law and economics. Virtually all law students, for example, at virtually all law schools, will receive, most likely in the very first semester of law school, some exposure to the logic and impact of the Coase theorem, economic arguments for and against strict liability, the economic understanding of the negligence system, and economic explanations for the primacy of the expectancy interest in contracts, to take just a few examples. All law students will be advised, at some point in their legal career, that it would behoove them to supplement this exposure with more sustained training in economic tools of analysis. Most top-tier law schools have at least one and usually more than one professionally trained economist on the staff. Any school that doesn't is seeking to acquire one, and all law schools strongly encourage their faculty to acquire basic training in at least microeconomics. If these indicia are any guide, it is certainly fair to say that the late-twentieth-century lawyer does at least *aspire* to be the "man of economics," just as Oliver Wendell Holmes, writing at the turn of the century, predicted he would.[1]

By contrast, no such claims are ever made regarding law and literature studies. Students are not advised that training in literary skills or some amount of familiarity with the literary canon is professionally *necessary*; at most, they are *told* that it may help them cultivate habits of mind and heart that may enrich their legal career;[2] and what they hear, if course evaluations are any guide, is that law and literature is a refreshing and fun course precisely *because* it is "nonlegal" and of virtually no professional use whatsoever.[3] The late-twentieth-century lawyer may be and may even typically aspire to be the man of economics Holmes urged him to become. He by no means is, nor does he aspire to be, a man of literature.

The first "project" of the "law and literature movement," both chronologically and in a sense logically is simply to change that state of affairs: to construct, at least as an "ideal type," a conception of lawyering which has at its center a *literary* rather than an economic sensibility. Although by this point a small community of law and literature teachers view this as their primary mission,[4] it has been James Boyd White, of Michigan Law School, more than any other, who has devoted the better part of his scholarly career to this end, and has had some measure of success in achieving it.[5] Central to White's jurisprudential perspective is the deep and foundational conviction that the language of law *can be* (and often is) the cultured language of community, of civility, of nobility, and of social justice — or, to borrow from the language of the title of his latest book, that law at its best can be an "Act of Hope."[6] To understand the law as an "act of hope" is, centrally, to understand it as a part of our literary culture. And to understand law as a part of culture, in turn, requires a fundamental reorientation of our conception of law, of legal language, and even of ourselves. To put it in a nutshell or a slogan, the law, for

White, is an *art*. It is not politics, and it is not social science.[7] The lawyer, White has argued again and again, and in a number of fora, is an artist,[8] and should learn to think of herself as such.

It is important to point out that this conception of the lawyer-as-artist, or, as I will sometimes call her, the "literary lawyer," is hardly without historical precedent. As Robert Ferguson argues in his masterful treatment of the subject,[9] this ideal conception of law as a part of high culture, and of the lawyer as engaged in the production of culture, was eminently familiar to the early-nineteenth-century elite "man of letters." If Ferguson's historical account is correct, it seems clear that the nineteenth-century "man of letters"—whom Ferguson calls the "lawyer-writer"—is at least an important historical analogue of the ideal type of lawyering White is laboring to construct. Like White, the nineteenth-century lawyer-writer, according to Ferguson's account, *also* viewed the seamless web of law and culture as expressive of an ethical and aesthetic ideal—law at its best is continuous with culture at its best. For the lawyer-writer as for White, the products of high culture accordingly could and should be used to illuminate just resolutions to legal inquiries, and, just as importantly, the products of law—the products of the "legal imagination"—are themselves literary, and should be understood, studied, and produced as such. White's project, against this historical backdrop, might best be understood as a "resurrection." White is in essence attempting to resurrect for the modern sensibility an ideal of what it means to be a good lawyer—both in the craft and moral sense—an ideal that was once familiar but, under the onslaught of attacks, first by legal formalists, then legal realists, and then law and economics, has now become not only antiquated but foreign.

To be sure, White brings to his project a decidedly twentieth-century commitment to social equality, a twentieth century critical and progressive eye, and—most important—a twentieth-century sensitivity to the magnitude of the historical and ongoing injustice wreaked upon our society by virtue of our history of slavery, racism, and discrimination.[10] Unlike his elitist, albeit "republican" nineteenth-century counterpart, White is liberal, progressive, and egalitarian in politics and spirit both. But nevertheless, the common ground White and his idealized literary lawyer, share with the nineteenth-century man of letters is striking. Most important, both White and his ideal lawyer share with their nineteenth-century predecessor a particular jurisprudential perspective which is at odds with *both* the legal realism *and* the legal formalism which have competed for dominance within the legal academy during the century that saw the end of the man of letters. Thus, White is obviously skeptical of the formalist claim that law either can or should be viewed as self-sufficient; that it needs recourse to no other field for its own completion. But he is equally skeptical of the realist claim that the language of economics, or the language of social science, should be employed to "fill in the gaps" so as to point us to justice.[11] Like the nineteenth-century man of letters—and really *only* like the nineteenth century man of letters—White is convinced that that part of law which cannot be or should not be understood positivistically can only be grasped through an understanding of its cultural, and more specifically its literary, foundation and potential.[12] Like the nineteenth-century man of letters, White aims to both "fill in the interstitial gaps" and fulfill the moral ambitions of law by recourse to a discriminating understanding of our cultural heritage.[13]

We might describe this Whitean project—the resurrection of the nineteenth-century lawyer-writer, or, more simply, the construction of the modern literary lawyer—programmatically in this way. White's attempted construction of the literary lawyer seeks to reinvigorate a vision of law that first, situates law, or embeds it, within the *humanities*—rather than within politics or the social sciences—and then analyses and uses law accordingly. It follows that a full understanding of a legal question, a legal dilemma, or a legal text requires a humanistic analysis, just as a full understanding of law requires a general knowledge of the culture from which the law emerged. It also follows that the *production* of a legal text—whether it be a case opinion, a contract, or a statute—is, potentially, a contribution to that culture and an expression of the author's literary sensitivity. For that production to be well done accordingly requires the marshaling and use of humanistic and literary skills. Pedagogically, an understanding of and therefore the teaching and learning of both canonical literature and the skills necessary to read it critically are necessary to the learning of law, because literature is itself a part of law, and law is itself a part of literature. Law is indeed an expression of power, but it is also an expression of a literary sensibility, and while the lawyer is inescapably political to whatever degree or amount of power she wields, she is also inescapably artistic. Her training should reflect that inevitability so that when she uses the literary language of law, she will use it well.[14]

What has been the response of feminists to this ambitious, Whitean project of renewal? With the important exception of Martha Nussbaum, whose work I will discuss in more detail below, feminists in law—perhaps unsurprisingly—have been for the most part wary of White's attempted resurrection of the man of letters. The suspicion stems in turn from a deep distrust of the literary "canon" that informs the view of law held by the cultural or literary lawyer, and more functionally, of the means by which some works but not others become canonized. For whom, exactly, does the man of letters speak? From which parts of "culture" does the cultural heritage of law emerge? To take an example, White has written eloquently on the literary properties of the phrase "We the People"[15] from the constitution's preamble. Angela Harris asks, in response, who the "we" in the phrase "we the people" precisely represents.[16] In the same vein, Judy Resnick and Carolyn Heilbrun, in an article on the intersections of law, literature, and feminism, question the worth of supplementing or interpreting the legal canon, with its notorious exclusions of outsider voices, with the equally exclusionary literary canon.[17] Susan Mann puts forward a similar critique in a thorough and thoughtful piece on the legal and literary canon in the *Stanford Law Review*.[18] Richard Delgado and Jean Stefancic voice the same complaint, both about the canon and the modern literary lawyer's explication of it, in their critical essay, "Norms and Narratives: Can Judges Avoid Serious Moral Error?"[19] The man of letters, all these critics argue, was elitist and exclusionary to the core, and both impulses were an integral part of his insistent reliance on the cultural canon as a source of quasi-legal authority. It's not clear that the resurrection of that part of his vision which seems worth salvaging can be reconciled with our twentieth-century democratic and egalitarian ambitions.

The root of this complaint might be put this way. Supplementing the legal canon with the literary, and the legal sensibility with a literary one, might very well cure the law of its anti-humanist penchant for stilted, deadened, wooden prose—a style that kills.[20] It might also push law's interpreters toward more humanistic understandings of the law's commands. But whether it can cure the law or the society law governs of its xenophobic intolerance of difference—including the difference of femininity—depends entirely on the content of the canon, and on the liberality of the liberal sensibility, and on both scores, history does not provide reasons for optimism. Women's voices have historically been censored from the language of literature and high culture at least as relentlessly as they have been banned from the language and courts of law. Supplementing the one with the other might leave both bigger and richer, but it won't leave either law or literature more inclusionary. The misrepresentations of women in law will only be magnified, should law turn to literature for guidance or inspiration, by the misrepresentations of women in literature and other forms of high culture. Law and literature may indeed come from a common cultural root, but that is the essence of the problem, not the solution. That shared commonality is an obstacle to overcome in the quest for true equality, not an overlooked reason for wedding the two.

To this criticism, White has responded with characteristic grace. "We the People," he argues, is a promise of inclusion, and its meaning transcends the particular, contingent limitations of the promisor.[21] That potential for *transcendence* is in the nature of language, and because it is in the nature of language, it is also in the nature of law, and it is in the nature of literature.[22] This is why the specific intent of authors can never be the last word on the issue of meaning. This is why law, with its genesis in conflict, compromise, and divisiveness, can be the vehicle for community, consensus, and peace. Language does not only *convey* promises. Language, by its nature, *is* a promise, and therefore, whatever we do with language has promissory potential, including our high-minded utterances—no matter how hypocritical or self-serving our intent. Language by its nature conveys the promise of the possibility of communal, shared understanding between speaker and listener. *That* promise, in turn, both presupposes and is constitutive of true and lasting communities. Those communities are in turn the wells of meaning from which both law and literature spring. We cannot and should not blind ourselves to the potential for justice which the promise holds out by insistently and perversely gazing only on the distance, often vast, between what was promised and what was delivered. The promise is what matters, and it is the promise which is in turn both grounded in, and ultimately only intelligible within, the meanings generated by our shared cultural artifacts, including both law and literature.

This is an elegant response, but it only partly satisfies. Even if we accept White's generous invitation to view law and literature in this

[185]

promissory way, nevertheless the *content* of the promise may be utterly compromised by its historical exclusionary genesis no matter how broadly we read its present incarnation. Surely we now understand the Bill of Rights, for example, as protecting the rights of "all of us," and it may be true that we might "just as well" read the Bill of Rights generously as containing, under the layers of its exclusionary history, a promise that speaks to that inclusive potential. But it's simply not that easy to shed the *consequences* of our brutally exclusionary past: the *content* of our rights, even if not their presently democratized scope, bears the mark of our history. Who is to say what the content of those rights might have been, or might be, had they been *authored* by as broad and representative a community as the community whose actions they now regulate, and on whose behalf, per White, we should now read their meaning?[23] Similarly, and more generally, we might happily claim the Western canon as the shared cultural property of our entire community in spite of its historical exclusionary impulses. But who is to say what the content of that canon might have been, had it been so inclusive from the outset? Our "culture" is indeed compromised by (as well as in part "constituted by") its historical patterns of exclusion and inclusion, as is our law. With a more inclusive past, our law and literature both might have been very different from their present incarnations, and given that we are *governed* by at least the former, whether or not the latter, that fact alone gives rise to a serious problem of justice. Blending "law" with a literary canon and heritage that suffers from the same flaw obviously doesn't cure the problem. Arguably, it magnifies it.

Let me quickly mention two additional jurisprudential problems—both of which should be of concern to feminists—with White's otherwise extremely appealing attempt to reinvigorate, for modern sensibilities and toward modern progressive ends, the "promise" of the nineteenth-century literary lawyer. Both problems stem from the literary lawyer's anti-positivist jurisprudence. The legal world the literary lawyer inhabits is decidedly *not* the positivistic world of sanctions, fines, prison terms, and executions.[24] Law, to the literary lawyer, is not, or at least not only, a manifestation of political power. White, contrary to any number of critiques of his work,[25] has never pointedly *denied* that law is power. What he has denied, and emphatically so, is that law is *nothing but* power: what he has denied, to put it differently, is that the "rhetoric" that accompanies the power is nothing but obfuscation, masks, legitimation, or other forms of disingenuity. For White, the literary, verbal "else"—the *expression* of law's power through language—is what holds out the hope, and it is the essence of his anti-positivistic jurisprudence to insist that we must study the language, as well as the politics, of law, and that to do so we must study the language humanistically and generously.

Nevertheless, although the anti-positivist invitation to focus on the ethics and aesthetics of the spoken legal word might humanize legal interpretation, and might push it in a more progressive direction, it is precisely the sort of invitation of which feminists—or anyone interested in more radical reforms of the law—should be extremely cautious. The literary lawyer may well be an improvement over other modern ideal conceptions of a general, day-to-day professional legal *practice.* But even if it is, it may nevertheless *not* serve as a workable ideal for the goals or practices of the legal *reformer.* Rather, a realistic, hardheaded, Holmesian, "bad man" positivism may be the better jurisprudential sensibility of legal reformers, and for utterly pragmatic reasons. To understand what laws need to be changed, overruled, cast out, or uprooted, we need to understand, foremost, their political impact, not their cultural heritage. We need to know who is hurt, and by how much, by the effect of law on the lives of its subjects. Such an inquiry is not analytically *incompatible* with a humanistic study of law's promise and of its cultural heritage, but it is most assuredly *different.* There is a difference, and an important one, between a conception of law as a branch of humanities, and therefore as something to preserve as well as improve upon, and a conception of law as a branch of politics, and therefore as something to use, reform, change, or challenge toward the end of improving people's lives. Holmes's positivistic insistence that to understand the law we should "wash it in cynical acid" and look at it from the point of view of the bad man if we wish to unsentimentally understand its true content, contains an important grain of truth for feminist reformers or any other legal critic who aims for positive change. The invitation to read law as literature, and to read literature as a part of law, does sometimes enlighten, and can *itself* be an important engine for reform: it alerts us, minimally, to alternative ways of reading and using extant legal authority. Where the needed reform "goes to the root," however, it can also distract us from the task at hand. Surely some feminist reform is of precisely such a nature.

The second problem with the anti-positivist invitation at the heart of so much of the law and literature movement is closely related. Whether or not the romantic notion, oft-repeated by White, that the "lawyer is essentially an artist" does an injustice to the ambition and self-esteem of artists, it may well do a disservice to *lawyers*. Lawyers ideally (like judges) aim toward justice, and they use law to do it, and feminists working in law are no exception: the central idea is to use law in an instrumental way toward the end of "gender justice." Artists, for the most part, don't "aim for justice," gendered or otherwise, and neither does the art which is their product. Whatever might be the nature of justice, it is surely not fully captured by any particular *aesthetic* ideal,[26] and the suggestion that it is seems to be simply a category mistake. Legal positivism, with its insistence on the difference between the political root of law and the idealistic ambitions of change, between the legal is and the moral ought, between our ethical ambitions and our legal compromises, between the power that we must contend with and the ideals we seek to realize, might be, perhaps ironically, precisely the jurisprudence which not only gives Caesar his due but which best captures the virtues which define the moral lives of feminist, as well as other legal advocates for change.[27] The anti-positivistic literary lawyer runs the risk of distracting the lawyer not only from the political root of the law which surrounds her, but also of the particular ideal—justice—which remains her distinctive goal.

MARTHA NUSSBAUM'S PROJECT

To date, the most promising attempt to further the reconstructive project initiated by White's groundbreaking scholarship, and in a way that answers all three objections raised above, comes from a feminist trained not in law but in classics and moral philosophy. The interdisciplinary and brilliant scholarship of Martha Nussbaum is unquestionably one of the most sustained attempts to put forward a humanistic account of practical reasoning—including, importantly, legal reasoning—which shares White's ambitions to reinstill in legal decision making a cultural familiarity with the teachings of the Western canon, and at the same time to do so in a way that will point us toward, rather than away from, a progressive understanding of community. Although Nussbaum's work *in law* is now only in its beginning stages, it is nevertheless worth briefly characterizing at least the direction that her ongoing study of law and culture seems to be taking, before moving on to the second and decidedly more critical project within law and literature studies.

The work that Martha Nussbaum has already done on the nature of moral decision making, as well as the work she promises to do in the future on more specifically legal forms of judgment, shares both deep and surface similarities with that of James Boyd White. To fulfill our ambitions of justice, Nussbaum argues, the judgments made in courts of law should be informed not only by legal precedent, but by the empathic knowledge we gain through the heart[28]—what she has called "Love's Knowledge"[29]—*and* by the learnings gleaned from a critical but sympathetic and engaged reading of our cultural heritage. They should be neither rigidly legalistic as positivists urge, nor rigidly rationalist as economists insist.[30] Nor should they be (nor must they be) mindlessly beholden to the arbitrarily held convictions of politically dominant subgroups, as is claimed in different ways by various wings of the critical legal community.[31] Echoing White, and echoing the nineteenth-century literary lawyer, they should be, and can be, in a word, *humanist:* they should bear the mark of immersion in our culture and of a learned sensitivity toward the communities that have created that distinctive culture. Were they to bear these marks, Nussbaum goes on to argue, they would not only be progressive rather than regressive in political orientation, but they would even be, surprisingly, *feminist.* When read generously, as they should be, our culture and its literary products, Nussbaum argues, counsel not only a message of equal respect for women, but even counsel forms of reasoning and judgment that resonate with modern descriptions of the feminine. The humanistic orientation at the heart of the literary lawyer would further, not hinder, feminist goals.

Nussbaum's project, in my view, is very likely one of the most heartening and inspiring, as well as inspired, projects on the legal academic horizon. If successful, her attempt to infuse legal and practical reasoning with both cultural knowledge and sympathetic listening would indeed go a long way toward answering the spiritually deadening relativism which now plagues both the left and right wings of the legal academy.[32] If successful, her work might also demonstrate the potential for internal, progressive transformation inherent in a rich literary canon in spite of its exclusionary history. But more to the point for these purposes, Nussbaum's project might also provide an answer to the two objections raised above to the anti-positivism in White's vision of the nature of law and lawyering. A rich, defensible, and noble conception of justice, Nussbaum might be taken to be arguing, simply *is* embedded in canonical culture, whatever might be the case of law. If wedded with law in the anti-positivist manner urged by both White and Nussbaum, and more broadly by the literary lawyer, it would point our *law* and not just our ideals in the direction of a just as well as beloved community. This is a project not only filled with ambition, but filled with *hope* and vision. There is no doubt but that it is vital work, and it is, I think, work which should be cheered by both the feminist and law and literature communities.

Nevertheless, and without in any sense wishing to impede the project, it is worth registering a cautionary note. As Nussbaum herself clearly recognizes, she is invoking the Western canon, in a sense, against a mode of reasoning which is itself a product of that canon.[33] The anti-historical, super-rationalist, and super-relativist mind-set that dominates the legal academy and which Nussbaum ambitiously, courageously, and entirely to her credit aims to dislodge, did not spring upon us from nowhere, it came from strands of authority firmly rooted in our cultural past. Before we employ the canon, and even the idea of a cultural canon, against the morally stunted relativism and rationalism in modern legal thought, we need to "root out the rot," and that itself may be no small task. If this feminist and feminized reconstruction of the Whitean project—the partial resurrection and reconstruction of a feminine literary lawyer—is to succeed, however, it is necessary work of some urgency. If we wish to *use* our cultural inheritance, and more specifically if we wish to use it in law, against the deadening impulse of relativism and more broadly toward the ends of a true community, we must first be willing to critically examine it. And we must be willing to examine it, among much else, for its profoundly misogynist underpinnings.

THE CRITICAL PROJECT: THE LITERARY CRITIQUE OF LAW AND LEGALISM

The second project within the law and literature movement—what I call the "critical project"—is in many ways the antithesis of the first. In fact, we might best characterize the critical project by *contrasting* it rather than comparing it with the project of the nineteenth-century literary lawyer. While the nineteenth-century literary lawyer "used" literary classics *for the most part to bolster* the law's authority, the twentieth-century law and literature scholar engaged in the "critical project" is far more inclined to "use" literature in such a way *as to call into question* the law's authority. The critical law and literature scholar uses literature as a means to open law to criticism, rather than to shield it from criticism within the protective shroud of high culture, and to push for greater democratization rather than greater elitism in legal processes.

In sharp contrast with White's and Nussbaum's clear pedagogical and professional ambitions, the major participants in law and literature's critical project have no real interest in either creating or revitalizing an idealized form of lawyering, whether literary or not. Indeed, they have little interest in participating in any reconstruction of professional ideals. Rather, they are interested in participating in the very different but equally central *critical* goal of both the legal and nonlegal academy: the criticism, from a nonlegal perspective, of particular laws, areas of law, entire historical legal eras,[34] jurisprudential theories, or most generally of the idea of the "Rule of Law" itself. What distinguishes these legal critics from others is simply their interest in literature as both a vehicle for this criticism, and a reflection of it.

The major premises of what might be called the "critical project" within the law and literature movement are clear enough. The basic argument or idea is simply that law is oftentimes a subject of literature, and at least occasionally the subject of great literature. Literature is replete with protagonists who are judges, lawyers, and other legal actors; trials that serve as vehicles for plots; and themes that seem to express well-developed jurisprudential conceptions of the nature of law. Literature, in brief, contains insights into the nature of law, of the legal profession, and of the legal persona. Those insights in turn are sometimes clearly critical, and sometimes radically so. It is now often remarked, by critical legal scholars as well as others, that if we want to examine law critically we need to somehow "get outside" the law's normative reach. That can be extremely difficult to do: law affects, and profoundly, not only our awareness of our legal rights and liabilities but our sense of justice and morality as well.[35] One way to achieve some critical distance on the law that undoubtedly in part constitutes the very critical ability we might use to judge it, is through the medium of literature—particularly that vast body of literature that portrays law in a seemingly critical light. Thus the ambition of the critical project: to cull from either canonical or noncanonical literature critical insights into the nature of law, whether that "nature" be oppressive or liberatory.

While Brook Thomas's important work, *Cross Examinations of Law and Literature,* [36] sparked interest among literary theorists in this critical project, it was Richard Weisberg's book, *The Failure of the Word,* [37] which in the early 1980s served the same function in law schools. Indeed, it seems fair to say that Weisberg's work has been as seminal to this critical project within the law and literature movement as has been James Boyd White's work to the reinvigoration of the literary lawyer. In *The Failure of the Word,* [38] Weisberg argues the neo-Nietzschean thesis that one of the most important if neglected constructions of modern Western literature is the articulate, even verbose, but pathologically resentful and spiritually stunted "lawyer-protagonist." The lawyer-protagonist of modern Western literature, Weisberg argues, is virtually *always* a moralistic and moralizing, psychologically twisted man who uses and misuses the language of law as a weapon against an impulsive and stronger man of action [39] and toward the fulfillment of ends defined not by the grandeur of law but by his own neurotic and perverse personal ambitions. Through close readings of Melville's novella *Billy Budd Sailor,* [40] Albert Camus's *The Stranger,* [41] Dostoyevsky's *Brothers Karamazov,* [42] and any number of other literary works, Weisberg has embellished this central claim: whatever its noble ambitions, precisely *because* it is so "wordy," law inevitably carries with it the potential for its own misuse toward the ends defined by the *ressentiment* of learned and academic but weak men. The result of Weisberg's labors has been a body of interpretive essays about literary lawyer-protagonists which consistently asserts a view of law, of legal language, of authority, and of rhetoric that is the antithesis of that put forward by White. The verbal, pontificating lawyer, according to Weisberg, makes his linguistic "promises" with neither the intent nor the effect of enhancing social life or strengthening community. Rather, he often—albeit not inevitably—makes them with the end, whether or not consciously realized, of overcoming the strength of natural action with the force of authoritative words; with the end of defeating impulse and health with neurotic deception; with the end of realizing, through the wordy forms of law, the neurotic personal ambitions formed of envy. If Weisberg's reading of literature is correct, and if the authors he interprets are saying something true about legalism, then the "promise" of liberal legalism—the governance of communities through the authority of impersonal law—is utterly compromised by—not embodied by—the inevitably twisted, envious, resentful, and wordy legal promises of the man of "law and letters."

Although he has not himself written on it, Weisberg's central, defining, critical thesis does resonate with at least some feminist concerns. Feminists too, both in law and even more emphatically in literature, have been suspicious of the "wordiness" of contemporary modernist authority—whether embodied in judges, priests, or fathers—and have struggled to unearth from history and family less patriarchal, as well as less "verbal" forms of power.[43] Feminists too have suspected that behind the apparent peace-seeking facade of the legalist's embrace of verbosity lies a resentful, envious neurotic longing for power, and destructive hatred of natural forms of life. Most recently, to take just one provocative example, J. C. Smith and Carla Ferstman have turned the misogynist Nietzsche to their own feminist ends, arguing that the entire patriarchal apparatus of male control of the female *is* largely the result of the attempt of men to use the power of the "word" to attain what they cannot naturally lay claim to, and that is possession of female sexuality and knowledge of their children's paternity.[44] There are obvious parallels which deserve greater exploration between this emerging neo-Nietzschean analysis of the verbosity of patriarchy and Richard Weisberg's neo-Nietzschean analysis of the "wordiness" of legalism.

Other early writings within this critical wing of the law and literature movement have been more explicitly driven by or influenced by feminist concerns. In *Legal Modernism*,[45] to offer just one particularly striking example, David Luban puts forward an interpretation of Aeschylus's trilogy *The Oresteia*[46] which owes much to feminist dramatizations of that work.[47] *The Oresteia*, of course, is widely read, and was probably intended to be read, as the first dramatization of the triumph of the idea of law, the Rule of Law, and legal process over the earlier and much more brutal and inefficient system of communal control known as private revenge.[48] On the other hand, it has *also* been widely read, at least by feminists, as a parable of the defeat of a political system of matriarchy by patriarchy: the revengers who are ultimately driven underground by the oracles of legalism are female, the crime which is the centerpiece of the famous trial is a matricide, and of course the defendant is eventually acquitted, to name just three of the many references in the play that suggest gender warfare as a central, if not the central, concern. In his essay in *Legal Modernism,* David Luban deftly ties these two strands of interpretation together, and the result is a profoundly feminist critique of the very ideals that go to the heart of legalism. What Aeschylus suggests in *The Oresteia,* Luban argues, is that the triumph of law, legalism, and legal process simply *was* the world historic defeat of the female sex. Rather than glorifying the virtues of law, Luban suggests, Aeschylus smuggled into the "subtext" of his masterpiece a devastating critique, according to which law is and has been skewed from its inception against the interests of the weak—including the politically weaker class of women. The purported "neutrality" of legal process, as dramatized in *The Oresteia* and as reenacted daily in courtrooms, is simply a sham. Its goal is not justice but civic order, or peace, the cost of which almost necessarily is a silencing of the voice, the rights, and the interests of women. Both in the trial depicted in *The Oresteia* as well as in modern courtrooms, Luban suggests, the cost of legalism's quest for civic peace is justice, and it is so because of its masculinist drive for dominance.[49]

Feminists have been both participants and critics of law and literature's critical project, which we might broadly define as the exploration of jurisprudential themes within literature toward the end of understanding and criticizing law and legal institutions. Martha Nussbaum, discussed above, has brought the teachings of the classics to bear on modern death penalty jurisprudence, arguing persuasively that by banishing or minimizing the role of mercy in such adjudications, the modern Court has compromised its standards of justice as well.[50] More generally, as discussed above, she has successfully employed the classics to mount arguments against what she sees as a modern skepticism that permeates both the law and economics movement and the critical legal studies movement in the legal academy.[51] Anita Allen finds in Brontë's masterpiece *Jane Eyre* a jurisprudential description of Eyre's private world as classically positivistic— a command society in which the law is laid down by the most powerful and habitually obeyed by the weak—and hence an important, and importantly jurisprudential, critique of positivism.[52] Lisa Weil reads Virginia Woolf's *To the Lighthouse* as a critique of formalist legal reasoning, and an endorsement of a more feminist, and feminine, approach to justice and legal inquiry.[53] Carrie Menkel-Meadow as well as others have examined Shakespeare's character Portia in *Merchant of Venice* both sympathetically and critically for evidence of the possibility that Portia reasons about legal issues "in a different voice"— with an ear and an eye more attuned to sympathetic engagement in the particular relational context of particular disputes, than to a discernment of hidden principles and rights.[54] Judy Koffler has written on the jurisprudential themes in Dante's *Inferno,*[55] Melville's *Billy Budd, Sailor,*[56] and a number of other canonical works from a clearly feminist perspective. I have looked at Kafka's short stories and parables about law to call into question the decisional rationality assumed by law and economics scholars.[57] This list of feminist participation is by no means exhaustive.

Feminists have also, however, noted the limitations of this critical project. The most important of these limitations is that it tracks the problem noted above with the use of the literary canon toward the end of ennobling and enriching legal reasoning. The literary canon is for better or worse elitist and exclusionary *by definition,* and it should come as no great shock to note that the voices of women have not been well represented within it. As a consequence, criticism of law by recourse to insights drawn from the literary canon might for that very reason be fairly tepid at best.[58] One cultural artifact is being critically pitted against another, but the two have more in common than what divides them. The literary canon will reflect the moral sensibilities of the same elite whose interests are reflected and served by law. Those moral sensibilities might, indeed, be in rebellion against the legal and political order of the day. But they are nevertheless the sensibilities of elites. The voices, experiences, and perspectives of outsiders will only rarely infiltrate, and a form of critique that depends upon the canon for its critical insights will reflect that limitation.

Let me give an example. It has become relatively commonplace within the law and literature movement, to cite Twain's masterpiece *Huckleberry Finn*[59] as a critique not only of the institution of slavery, but also of the laws and legal sensibilities, as well as the positivistic, legalistic, and property rights-minded view of morality, that supported it.[60] But it also seems fair to say that *Huckleberry Finn* expresses the revolt of conscience against slavery which was experienced by and articulated by *whites.* Huck is a developed character, and a moral rebel, in the story; Jim, by contrast, is not. Rather, Jim is developed to precisely the degree necessary to constitute a dramatic contrast to Huck: he is a loyal friend (while Huck's loyalty waivers); he is a devoted family man (while Huck's family is dysfunctional) and he is, from the outset, a truly morally just and upright human being (while Huck must *become* moral through acts of rebellion). He is also, of course, a wronged victim by virtue of skin color while Huck is not. But for all these attributes, he is nevertheless a two-dimensional character. The reader learns much of Huck's mind-set and subjectivity, and little of Jim's. This is a story, in short, *about* a runaway slave; it is not a story *of* a runaway slave. It was not Twain's intent, nor his accomplishment, to provide the slave's perspective. This is Huck's story, not Jim's. While *Huckleberry Finn* conveys a powerful jurisprudential critique of slavery, it is a critique by and of a white man of conscience. It is not itself a slave narrative. Use of works such as *Huckleberry Finn* in the canon of literature critically employed against legalism highlights, rather than cures, the exclusionary history of the literary canon. We might usefully call this complaint—that even canonical literature which is squarely critical of extant legal institutions, such as *Huckleberry Finn,* will convey at best the critical perspective and the reservations of conscience experienced by the relatively powerful—the "outsider's lament."

How forceful is this objection? As critique, it seems clear, even obvious, that the outsider's lament has force only to whatever degree the literary canon is itself resistant to change and supplementation from the voices of "outsiders." As the canon "opens up," we should expect to find critiques of law not only sympathetic to the plight of outsiders such as Jim, but more specifically critiques which speak with their voice and from their perspective. The canon may, of course, prove resistant to change. Indeed, there is an inevitable and much remarked upon tension between the idea of a canon and egalitarian, inclusive democratic ideals: as Bloom and others have pointed out, full inclusion defeats not only the idea of a canon but the idea of culture.[61] There is *also,* however, a less remarked upon but equally inevitable tension between the idea and ideal of excellence and a steadfast, frozen *resistance* to change: a canon that cannot expand to include new entries as well as new standards of excellence is not only no longer canonical, it is no longer a measure of excellence. To whatever degree the canon truly remains canonical, it *must be* open to amendment and change so as to include the works of those artists once considered outsiders. And to the degree that it is open, the force of the outsider's lament is weakened. As the force of the critique weakens, the case for feminist participation in, rather than criticism of, the law and literature movement's critical project becomes stronger.

There is, though, a deeper problem with the critical project, which inclusion of noncanonical or outsider literature ironically highlights. A contrast of *Huck Finn* with Toni Morrison's masterpiece *Beloved*[62]—by now surely no less canonical than Twain's novel—illustrates the point. Unlike Twain's Jim, Morrison's protagonist, the escaped slave Sethe, *is* fully developed: *Beloved* is indeed the story *of*, rather than about, a runaway slave, and in *Beloved* we do indeed confront many of Huck's moral dilemmas, though from the slave's perspective. And the contrast is stark. Sethe's utterly "outsider" world is indeed a very different, more vicious and more tragic one than even the world the rebellious Huck confronts. Including study of *Beloved* alongside study of *Huck Finn* at least addresses the exclusionary objection—the outsider's lament—raised above.

However—and herein lies the irony—one of the most striking features of Sethe's world is not only that it is so much more horrific than Huck's—or Jim's—but it is also considerably less *textual*, and even less verbal, than the world inhabited by Huck and his friend Jim.[63] To put it differently, Sethe's world, to which Morrison's *Beloved* gives us access, is *itself* less governed by ruling verbal canons from *any* community, and it is utterly ungoverned by the ruling canon—legal or literary—of the white world. Sethe's family, community, and friends communicate in many ways, but strikingly they communicate in many more *nonverbal* ways than do Huck's. They communicate through dance. They communicate through signs and cues when gags prevent speech. They communicate through the marks left by whips on their backs. They communicate through ghosts and visions across the divide of death. Only at the end does a central character—Sethe's surviving daughter—learn to read, and hence take tentative steps toward joining the white world of governing canonical texts.[64] Until that point, the communities in *Beloved* are built not around textual consensus, but around direct and physical, or indirect and psychic, *interactions*—communal and life-sustaining interactions between the living and the dead; between mother and infant; and between man and woman, and oppressive and threatening interactions between master and slave, slave catcher and escaped slave, white and black. Among much else, what *Beloved* teaches is that the spirituality, the sense of selfhood, and the communities created through silent and silenced interactions—through dance, through laughter, through death, birth, sign, and touch—are as morally important and constitutive as the textually saturated pontificating "individuals" and communities created by a literary canon, whether critical or celebratory of the legalism with which it interacts. What *Beloved* teaches, again, among much else, is that we should attend to those nontextual and even nonverbal interactions and the communities they create, and not only to the texts we produce if we want to understand and assess the moral quality of our governing institutions.

There is, then, contained in *Beloved,* a quite powerful critique of the critical project itself—which in essence simply advocates the use of one verbal construct (literature) to criticize yet another (law). Our moral foundation, *Beloved* teaches, emanates not only from the verbal lessons we inherit, but also from our profoundly nonverbal interactions, from birth to friendship, mothering, sexuality, touch, and death. One lesson of at least this canonical "outsider" work is that the use of verbal "canons" of *any* sort—outsider, insider, or in-between—gives short shrift to our nonverbal forms of interaction and the nonverbally based communities they form. If that is right, then even the "critical project" arguably occasions a critical injustice of its own. It pits the lessons of one sort of verbal text—literature—against that of another—law. What is elided entirely are the lessons of our nonverbal interactions, whether oppressive, intimate, or liberatory, and the communities of oppression, intimacy, and liberation those interactions create.

Susan Glaspell's early-twentieth-century novella, *A Jury of Her Peers* [65] gives rise to a similar dilemma. *A Jury of Her Peers* is about the spousal murder of a husband by an emotionally abused wife, as told through the eyes of two neighboring women from the larger community. The two women have accompanied the group of men—including a prosecutor and a sheriff—to the farmhouse to investigate the crime, and eventually, while sitting in the guilty woman's kitchen, discover and then suppress incriminating evidence, deciding on their own that the murder was justified. [66] Although not by any means as great a work as *Beloved, A Jury of Her Peers* is nevertheless "canonical" at least within feminist communities: it is much taught, discussed, and criticized as a foundational text of twentieth-century feminism. It is a natural candidate for *inclusion* in any canon of critical works on law. It is a story about political marginalization and emotional abuse, and it is unquestionably jurisprudential. It can readily ground a jurisprudential critique of law, and it does so squarely from the perspective of an outsider.

Yet, like *Beloved,* the actual message of *A Jury of Her Peers* uncomfortably undercuts even an expanded conception of the critical project. *A Jury of Her Peers* is about many things, but one thing it is about is silence, and silent protest. The women who sit in judgment in that farmhouse kitchen of the clearly guilty farmwife, refuse to convey to the sheriff and prosecutor the evidence they have uncovered of the wife's guilt. This is itself a crime of silence. The evidence they uncover and refuse to disclose is a strangled songbird—its song needlessly and cruelly silenced by the woman's husband, apparently in an act of rage which in turn prompted his own killing at the hands of his silent wife. The childless, friendless, isolated farmwife who committed the homicide had lived in a silent and emotionally dead world with a noncommunicative and abusive husband, and she responded to her silent hell with a crime of silence—strangling her husband in the middle of his sleep. The wives who visit the farmhouse after the homicide fault themselves for their neglect of their neighbor's silent suffering. And all this action takes place, of course, against the backdrop of a legal system which itself silences, by excluding, the views, perspectives, and voices of women from juries in properly constituted courts of law.

To be sure, *A Jury of Her Peers* is clearly critical of all this *silence.* Nevertheless, not only the homicide itself, but every other morally significant act in the novella is an act of silence, from the strangling of the bird to the refusal to turn over the evidence. The *speech* in the story, in fact, stands in marked contrast: both the speech of the sheriff and prosecutor as they search the home, and the speech of the women in the kitchen is pointedly banal. The norms to which they give expression are insipid. In this novella, as in *Beloved,* it is the acts of silence that form the communities that matter—communities of oppression, of solidarity, of loyalty, of life, and of death. It is the acts of silence, not the pontificating acts of verbosity, that constitute the contours of the lives for which the reader learns to care.

It is not, however, fatal to the critical project that the included voices of outsiders in a newly invigorated and more inclusive canon at least on occasion counsel greater attentiveness to actions and to silences, and to the communities thereby created, and a little less to "what we say." First, of course, it is in keeping with the "anti-wordiness" message of Weisberg's seminal contribution to the critical project. It is also in keeping with the late Robert Cover's impassioned and eloquent plea that the law and literature movement heed the violence law *does,* not only the principles it expresses.[67] Most important, though, it is in keeping with at least one goal (if not the only goal) of literature, whether canonical or not: to shed light not on our subjective "texts," but on the quality of our internal lives. That outsider literature, like outsider jurisprudence, directs and enables us forcefully toward an examination of those lives, as much as possible unfiltered by the disorienting gaze of the dominant culture's defining texts, is a reflection of that literature's strength.

THE LEGAL SUBJECT, LEGAL INTERPRETATION, AND LEGAL AUTHORITY

Legal scholars with even passing familiarity with trends in English and literature academic departments could not help but notice the last twenty years' explosion of scholarship within those disciplines on the nature of literary interpretation: during those years, the so-called "theoretical" work on the nature of literary interpretation came to overshadow interest in literature itself. Whatever the value of this "turn toward theory" and away from literary texts themselves in literary disciplines, the temptation *in the law schools* to borrow from that thriving industry of learning so as to elucidate problems within law concerning the nature of legal interpretation, has proven to be irresistible. Law, like literature, is centrally concerned with texts, words, interpretations, conflicting interpretations, and the problem of interpretive authority. Indeed these issues *in law* have an immediacy and a political significance that at least at first blush are not present in literary battles. It was surely not unreasonable to assume, as did scores and perhaps hundreds of legal scholars over the last couple of decades, that the legal academy could learn something about the nature of legal interpretation by looking over their shoulders at the work being done in literature departments on the nature of literary texts, interpretation, and authority.

The third project of the law and literature movement, then, is unquestionably the project that has drawn the largest number of participants, namely, an attempt to further our understanding of the nature of legal interpretation, legal texts, and legal authority by turning to the substantial body of scholarship created in other disciplines—but most importantly, literature—on the nature of literary interpretation. A number of extremely influential scholars both inside and outside the law and literature movement per se, made the "interpretive turn" quite explicitly. Owen Fiss declared, in an influential piece attacking the critical legal studies movement, that adjudication simply *is* interpretation—and that because interpretation must be "objective" to be authoritative, so too must adjudication.[68] In a piece entitled "How Law Is Like Literature," Ronald Dworkin declared the common law method of judging to be essentially like a chain-produced novel, and drawing on that analogy, compared interpretation (as well as creation) of common law cases to literary creativity and interpretation.[69] Stanley Fish famously applies to the problem of legal authority and legal interpretation a controversial view of the nature of interpretation drawn from his study of literary texts.[70] Walter Benn Michaels moves seamlessly from his insistence on originalism in literature to an argument for originalism in law.[71] And the entire critical legal studies movement has drawn sustenance and inspiration from the "deconstruction" movement originating in various departments of literature, finding in the lessons of indeterminacy the premises of a weighty attack on the political legitimacy of law.[72]

More generally, as literary critics, professors, and theorists moved, through the course of the second half of the twentieth-century, from intentionalism, to new criticism, to structuralism, to post-structuralism, postmodernism, deconstructionism, and reader- or community-response theories about the nature of literary interpretation, the parallels between each of these competing theories and a comparable view of the nature of legal interpretation were painstakingly elaborated by legal scholars. Thus, intentionalism, as a theory of literary meaning, seems to have a clear mirror image reflection in originalism as a theory of legal and constitutional meaning: both identify the meaning of a text with its author's intended meaning, and both ascribe "authority" to the text by reference to the authority of the author.[73] "New criticism" appears to rest on a literary equivalent of a "plain meaning" view of textual meaning in law,[74] and "structuralism" has at least surface similarities with a four-cornered approach to contract, statutory, and even constitutional interpretation.[75] Post-structuralism and reader-response theories of interpretation tend to lend support, however indirect, to a robust, activist judiciary which, in post-*Brown* days, must look elsewhere than to the original intent of the constitution's authors for many of its most important constitutional interpretations.[76] Literary deconstruction and indeterminacy theories obviously give some weight to the suspicions of many critical legal scholars (and others) that the apparent rationality of judicial interpretive decision making as well as the apparent constraints—whether of reason, text, role, or duty—are illusory.[77]

Given the seeming intractability and political significance of interpretive quandaries in law, and the heightened interest in the nature of interpretation in literary studies, substantial borrowing between the disciplines was inevitable. The sentiment is perhaps best captured in an article by Thomas Grey, from the early 1980s, in which he ringingly declares that, in the aftermath of the so-called "interpretive turn" in various humanistic disciplines, "we (in the legal academy) are all interpretivists now"—the issue is not *whether* judges interpret, but rather how they do so, and what it means that they do so.[78] The law reviews of the last fifteen years have certainly borne out his declaration. Articles of the form: "because interpretation is thus-and-so, which we know from looking at literary interpretive theories, *legal* interpretation must also be thus-and-so, from which it follows that judges are doing the right thing, the wrong thing, or the right thing for the wrong reason," number in the hundreds. Just as literary scholars seemed to turn away from literature itself in the turn to theory, so legal scholars seemed to turn away from law. Arguments for or against the outcome in a case or in a particular line of cases, for or against judicial review, for or against particular lines of authority on hot topical issues, had to make room for what appeared to all to be of paramount, overriding importance: the nature of interpretation and the need to plumb the depths of theoretical writing in other disciplines, but primarily literature, to glean some greater insight into its mysteries.

Some of us (including myself), it might be worth noting, dissented, arguing that the entire comparative project was based on a false assumption about the nature of the legal subject, as well as a false assumption about the nature of law. Briefly, the dissent went, the interpretive turn *in law,* whatever may be the case in literature, wrongly assumed that adjudication *should be viewed* as primarily an interpretive exercise rather than an exercise of some other sort entirely (such as a political act), and accordingly that the judge should be viewed as primarily an interpreter of texts rather than someone who holds and uses power to resolve, or at least in some fashion terminate, disputes.[79] Those dissents, however, did not ring loudly. For the most part the overwhelming consensus within the law and literature movement as well as the larger legal academic community was that whether or not lawyers and legal theorists had much to learn from literature itself, they unquestionably had something to learn from literary scholars, and what they had to learn concerned the nature of interpretation quite generally. Indeed, for many of its most prominent members interest in the nature of interpretation, and a willingness to borrow from literary studies to further that inquiry, are *defining,* not just incidental, features of the law and literature movement itself. Perhaps more importantly, for many, perhaps most, legal academics outside the law and literature movement, that movement is quite firmly identified with the "interpretive project": the attempt to understand something about the nature of law by understanding legal decision making as a species of a more general genus of human activity, to wit, interpretation of written texts.

Perhaps surprisingly, while this interpretive project of the law and literature movement without question has attracted the largest number of interested legal theorists, it has also generated the least interest among feminists. To be sure, feminists have from time to time weighed in on various sides of what might be called the "interpretation wars." Thus, Suzanna Sherry, Lynne Henderson, and others have noted and decried the not-so-hidden authoritarian impulse in originalist approaches to constitutional authority,[80] and Clare Dalton has quite nicely exposed the tensions in plain-meaning and four-cornered approaches to contractual interpretation, also from an explicitly feminist perspective.[81] Drucilla Cornell has argued against the nihilistic tendencies of the deconstruction movement and in favor of a neo-Hegelian, teleological, and communitarian approach to legal interpretation.[82] Of more immediate relevance to feminism, Catharine

MacKinnon, no doubt speaking for many, complained of the critical legal scholars' compulsive attraction to the indeterminacy thesis, noting that, at least from the perspective of severely oppressed women, legal doctrine has "all the indeterminacy of a bridge abutment hit at sixty miles per hour."[83] She might have added (and would no doubt have been speaking for many) that for feminist reformers concerned with doing something with law to end patriarchy, as a tool of analysis deconstruction has all the usefulness of an unhinged steering wheel in avoiding a collision with a wall. Drucilla Cornell, David Luban, and I have all argued, albeit in very different ways, that Stanley Fish's discipline-response view of interpretation does little but reinscribe as interpretation the interests of the relatively empowered, and that such a view does a disservice to politically marginalized groups.[84] I have made a comparable critique of Owen Fiss's far more liberal and generous conception of legal interpretation as bounded by the moral principles and practices of the social community from which the law emerges.[85]

For the most part, however, feminists have been rather strikingly uninterested in or at least absent from these interpretive battles. Nevertheless, if we broaden the camera angle it becomes apparent that feminists and the "interpretation theorists" have shared, over the last twenty years, a common interest in the *set of problems* that prompted the mainstream theorists to turn to theories of interpretation in the first place. Thus, feminists have been no less interested than interpretivists in the nature of the "legal subject," and when so broadened, it's clear that feminists and interpretivists are in fact on common ground. Despite their comparative lack of interest in the "nature of interpretation," in other words, feminists share with interpretivists an interest in the more general question of how it is that judges or lawyers go about the task of applying the law to disparate factual situations. But while the protagonists in the interpretive wars have generally understood that project in one way, feminists have understood it very differently. Interpretivists have looked to theories of interpretation to shed light on how it is that judges or other legal interpreters resolve legal issues when the relevant legal texts—legal rules and principles—appear to conflict. Thus the relevance of literary theories of interpretation. Feminists who have developed an interest in the reasoning processes of judges and other legal actors, have looked elsewhere—and, notably, to other disciplines—for help in resolving this question.

Partly—but only partly—inspired by Carol Gilligan's groundbreaking work *In a Different Voice,*[86] feminists have tended to pose the issue that prompted the interest in interpretation—the nature of judicial decision making—not so much in terms of conflicting textual rules and principles—hence inviting examination of conflicting theories of interpretation—but rather in terms of conflicting roles, responsibilities, stories, and avenues for giving care—and hence inviting inquiry into conflicting accounts of what might be called "judicious care." Just as Gilligan's research subject Amy famously responded to the Heinz dilemma by requesting more facts,[87] so feminists interested in judicial quandaries have argued that judicial as well as legal decision making requires, foremost, not so much an ability to manipulate legal principles as sensitivity to various, and conflicting, *stories* situated in various, and conflicting *contexts.* According to feminists working in the area, the legal subject—the lawyer or judge—who seeks a resolution to a legal dilemma faces not so much conflicting texts requiring Herculean interpretation, however understood, but conflicting "stories" requiring a sensitive "resolution." Focus is on the facts that give rise to the conflict, and the possibility of peaceful resolution, not the principles which will at best give a victory to one side and defeat to the other. Attention is devoted to the context of disputes, not the principles for which they stand. And the judicial ideal is captured by the judge who works carefully—and caringly—to responsibly resolve conflict in a manner which can preserve or restore to the greatest degree possible civic or even harmonious relations between the parties, rather than to the Herculean judge who scales the mountain of conflicting principle and pronounces the victorious interpretation, along with the victorious litigant.

Toward this end, feminist legal theorists have begun to "construct" a quite different image of the judge as legal subject, and one which contrasts with the Herculean judge at the center of the Herculean wars—*whatever* be that judge's interpretive theoretical disposition. Thus, Lynne Henderson has argued the case for the importance of *empathy* to good judging, in part to balance and in part to counter the overacknowledged need for certainty, principle, and predictability in the Herculean, interpretive model.[88] Martha Minow has argued in a number of articles and then a book for the importance of a sensitivity to the context within which each decision is made, again in part to balance and in part to counter the striving for universality and abstraction at the heart of the Herculean, interpretive model.[89] As discussed above, in a series of books on classical and Western philosophy, Martha Nussbaum has shed light on what she calls "Love's Knowledge"[90]—the knowledge we gain through the heart, and from immersing ourselves in the stories of others—and has recently begun to apply those lessons to the puzzles of judicial decision making.[91] Speaking directly to and of women in the judiciary, Suzanna Sherry has called for a feminine style of judging that would explicitly draw on the virtues of compassion and care while respecting the demands of abstraction and justice.[92] Judy Resnick and others have called for greater attention to the role of what might be called a justified maternalism in the construction of our code of judicial ethics.[93]

This composite, constructed, idealized feminist and feminine judge is, ironically, in many ways engaging in a type of decision making which owes more to a literary and narrative sensibility than the interpreting judge at the heart of the nonfeminist "interpretation wars." While the interpreting judge finds himself facing conflicting rules, principles, and theories of interpretation, the idealized feminist or feminine judge finds herself facing interlocking webs of *stories* which she must somehow weave together and then complete. She must be, quintessentially, a good listener and a good teller *of stories.* She must find the ethical heart, so to speak, of each of these stories, and redirect them toward the end of justice, and if she is to do that well, she will do it *gently.* Finding that ethical heart in turn does indeed require immersion in the rules, principles, and lines of authority discovered in cases, statutes, and constitutions. But the goal is completion of the story, and the story in turn is not a story of or about emerging legal doctrine. It is a story of the life and lives of individuals and communities, and of conflicts and resolutions. Judging, on this view, is a practical art, not a literary one—but it is a practical art with narrativity at its ethical core.

The "construction" of this feminist and feminine conception of the act of judging receives considerable support from the scholarship of law and literature participants who for different reasons are *not* under the sway of the postmodern "interpretive turn" in various academic circles. As that scholarship teaches, it is, at least arguably, a central lesson not only of relational feminism but also *of the humanities themselves*—of Western culture—that judging is and ought to be an empathic, as well as a rational, act, informed by a sympathetic engagement with the lives and interests of the competing litigants, tempered with mercy, and guided by care. Martha Nussbaum's work on the nature of judging and knowledge, for example, unquestionably resonates with the alternative view of judging propounded by feminists in law,[94] even though it is a conception of judging and knowledge that is a product of the study not of *women's* unique modes of reasoning, but of the lessons of the classics of Western culture. The moral philosopher Wai Chee Dimock's book *Residues of Justice* similarly articulates alternative conceptions of moral knowledge, which like Nussbaum's are in important respects similar to those put forward by feminist scholars, but are culled not from those sources but from both canonical and noncanonical nineteenth-century stories.[95] Similarly, James Boyd White's careful construction of the literary nature of the judicial and legal decision, as well as his more specific critique of economic modes of decision making in law, sound many of the themes that recur in feminist critiques of economic rationality.[96] All three of these writers, for various reasons, have eschewed the "interpretive turn" that captured the attention and commitment of much of the law and literature movement in the 1980s, accepting instead Richard Weisberg's insistent plea that the law and literature scholars return their attention to the literary text.[97] Their work clearly demonstrates that when divorced from the "study of interpretation," humanistic inquiry produces a conception of the "legal subject" and of legal decision making that informs and enriches rather than detracts from, the conception of judging, reasoning, and knowledge at the heart of much feminist analysis.

THE NARRATIVE VOICE

The fourth "project" of the law and literature movement—analysis of, explication of, and *expansion of* the "narrative voice" in law and legal scholarship—is the only one of the four which originated not in the law and literature movement but in feminism and its sister "outsider" jurisprudential movement, the critical race theory movement. Reflecting that point of origin, it is also the only one of the four in which the participation of feminists and critical race theorists outstrips that of law and literature scholars. Narrative jurisprudence is for that reason at least as often, perhaps most often, identified as a branch or wing of feminist and critical race scholarship rather than of the law and literature movement per se. Of the four, it is also the most overtly political, and the farthest removed from the constraints and rules which define traditional scholarship. For all these reasons, as well as others, it is the only one of the four which has attracted the ire and the angst of the mainstream legal academy.[98]

For these purposes narrative jurisprudence might be narrowly defined as involving the use, in otherwise traditional legal scholarship, of the narrative voice, sometimes autobiographical, to further particular legal and/or political arguments, and the explication and defense of that departure from standard forms of argument. So defined, there is obviously nothing about narrativity which necessarily ties it to feminism. Nevertheless, it is clear that narrativity has come to play a relatively large (and certainly noticeable, and much noticed) role in both feminism and critical race theory. Both feminists and critical race theorists, far more often than other legal scholars, infuse their writing with narrative accounts of their own lives or those of others.[99] This narrative jurisprudence is by this point far too vast a field to summarize in any coherent manner, and I will not attempt to do so. What I will do, instead, is put forward a tentative explanation for the disproportionate inclusion in feminist scholarship of narrativity and autobiography.[100]

My *own* view is that there are four major reasons. First, feminists tend to employ narrative and autobiography in feminist legal scholarship in part because the *injuries* which are the subject matter of a good bit of that scholarship have been so thoroughly "privatized" that there is no societal understanding of their nature, their prevalence, their effects, or their history. Narrative and anecdote is one sometimes effective way to communicate both the nature and extent of these injuries: more quantitative measures quite literally "don't tell the story." The impulse to tell stories to try to communicate the nature of overly privatized, silenced, and hidden injuries is largely a response to felt necessity in the face of widespread ignorance and incomprehension. Let me quickly illustrate with an example the sort of ignorance for which, it is often hoped, narrative might provide a partial cure.

In the *New York Times Book Review* of June 25, 1995[101] there appears a book review by Stephen Carter of Yale Law School of a book, *A Man's World: How Real Is Male Privilege—And How High Is Its Price?* [102] which in turn attacks feminism for various sins of omission and commission. In his review, Carter notes approvingly how the author of the book complains that feminists tend to exaggerate. As an example of their tendency to exaggerate, Carter cites the book's complaint that feminists don't seem to "distinguish between a slap on the face and a life-threatening beating." [103] When I read that sentence, to resort to just a bit of narrative, it felt like a (metaphoric) kick in the stomach. My relaxing morning on the couch with the *Times* was over. The sentence itself is (metaphorically) assaultive. Why?

The sentence feels so assaultive, I think, partly because it so glibly captures, recalls, and threatens to reenact an age—an age, one would have hoped, in the past—when domestic violence was routinely regarded, and treated, *as a joke,* on the firmly held and erroneous assumption that at least most domestic violence—the common kind, so to speak—was relatively harmless: the "slap on the face" variety, not the life-threatening variety. But second, it feels assaultive because its accusation of ignorance is so woefully, and tragically, and dangerously, misdirected. I know many feminists who write on, work with, litigate over, and legislate around, domestic violence, as well as a good number of women who are or have been victims of domestic violence, and I do not know *anyone* who doesn't know the difference between life-threatening and non-life-threatening violence. On the other hand there are obviously many people who do not know that a "slap on the face" can dislocate a jaw, dislodge teeth, and leave a bruise. Many, many people do not know that a slap on the face, when undeterred, when unacknowledged, when hidden, when societally *condoned,* will often *escalate.* Way too many people, including the women who sustain them, think that a slap on the face is normal, ordinary, unexceptional, or deserved. Way too many people do *not* know that a slap on the face administered in anger from someone with whom you live is profoundly damaging. Too many people do not even know that it is *criminal.* Many, many people do not know, most importantly, that there is in fact *not* a sharp line between a slap on the face and a life-threatening beating—there is only a continuum. Too many people do not know that the *only* sharp line that matters, and should matter, in domestic relations, is between violence and nonviolence, not between bad violence and okay violence. No level of violence is acceptable; none should be tolerated.

That ignorance is appallingly widespread, and my sense is that one reason—perhaps the main reason—that narrativity shows up in so much feminist legal writing is the somewhat desperate sense that maybe narrative writing will help cure it. It is not an unreasonable strategy, for two reasons. First, many people are simply unaware of the prevalence—the bare statistical occurrence rate—of even "life-threatening" domestic violence. The straightforward premise of much of the narrative in feminist jurisprudence is simply the belief that the telling of stories of such violence in any possible medium will change the prevalent and false view—itself perpetuated by constraints of silence, privacy, and need—that such violence is rare. But second, and perhaps more importantly, many people—including Ellis Cose and apparently including Carter as well—may well be aware of the prevalence of the non-life-threatening "garden-variety" type of domestic violence, but are clearly unaware of the damage it causes. At least some of the narrative in feminist jurisprudence is premised on the belief that this kind of writing might cure that ignorance as well. If people don't know what it means, what it feels like, and what it does to be slapped on the face at home by someone you once trusted to love and cherish you, then for heaven's sake *tell them.* The narrativity in feminist writing—at least the narrative surrounding issues of violence—often comes, I think, from this sense of bewildered urgency. If we can address the ignorance, then the law will address the injury—that is, after all, supposed to be the way the law works. If the ignorance concerns the subjective "feel" of an injury—if the ignorance concerns the very *existence* of an injury caused by what are wrongly taken to be innocuous or mundane transactions—then narrative is obviously the way to address the ignorance.

Thus, the first reason for narrativity in feminist jurisprudence is purely strategic, and entirely consistent with instrumental assumptions about the nature of law: it is an attempt to make the reader aware that these injuries *happen,* and that they happen to people known to the reader, and that they are devastating, on the assumption that if the reader knows those facts, she may be prompted to use law to do something about it. It is primarily for that reason that feminist scholarship is filled with stories of injury—of first-person accounts of rape,[104] of domestic violence,[105] of illegal abortions,[106] of botched deliveries by arrogant and unsympathetic obstetricians,[107] of sexual harassment on the job,[108] of harassment on the street,[109] of incest and the sexual abuse of children,[110] of, in short, appalling levels of abuse. The point is simply to get the elite readership of law reviews (and law-related books) to understand that abuse, care about it, and act on that knowledge. Whether or not it is successful, of course, is another question entirely. The book and book review above referenced are not good signs that any of this scholarship is making much of a dent. But then again, there are also reasons for optimism: both public awareness and reporting of domestic violence, at least, seem to be on the up-swing.

The second reason for including narrative and autobiography in feminist scholarship is also strategic, but toward a somewhat different end, and that is to "debunk" what might be called the "stock stories" of mainstream legal scholarship. As Chris Littleton and Catharine MacKinnon have wryly noted, mainstream theorists tend to bury their narrative presumptions, but they nevertheless do their work on a foundation which is narrative to the core.[111] When legal doctrine, whether a case or an entire area of doctrine, is grounded in reliance on the universality of those unstated stock stories, anyone caught within the scope of the rule, but whose "story" departs in significant ways from the assumed narrative which grounds it, may suffer an injustice. Let me give two examples.

One "stock story" that lies at the heart of scores of legal rules is the story of "typical human development": boy grows into manhood, marries, takes a job or begins a career, while his wife bears his children, raises them, and keeps his home running. Vast areas of law that affect the relationship between our work life and our home life, from social security law and employment law to family law and even constitutional law, are explicitly or implicitly built on the foundation of the assumed typicality of this story of human development. There are, of course, two obvious problems with this stock story. The first is that even within that universe of people whose lives fit the contours of the narrative, the stock story obliterates the perspective, experiences, wisdom, sorrows, and interests of the wife and mother. She is an object within the stock story, not the subject of it, and it is for that reason not surprising that the law built on this narrative is not responsive to her needs and interests.

But the second problem is that the stock story obliterates the very different story of all those—men and women—who do not fit the narrative: the working *woman,* rather than man, who is also a mother, and who does not have a wife at home to raise the children and keep the home running; the worker of either sex who is not married; the gay or lesbian worker with or without children but who does not have a "spouse" or significant other of the opposite sex; the single parent; or for that matter even the married man who shares equally with his working wife the burdens of home maintenance and child raising. Entire areas of law are badly skewed against the interests of vast numbers of people simply because of the law's steadfast but unstated reliance on this unrepresentative stock story of human development. To take just one example, but one familiar to readers of this book, think how different tenure and partnership tracks would look, and how different the law regulating those tracks would look, if the stock story on which those employment policies were built was of the working *mother,* with finite childbearing years and disproportionate child-raising responsibilities, rather than the stock story of the working husband-father with a supportive wife to mother his children and keep his home.

The criminal law of justified self-defense is also squarely based on a stock story, this time of the nature of violence: a stranger is accosted in a public place, such as a bar or street, and if possible, retreats, but if retreat is impossible, he justifiably defends himself. The intricate rules in criminal law governing the justified use of force to defend oneself are tailored to this story. They do not fit well—or at all—violent encounters that depart from it. They do not fit well, for example, the violent encounters between intimates that occur in a home: there is nowhere to "retreat" when one's attacker is an intimate and when the "safe haven" to which retreat is required is where the violence occurs.[112] Whatever might be the case with respect to the now much battered "battered wife syndrome" defense to criminal homicide,[113] at least this much is clear: the rules of self-defense, the inadequacy of which prompted creation of the battered spouse defense in the first place, would look very different if those rules had been crafted around the stock story of domestic violence between intimates rather than the stock story of barroom or playground violence between strangers. Some number of those "syndrome"-induced acts of violence—at best, under current law, *excused* as acts of a nonresponsible actor—might be better viewed as fully justified acts of self-defense. The injustice occasioned by unthinking reliance on unrepresentative stock stories of this sort is rampant. Part of the "point" of narrativity in feminist writing is simply to address that injustice.

African American feminists, lesbian feminists, and others who are marginalized within academic feminism, have made precisely the same argument about feminism itself that feminists as a group have made about mainstream legal theory and law. Consequently, black feminism, lesbian feminism, and other intrafeminist strands are similarly characterized by an attempt to address, through narrative, the unrepresentative but purportedly universal stock stories of feminist legal theory. The standard or near-standard feminist analyses of rape,[114] of sexual violence quite generally,[115] of discrimination in the workplace,[116] and of any number of family-related issues[117] seem to be built upon a narrative foundation of stock stories which are as untrue of black women's lives as the stock stories of legalism are untrue of women's lives. To take just one example, think how different the misleadingly simple stock story "a woman is raped by a man" is, where the woman is white and the man black, or where both protagonists are black, or where the woman is black and the man is white, both in terms of the protagonists' own experiences as well as the perception of the attack by the larger white and black worlds.[118] Feminist attempts to rethink criminal law by centralizing a woman-centered stock story of rape do an obvious injustice to women whose experience of rape and rape accusations differs from the dominant. To take a related example, think how different the feminist stock story of the quite general phenomenon of *fear* is when the woman is black: it is a recurrent part of black women's experience to be not only fearful of men, but themselves feared by whites solely because of their color.[119] African American feminists have responded to these injustices of exclusion, again, with narratives—often with full awareness that the cycle is bound to repeat, as the stock stories of those arguments as well are revealed to be partial.

The third reason for the disproportionate amount of narrative, particularly first-person narrative, in feminist jurisprudence is simply that feminists are more inclined to distrust the pretense of detached objectivity that characterizes traditional jurisprudence. For some, particularly for feminists influenced by postmodern and post-structuralist turns in philosophy and literary studies, the distrust is principled, and (paradoxically) foundational: objectivity itself is found objectionable.[120] For others, and I suspect for most, although there's no easy way of knowing, it is not objectivity itself but the appearance of it that rankles. For this group, objectivity remains an ideal, but it is an ideal best attained not by hiding one's perspective but by openly declaring it. Correspondingly, it is an ideal which is frustrated, not furthered, by the annoying, grating practice, within mainstream discourse, of intellectual and emotional detachment from whatever issue is under discussion.

Partly, the open declaration of one's own history and stance with respect to a particular issue is simply a matter of correcting for errors in turn caused by underrepresentation. Objectivity is obviously frustrated, not furthered, by banning from all discussion of rape, for example, anyone who has herself been raped, on the spurious ground that rape survivors cannot, by definition, be dispassionate in their understanding of the issue. The rape survivor is often the person *best* qualified to speak on any number of matters of direct relevance to the legal issues surrounding rape. Excluding that class of interested persons will skew the legal analysis, and furthermore will skew it in a particular direction—namely, against the interests of victims. There is, of course, a risk that one's own victimization will skew one's assessment of the interests that run counter to the seemingly compelling imperative to stop the violation one has suffered from recurring. But that is a risk to be minimized, not run away from, and like many other risks that should be familiar to lawyers and law professors, it is a risk that must be *balanced* against the opposing risk of error that comes from excluding the relevant information altogether. It is also, of course, a risk that can never be reduced to zero. One's own *nonvictimization*—the fact that one has gone through life never having been raped, or the fact that one realistically faces no significant risk of being raped in the future—will *also* affect one's assessment of relevant interests. Both risks—the risk of distortion occasioned by one's having been oneself a victim, as well as the risk of distortion occasioned by one's good fortune not to have been—are magnified, not diminished, by thrusting oneself into a dialogue, and in the name of a false objectivity, refusing to reveal either to others or to oneself the experiences that inform one's own perspective.

For other feminists, the distrust of the pretense of objectivity comes from a different source. Feminist legal scholarship is, oftentimes, differently *motivated* than nonfeminist scholarship. Feminists working in law are, in fact, deeply "interested" in the work they produce. To put it bluntly, a felt moral imperative, and in extreme cases an instinct for survival itself, far more than curiosity, the fun of puzzle solving, or the fact that like Mount Everest the challenge is there, motivate a good bit of feminist work in law, and that is largely because of women's personal experiences with the events, social structures, and institutions regulated by the legal constructs in question. Where that's the case, it seems appropriate to simply say so. This does not destroy objectivity. Quite the contrary: by more carefully explicating the observer's perspective, it goes a long way toward creating it.

The fourth reason narrative appears disproportionately in feminist legal theory is the least strategic, and in many ways the most "nonlegal." In a quite different context, the law and literature scholar Milner Ball has argued that narrativity in religious discourse often serves the purpose of creating, or opening, a mental "space" where none had earlier existed: prior understandings are challenged, not so much to be replaced with different understandings as simply to open the mind and heart to new ways of being.[121] I think something similar motivates some of the narrativity in feminism (and a good bit more in critical race theory). Marie Ashe's stunning narrative piece *Zig-zag Stitching*[122] is, I believe, best understood in this way. In that piece (among much else) Ashe relates a narrative of the home and hospital births of her own children. Critics have complained of the piece that Ashe fails to connect her narrative to a particular legal argument regarding reproductive rights, and the criticism is well taken: she doesn't.[123] On the other hand, the power of the piece may lie precisely in that "failure." What she does in the piece, to my mind spectacularly, is "open a space" for new understandings of the heretofore utterly hidden, privatized, and unmistakably dangerous experience of birth. Patricia Williams's writing is often powerful for the same reason. Williams often fails, or simply refuses, to "connect" her stories of her own encounters with racism, poverty, and commerce with concrete legal arguments. The power of those stories, however, may lie in part in that refusal. What Williams accomplishes with her narrative is a *dislodging*, rather than a creating, of understanding. What she has created is an "open space": an open space for a different learning, for new knowledge, for a better way of being, or for higher and decidedly more noble aspirations toward social, economic, racial, and gender justice.

[215]

CONCLUSION

As a very general, disciplinary matter, it's fair to say that feminist legal scholars have participated in, criticized, and enriched law and literature studies, and law and literature scholarship has enriched feminist legal scholarship as well. By way of conclusion, let me just note three structural reasons why it is safe to predict that these interconnections between the two fields will continue, and strengthen, over time.

First, both law and literature and feminist legal studies are interdisciplinary fields, the first by definition and the second by necessity. The shared interdisciplinarity of both movements is underscored by their overlapping projects. Both movements are seeking to expand the contours of legal scholarship by bringing in heretofore excluded voices. Both are interested in the nature of legal and moral decision making, and the role of narrativity in that activity. Both have mounted challenges to the conception of decision making, and the complex notion of rationality behind it, that dominates liberal and economic understanding of legal, moral, and practical reasoning. Both are interested, albeit for somewhat different reasons, in seeking understandings of the subjective experience of objective legal norms, and both seek to do so through modes of inquiry that go beyond traditional forms of legal analysis. Both are interested, again for somewhat different reasons, in the practices of narrativity, and both seek an understanding of those practices through disciplines located outside as well as inside the legal academy.

Second, at least at this point in their development, both movements stand in a generally critical relationship to the "law" which is their shared focus. This is, of course, a contingent, not a necessary truth for each. The literary lawyer of the nineteenth century, for example, overwhelmingly viewed literature as a means to bolster legal authority, not as a means to challenge it. And at least in the eyes of some of its critics, strands of the modern law and literature movement tend excessively toward an attitude of conservative complacency, if not celebratory adulation, toward the law which is its subject.[124] Feminist legal theory in a future age of improved relations between the sexes might similarly lean toward celebration rather than critique of legalism. But for now, at this point, it's fair to say that at least a good deal of the law and literature movement and virtually all feminist scholarship aim to provide critical, not celebratory perspectives on law. This fact alone puts them on common ground: it accounts, in short, for their shared marginality in legal education.

Lastly, both feminist legal studies and the law and literature movement stand in an *interested* but *ambivalent* relationship to the virtue of justice. Echoing the stance of Marxist legal critics (whose politics they sometimes share), law and literature scholarship is often moved by a passion for justice that is explicitly conjoined with a distrust of dominant, property-obsessed conceptions of that virtue. Brook Thomas's writings on the law and literature of the antebellum era are a striking example.[125] James Boyd White's communitarian, universalist conception of the virtue of justice as explicated in his book *Justice as Translation*[126] bears only a tenuous relation to the felt imperative— the "thirst"—for retribution and compensation that often goes by that name. Richard Weisberg's writing is perhaps the most overtly critical of the pretense of justice, but it too is unquestionably motivated by the quest for a truer, if more naturalist, realization of the same virtue.[127] Feminist writing reveals the same ambivalence. Feminists as diverse as Martha Minow,[128] Catharine MacKinnon,[129] and Carol Gilligan[130] all in very different ways characterize and criticize the quest for justice that is the raison d'être of the legal system as polluted by a false and disingenuous pretense of neutrality. There is nevertheless little doubt that the entire jurisprudential work of all three theorists is aimed toward the realization of some conception of "gender justice." The common ground, then, of feminist legal scholarship and the law and literature movement is precisely this ambivalence. Both movements, coming from different points of origin, converge on a common project: the realization of a just society, but through, among many other things, a thorough reconstruction of the flawed theory of justice we have inherited, and which of necessity guides the effort.

CHAPTER FOUR

Invisible Victims: Herman Melville's Bartleby the Scrivener *and* Susan Glaspell's Jury of Her Peers

Somehow, by some process, some of the pains and suffering we sustain in life become cognizable legal injuries: if we are hurt through the defamatory utterances of others, we might seek compensation; if we suffer a whiplash in an automobile accident when we're rear-ended on the road, we might seek compensation for the pain we're put in; if we lose profits we might have made but for the interference of some third party with a contract we've entered, we might recover that loss. Other pains, although admittedly injurious, and even admittedly "caused" by some blameworthy individual or entity, are not cognizable: perhaps because they are too trivial, or too easily faked, or because they happened too long ago, or for any number of other reasons, the societal costs of fashioning a remedy exceed the benefits to the injured individual of recognizing one. Still others are also admittedly injurious, but nevertheless not cognizable because they were not in fact caused by a culpable individual: the pain of grieving the non-negligently caused death of a beloved, or the pain inflicted by the strike of lightning or some other "act of God," are such pains. Toward all this uncompensated suffering, the law stands, so to speak, respectfully mute: although not compensated, the pain of grief, or of lightning, is at any rate not denied.

There is, however, another type of suffering—another "category" of harms—toward which the law stands in a quite different relationship. As a number of critical legal scholars have argued, some of the

sufferings of daily life—some of the harms individually sustained—
are not simply not compensated by our positive law, but their very
existence is aggressively denied, trivialized, disguised, or legitimated
by our legal rhetoric.[1] These harms tend, not coincidentally, to be the
byproduct of institutions, social systems, and structures of belief
which overwhelming serve the interests of powerful individuals,
groups, or subcommunities. Although law does not cause these harms
it is complicit in the process by which they become "legitimate"—an
accepted part of the terrain of daily living—and hence become invisible, often even to the individuals who sustain them. Particularly from
a perspective internal to the legal system, such harms can be extremely hard to discern.

For some time now it has been the contention of at least some
practitioners of the law and literature movement that narrative literature may be one means by which the contours and dimensions of the
subjective experience of persons regulated and governed by law become articulated. If so, and if the critical scholars are correct in
arguing that a part of our subjective experience is of harms legitimated
and thereby made invisible by legal rhetoric, then it seems that one
use to which narrative literature might be put, is to give voice to the
victims of invisible harms legitimated by law. And in fact, at least one
prominent law and literature scholar heavily influenced by the critical
legal studies movement—Brook Thomas—argues for precisely such a
thesis in his seminal study on nineteenth-century American fiction,
*Cross Examinations of Law and Literature: Cooper, Hawthorne,
Stowe, and Melville.*[2] In that work, Thomas argues persuasively that
all four of these prominent literary figures explored in their fiction
the suffering of persons hurt by various social hierarchies, and the
complicity of law in legitimating and masking that pain.

In this chapter, I hope to take this Thomasian claim one step
further. I will argue that two short novellas, Herman Melville's *Bartleby the Scrivener*[3]—which Thomas does discuss[4]—and Susan Glaspell's *A Jury of Her Peers*[5]—which he does not—not only seek to
articulate and give voice to the victims of such legitimated harms in
the way Thomas suggests, but that they also quite directly concern
the process of legitimation *itself.* Thus, legitimation as well as the
invisible pains that are legitimated are the subject matter of both
stories. Both stories do indeed aim to make more visible the suffering
of two groups of people in classically liberal societies: in *Bartleby,*

employees in certain kinds of labor markets who bear the brunt of the pain of alienating and commodifying the products of labor, and in *A Jury of Her Peers,* wives in traditional, patriarchal marriages who bear the weight of the institutionalized loneliness, abuse, and injustice that such marriages often entail. But this exposure of otherwise hidden suffering is not all these stories do: both novellas are also centrally and undeniably concerned with legal process. They are clearly about *law* as much as they are about labor markets or patriarchy. And yet neither story offers a clear-cut *indictment* of law. Neither story portrays law—or even a legal actor—as the cause of the suffering it describes. Yet law is obviously complicit in the suffering of Bartleby in Melville's tale, and Minnie Foster in Glaspell's. What both novellas, each written by astute and critical professional legal observers, aim to show is the way in which law masks or obfuscates this suffering. Both novellas, in short, aim to depict the "process of legitimation."

In neither case, however, is the process of legitimation a simple one. The law does not stamp these institutions, and the suffering they prompt, with a good housekeeping seal of approval to which all involved parties quietly nod in acquiescence. Rather, in both cases, the law, through noninterference as well as positive acts, creates a private "space" within which the strong can dominate the weak free of the threat of state or community intervention, and within which the only check on such domination is either the moral conscience of the strong, or some sort of concerted political action by the weak. In both cases, there are significant obstacles to either of these checks being exercised, the most important of which, arguably, is ideological: as both novellas make clear, the "individual" wage worker, employer, wife, and husband are characterized within each societal context in such a way as to render either a political response by the weak, or a moral act by the strong, unlikely. Legal rhetoric as well as positive law contribute, and mightily, to that characterization. As a result, the misery felt within these private relationships and private spaces proceeds unabated.

The first part of this chapter takes up Melville's *Bartleby the Scrivener,* and the second concerns Glaspell's *A Jury of Her Peers.* In each part, I will first examine the institution depicted in the novella, with a focus on the social construction of the "individual" which thereby emerges, and then on the injury, or simply the suffering, each institution entails and which each story depicts. I then look in each case at the process of legitimation. In the conclusion I will comment briefly on the lessons these stories might impart with regard to our own peculiarly modern, and even postmodern, habits of thought and action.

BARTLEBY THE SCRIVENER

The plot of Melville's *Bartleby the Scrivener* can be readily summarized. The narrator of the story is a lawyer "of Wall Street" in the 1850s, who, in response to an increase in his business, finds himself in need of an additional copyist, or scrivener. After placing an ad, the narrator hires the first to respond: a despondent, pale, gauntly creature named Bartleby. Although even from the outset clearly eccentric in appearance and taste, Bartleby is initially a good worker—a careful, quiet copyist about whom the lawyer has no complaints. The narrator in fact commends his productivity:

> At first Bartleby did an extraordinary quantity of writing. As if long famishing for something to copy, he seemed to gorge himself on my documents. There was no pause for digestion. He ran a day and night line, copying by sun-light and by candle-light. I should have been quite delighted with his application, had he been cheerfully industrious. But he wrote on silently, palely, mechanically.[6]

In a very short time, however, Bartleby becomes uncooperative. He initially refuses to take on all assigned tasks other than the copying itself (such as proofreading), saying simply and repeatedly that "he prefers not to," in response to all requests. Even more galling, it becomes clear to the employer that Bartleby has no place of residence, and is in fact living in the law office. Eventually Bartleby announces that he will do no copying at all, and in fact that he "prefers not to" do any work whatsoever. Bartleby does nothing but stand mute and expressionless, all day long, in the middle of the office. Understandably, this situation eventually becomes intolerable to his employer. Although tolerant of Bartleby's eccentricities, and even sympathetic to his plight, the lawyer, who is described throughout the book as above all a *prudent* man, cannot abide the presence of a ghost like figure in his law office who does literally no work and never leaves the premises. The lawyer tries to convince Bartleby to leave, and offers him severance pay to facilitate his departure. But Bartleby prefers not to go. The narrator, an amiable and likable figure, is unable to bring himself to call the police and have Bartleby physically hauled off the premises. In desperation, he responds to the dilemma by literally *moving his office*—thus leaving Bartleby standing mute, expressionless, and unmoving in the empty office suite. Eventually the narrator receives word that Bartleby, after refusing to leave the office building, has been arrested for vagrancy at the insistence of the new, bewildered tenant, and placed in the city "tombs." Moved by charity and humanitarian impulse, he visits him there, twice. On the second visit he learns that Bartleby has refused to take all offers of food, and has starved himself to death.

Whatever else this enigmatic story may be "about," it is most assuredly about an employment relationship between a lawyer and a scrivener, and in a highly particularized context. Indeed, Melville subtitles his story *A Story of Wall Street,* and the subtitle is significant. The lawyer-narrator of Bartleby's story is not just any lawyer, he is a Wall Street lawyer, who does, in his own words, "in the cool tranquillity of a snug retreat, [a] snug business among rich men's bonds and mortgages and title-deeds."[7] We are also told by the lawyer, in a brief aside which has proven to be of interest to legally sophisticated critics, that "The good old office, now extinct, in the State of New York, of a Master of Chancery, had been conferred upon me. It was not a very arduous office, but very pleasantly remunerative."[8] We should not, though, confuse the equitable tilt of Chancery for a similar inclination in the narrator, as his next comment makes clear:

> I seldom lose my temper; much more seldom indulge in dangerous indignation at wrongs and outrages; but I must be permitted to be rash here and declare, that I consider the sudden and violent abrogation of the office of Master in Chancery, by the new Constitution, as a _____ premature act; inasmuch as I had counted upon a life-lease of the profits, whereas I only received those of a few short years. But this is by the way.[9]

The "rich men" whose exchanges of property provide the narrator with a livelihood, however, remain in the background throughout the story. We never see or hear them. Indeed, even the narrator's own work—the reduction, through law, of "property" into verbal formula, so as to facilitate their exchange and conversion into profit—remains in the background. What this "story of Wall Street" is about, at least at first blush, is not the bonds and mortgages themselves (and much less, the holders of the bonds and mortgages) but the individuals charged with the *mechanical* aspects of the work required to produce those bonds and mortgages: the scriveners who copy, and recopy, and recopy, in longhand, the requisite documents, some of them hundreds of pages long. The narrator himself makes the subject matter clear in the opening paragraph:

> I am a rather elderly man. The nature of my avocations for the last thirty years has brought me into more than ordinary contact with what would seem an interesting and somewhat singular set of men, of whom as yet nothing that I know of has ever been written:—I mean the law-copyists or scriveners. I have known very many of them, professionally and privately, and if I pleased, could relate divers histories, at which good natured gentlemen might smile, and sentimental souls might weep. But I waive the biographies of all other scriveners for a few passages in the life of Bartleby, who was a scrivener the strangest I ever saw or heard of.[10]

The work of the "mere copying," as opposed to the "original drawing up of the legal documents" is unenviable. In one passage, the narrator explains:

> It is, of course, an indispensable part of a scrivener's business to verify the accuracy of his copy, word by word. Where there are two or more scriveners in an office, they assist each other in this examination, one reading from the copy, the other holding the original. It is a very dull, wearisome, and lethargic affair. I can readily imagine that to some sanguine temperaments it would be altogether intolerable. For example, I cannot credit that the mettlesome poet Byron would have contentedly sat down with Bartleby to examine a law document of, say, five hundred pages, closely written in a crimpy hand.[11]

Of course, Byron is not the only one who would find the work intolerable. Bartleby himself eventually "prefers not" to do it. Indeed, it's hard to think of a more deadening, spirit-murdering employment of language than the task of copying out, longhand and in quadruplicate, hundred-page-plus deeds of trust, mortgages, and bonds. The copied word is the antithesis of the creatively spoken utterance which, at least according to any number of linguists, is the defining attribute of biological human life. The work of copying words which themselves reduce nature to profit might be seen to be thus doubly or even triply alienating: the natural human instinct to play creatively with language, the creative relationship of the individual to the natural world through work, and the natural world itself, are all alienated by the commodifying and tedious process of reducing, through copied words, nature to property, and property to security for loans, and loans to profits.

In a moment I will focus on the various injuries, both physical and spiritual, suggested by this sort of employment. Preliminarily, however, it is worth noting that Melville supplies at the end of the novella a telling metaphor for the very idea of frustrated, futile, impotent, and indeed "dead" communication. In an addendum to the main story, the narrator explains a rumor heard about the mysterious Bartleby, to wit, that prior to his employment as a scrivener, Bartleby had worked in the "Dead Letter Office" in Washington, D.C. The image of Bartleby sorting and destroying dead letters prompts from the narrator a curious and confused passion:

> The report was this: that Bartleby had been a subordinate clerk in the Dead Letter Office at Washington, from which he had been suddenly removed by a change in the administration. When I think over this rumour I cannot adequately express the emotions which seize me. Dead letters! Does it not sound like dead men? Conceive a man by nature and misfortune prone to a pallid hopelessness: can any business seem more fitted to heighten it than that of continually handling these dead letters, and assorting them for the flames? For by the cartload they are annually burned. Sometimes from out the folded paper the pale clerk takes a ring: the finger it was meant for, perhaps, moulders in the grave; a bank note sent in swiftest charity: he whom it would relieve, nor eats nor hungers any more; pardon for those who died despairing; hope for those who died unhoping; good tidings for those who died stifled by unrelieved calamities. On errands of life, these letters speed to death.
>
> Oh Bartleby! Oh Humanity! [12]

The Dead Letter rumor, however, is a rumor, and an afterthought to the story. In the main, the story is about Bartleby's work as a scrivener, not a postal clerk. Now the point—the raison d'être—of the contract of employment between the narrator and Bartleby, of course, is to produce copied words—*many* of them, and without mistake. At the heart of this relationship, as at the heart of all relationships of employment, is an imperative of what might be called "free productivity." For the employee to continue *to be* an employee, he must be, by his own free choice, *productive*. What he must be is freely productive. Putting it differently, what it means *to be* an individual within these relationships is *to be* productive. When the employee ceases to be productive he ceases to be. It is his productivity—not his biological and certainly not his social identity—that defines his essence.

The point is underscored repeatedly by Melville's descriptions of Bartleby, the unproductive scrivener. As Bartleby becomes increasingly unproductive, he becomes increasingly, in the narrator's eyes, "cadaverous." When the narrator first employs Bartleby, he is described as "pallidly neat, pitiably respectable, [and] incurably forlorn" [13]—but not deathly. His productivity, as noted above, is praised, and it is praised *in organic terms* as ravenous: he "gorged himself" on documents, with "no pause for digestion." [14] It is only when he begins to refuse to work that the tone of these descriptions shifts toward the macabre. When Bartleby first begins to refuse to work he is compared by the narrator to the bust of Cicero that decoratively adorns the office. [15] When he eventually refuses to leave the office, he is first compared to a millstone around the narrator's neck, [16] and then to the "last column of a ruined temple." [17] By the time he refuses all work, he is described, and repeatedly, as cadaverous. [18] Before he actually dies in the tombs, he has become dead in the office. As his freely chosen "preference," in response to requests to produce, is "not to," he becomes organic—but dead—matter. He is of human substance, but that is all—his formal humanity is negated by his unproductivity.

What this employee becomes when he becomes unproductive is *nothing but* a repository of organic need. He needs shelter, which he takes from the lawyer's office space, and he needs food, which he buys from his savings squirreled away in his desk cubbyhole. Coupled with his unproductivity, this neediness makes him infantile, and toward the end the narrator does in desperation offer to take him home simply to care for him—an offer Bartleby prefers to refuse. [19] But Bartleby does not become, in the eyes of the narrator or anyone else, particularly innocent, or even animalistic. As he becomes nothing but his biological, organic needs, he becomes, rather, increasingly deathlike. To the reader, his actual biological death, freely chosen, at the end of the story, seems inevitable, and even anti-climactic.

By steadily shedding himself of them, Bartleby thus places in relief both prongs of the definition of the individual at the heart of contractual employment: free agency and productivity. Let me take them one at a time. First, as Brook Thomas has ably argued in his study of Melville's legal fiction, the laissez-faire assumption of free agency at the heart of classical liberalism's conception of the labor contract is directly challenged by the portrayal of both Bartleby and his employer, both of whom seem to be utterly constrained by the economic circumstances in which they find themselves.[20] In fact, although Thomas doesn't note it, the narrator *himself* remarks upon the sheer *oddity* of one of the central conceits of the picture of freedom assumed by liberalism's conception of the labor contract, to wit, the notion of a deal for labor as meaningfully manifesting "preferences" of the free individuals that enter into them. In a prescient passage which speaks directly to a striking feature of contemporary legal and economic discourse, the narrator and his employees comment on the perversity of using the verb "to prefer" in all sorts of inappropriate contexts:

"Say now that in a day or two you will begin to be a little reasonable:— say so, Bartleby."

"At present I would prefer not to be a little reasonable," was his mildly cadaverous reply. Just then the folding-doors opened, and Nippers approached. . . . He overheard these final words of Bartleby.

"Prefer not, eh?" gritted Nippers—"I'd *prefer* him, if I were you, sir," . . . "What is it sir, pray, that he prefers not to do now?"

Bartleby moved not a limb.

"Mr. Nippers," said I, "I'd prefer that you would withdraw for the present."

Somehow, of late, I had got into the way of involuntarily using this word "prefer" upon all sorts of not exactly suitable occasions. And I trembled to think that my contract with the scrivener had already and seriously affected me in a mental way. And what further and deeper aberration might it not yet produce? This apprehension had not been without efficacy in determining me to summary means.

As Nippers . . . was departing, Turkey . . . blandly approached. . . .

"[A]bout Bartleby, I think that if he would but prefer to take a quart of good ale every day, it would do much towards mending him, and enabling him to assist in examining his papers."

"So you have got the word, too" said I, slightly excited.

"With submission, what word, sir?" asked Turkey . . .

"I would prefer to be left alone here" said Bartleby, as if offended at being mobbed in his privacy.

"*That's* the word Turkey," said I, "*that's* it."

"Oh, *prefer?* oh, yes,—queer word. I never use it myself. But sir, as I was saying, if he would but prefer—"

"Turkey," interrupted I, "you will please withdraw."

"Oh, certainly sir, if you prefer that I should."[21]

However, it is not only the purported free agency of the labor contract that is thrown into question by Bartleby's extreme malady. The obsession with productivity is as well. What defines the employment relationship, which is itself of course both defining and necessary to the employee's life, is production; biological and social needs are incidental and noteworthy only as they impact upon production. Bartleby's metamorphosis highlights this in a negative sense: over the course of the story he deadens as he refuses to produce copy. But Melville also describes the process positively: the lawyer does indeed notice the temperament, the diet, the ages, and the ambitions of all his copyists—not only Bartleby—but he notices them distinctively in the context of their impact on their rate of production. Although engaging, humorous, sympathetically drawn, and introspective, the narrator is steadfast in his pursuit of profit through the commodified, and commodifying, word. His bantering and good-natured interaction with his copyists—at least until Bartleby forces him into a crisis of conscience—is entirely directed toward that end.

THE INJURY

Bartleby's work—the job of the scrivener in the law office—is surely injurious physically, mentally, and spiritually. Yet, even left-wing critics are loath to suggest that the injury inflicted by this sort of employment upon the bodies and minds of office workers is in any way what this story is actually *about*—such an interpretation seems to diminish the work, as well as ignore its peculiarities. Brook Thomas's reading noted above, which is heavily influenced by Morton Horwitz's history of the common law during the nineteenth century, certainly comes closest: Thomas reads *Bartleby* as largely about, and critical of, the myth of free agency in the laissez-faire ideology of contract so prevalent in mid-nineteenth-century law.[22] But even Thomas stops short of the most political, albeit most literal lesson one can possibly draw from this story, which is that the work of being a scrivener in a Wall Street law office is both injurious and profoundly alienating. Clearly anxious not to have his interpretation reduce Melville to the status of being an agitator for improved working conditions in offices,[23] but just as anxious to insist that the story is indeed about the alienation of labor, Thomas argues that we should understand the character Bartleby as essentially a stand-in, or representative, of an "underworld" of oppressed workers, knowledge of the existence of which both the narrator and his rich clients must quite actively repress if they are to continue comfortably with their "snug business" on Wall Street.[24] By reading Bartleby as a stand-in for oppressed workers from all sorts of industries, Thomas can then read the story as containing an implicit condemnation of the handful of doctrinal developments in the common law which were contemporaneous with the story's setting. These did indeed dramatically undermine the position of workers badly injured on the job, and correspondingly benefited the interests of capital during the industrial revolution: most notably the fellow-servant rule,[25] but also, as Thomas argues, the doctrine of charity,[26] and abolition of the "office of equity."[27] Of course, it also frees Thomas of the need to describe the work Bartleby actually *does*—copy words in an office—as particularly alienating or particularly injurious (or particularly anything). His status as wage laborer suffices to confer upon him his role as representative of the working class.

By his own account, Thomas is moved to this abstraction—Bartleby as representative of a larger class of oppressed workers—in part because of his discomfort with the constraints of the story. Most notably, Thomas seemingly agrees with his critics that there don't seem to be any work-related injuries in *Bartleby* anyway, and surely nothing for which compensation would have been barred by the fellow-servant rule.[28] In fact, Thomas suggests, there's little from which Bartleby suffers that would have been compensable under *either* the more paternalistic rules of the preclassical contracts era *or* the more regulated regime of the twentieth-century workplace. Viewing Bartleby as a stand-in for a class of workers, of course, removes this interpretive difficulty: even if *he* doesn't suffer from uncompensated injuries, he is a stand-in for other (more dramatically) maimed and oppressed factory workers who clearly do suffer such injuries and very likely would have been compensated for them, either before or after the heyday of laissez-faire ideology which Thomas reads as the real target of the story. Thus the need to abstract: *Bartleby* is about wage labor, not office work.[29] The reading he's left with—that Bartleby

[228]

represents a class of unseen oppressed workers, knowledge of the existence of whom the narrator and his capitalist rich clients must deny to maintain their own moral equanimity—is a perfectly sensible one: there's plenty in the story to support it. But there are at least two problems with it.

The first is simply interpretive: it denies the specificity and the detail of Melville's narrative. I will return to this problem with Thomas's reading in greater detail in the next section below. The second and more fundamental problem is that the strained abstraction away from office labor to the class of laborers in order to preserve the utility of the story as a parable of wage labor alienation, is based on a false premise, and hence is simply not necessary. The office work Bartleby is required to do is plenty injurious and alienating. There's no need to think of it as representative of more truly harmful and oppressive labor.

What are those injuries? First of all, although not central to the action, it is certainly worth pointing out that Thomas and his critics are simply wrong in assuming that whatever suffering Bartleby and his colleagues endure, none of it can be traced to injuries which were or might be compensable by decent legal institutions. In fact, there are at least two injuries, quite physical and clearly work-related, that are referenced in the short novel, either of which might be compensable under a paternalistic pre-laissez-faire regime of the sort that predated the classical era, or under a "regulatory" regime like that which followed it. Thus, in describing the junior copyist, Nippers, at the beginning of the story, the narrator explains:

[His] indigestion seemed betokened in an occasional nervous testiness and grinning irritability, . . . and especially by a continual discontent with the height of the table where he worked. Though of a very ingenious mechanical turn, Nippers could never get this table to suit him. He put chips under it, blocks of various sorts, bits of pasteboard, and at last went so far as to attempt an exquisite adjustment by fine pieces of folded blotting paper. But no invention would answer. If, for the sake of easing his back, he brought the table lid at a sharp angle well up toward his chin, and wrote there like a man using the steep roof of a Dutch house for his desk—then he declared that it stopped the circulation in his arms. If now he lowered the table to his waistbands, and stooped over it in writing, then there was a sore aching in his back. In short, the truth of the matter was, Nippers knew not what he wanted. Or, if he wanted anything, it was to be rid of a scrivener's table altogether.[30]

[229]

It may be that Nippers's discomfort, as the narrator insists, is rooted in his unappealing ambition to rise above the status of being a mere scrivener and usurp the work of the lawyer in the "original creation" of the mortgages and bonds which he can but copy. Or it might be that his discomfort, his back pain, and the poor circulation in his arms were all quite real, and symptoms of carpal tunnel syndrome. If so, Nippers was right—adjusting the angle and height of the scrivener's table was as close as he would come to resolving the problem and minimizing this unambiguous work-related injury.

Second, when Bartleby first refuses to do any writing, the narrator intimates yet a second injury:

> The next day I noticed that Bartleby did nothing but stand at his window in his dead-wall revery. Upon asking him why he did not write, he said that he had decided upon doing no more writing.
> "Why, how now? What next?" exclaimed I, "do no more writing?"
> "No more."
> "And what is the reason?"
> "Do you not see the reason yourself?"
> I looked steadfastly at him, and perceived that his eyes looked dull and glazed. Instantly it occurred to me, that his unexampled diligence in copying by his dim window for the first few weeks of his stay with me might have temporarily impaired his vision. . . .
> . . . added days went by. Whether Bartleby's eyes improved or not, I could not say. . . . At all events, he would do no more copying.[31]

There is no shortage of work-related injuries in this Wall Street law office. There is accordingly no need to extrapolate from the office to the factory to read *Bartleby* as an indictment of the uncompensated injuries occasioned by wage labor in a laissez-faire economy.

Of course, Thomas and his critics are right to suspect that the crisis of conscience which ultimately is the result of Bartleby's presence in this law office is not a function of these uncompensated work-related injuries. Thomas is wrong, though, to conclude from this that Bartleby must therefore be representative of a class of more seriously oppressed factory workers. Rather, what Bartleby's unproductive presence brings to the fore is the injurious nature of the work *itself,* and it is *that* injury which Thomas's reading of Bartleby as a working-class representative curiously masks. Bartleby forces upon us direct knowledge of the unpalatability of the choice the labor contract has imposed upon *him*. It is a choice the unpalatability of which would certainly survive the transition away from the laissez-faire assumptions of the classical era to the more regulated work environment of the twentieth century: Bartleby must either be forcibly removed from the premises, in which case he will apparently starve, or he must be productive. The first choice starkly reveals the barbarism of the disingenuously equal and free contract of labor: the choice to work or not work is not much of a choice where the alternative to labor is death. Again, where the essence of the individual is his productivity rather than his biological or social self, his nonproductivity reduces him to biological need, and if his wage is his only means of satiating those needs, then to death.

But the second choice as well—the choice of free productivity in the office—is also unpalatable, and this unpalatability, no less than its barbarous alternative, is at least in part the subject matter of this most peculiar tale. Again, the work *itself* is injurious. Rather than burning "dead letters" which were on "missions of life," as he had done in the Dead Letter Office, as a scrivener Bartleby produces dead letters on a mission of death—the commodification, through the mechanical production of deeds, mortgages, and "rich men's" trusts, of language, work, property, nature, and life itself. Through a series of metaphors, Melville makes clear that while the alternative is literal death, the work required of this scrivener is indeed a kind of "living death": the work *preserves* biological life, but without *sustaining* it. The office itself, the narrator tells us, resembles just such a preservative container more than a site for life:

My chambers were upstairs at No —— Wall Street. At one end they looked upon the white wall of the interior of a spacious sky-light shaft, penetrating the building from top to bottom. This view . . . [was] deficient in what landscape painters call "life." But if so, the view from the other end of my chambers offered, at least, a contrast, if nothing more. In that direction my windows commanded an unobstructed view of a lofty brick wall, black by age and everlasting shade; which wall . . . for the benefit of all near-sighted spectators, was pushed up to within ten feet of my window panes. Owing to the great height of the surrounding buildings, and my chambers being on the second floor, the interval between this wall and mine not a little resembled a huge square cistern.[32]

The space in this office assigned to Bartleby is even more coffinlike:

> I resolved to assign Bartleby a corner by the folding-doors. . . . I placed his desk close up to a small side-window in that part of the room, a window which originally had afforded a lateral view of certain grimy back-yards and bricks, but which, owing to subsequent erections, commanded at present no view at all, though it gave some light. Within three feet of the panes was a wall, and the light came down from far above, between two lofty buildings, as from a very small opening in a dome. Still further to a satisfactory arrangement, I procured a high green folding screen, which might entirely isolate Bartleby from my sight, though not remove him from my voice.[33]

The brick wall that bars any further view out the windows of the office is routinely referred to by the narrator as the "dead wall," particularly when it is the object of Bartleby's gaze. The confining, coffinlike architecture of the office is finally echoed in the end, in the narrator's description of the "tombs," or prison, to which Bartleby is dispatched:

> Being under no disgraceful charge, and quite serene and harmless in all his ways, they had permitted him freely to wander about the prison, and especially in the inclosed grass platted yards thereof. And so I found him there, standing all alone in the quietest of the yards, his face toward a high wall—while all around, from the narrow slits of the jail windows, I thought I saw peering out upon him the eyes of murderers and thieves.[34]

Bartleby's free choice, then, is between imprisonment as a vagrant or biological death in the elements, or sustained, preserved life in a cistern in which he produces copied words which both describe and themselves constitute the properties and profits of others. It is a barbaric set of options. Those who sanely and rationally choose to produce dead letters in a coffinlike office rather than risk death or imprisonment, do so at the cost of a tremendous amount of suffering. *Bartleby* makes the true nature of the choice, and hence the suffering it entails, starkly visible.

LEGITIMATION

It has for some time now been the contention of the critical legal studies movement that law perpetuates hierarchical social and economic relations and the suffering they cause in at least two ways: first by brute force, and second by influencing the consciousness of both the empowered and the weak. Melville's *Bartleby* explores both. First, the narrator gives voice to the limits of Bartleby's *rights,* which, when reached, justify the law's forceful intervention. Either the possession of private property or the provision of labor confers legal rights. In the absence of either there simply is no legally recognized entitlement to shelter:

> "Will you, or will you not, quit me?" I now demanded in sudden passion, advancing close to him.
>
> "I would prefer *not* to quit you," he replied, gently emphasizing the *not.*
>
> "What earthly right have you to stay here? Do you pay any rent? Do you pay my taxes? Or is this property yours?"
>
> He answered nothing.
>
> "Are you ready to go on and write now? Are your eyes recovered? Could you copy a small paper for me this morning? or help examine a few lines? or step round to the Post Office? In a word, will you do any thing at all, to give a colouring to your refusal to depart the premises?"[35]

Without a legal right to have basic needs met, the individual is left to the vagaries of private charity, or to fend for himself against nature. It is obviously by virtue of that harsh and immediate consequence of positive law that the inequalities in labor contracts self-perpetuate. Law quite literally enforces the inequalities engendered by these economic exchanges.

The enforcement of positive law, though, although necessary is not sufficient to account for the phenomenal degree of compliance with law that distinguishes liberal legal societies, or at least it has been the distinguishing and persistent claim of the Gramscian wing of the critical legal studies movement to so maintain. Rather, what accompanies the application of force, and together sufficiently accounts for compliance, is the creation through rhetoric of a consciousness, or a frame of mind, or a set of beliefs, within which the weak feel that they are freely complying, and therefore that their choices manifest and evidence their autonomy, and allow the strong to feel justified in their positions of privilege. The complicity of law in the creation of this state of consciousness is partial and indirect. The narrative, expository, normative, rhetorical part of law—not the guns and prisons, but the words, the holdings, and the stories—is but a part of a larger cultural apparatus. That cultural apparatus overwhelmingly and at times unwittingly constructs individuality and individual consciousness in such a way as to render compliance seemingly natural and free on the part of the weak, and morally unproblematic on the part of the strong.

Melville's *Bartleby* dramatizes both ends of this process of legitimation. First, as suggested above, by the prescient and insistent use of the verb *prefer,* Bartleby's suicide is marked as consensual, as is the choice of the other copyists to produce rather than starve. To *prefer* is to express a choice, and to express a choice is to do so freely; hence both Bartleby and his colleagues' fates are chosen rather than duressed. In fact, Melville is insistent that *all we know* of Bartleby is that he makes these odd choices; we are on several occasions reminded that the narrator lacks all knowledge of Bartleby's history.

The protagonist of this story, however, is clearly not the enigmatic Bartleby, of whom we know truly nothing other than that he prefers not to produce (until the end, when we learn of his prior work in the Dead Letter Office). Rather, the protagonist is the narrator, and of the narrator we learn a great deal. This story of Wall Street is at bottom a story of the self-justification of privilege within a liberal market economy. In the absence of any legal claim to entitlement, Bartleby is at the mercy of the narrator's charity. *Whatever* course he takes, the narrator must deal with Bartleby in a noncontractual and therefore unscripted manner; this above all else prudent lawyer must somehow come to grips with a nonproductive, seemingly irrational, and eventually quite disruptive presence in his law office. The narrator must somehow justify either his decision to support Bartleby in spite of his nonproductivity, or his decision to abandon him.

Over the course of the novella, the narrator explores a number of such justifications, and by so doing eventually develops a quite intricate "empathic calculus" to suit the decision of the moment. Those various self-justifications constitute, collectively, a compelling and even exhaustive account of the many ways in which economic privilege is still squared, today, with utterly visible and widespread economic deprivation. Thus, when the narrator first resolves to indulge Bartleby's eccentricities (at a point when Bartleby had refused only some but not all work, so that his crime was insubordination rather than total nonproductivity) the narrator introduces his first egoistic account of his own charitable impulse:

> I regarded Bartleby and his ways. Poor fellow! thought I, he means no mischief; it is plain he intends no insolence; his aspect sufficiently evinces that his eccentricities are involuntary. He is useful to me. I can get along with him. If I turn him away the chances are he will fall in with some less indulgent employer, and then he will be rudely treated and perhaps driven forth miserably to starve. Yes. Here I can cheaply purchase a delicious self-approval. To befriend Bartleby; to humour him in his strange wilfulness, will cost me little or nothing, while I lay up in my soul what will eventually prove a sweet morsel for my conscience.[36]

Later in the story, as Bartleby's "eccentricities" become more trying, the narrator reintroduces his prudential account of charity, but this time as a means of checking his own anger:

> But when this old Adam of resentment rose in me and tempted me concerning Bartleby, I grappled him and threw him. How? Why, simply by recalling the divine injunction: "A new commandment give I unto you, that ye love one another." Yes, this it was that saved me. Aside from higher considerations, charity often operates as a vastly wise and prudent principle—a great safeguard to its possessor. Men have committed murder for jealousy's sake, and anger's sake, and hatred's sake, and selfishness' sake, and spiritual pride's sake, but no man that ever I heard of, ever committed a diabolical murder for sweet charity's sake. Mere self-interest, then, if no better motive can be enlisted, should, especially with high-tempered men, prompt all beings to charity and philanthropy. At any rate, upon the occasion in question, I strove to drown my exasperated feelings toward the scrivener by benevolently construing his conduct. Poor fellow, poor fellow! thought I, he doesn't mean any thing; and besides, he has seen hard times, and ought to be indulged.[37]

However, there are limits to sympathy, and limits upon the charitable impulse, particularly in the public world of work rather than the private world of home or worship. The first such limit, of course, is professional appearances. The narrator tells us in the first paragraph that he is, above all else, an eminently *safe* man who "from his youth upward, has been filled with a profound conviction that the easiest way of life is the best."[38] And what this safe man of prudence comes to understand is that his business will suffer, and badly, if he continues to indulge Bartleby's unproductive presence. It is this inescapable fact that finally impresses upon the his consciousness the need to restore "normalcy" in his office, and eventually spurs him on to more definitive action:

> I believe that this wise and blessed frame of mind would have continued with me had it not been for the unsolicited and uncharitable remarks obtruded upon me by my professional friends who visited the rooms. But thus it often is, that the constant friction of illiberal minds wears out at last the best resolves of the more generous. Though to be sure, when I reflected upon it, it was not strange that people entering my office should be struck by the peculiar aspect of the unaccountable Bartleby, and so be tempted to throw out some sinister observations concerning him.[39]

Perhaps more ominously, the narrator explains, even apart from prudential concerns of business, there is a "prudential" limit to the sympathetic response itself. We quit sympathizing with those in need of our charity where the pain of doing so exceeds the "morsel of self-approval" we might glean from the charitable act itself. And we reach that point rather quickly when it becomes clear that the object of our charitable impulse is failing or refusing to respond in the appropriate and hoped-for way:

> Revolving all these things, . . . a prudential feeling began to steal over me. My first emotions had been those of pure melancholy and sincerest pity; but just in proportion as the forlornness of Bartleby grew and grew to my imagination, did that same melancholy merge into fear, that pity into repulsion. So true it is, and so terrible too, that up to a certain point the thought or sight of misery enlists our best affections; but, in certain special cases, beyond that point it does not. They err who would assert that invariably this is owing to the inherent selfishness of the human heart. It rather proceeds from a certain hopelessness of remedying excessive and organic ill. To a sensitive being, pity is not seldom pain. And when at last it is perceived that such pity cannot lead to effectual succour, common sense bids they should be rid of it. What I saw that morning persuaded me that the scrivener was the victim of an innate and incurable disorder. I might give alms to his body; but his body did not pain him; it was his soul that suffered, and his soul I could not reach.[40]

Having resolved that Bartleby's needs were spiritual rather than physical, the narrator more readily reaches the prudential conclusion that neither moral nor divine law precludes him from barring Bartleby from his office.

However, the constraint on charity that proves decisive in Bartleby's case is neither economic nor psychological prudence, but rather the narrator's consciousness of his own legal entitlement. It is that consciousness—a concern that his legal property is threatened by his charitable impulse—that cabins his impulse toward charity and propels him toward his repulsion of Bartleby. It is in this sense that the story "unmasks" the role of law and legal rhetoric in the construction of a quite specific consciousness that legitimates and masks human suffering. In the pivotal psychic action of the story, the narrator makes clear that although the meek may indeed some day inherit the earth, he, the narrator, has neither the desire nor the intention of allowing them to inherit his part of it. Ultimately, it is his own felt entitlement to property that fully checks, and trumps, his impulse to charity:

> [A]s the idea came upon me of [Bartleby's] . . . possibly turning out a long-lived man, and keep occupying my chambers, and denying my authority; and perplexing my visitors; and scandalizing my professional reputation; and casting a general gloom over the premises; keeping soul and body together to the last upon his savings, (for doubtless he spent but half a dime a day), and in the end perhaps outlive me, and claim possession of my office by right of his perpetual occupancy; as all these dark anticipations crowded upon me more and more, and my friends continually intruded their relentless remarks upon the apparition in my room, a great change was wrought in me. I resolved to gather all my faculties together, and for ever rid me of this intolerable incubus.[41]

What he could not do, however, was force Bartleby from the premises. He simply *could* not, morally, do something so barbaric:

> What shall I do? What ought I to do? What does conscience say I *should* do with this man, or rather ghost? Rid myself of him, I must; go, he shall. But how? You will not thrust him, the poor, pale, passive mortal,—you will not thrust such a helpless creature out of your door? you will not dishonour yourself by such cruelty? No, I will not, I cannot do that.[42]

By force of this reasoning, the narrator is led to his bizarre, somewhat pathetic, absurd, but utterly legalistic conclusion: he moves his offices, leaving Bartleby on the premises, since he can't bring himself to forcibly eject Bartleby from the office. Shortly thereafter, Bartleby is taken to the Tombs where, after preferring not to eat, he dies.

What to make of this peculiar story? Richard Weisberg, surely the foremost contemporary Melville authority attuned to the complex legal and jurisprudential themes so often explored in Melville's fiction, compares *Bartleby* to *Billy Budd, Sailor*. [43] In Bartleby, in Weisberg's judgment, Melville presents simply a gentler rendition of the legalistic themes explored in more depth in the later story: Bartleby, no less than Billy Budd, then, if we spell out the extrapolation, tells the story of a wordy lawyer's disingenuous, subtle, and resentful persecution, and ultimately destruction, of a nonverbal, paganistic man of paganistic nature. But even if one accepts Weisberg's controversial reading of Budd,[44] there's something amiss in extending this theme to embrace *Bartleby* as well. *Unlike* the character of Captain Vere in *Billy Budd, Sailor,* the lawyer in this story of Wall Street is for the most part a sympathetically drawn character. He is insightful, somewhat self-deprecatory, generous to his employees, for the most part charitable to Bartleby, and charming. He does not have the asocial, bookish, twisted, complicated psyche of the "starry-eyed Vere." Unlike Vere he is good company. He does not seem to be filled with *ressentiment*. Nor does he order Bartleby executed or anything remotely close: the worst he does is to stand on his rights, and he does that, ultimately, only after first offering to care for Bartleby in his own home. And, to continue the contrast, unlike the character of Billy Budd Bartleby does not exude an appealing childlike innocence, or an instinctive talent for peacemaking, or a natural love of his fellows. Perhaps most tellingly, and in the sharpest contrast to "Baby Budd," Bartleby is anything but physically beautiful. He is deathly and pale, not joyful and radiant. We are more drawn to the narrator of this tale than we are to Vere, and we are most assuredly more repelled by the character of Bartleby than by the portrait of Budd. Whatever this story is about, it does not seem to be simply a rehearsal, or an echo, of the themes of ressentiment and legal perversion so thoroughly explored in *Billy Budd, Sailor.*

Brook Thomas's reading, discussed above, seems more convincing:

Thomas reads *Bartleby* as in some way about the existence of an alienated workforce brought on by the industrial revolution, and the complicity of law, and particularly the common law of contracts and torts, in legitimating that alienation. But like Weisberg's, Thomas's reading also requires him to depart from the narrative story line itself. As noted above, Thomas reads the character of Bartleby as a *stand-in* or representative of the existence of an alienated workforce, rather than more simply reading the character as a member of it:

> Allotted machinelike roles, neither the lawyer nor the scrivener is a free agent. Nevertheless, they receive unequal rewards for fulfilling their tasks. Bartleby's job implicitly links him to the world of exploited workers produced by the same market system that allows the lawyer to live a comfortable life serving the rich. Thus, another possible reason for the lawyer's keeping Bartleby out of sight is that he is trying to repress his awareness of the existence of this repressed labor force. . . .
> Bartleby shows that the underworld exists within the world of Wall Street itself. To be sure, that world is present in the story before the arrival of Bartleby, in the person of the lawyer's three other employees, but their ultimate submissiveness allows the lawyer to continue to repress his awareness of its existence. . . . Bartleby's eccentricity does not. Hauntingly present, Bartleby becomes a bizarre representative of the existence of an underworld of workers that the lawyer and his class tried to ignore.[45]

Thomas goes on to argue that the story should be understood as, in part, a critique of the displacement of paternalism with a laissez-faire tilt in torts and contracts, as evidenced by such nineteenth century inventions as the fellow-servant rule. I have already discussed one problem, also noted by Thomas's critics, with this reading: the actual physical injuries Bartleby sustains (if any) have nothing to do with the fellow-servant rule, and the more serious psychic injury he endures is surely not the sort of injury that might have been compensated under either a more paternalistic understanding of master-servant relations or a more regulatory regime governing the workplace.[46] The second problem, however, less noted by Thomas's critics, is that by making Bartleby a stand-in, essentially, for factory workers who *were* maimed, killed, and grotesquely uncompensated by nineteenth-century tort and contract law, Thomas gives the story straightforward thematic content, but in so doing has lost sight of its particularity: its focus on the work of copying deeds and trust agreements in a Wall Street legal office in the middle of the nineteenth century. If Melville had wanted to write about oppressed factory workers he surely could have, and in fact did in a story written right after *Bartleby,* entitled "The Paradise of Bachelors and the Tartarus of Maids." In that story Melville does indeed quite vividly contrast the luxurious life of lawyers with the hellish conditions of the factories that produce the paper on which the lawyers rely, and the women who labor in those factories. But that story is not this one.

By combining, in a sense, parts of Thomas's reading with Weisberg's (implicit) one, we reach, I think, an understanding of the story stronger than either standing alone. Weisberg is surely right that this story, like *Billy Budd,* is about the psyche of the lawyer, and Thomas is surely right that the story is in some sense about the exploitation of workers. But we don't need to view the "psychic story" as a story of ressentiment, and we don't need to view the "exploitation story" as a story about the effect of the fellow-servant rule on injured factory workers. In fact to do so renders Bartleby peculiarly *redundant:* Melville explores the theme of ressentiment in *Billy Budd* and, as noted above, explores the exploitation of factory workers in "The Paradise of Bachelors and the Tartarus of Maids." Rather, the psychic story told in *Bartleby* is the story of *legitimation,* not ressentiment. What is driving the narrator in *Bartleby* is not ressentiment—a jealous, wordy urge to conquer and displace natural paganistic heroism—but a need to legitimate his own wealth and position of comparative privilege. And the story of exploitation told in *Bartleby* is the story of the exploitation of office workers—workers doing the mechanical work of producing copied words which themselves mechanically convert nature into property and profit. There is no need to view the office worker as a stand-in for the maimed factory worker, injured by a machine for which, under the auspices of the fellow-servant rule, the employer need not take responsibility. Office work is the subject matter of the story, and the subject of its implicit political critique.

Such a reading, I think, preserves the integrity of the narrative and also explains the modern reader's affective attachment and repulsions to the characters in the story. The narrator of this story is simply not as evil, or as *twisted,* or as psychically damaged, or, ultimately, as destructive, as Captain Vere. The "story" of legitimation, unlike the story of ressentiment, is not a story of the viciousness and moral hypocrisy of men of letters. In short, we like the narrator of this story—even if he does do a "snug business with rich men's bonds and morgages"—because he's really *not* such a bad guy. Likewise, Bartleby is not an exploited, maimed, victimized factory worker, nor does he "represent" them. He is who he is—an office worker who refuses to be productive, eventually refuses even to accept charity, and in short refuses to behave rationally. Our exasperation with him, like the narrator's own, is not a pale reflection of the factory owner's exploitative failure, sanctioned by the law, to take responsibility for the injuries caused by his machines. It is an entirely understandable frustration over the refusal of someone to play according to a social and political script we've all come to accept as relatively unproblematic, and in any event more or less inevitable.

To conclude by stating the obvious: the professional, legal, educated reader of this story likes and identifies with this narrator, whether or not he identifies with Vere, for the simple reason that he so resembles us. We like him because we are like him. Whether or not "we"—the professional or educated readers of these stories—suffer from the ressentiment that afflicts Vere, we all legitimate our own privilege, and like the narrator we all do so in part by repressing our awareness of Bartleby's physicality, and his need for biological sustenance. There are elements of Bartleby's obstinate refusal to produce, to *help himself,* to stand on his own, to even accept help from others, in every panhandler, homeless person, drug addict, chronically un- and underemployed, and mentally deranged person we pass on the street. Their suffering is not a stand-in for the suffering of more economically exploited factory workers; their suffering is their own. And we legitimate it with the same psychic stratagems employed by the narrator: we ascribe to them either free agency or an "incurable malady," we insist that the cause of their illness is spiritual rather than physical need, we limit our felt capacity for empathy, and most of all we police the moral entitlements of the meek by reference to the legal entitlements of the propertied, including our own. Whatever the meek might inherit, they won't inherit *mine,* and my charitable reactions are cabined accordingly. All these stratagems feel morally unproblematic when we encounter them in this narrative because they feel so utterly familiar; that the narrator employs them makes him no worse than ordinary. Our identification with and sympathy for the narrator is by no means evidence of our own mendacity.

It *is,* however, evidence of our own complicity, and it is complicity in a system which *vigorously* legitimates the suffering and exploitation of wage workers not only in factories and on farms, but in offices as well. For while the narrator in *Bartleby* is no villain—as Thomas notes, he is no Dickensian evil capitalist—he is also no hero. He does indeed, as Thomas insists, lack agency—thereby precluding either heroism or villainy. His resolution of his moral dilemma—to remove his office from Bartleby, since he can't remove Bartleby from his office—is truly comical: one pictures a small-bodied man, empowered by law but lacking in physical strength, literally running down Wall Street, leading a small horde of packers and movers carrying furniture, all so as to escape the unappealing need to remove an oppressive mentally ill but utterly harmless individual from an office building. He also lacks imagination: he can't fathom alternative solutions to his problems.

But what he most lacks, of course, is critical distance from the underlying economic and political causes of not only Bartleby's malady, but his own as well. He cannot question the deeper premises of a system which led him and Bartleby to their point of crisis. He can more easily abandon Bartleby than his own consciousness, and his consciousness, structured and constrained by legal entitlements, is what (penultimately) points him away from common humanity—in the form not only of Bartleby's need, but also in the form of his own impulse to care.

A Jury of Her Peers

A Jury of Her Peers, or *Trifles* as it was alternatively entitled, tells the story of the investigation of the murder of a farmer, killed in his sleep by a rope around his neck, in the second decade of the twentieth century. The farmer's wife is the chief suspect. The story opens as the murder is being investigated inside the home, from which the wife has been removed, by the sheriff, a neighbor, and the prosecutor. The men have brought two women with them: the sheriff's wife, a Mrs. Peters, and the neighbor's wife, Mrs. Hale. These two women sit in the kitchen and talk while their husbands examine the rest of the house for some evidence that might supply a motive with which to incriminate the wife in her husband's murder. The women's conversation and actions in the kitchen constitute the entire action of the story, and the dialogue of the play.

While sitting in the kitchen the women discover precisely the evidence of motive the men are in search of. Amidst the various "trifles" contained in a kitchen which the men, in their condescending dismissal of women's concerns, overlook, the women find what is for them clear evidence of a severely disturbed and abusive relationship: the kitchen is in disarray, the table half cleaned, quilting blocks are oddly and badly sewn—all of which, they conclude, evidence domestic work abruptly interrupted. They eventually happen upon the clinching piece of evidence: a hidden songbird which had clearly been wrenched from its cage and strangled to death. The women reason that the strangled bird had been treasured by the desperately lonely farmwife for its companionship and killed at the hands of her husband, and must have been the proverbial last straw prompting the wife to kill her abusive husband.

However, through the course of their conversation they also realize that they each (for somewhat different reasons) strongly sympathize and identify with the farmwife. The very evidence which, in the mens' eyes, would inculpate the wife—providing the decisive and necessary evidence of motive—the women view as exculpatory. This metaphorical jury of one's peers metaphorically acquits the farmwife of the murder of her husband, finding the homicide either justified or excused. In a climactic moment of political solidarity with the farmwife, they hide the evidence, insuring that she will not be brought to trial.

Like Melville's *Bartleby,* Glaspell's *A Jury of Her Peers* can be read as a study of the societal and legal legitimation of human suffering— legitimation of the suffering caused, in this case, not by the institution of wage labor but rather by the institution of marriage. The story is structurally parallel to *Bartleby* in a number of respects. In *Jury* as in *Bartleby,* we are given an evocative description of the injury and suffering brought on by a social institution, which is itself defined by law as well as custom. Both stories provide an account of the ways in which law legitimates that suffering. Unlike *Bartleby,* however, which gives us an inside look at the legitimated consciousness of the privileged, *A Jury of Her Peers* provides, through the wives' conversation, an examination of the legitimated consciousness of the oppressed. What *Jury* provides, ultimately, is an account of the ways in which political action between oppressed women is frustrated—in large part by the construction of individuality implicit in the role of the wife.

THE INJURY

This novella—which for any number of obvious reasons has become canonical within the feminist legal community—contains, among much else, a particular and highly critical portrayal of the institution of marriage. Through marriage, the story suggests, young girls are separated from their communities and families of nurturance, and isolated within heterosexual relationships in which they are expected to altruistically sacrifice their own needs and subordinate their own wills, and which are often—typically?—far less emotionally nourishing than the communities from which they came. That lack—the absence of emotional nourishment—is severely injurious. Whether or not a marriage is physically abusive, a marriage in which a woman's need for intimacy and emotional companionship is not met, and which simultaneously severs her from sources of emotional nourishment, is profoundly damaging. It entails immense amounts of human suffering, most or all of which, like the suffering incident to wage labor, goes entirely unnoticed, unrecognized, and uncompensated by the law.

The injury occasioned by such a marriage in Minnie Foster's life was extreme. Minnie Foster, the women's conversation in the kitchen makes clear, moved from girlhood to an early marriage to an incommunicative, cold man, and more generally, from a life of delight and pleasure to a life dominated by loneliness and ugliness. It is that loneliness and ugliness, more than any other feature of the marriage, to which Mrs. Hale and Mrs. Peters return again and again in their attempt to make sense of the apparent murder that faces them. Thus, in the opening paragraphs, the narrator explains that the house itself was lonesome:

> [T]hey had gone up a little hill and could see the Wright place now, and seeing it did not make her feel like talking. It looked very lonesome this cold March morning. It had always been a lonesome looking place. It was down in a hollow, and the poplar trees around it were lonesome-looking trees.[47]

The lonesomeness endured by Minnie Foster in this house (aggravated by her husband's refusal to install a telephone), was further underscored by the ugliness and hardness of life in a home pressed for cash, and without light, liveliness, or delight. Mrs. Hale, the neighbor, comments:

> "Wright was close!" she exclaimed, holding up a shabby black skirt that bore the marks of much making over. "I think maybe that's why she kept so much to herself. I s'pose she felt she couldn't do her part; and then, you don't enjoy things when you feel shabby. She used to wear pretty clothes and be lively—when she was Minnie Foster, one of the town girls, singing in the choir. But that—oh, that was twenty years ago."[48]

In a similar mode, she comments on the stove:

> "How'd you like to cook on this?"—pointing with the poker to the broken lining. She opened the oven door and started to express her opinion of the oven; but she was swept into her own thoughts, thinking of what it would mean, year after year, to have that stove to wrestle with. The thought of Minnie Foster trying to bake in that oven—and the thought of her never going over to see Minnie Foster . . .
> She was startled by hearing Mrs. Peters say: "A person gets discouraged—and loses heart."[49]

The absence of objects of beauty in such a life is an assault on the senses, and an injury itself. In putting together sewing materials to take to Minnie Foster, Mrs. Hale comments:

> "Here's some red," said Mrs. Hale, bringing out a roll of cloth. Underneath that was a box. "Here, maybe her scissors are in here—and her things." She held it up. "What a pretty box! I'll warrant that was something she had a long time ago—when she was a girl."[50]

The grimness of this life—surely bearable if undertaken within a companionable marriage—became intolerable when coupled with her husband's personality and character. The women repeatedly make the point by contrasting Minnie's life before and after her marriage:

> "Not having children makes less work," mused Mrs. Hale. . . . "but it makes a quiet house—and Wright out to work all day—and no

company when he did come in. Did you know John Wright, Mrs. Peters?"

"Not to know him. I've seen him in town. They say he was a good man."

"Yes—good . . . he didn't drink, and kept his word as well as most, I guess, and paid his debts. But he was a hard man, Mrs. Peters. Just to pass the time of day with him—." She stopped, shivered a little. "Like a raw wind that gets to the bone." Her eyes fell upon the cage on the table before her, and she added, almost bitterly: "I should think she would've wanted a bird!" . . .

"She—come to think of it, she was kind of like a bird herself. Real sweet and pretty, but kind of timid and—fluttery. How—she—did—change."[51]

In contemplating the significance of the strangled songbird, both Hale and Peters eventually identify with, and sympathize with, the injury occasioned by this forced, quiet, loneliness:

Mrs. Hale had not moved. "If there had been years and years of—nothing, then a bird to sing to you, it would be awful—still—after the bird was still . . ."

"I know what stillness is," [Mrs. Peters] said, in a queer, monotonous voice. "When we homesteaded in Dakota, and my first baby died—after he was two years old—and me with no other then—" . . .

"I wish you'd seen Minnie Foster," [Mrs. Hale responded] . . . "when she wore a white dress with blue ribbons, and stood up there in the choir and sang."[52]

What, exactly, is Minnie Foster's injury? In a rich and informative historical analysis, Marina Angel argues persuasively that Susan Glaspell was moved to write *Jury* as the result of a trial on which she had reported as a journalist, which involved the murder of a husband by a physically abused wife.[53] Angel shows that the dominant issue of the trial—and in this respect, apparently, the trial was typical—concerned the prosecutor's attempts to *introduce* evidence of that abuse so as to provide precisely what was missing in the fictional story: evidence of motive. The defendant and loyal family members tried just as strenuously to keep evidence of the abusive quality of the marriage *out*—the result being a curious reversal of contemporary tactics. The defendant and witnesses would offer sometimes perjurious testimony of the *contentedness* of the marriage, to support the inference that the murder must have been committed by a third party. The prosecutor would try to show the abuse.[54] The defendant and her witnesses were thus involved in precisely the tactics employed by Mrs. Hale and Mrs. Peters: manipulation and destruction of evidence so as to lead to the false inference at trial that the wife lacked a motive for her husband's murder. Angel's historical context provides an important clue to Glaspell's intended meaning. Clearly as a journalist and feminist Glaspell was taken by this profoundly unjust alignment of tactic and end result: to achieve the right result, the trial had to be illegally manipulated, so as to *underscore* the legitimacy of the institution responsible for the woman's suffering. An abused woman had to aggressively deny her own abuse—she had to wrongly claim she was happily married—in order to win a just result. This is, of course, legitimation with a vengeance.

Against this historical backdrop, A Jury of Her Peers can indeed be seamlessly read as a straightforward indictment of a score of sexist and misogynist doctrines of law, all of which Angel skillfully lays out. Obviously, it is an indictment of the exclusion of women from juries and voting booths (Glaspell was an active suffragist). But just as clearly it is an indictment of the system's utter hypocrisy: remember, at the same time women were routinely prosecuted and convicted for murdering violently abusive husbands, husbands were just as routinely *released*—with no criminal charge whatsoever—for murdering adulterous wives. And just as *Bartleby* can be read, and Thomas so reads it, as an indictment of the law's failure to incorporate ameliorative doctrines (such as workers' comp) to remove the harsh edges of wage labor, so *Jury* can be read, and Angel so reads it, as an indictment of the law's failure to incorporate ameliorative doctrines (such as battered spouse syndrome) to ameliorate the harshness of patriarchy. As *Bartleby* can be read as a "stand-in" for the more *truly* oppressed worker, so Minnie can be taken as a "stand-in" for the more profoundly injured battered spouse. And it's worth noting that Angel has considerably more historical evidence for her abstraction than Thomas has for his: Glaspell really *did* report on, and dwell on, *precisely* these cases—cases involving what we would today recognize, and "class"ify as, battered women who kill. By reading the fictional Minnie as a stand-in for the historically real battered women who killed, the story can be given seamless thematic content. On this reading, the evidence Hale and Peters hide is evidence of the violent *abuse* of Minnie Foster by her husband. That is the injury she sustained, evidence of which should have exculpated instead of inculpating her. Such a trial, and such a system—in which evidence of violent abuse disserves rather than serves the interest of the woman who kills so as to defend herself against it—quite aggressively and bald-facedly legitimates that violence, and directly legitimates, and masks, the unutterable amounts of human suffering it causes. Such a system is egregiously out of line with fundamental norms of justice, and this story's dramatic action reveals it as such.

There is, though, a problem with Angel's reading, and it parallels the problem noted above with Thomas's: it is curiously at odds with the facts of the story. The women in the kitchen never explicitly conclude that Minnie Foster was violently abused. They never even suggest it. We have no more evidence that she has been physically abused than we have of Bartleby having been maimed by factory machinery. Again, it is only by reading her as a stand-in—a representative—that we can make sense of this story as about the sorry legal predicament of battered women who killed their abusers at the turn of the century.

But why make this abstraction? Minnie Foster's *own* injury is described, repeatedly and convincingly: she's *lonely*. She's isolated. She has no light, liveliness, loveliness, delight, conversation, or companionship in her life, and that is enough to create a living hell. In fact, she is enduring a living death in her farmhouse, no less than Bartleby and his coscriveners are enduring a living death at their desks in their work cubbies. Her emotional needs for intimacy are as trampled upon by this man, and this patriarchal regime that produced him, as Bartleby's physical needs for shelter and food are trampled upon by laissez-faire capitalism. We don't need to view Minnie as a stand-in for battered women any more than we need read Bartleby as a stand-in for maimed factory workers. The injury the story actually depicts—the utter, lonely isolation of an emotionally dead marriage—is bad enough. It is Hale and Peters' sympathy and understanding with the sufferance of *that* injury, I think, which leads them to hide evidence of it. And it is the reader's sympathy and understanding of it as well, furthermore, which lead us to believe, at least for a moment, that perhaps they were right to do so.

At any rate, if we at least permit an alternative and more literal reading of this story as being not about the physically abused wife, but about the emotional and psychic injury of living in a marriage that is empty of emotional succor, a quite different set of meanings emerges. If we view the injury as emotional rather than physical, the story is not simply a prescient tract for incorporation of a battered spouse syndrome defense into the criminal law, or even more broadly the refusal of the legal system to amend itself to incorporate perspectives distinctive to women's lives, and thus render it more just. What it is about is the injury done to women through the rending of their emotional attachments to their largely female communities of origin, and of friendships, and the displacement of those communities with the too often isolating, cold, and nonsustaining relationship of heterosexual marriage. And although the story is unambiguously about *law*, it is not simply about the law's failure to incorporate doctrines that would ameliorate its harshness in dealing with the extreme injuries sustained within these marriages by battered women who kill. It is, rather, as I will argue below, about the complicity of law in constructing the consciousness of privilege and deprivation that renders such suffering invisible.

THE LEGITIMATION

How, then, is the suffering within abusive marriages, whether the abuse is emotional or physical, legitimated? Partly, of course, it is legitimated by brute legal force: a wife who rebels against this suffering by killing her husband will be charged with murder, and evidence of his abusiveness against her—even if violent, at the time of this story— most assuredly will be inculpatory evidence of motive. If Marina Angel is right, then the women in this story took an action which at the time was not unheard of: family and friends of women accused of killing their husbands often conspired among themselves to keep evidence of the abusive character of the slain spouse out of the trial. Such evidence would help, not hurt, the prosecution by supplying a motive. Likewise, the exclusion of women from juries quite brutally and forcibly legitimated the exclusion from the public consciousness of awareness of the obvious fact that constant abuse, belittlement, and condescension, can indeed drive someone to kill. Exclusion of women from juries and from public life in general barred from public consciousness awareness of the overwhelming hypocrisy in allowing knowledge of a wife's adultery to constitute, in any number of jurisdictions, a full defense to a husband's murder of his wife, while even physical abuse of the wife by the husband constituted inculpatory evidence of motive, rather than exculpatory evidence of justification and excuse. In a system so blatantly skewed, it was inevitable that women would and did hide evidence in precisely the manner of Mrs. Hale and Mrs. Peters, and as recorded both journalistically and in fiction by Susan Glaspell.

A Jury of Her Peers was certainly intended to be read as, and certainly should be read as, a condemnation of this exclusionary unfairness. Nevertheless, the novella is not only a tract for women's equality, nor for battered spouse defenses, nor for women's participation on juries—although it is most assuredly in part all of these. Like *Bartleby*, what this story vividly records is not so much the forced oppression of a class of people by law, as their ideological oppression by a cultural system of meanings in the construction of which law is complicit. But whereas *Bartleby* chronicles the system of meanings which cabin and constrain the charitable instincts of the powerful, *Jury* chronicles the system of meanings which cabin and constrain and frustrate the political consciousness of the weak. What *Jury* is about are the formidable obstacles—overwhelmingly ideological and psychic—confronting the political act ultimately taken by Mrs. Peters and Mrs. Hale. The act of defiance and solidarity taken by these two women is as difficult and "unnatural" for them as is the act of charity for the narrator in *Bartleby*. What the novella does is provide a descriptive account of the women's state of mind, which might explain why this is so.

What are those obstacles? What *is* the content of the "false consciousness" of the oppressed, which renders their acquiescence so seemingly natural and voluntary? First, and as suggested by the title of the play—*Trifles*—on which the novella is based the women have indeed to some extent internalized the trivialization of their interests, concerns, and perspectives so consistently voiced by the men in the story. The sheriff and county prosecutor in *Jury*—the only male characters—are indeed two-dimensional, as male students who read the work in my "Law and Literature" class invariably complain, but their habitual belittlement, negation, bantering abuse, and condescension of their wives and female neighbors is surely not unfamiliar to even modern readers. This bantering abuse takes its toll—if you hear it often enough, you do begin to believe it. And these women hear it,

Glaspell makes clear, relentlessly. It is as present to them as the air they breathe.

But on the other hand, we shouldn't make too much of it—the women themselves do not. Interestingly, the women's response to their own belittlement from the men they marry is ambiguous. Sometimes the women's comments and their self-reflections do echo it, evidencing a badly diminished self-concept. At other times, however, they clearly resist it, gaining strength from each other in so doing:

> The sheriff . . . looked all around . . . "Nothing here but kitchen things," he said with a little laugh for the insignificance of kitchen things.
>
> The county attorney was looking at the cupboard—a peculiar ungainly structure . . . As if its queerness attracted him, he got a chair and opened the upper part and looked in. After a moment he drew his hand away sticky.
>
> "Here's a nice mess," he said resentfully.
>
> The two women had drawn nearer, and now the sheriff's wife spoke.
>
> "Oh—her fruit," she said, looking to Mrs. Hale for sympathetic understanding. She turned back to the county attorney and explained: "She worried about that when it turned so cold last night. She said the fire would go out and her jars might burst."
>
> Mrs. Peters' husband broke into a laugh.
>
> "Well, can you beat the women! Held for murder, and worrying about her preserves!"
>
> "Oh, well," said Mrs. Hale's husband, with good natured superiority, "women are used to worrying over trifles."
>
> The two women moved a little closer together. Neither of them spoke. The county attorney seemed suddenly to remember his manners—and think of his future.
>
> "And yet, said he," . . . "for all their worries, what would we do without the ladies?"
>
> The women did not speak, did not unbend. He went to the sink and began washing his hands. He turned to wipe them on the roller towel—whirled it for a cleaner place.
>
> "Dirty towels! Not much of a housekeeper, would you say, ladies?"
>
> "There's a great deal of work to be done on a farm," said Mrs. Hale stiffly. . . . "Those towels get dirty awful quick. Men's hands aren't always as clean as they might be."
>
> "Ah, loyal to your sex, I see," he laughed.[55]

The men's attitude toward their wives and toward women's work accounts for their own obtuseness, but it does not entirely account for the women's difficulty in forming common cause with Minnie Foster. Of far greater importance, at least in Mrs. Hale's mind, was the physical and emotional isolation of each woman from every other. Mrs. Hale returns to this isolation—this failure, or inability, on the part of the women to sustain a community among themselves—again and again, and she returns to this theme, throughout the story, with increasing degrees of remorse. She first comments on it in a fairly matter-of-fact tone:

> Time and time again it had been in her mind, "I ought to go over and see Minnie Foster"—she still thought of her as Minnie Foster, though for twenty years she had been Mrs. Wright. And then there was always something to do and Minnie Foster would go from her mind.[56]

Later, she ascribes her reluctance to visit Minnie to the *cheerlessness* of the household, although at this point for no clearly articulated reason. By now she is uncomfortable with the insight, and refrains from discussing the matter in the presence of the men:

> "But you and Mrs. Wright were neighbors. I suppose you were friends, too."
> Martha Hale shook her head.
> "I've seen little enough of her of late years. I've not been in this house—it's more than a year."
> "And why was that? You didn't like her?"
> "I liked her well enough," she replied with spirit. "Farmers' wives have their hands full, Mr. Henderson. And then —" she looked around the kitchen.
> . . . "It never seemed a very cheerful place," said she, more to herself than to him.
> "No," he agreed; "I don't think any one would call it cheerful. I shouldn't say she had the home-making instinct."
> "Well, I don't know as Wright had, either," she muttered.
> "You mean they didn't get on very well?" he was quick to ask.
> "No, I don't mean anything," she answered. . . . "But I don't think a place would be any the cheerfuller for John Wright's bein' in it."[57]

Later, when the men have left the room, she explains in more detail her own motives and regret for having abandoned Minnie Foster, to Mrs. Peters:

"But I tell you what I do wish, Mrs. Peters. I wish I had come over sometimes when she was here. I wish—I had. . . . I stayed away because it weren't cheerful—and that's why I ought to have come. I . . . never liked this place. Maybe because it's down in a hollow and you don't see the road. I don't know what it is, but it's a lonesome place, and always was. I wish I had come over to see Minnie Foster sometimes. I can see now—" She did not put it into words.[58]

Eventually, she suggests a more ominous reason for her reluctance to involve herself—her suspicion that Foster's problems are not altogether different from her own. By this point, almost at the end of the story, she is clearly panicked and guilt-ridden by her belated recognition of her neglect of her one-time friend:

The picture of that girl, the fact that she had lived neighbor to that girl for twenty years, and had let her die for lack of life, was suddenly more than she could bear.

"Oh, I *wish* I'd come over here once in a while!" she cried. "That was a crime! That was a crime! Who's going to punish that?"

"I might'a *known* she needed help! I tell you, it's *queer,* Mrs. Peters. We live close together, and we live far apart. We all go through the same things—it's all just a different kind of the same thing! If it weren't— why do you and I *understand?* Why do we know—what we know this minute?"[59]

Third, the women in *Jury* are reluctant to act in solidarity and on the basis of their knowledge because of their sense of the futility of political effort—the sheer weight of the given. "The law's the law," Mrs. Peters repeatedly reminds Mrs. Hale—even if, as Mrs. Hale retorts, "A bad stove's a bad stove."

The major obstacle, however, facing the women's groping attempts toward solidarity with Minnie Foster is ultimately voiced by the men. Each woman is isolated from every other, not only by physical distance, but through the legally created and perpetuated institution of marriage itself and the state of mind that it inculcates. Mrs. Peters in particular is continually described as a sheriff's wife—even if, as Mrs. Hale opines at the outset of the story, she doesn't quite look the part. "Of course, Mrs. Peters is one of us" the county attorney remarks, "in a manner of entrusting responsibility."[60]

At the dramatic climax of the story, the county attorney returns to the matter of Mrs. Peters' legal status, driving the point home. The women watch in fascinated, suspended horror as he narrowly avoids accidentally uncovering the hidden dead bird, while he explains his reasons for not feeling the need to examine with any care the items the women have gathered to take to the accused farmwife. Part of the reason is the trust he places in Mrs. Peters as a representative of the law:

> "No, Mrs. Peters doesn't need supervising. For that matter, a sheriff's wife is married to the law. Ever think of it that way, Mrs. Peters?"
> . . . Mrs. Peters had turned away. When she spoke, her voice was muffled.
> "Not—just that way," she said.
> "Married to the law!" chuckled Mrs. Peters' husband.[61]

The county attorney is surely right. It is precisely her "marriage to the law" and the law's marriage to patriarchy, that more than any-thing—certainly more than a falsely diminished view of herself—keeps her loyal to him and his sex, rather than to Minnie Foster and her suffering. The function of law, in this story, is not only to hypocritically and unequally punish Minnie Foster for the justified or excusable murder of her husband, where it would not have punished a cuckolded man. The function of law is to validate, through the institution of marriage, the isolation of women from each other.

Conclusion: Breaking Away

Neither of these stories is tragic. *A Jury of Her Peers*, in fact, ends somewhat triumphantly: the two women do ultimately join forces with each other and in solidarity with Minnie Foster, protecting her from her legal fate. Throughout the story, at each moment of dawning comprehension of the commonness of their fate, the women's eyes meet in recognition, bringing them the physical proximity to each other that their own marriages have torn asunder. As they first ac-knowledge the unevenness of Minnie Wright's sewing—and the import of that sewing—their eyes meet:

> "The sewing" said Mrs. Peters, in a troubled way. "All the rest of them have been so nice and even—but—this one. Why, it looks as if she didn't know what she was about!"

Their eyes met—something flashed to life, passed between them; then, as if with an effort, they seemed to pull away from each other. A moment Mrs. Hale sat there, her hands folded over that sewing which was so unlike all the rest of the sewing. Then she had pulled a knot and drawn the threads.

"Oh, what are you doing, Mrs. Hale?" asked the sheriff's wife, startled.

"Just pulling out a stitch or two that's not sewed very good," said Mrs Hale, mildly.[62]

Similarly, when they first find the broken door of the birdcage, their eyes meet in recognition:

"Look at this door," [Mrs. Peters] said slowly. "It's broke. One hinge has been pulled apart."

Mrs. Hale came nearer.

"Looks as if some one must have been—rough with it."

Again their eyes met—startled, questioning, apprehensive. For a moment neither spoke nor stirred. Then Mrs. Hale, turning away, said brusquely:

"If they're going to find any evidence, I wish they'd be about it. I don't like this place."[63]

When they discover the dead bird, the same action is repeated:

The sheriff's wife again bent closer.

"Somebody wrung its neck," said she, in a voice that was slow and deep.

And then again the eyes of the two women met—this time clung together in a look of dawning comprehension, of growing horror. Mrs. Peters looked from the dead bird to the broken door of the cage. Again their eyes met.[64]

And finally, when the women act in joint conspiracy, their eyes actually seem to direct their physical actions:

Again—for one final moment—the two women were alone in that kitchen.

Martha Hale sprang up, her hands tight together, looking at that other woman, with whom it rested. At first she could not see her eyes, for the sheriff's wife had not turned back since she turned away at that suggestion of being married to the law. But now Mrs. Hale made her turn back. Her eyes made her turn back. Slowly, unwillingly, Mrs. Peters turned her head until her eyes met the eyes of the other woman. There was a moment when they held each other in a steady, burning look, in which there was no evasion nor flinching. Then Martha Hale's eyes pointed the way to the basket in which was hidden the thing that would make certain the conviction of the other woman—that woman who was not there and yet who had been there with them all through that hour. . . .

There was the sound of a knob turning in the inner door. Martha Hale snatched the box from the sheriff's wife, and got it in the pocket of her big coat just as the sheriff and the county attorney came back into the kitchen.[65]

In recognition of the women's triumph, the story ends almost comically, affirming both the political solidarity, but also the secrecy and commonality of women's shared labor. Referring to an earlier conversation in which the men had mocked the women's interest in Minnie's quilting, and more specifically in what quilting technique she might have intended for the completion of the unfinished project, the county attorney asks:

"Well, Henry," . . . "at least we found out that she was not going to quilt it. She was going to—what is you call it, ladies?"

Mrs. Hale's hand was against the pocket of her coat.

"We call it—knot it, Mr. Henderson."[66]

Bartleby as well—although a much sadder story—ends on a note of solidarity, which has also been foreshadowed in earlier scenes. In fact, throughout the story, the narrator has moments of acting against the script of arm's-length contractual behavior, just as Hale and Peters have moments of acting against the script of obsequious wifely submissiveness. The narrator's moments of sympathy for Bartleby, and his feeling of common brotherhood with him, although invariably short-lived, are seemingly genuine. Upon discovering that the unproductive scrivener has also become a tenant, after registering shock, the narrator remarks sympathetically upon his poverty, his loneliness, and his manifest misery:

What miserable friendlessness and loneliness are here revealed! His poverty is great; but his solitude, how horrible! Think of it . . . here Bartleby makes his home . . .

For the first time in my life a feeling of overpowering stinging melancholy seized me. Before I had never experienced aught but a non-unpleasing sadness. The bond of a common humanity now drew me irresistibly to gloom. A fraternal melancholy! For both I and Bartleby were sons of Adam. I remembered the bright silks and sparkling faces I had seen that day, in gala trim, swan-like sailing down the Mississippi of Broadway; and I contrasted them with the pallid copyist, and thought to myself, Ah, happiness courts the light, so we deem the world is gay; but misery hides aloof, so we deem that misery there is none. These sad fancyings . . . led on to other and more special thoughts, concerning the eccentricities of Bartleby. Presentiments of strange discoveries hovered round me. The scrivener's pale form appeared to me laid out, among uncaring strangers, in its shivering winding sheet.[67]

To what modern use might these stories be put? They remind us, minimally, of "the misery that hides aloof," and guard against the temptation of concluding that "misery there is none." They also guard against a quite specific and specifically modern tendency—and temptation—to validate and legitimate suffering by denying the existence of large groups of victims. I am thinking here not of the "blame the victim" excesses of the modern political right, but of modern *liberatory* discourses, and particularly the writings of a number of modern feminists who urge feminists generally to eschew the focus on women's victimization which has unquestionably been at the core, historically, of virtually all strands of twentieth-century feminism. To insistently describe women as "victims," victimized by their common conditions, we are told, is to deny each individual in that group "agency," to demean her in her uniqueness, to insult her self-possession, awareness, and autonomy, and to deny her felt freedoms.[68] But what if there are, in fact, just such victims, who have, in fact, little if any autonomy, no sense of self-possession, and no "agency" to speak of beyond the false freedom to deny their own victimization? If so, then there are groups of women suffering who possess neither heroism nor villainy but are rather, and simply, victims. And if so, then our refusal to see, discuss, or relieve that victimization is complicity, and it is a complicity against which we should be on guard.

Tort and contract, criminal law, and constitutional law, despite their purported aim of relieving harm, do little to remind us of the presence of such victims among us, and in fact their legitimating discourses do much to worsen the problem. Oddly, it is now *fiction*—including the stories of Bartleby and Minnie Foster—that can most strikingly remind us of the presence of real victims—nonheroic, non-villainous, real people suffering serious but invisible injury. In a curious inversion, we now increasingly demand of actors in true legal dramas either villainy or heroism—or at a minimum, true *agency*—and can only turn to narrative fiction—the well from which we drew stories of heroism in our childhoods—with which to relieve the doldrums of blandness and ambiguities of real life—for depictions of the real suffering of those who have been rendered invisible by the silencing and fictional legitimating discourses of law. *Bartleby* and *Trifles* remind us of the presence and reality of human beings—neither heroes nor villains, and neither free nor in chains—suffering the burden of institutions legitimated by the Rule of Law we hold so dear.

Bartleby and *Trifles* remind modern readers as well, of course, of possibility: the possibility of breaking free of those bonds of complicity. Moments between women, in which women truly look at each other without "evasion or flinching," *are* rare, even in fiction, and certainly in law. Moments of true charity, of true "fraternal melancholy," in which the strong, like the narrator, offer food and shelter to the weak, are rarer still. But they do occur, and they occur in each of these stories: the narrator's charity in *Bartleby* is cabined by his sense of his own legal entitlement, but he nevertheless behaves charitably at the end of the day: he offers Bartleby the shelter of his own home and the warmth of his own embrace, although both offers come too late. Mrs. Hale and Mrs. Peters do forge a common cause with Minnie Foster, despite being married to the law. These moments do not seem to be particularly transcendent, or fantastic; they seem quite realistic, even familiar. *Bartleby* does in the end serve, as Brook Thomas argues, to make the forces of legitimation that constrain the narrator's responses and validate his capitalist privilege seem strange and indefensible. But it does more: it also serves to make the moment of common humanity seem familiar, and even inevitable. *Trifles* likewise does serve, as Marina Angel argues, to render the legitimation of marital violence foreign and unjust. But it too does more: it makes the moment of common cause, albeit fleeting, utterly recognizable. It is in the end a *relief* when the narrator finally recognizes Bartleby's humanity, and it is a relief when Mrs. Hale and Mrs. Peters act in concert on Minnie Foster's behalf. Both stories remind their reader of our recognition of that common bond and that common purpose. And both do so against the considerable weight of legal habit—both the characters' habits and our own.

CHAPTER FIVE

Feminism, Postmodernism, and Law

Postmodern social theory has revolutionized the way critical legal scholars and, to a lesser extent, mainstream legal scholars think of the most fundamental categories of legal theory. By contrast, postmodernism has proven to be far more controversial among feminist legal theorists. This chapter tries to explain and defend the lack of enthusiasm among at least some feminist legal theorists for the great transformative ideas of Michel Foucault, Roberto Unger, and other critical social theorists who have so energized critical legal thought. I will urge that the four central ideas of postmodern social theory that have proven to be of most interest to critical legal theorists—ideas that center around the nature of power, of knowledge, of morality, and of the self—will not further our understanding of patriarchy, and will frustrate rather than further our attempts to end it.

POWER

The first and most defining tenet of postmodern social theory is, to quote Foucault, that "power comes from everywhere."[1] It immediately follows that power is not, for the most part, occasional, censorial, and repressive. Nor are its primary manifestations censorship and repression, as an excessively juridical view of power had taught both legal and social scholars of earlier generations to believe.[2] Rather, according to the critical social theorists, repression is just one form that power might take. Whatever may have been the case historically, in modern times power far more typically takes a positive, inventive, and creative form, the consequences of which are not censorship, silence, or oppression, but rather a multiplicity of positive social inventions. These inventions include knowledge, the concept of knowledge, the liberal self, and the idea of objectivity. Foucault puts the point this way:

> The individual is no doubt the fictitious atom of an "ideological" repre-sentation of society; but he is also a reality fabricated by this specific technology of power that I have called "discipline". *We must cease once and for all to describe the effects of power in negative terms: it "excludes," it "represses," it "censors," it "abstracts," it "masks," it "conceals." In fact, power produces; it produces reality; it produces domains of objects and rituals of truth. The individual and the knowl-edge that may be gained of him belong to this production.* [3]

Foucault's quintessentially social and critical directive—to "cease once and for all to describe the effects of power in negative terms"—has become a unifying methodological commitment of the critical legal studies movement. Indeed, the claim seems tailor-made for the study of law. Following Foucault's mandate, critical legal scholars collectively have taught all of us to think of the productivity rather than the negativity of legal power. They have taught us to see not only our legal institutions and legal outcomes, but also (and more centrally) our legal imaginative constructs and legal knowledge as the inventions and products of a positive political will and *not* as the reflection of a deep social or biological logic, as the accommodation of discrete inter-ests, or as the working out of a necessitarian historical pattern.[4] Largely due to Foucault's influence, the critical legal academy has taught us to think of law as a form of knowledge that is *both* a product of politics and itself a political force which in turn generates other forms of knowledge. To the credit of the critical legal studies move-ment, we have indeed to a considerable degree quit thinking of legal power in negative terms. The result has been an increasingly sophisti-cated understanding of the positive, constructed inventions of law and legal ideology.

Is Foucault's suggestion, though—that we should quit talking about power in negative terms—something feminist legal scholars should heed? Is its underlying assumption—that modern power is creative and productive rather than negative and censorial—as true of modern *patriarchal* power as it seems to be of *legal* power? It is not at all obvious that it is. It certainly does not follow logically from any of the particularized inquiries critical social theorists have made into the various forms of social, legal, intellectual or economic power of the modern era that their general claim will be true of *patriarchal* power as well. It may be, in other words, that a profoundly negative, censorial, patriarchal power lies behind the positive and creative forms of modern social and legal power which are the subject of critical legal or social analysis. If so, we should hardly expect theorists to see this, or to adjust their theory accordingly. But more importantly, if modern patriarchal power is different in this way from other forms of modern social power, then while feminist legal theorists may be well advised to quit thinking of legal power in negative terms, it would be disastrous if we unwittingly generalized from Foucault's suggestion and quit thinking of *patriarchal* power in negative terms.

I want to urge, even plead, that we turn down the Foucauldian invitation to think of power in primarily positive terms. My reason is very simple: women's experiences of patriarchal power, told and re-told in feminist texts, are profoundly unlike anything imagined in Foucault's philosophies. Unlike the institutional "disciplines" that are the subject of Foucault's histories of the workings of power, and unlike the ideological and imaginative forms of power reflected in the legal ideologies, processes, and decisions that are the subject of study for the critical legal studies movement,[5] patriarchal power is experienced by modern women as intensely nondiscursive, as utterly unimaginative, as profoundly negating, and, in short, as frighteningly and pervasively *violent.*[6] So long as this is the case—so long as the experience of violence rather than that of discursive productivity is central to the female experience of patriarchal control—then no matter how appropriate it may be for the study of legal history and legal ideology, Foucault's appeal to cease talking about power in negative terms is of little use to feminism.

This is not to say that patriarchy does not have it positive, productive side, or that we could not study it. We could look at the "discursive truths" patriarchy has manufactured in its struggle to maintain itself. We could look, as some postmodern feminists want us to do, at patriarchy's discourses of gender[7] and study the "truths" produced by patriarchy about women: "truths" about women's inferiority, women's nature, men's culture, men's superiority, and so on. We could end-lessly deconstruct, to take a legal example, Supreme Court sex dis-crimination doctrine so as to cull and then reverse its "suppressed differences."[8] All this might well be important work. However, if it comes to exhaust the feminist agenda—even the feminist theoretical agenda—it will surely distort the object of its own study.

If feminist legal theorists want to understand, much less challenge, patriarchal power, we need to come to grips with its utterly nondiscur-sive and silencing violence. Particularly if we want to understand it from women's point of view, we must not focus obsessively on its talkative, pontificating, and no doubt internally contradictory blab-ber.[9] To understand patriarchy we do indeed need archaeologies, but not of the positive creations of power—not of the "discourses" and "selves" patriarchy has produced, created, or invented. We need ar-chaeologies of the discourses patriarchy has silenced, of the selves it has not allowed to be, of the subjectivities it has denied, of what it has forbidden, and what it has destroyed.

Beyond simply bettering our understanding of patriarchy, there are also political reasons feminist legal theorists should keep our focus on patriarchal violence rather than patriarchal constructs. The first of these reasons is decidedly local. It is extremely difficult, as feminists inside and outside of law know, to communicate to men, including critical legal scholars, the defining role that sexual violence and the fears of sexual violence play in women's and girls' lives. The reason for this, I suspect, is to some degree self-interest. To be blunt, it is almost impossible not to blind oneself to the violence in the world of which you are an indirect if not direct beneficiary, and most men do indeed benefit, at least in the short run, from the sexual violence which many women fear or from which they suffer.[10]

In addition to the psychic and political motives for denying the centrality of violence to women's oppression, critical legal scholars increasingly resort to a decidedly hip philosophical and intellectual justification for their selective blindness. If the central insights of social theory hold for patriarchal power as they seem to hold for legal power, they argue, then to understand patriarchy, as well as to understand law, we should be examining what it has invented rather than what it has destroyed. Why talk about something as banal as violence when there are so many "social constructs" to deconstruct? Social theory, in short, has become yet another excuse for men to blind themselves to the violence of patriarchy, the destructivity of misogyny, and the absolute moral imperative for positive legal intervention on behalf of women. For this reason if for no other, we need to resist the false comparison between legal and patriarchal power that the univocality of social theory invites.

There is another reason why Foucault's mandate is peculiarly inapposite to the concerns of feminism. At least since the English legal positivists began focusing on force, sanction, and legal violence as the defining core of legal power, it has been the positive power of legal *discourse* rather than the negative power of legal violence which has been least visible. Hence it is appropriately the submerged positive effects of legal discourse rather than the more visible impact of legal violence that the critical legal scholars, following Foucault, now highlight. With respect to patriarchal power, though, the situation is the reverse. In patriarchy it is the negative, negating violence rather than the positive discourse which is privatized, muffled, denied, and invisible. We therefore should be highlighting the effects of the invisible violence against women rather than the relatively visible discourse. The discursive, positive impact of "stereotyping" magazines, fairy tales, school lessons, and so on, is gradually becoming more visible in this culture. It is the censorial, negative power of patriarchal violence that is still so adamantly denied. Thus the invisibility and privacy of sexual violence is to patriarchy much as the invisibility of discursive power is to legalism.

The most important reason, however, that feminist legal theorists should resist critical legal scholars' tendency to conflate forms of power into one "inventive, creative mode," is that if we indulge in this conflation, we will bypass a significant opportunity to diminish concretely the violence women do in fact suffer. For it is distinctively *because* of this central *difference* between law and patriarchy that law becomes a tool with which patriarchal power can be resisted. Put another way, it is because of the difference between legal and patriarchal power that law, with all its positivity—its socially constructed rights and its ideological, imaginative, and institutional inventions—is a potent weapon against the destructivity and negativity of patriarchy.[11] Patriarchy is, in both a philosophical and to some degree literal sense, illegal: its destructive, negating, censorial violence is paradoxically both facilitated by but also contrary to the constructive, positive, creative, and inventive essence of legality. There is no question but

[263]

that we can and should use the instrumental inventiveness of the law to counter the damage of patriarchal violence.

The situation of feminist legal theorists is admittedly complicated. While as feminists we need to be attuned to the violence and negativity of patriarchy, as legal theorists we must also be attuned to the positivity and creativity of law in precisely the way the critical legal scholars have urged. In fact, we must do *both* if we are to understand that incredible endurance of patriarchy within as well as outside legal culture. Just as we need understandings of the brutal and silencing power of patriarchy, we also need to understand what it is that legal discourse has positively created or invented to *facilitate* the radically contrasting negativity and destructiveness of patriarchal violence. We need to understand, for example, how, through "privacy rights," constitutional guarantees,[12] the private/public distinction, and a host of other mechanisms, law as well as other forms of social power create a safe haven in which patriarchal domestic violence, for example, proceeds unabated and largely unnoticed even by progressive men. We need to understand the "marital rape exemption" both from a legalistic viewpoint of what it creates and the raped woman's viewpoint of what it destroys.[13] We need to understand how, and if, the constitutional protection of (some) pornography creates a positive legal space within which the negativity of patriarchal power is unleashed.[14] We need to understand, that is, not how these legal constructs "invent" us—because they don't—but rather how they create zones of protection within which patriarchal violence is freed to destroy us. What legal power distinctly "creates" that is of interest to feminists is space into which the law's ordinary protections against violence will not be allowed to penetrate. Feminists working in and thinking about law are uniquely positioned to provide this understanding. We numb ourselves to it, however, if we are unwilling to confront the violence that is at the core of patriarchal power.

KNOWLEDGE

The second tenet of postmodern social theory (immediately implied by the first) is that we create—we do not discover—objects of knowledge, and we do so discursively.[15] Through discourse, according to postmodernism, things and objects, as well as concepts and ideas, are manufactured, invented, made, and remade. By now it may be superfluous to note that this central Foucauldian insight has radically transformed not only our understanding of legal power, but also and perhaps more centrally our understanding of legal knowledge. The critical legal scholars' relentless focus on legal texts, their commitment to deconstructive methodologies, their use of interpretation as both method and object of inquiry, and their embrace of legal pragmatism all stem, directly or indirectly, from the Foucauldian mandate to focus on knowledge rather than violence as the primary product of power. Critical legal scholars have taught all of us to take our legal texts, legal discourses, and legal doctrines—and the contradictions they seem to contain—very seriously indeed. In short, the postmodernist's focus on knowledge and discourse as political products of power has opened up our understanding of the "politics of legal texts," and has cleared the way for an understanding of the productivity of power.

I want to pose the same question with respect to knowledge that I asked regarding power: is postmodernism's focus on knowledge, texts, and discourses a helpful focus for feminism? First, is the implicit claim that knowledge and discourse are the paradigmatic products of modern forms of power as true of *patriarchal* power as is it of *legal* power? It is a hard question but the answer, I believe, might be no. While patriarchy has no doubt produced massive amounts of discourse and massive numbers of "truths" about men and women's nature, patriarchy has not, for the most part, produced this discourse *from women* at all. Patriarchy has mostly produced silence from women, and it is for precisely that reason that feminists not yet taken by postmodernism have theorized so extensively about women's silence rather than women's discourse.[16] Much of our feminist work both in and outside law is beginning to show that silence is and has been to modern women's lives what Foucault has argued knowledge and discourse are and have been to modern men's: the major product of the most significant power that shapes us. So long as silence rather than discourse remains the primary product of modern patriarchy, then whatever else it has going for it, the postmodern social theorist's focus on discourse and speech is an entirely misguided entry into the study of modern women's lives. We ought instead to study the production of silence.

Let me give some examples of what might be revealed, and what has been revealed, by the feminist study of women's silence as the primary product of modern patriarchy. First, both Adrienne Rich[17] and Andrea Dworkin[18] have written extensively on the silence produced by both government and market censorship, particularly of lesbian writers and speakers. Ellen Bass,[19] Louise Thornton,[20] Florence Rush,[21] and many others have probed the silence produced by the double injury of sexual abuse and violence, followed by the societal nonresponsiveness toward that abuse.[22] Other feminists have written on the modern silence produced by flattened female self-esteem and lack of entitlement,[23] by our lingering status as primary caretaker of the young,[24] by our "helpmate" role,[25] and by our continuing exclusion from professional, academic, literary, and artistic life.[26]

One remarkable study of modern women's silence requires more than a mention. Intending to write a book on women's literary contributions over the last century, Tillie Olsen instead found herself overwhelmed by the silence, and wrote a book entitled, simply, *Silences*.[27] In marked contrast to Foucault's deservedly heralded attempts to explain the masculine verbosity of modernity, Olsen attempts to explain not verbosity but the relative silence of women over roughly the same time period. Why is it, she asks, that women have produced only "one out of twelve" of the world's modern literary classics?

Olsen's analysis attributes women's creative silence not to our differing biology but to our differing history. Her brief summation of that history makes powerfully clear why feminists should heed neither the social theorist's command to cease talking of power in negative terms, nor his command to focus on knowledge rather than silence as its major product:

> Evidently unknown to or dismissed by . . . [those who regard biology as that which blunts female creativity] . . . [is] *the other determining difference—not* biology—between male and female in the centuries after; the *differing past of women*—that should be part of every human consciousness. . . . Unclean; taboo. The Devil's Gateway. The three steps behind; the girl babies drowned in the river . . . Buried alive with the lord, burned alive on the funeral pyre, burned as witch at the stake. Stoned to death for adultery. Beaten, raped. Bartered. Bought and sold. Concubinage, prostitution, white slavery. The hunt, the sexual prey . . . Purdah, the veil of Islam, domestic confinement. Illiterate. Denied vision. Excluded, excluded, excluded from council, ritual, activity, learning, language. . . .
>
> Neither was the man created for the woman but the woman for the

man. . . . The Jewish male morning prayer: thank God I was not born a woman. Silence in holy places, seated apart, or not permitted entrance at all; castration of boys because women [are] too profane to sing in church.

And for the comparative handful of women born into the privileged class; being, not doing, man does, women is; . . . Isolated. Cabin'd, cribb'd, confin'd; the private sphere. Bound feet: corseted, cosseted, bedecked; denied one's body. Powerlessness. Fear of rape, male strength. Fear of aging. . . .

Vicarious living, infantilization, trivialization. . . . Shut up, you're only a girl. O Elizabeth, why couldn't you have been born a boy? For twentieth century woman: roles, discontinuities, part-self, part-time; conflict; imposed "guilt"; a man can give full energy to his profession, a woman cannot."[28]

If this is women's history, another question remains: What "produces" *modern* women's silence? There are surely many causes, as there are many silences. The psychologists Belenky, Clinchy, Goldberger, and Tarule argue in *Women's Ways of Knowing*[29] that for many modern women retreating into the numbing world of silence is not only an occasional decision or strategy, but also a full-fledged epistemic "way of knowing."[30] This silence-as-a-way-of-knowing, the authors maintain, is commonly "produced" in modern women (far more numerous, one suspects, than assumed by Belenky and her colleagues) who have known abusive and violent childhoods.[31] When it becomes a way of knowing, silence leads to passivity in the face of violence in adult life as well. Thus, trying to explain why she had stayed with a batterer for ten years one woman respondent in the study recalled her own voicelessness:

You know, I used to only hear his words, and his words kept coming out of my mouth. He had me thinking that I didn't know anything. But now, you know, I realize I'm not so dumb. . . . And my own words are coming out of my mouth now.[32]

Another woman, Ann, also explained her imprisonment in a violent childhood in terms of her experience of what the researchers came to call being "deaf and dumb," without voice, and without understanding:

I could never understand what they were talking about. My schooling was very limited. I didn't learn anything. I would just sit there and let people ramble on about something I didn't understand and would say,

Yup, yup. I would be too embarrassed to ask, What do you really mean?
. . . I had trouble talking. If I tried to explain something and someone
told me that it was wrong, I'd burst into tears over it. I'd just fall apart.[33]

It is not only overt violence, however, that produces the silence of
modern women. The more subtle coercion of an alien and hostile
"dialogue" can have the same effect. Very contemporary and relatively
privileged women law students, for example, apparently opt for or are
pushed toward silence in very contemporary law school classrooms,
and in significantly greater numbers than are men. Thus, at the other
end of the economic and social spectrum from Ann, quoted above, a
woman student at Yale Law School describes her experience in the
classroom in language strikingly similar to Ann's. Like Ann, this Yale
law student was also "deaf and dumb" in the classroom:

I felt unable to keep up with the class and terrified of being exposed to
the rest of the class as unable to match them. . . . I was very, very quiet,
very reserved. . . . I basically felt inadequate in all classroom settings,
unable to make comments or to project myself into the conversation,
often unable to think as quickly as I thought others did, to come up
with insightful or relevant things to say, . . . and focusing always on
what was previously said and trying to understand it rather than sitting
back and playing with ideas in a reckless way. The recklessness, the
casual "well let's look at it this way, let's spin it around and look at it
from this angle" stance that others seemed to achieve—I just couldn't.
So my first weeks I was really in shock. . . . I felt like I was missing some
gene or protein. Everyone else could spew forth arguments which I
couldn't do.[34]

Modern women's silence is often the product of a profound sense of
lack of entitlement. Indeed, the massive production of "unentitled
silence" regarding female sexual violation stands in marked contrast
to the near-manic production of a "discourse" on male sexual pleasure
so carefully documented by Foucault.[35] As Florence Rush asks:

Why is it that children who have been molested, sexually abused, or
even raped rarely or never tell? They never tell for the same reason that
anyone who has been helplessly shamed and humiliated, and who is
without protection or validation of personal integrity, prefers silence.
Like the woman who has been raped, the violated child may not be
believed (she fantasized or made up the story), her injury may be
minimized (there's no harm done, so let's forget the whole thing), and

she may even be held accountable for the crime (the kid really asked for it).[36]

Modern women's silence is also a product of conflicting demands on our time and energy: women are silent because we do not have the time, the atomistic self-possession, the luxury, or the rooms of our own in which to speak. In marked contrast to the postmodern social theorist's certitude that language, speech, and discourse generate all else, women know that there is a nonlingual domestic world of human needs that compels fulfillment—a world of bodies, of babies, of babies sucking milk, of babies' shit, of babies' sleeplessness, of children, of children's needs, of children's appetites—lurking beneath. We know about this nondiscursive world because we live there. It is not always a pleasant place. There are too many dishes in that world, too much laundry, too many children, too many cares, too many problems. Without more help—a great deal of help—there is just too much of this nonlingual, demanding domestic world for women even to begin to make the numbers that concern Tillie Olsen better than one in twelve. In *Silences,* for example, Olsen quotes from Harriet Beecher Stowe:

> Our children are just coming to the age when everything depends on my efforts. *Can* I lawfully divide my attention by literary efforts? . . . All last winter I felt the need of some place where I could go and be quiet and satisfied. I could not there [the dining room], for there was all the setting of tables, and clearing up of tables, and dressing and washing of children, and everything else going on. . . . Then if I came into the parlor where you were, I felt as if I were interrupting you, and you know you sometimes thought so, too.[37]

Olsen explains Stowe's relative silence thus:

> [S]he became more and more habituated to rapid, unripened (usually made-to-order) work. The book she wanted to write "to make this whole nation feel what an accursed thing slavery is" waited and waited. "As long as the baby sleeps with me nights I can't do much at anything, but I will do it at last," she vowed in a letter. There was "many a night weeping, the baby sleeping beside me, as I thought of the slave mothers whose babes were torn from them," but nothing was translated onto paper.
> Stowe was thirty-nine before she got to *Uncle Tom's Cabin*—at last. She wrote it in magazine serial installments—in between—when weary

with teaching the children and tending the baby and buying provisions and mending and darning; much of it on the kitchen table as the younger Harriet Beecher Stowe had, when trying to get writing done fourteen years before.[38]

Finally, modern women's silence is produced by our silence: the consequence of our silence is its own perpetuation. Masculine discourse dominates the conversational space, thus generating male social constructs that in turn further women's silence. As Sallyanne Payton describes the cycle:

> For centuries now, women's voices and women's realities have been entombed in silence. Think about it: all of the official versions of reality ... are made by men. It is male perceptions, male feelings, male patterns of behavior, masculine preferences and need, that account for everything from the shapes of buildings to the shapes of careers. Male patterning ... is implicit in much of this culture, but largely by default, there being no female patterning to challenge it. I confess that I do not know what that female patterning might look like; but I am quite certain that we will never know until the female voices in this society succeed in telling stories about female realities.[39]

A central passage from Foucault's magnificent and unfinished postmodern treatise, *The History of Sexuality*,[40] starkly and unwittingly highlights the contrasting roles of silence and discourse in women's and men's lives, and how attention to one but not the other has distorted the critical social and legal theorists' understanding of both. Foucault set out in that treatise to show that sexuality, far from being a pregiven, natural activity or biological state that social forces either repress or free, is instead a social construction produced by modern forms of social power. Foucault's most recurrent image or metaphor for this production of discourses on sexuality is a true story about a nineteenth-century half-wit who fondles a young girl and is consequently arrested. Foucault's interest is in what happens next. Far from having his pregiven sexuality "repressed" or "driven underground," Foucault argues that the half-wit is forced to speak and speak and speak—literally for the rest of his life and metaphorically for centuries—of his own sexuality. He speaks of his sexual pleasures first to the constabulary, then to the judiciary, then to the priesthood, then to the medical community, and finally to the psychoanalytic and psychiatric establishment.[41] The half-wit became

[270]

the object not only of a collective intolerance, but of a judicial action, a medical intervention, a careful clinical examination, and an entire theoretical elaboration. The thing to note is that they went so far as to measure the brainspan, study the facial bone structure, and inspect for possible signs of degenerescence the anatomy of this personage who up to that moment had been an integral part of village life; that they made him talk; that they questioned him concerning his thoughts, inclinations, habits, sensations, and opinions. And then, acquitting him of any crime, they decided finally to make him into a pure object of medicine and knowledge—an object to be shut away till the end of his life in the hospital at Mareville, but also one to be made known to the world of learning through a detailed analysis. . . . So it was that our society . . . assembled around these timeless gestures, these barely furtive pleasures between simple-minded adults and alert children, a whole machinery for speechifying, analyzing, and investigating.[42]

In the twentieth century, Foucault continues, the half-wit is still speaking: we speak of the "unspeakable" subject—sex—more than absolutely anything else. This is the irony which consumed Foucault, and which he explores so forcefully in his history.[43] This quintessentially modern, relentless production of juridical, moral, psychological, theological, medical, and psychiatric discourses on the supposedly unmentionable subject of sex, Foucault argues, is what has given "sexuality" both its form and its content, making it, so to speak, a part of an "inner truth" about the "nature of man." As Foucault recounts the lesson he draws from the tale:

Since the eighteenth century, sex has not ceased to provoke a kind of generalized discursive erethism. And these discourses on sex did not multiply apart from or against power, but in the very space and as the means of its exercise. Incitements to speak were orchestrated form all quarters. . . . Sex was driven out of hiding and constrained to lead a discursive existence. From the singular imperialism that compels everyone to transform their sexuality into a perpetual discourse, to the manifold mechanisms which, in the areas of economy, pedagogy, medicine, and justice, incite, extract, distribute, and institutionalize the sexual discourse, an immense verbosity is what our civilization has required and organized. Surely no other type of society has ever accumulated— and in such a relatively short space of time—a similar quantity of discourses concerned with sex. It may well be that we talk about sex more than anything else. . . . It is possible that where sex is concerned, the most long-winded, the most impatient of societies is our own. . . . What is peculiar to modern societies is not that they consigned sex to a shadow existence, but that they dedicated themselves to speaking of it *ad infinitum,* while exploiting it as *the* secret.[44]

It is indeed a great irony that we talk so much about an unspeakable subject. But there is a greater irony revealed by Foucault's story: with all the attention given to "discourses," neither the French officials, nor Foucault himself, nor the vast majority of social and legal critics he has influenced, have yet heard scarcely a word from the child who was molested in that eerie scene or from the millions of children who have been molested since. Sadly, for all his close attention to detail, Foucault did not seem to *notice* the contrast between the speechifying and speechified half-wit and the entirely, utterly silent child.[45] "We" may "talk about sex more than anything else,"[46] as Foucault says, so long as "we" means "men," but we have yet to end the silence of the child, and to a lesser degree, of women, from whom sex is taken, as an "inconsequential matter of course,"[47] as from an object or indeed as from property. While we discourse endlessly on the *pleasure* of sex so central to masculine sexuality—whether to condemn it, censor it, praise it, analyze it, understand it, rechannel it, repress it, or simply indulge it—we still speak almost not at all of the violence of sex so central to childhood and femininity. This constitutes a huge omission in our understanding of both the "discourses" we have produced and of sexuality, postmodern or otherwise, and a gross injustice to women and children. Surely we need to understand not only the speaking (male) sexuality and its possessor, the subjective (male) self created by all our discourse on sexuality, but also the silence of the objective (female) being, also "created" by both the sexualized discourse and the patriarchal power behind it. We need, in other words, to understand the modern societal inclination to keep the "alert children" silent, no less than the modern need to make the adult speak.

This inattentiveness to silence is not only a massive injustice, but it also distorts understanding. At least in part because of this characteristic selective attention to discourse and inattentiveness to silence, Foucault unwittingly commits himself in his study to a profoundly partial and hence false account of sexual pleasure. Thus at various points in his argument, Foucault refers to the "inconsequential bucolic pleasures,"[48] "barely furtive pleasures,"[49] "timeless gestures,"[50] and "bodies and pleasures"[51] that are transformed and rei-

fied into "discourses of sexuality." The implicit argument seems to be
that societal power has transformed bare pleasures into "discourses,"
which have in turn constructed "sexuality" as one of its objects. But
is it true, as Foucault suggests, that it is "pleasures" that are societally
transformed, and are they transformed into "discourse"? Is it as true
of the "alert child" as it is of the half-wit? Or is this Foucauldian
"truth" about how "natural-pleasure-is-transformed-into-socially-con-
structed-sexuality" only maintainable because of the alert child's silence? Is it, for the "alert children" and for many adult women as well,
not *pleasure* at all, but something very different that is transformed,
and is that *very different thing* that is transformed, transformed not
into discourse but rather into silence? What would the "alert child"
have said, if she, rather than he, had been the one to transform into
discourse that "timeless gesture," that "barely furtive pleasure" that
transpired between herself and the half-witted adult?

If we had listened, analyzed, and speechified the experience of the
alert child in that French village rather than the experience of the
half-witted adult, a radically different picture of what Foucault calls
these "inconsequential pleasures" from which "sexuality" is derived
might have emerged. There are, of course, any number of possible
stories the alert child might have told. All those stories are different
from the adult's, and all of them have been viciously repressed during
the same era that so energetically produced sexualized adult discourse. First, it is possible that behind all the discourse—the analyzing, categorizing, and speechifying—lay not pleasure but violence,
abuse, and terror for the silent child. The significance of this cannot
be overstated. Maybe, if we had listened to the child rather than
the half-wit, we might have had an account of "furtive violence" to
analyze, categorize, speechify, medicalize, theologize, philosophize,
psychologize, and agonize over rather than an account of "furtive
pleasure." Maybe, for example, what the half-wit felt as an "inconsequential pleasure" was, for the alert child, similar to Jill Morgan's
experience of "furtive moments" with her father, recounted in *I Never
Told Anyone:*

> It began for me the summer I was four years old. . . . He would . . . call
> me in from play in order to undress me in the empty house and then,
> with hurried injunctions not to tell mama, send me out to play again.

His hands undressing me this time were harsh and angry; his voice was abrupt and vicious. I was frightened and questioned him. With a harsh slap, he silenced me. . . . With no words and no warning, he spread my legs and entered me dry. My screams started the dog barking. I must have passed out. . . . My memories here are sketchy. I really don't even remember the pain yet. When he was through with me, he dropped me on the floor like a discarded dishrag. Then with belt in hand he began beating me. When the belt stopped its endless rise and fall, he took me in the bedroom, re-dressed me in the same play clothes, and put me into my bed with a strict injunction to stay there.[52]

Why, with all the speechifying to which Foucault attests, do we only have this story from the half-wit's point of view? Why, with all the speechifying, do we still have only half the story? Maybe the "alert" child's attempts to be heard were met with a nineteenth-century version of the resistance Morgan encountered:

I told adults of the horror I was enduring, but NO ONE listened. . . . Or they believed that my parents were such pillars of the community that they could not be guilty of the crime. Later, therapists referred to Oedipal fantasies instead of listening to what I was saying.[53]

Other stories, less violent, are also possible. Perhaps, as Foucault's telling of the story seems to suggest, the alert child did not really feel violated, frightened, or scared. Perhaps her story would have been somewhat like Jean Monroe's, also told, with self-admitted fear and trepidation, in *I Never Told Anyone:*

I go to the garage to get my bike and he is there, working in his lighted corner. I know I am trapped. "Honey, come back here a minute." I slide between him and the car fender and when he asks I lift my T-shirt. He touches them and I smile when he looks at my face. I must show him it is all right with me. But I don't like it. They are larger and more embarrassing, cold puckering the skin around the nipples. He is funny, breathless and giggly, different from his usual stern self. But it's not hurting me, and if I object, it will hurt him. He would see then that I know it is wrong. I couldn't bear for him to think that. . . . "Remember," he says, his huge finger over and over the protruding nipple, "remember, this is just between you and me. Don't tell anyone. Especially mama." He likes to take his thing out of his pants for me to look at it. He seems to love it. "Isn't it nice?" . . . I hate it most in the winter when the air is cold and shrivels the skin. I'm embarrassed. But he says they're beautiful. Never tell, honey. I love you. I never will, daddy, I promise. They are getting so big. You are beautiful.[54]

How, I wonder, did the "alert child" feel about the incident? How would she feel about the adults in her world, whom she could not tell for fear of hurting daddy—or the half-wit? Maybe, like Jean Monroe, she felt not fear but a chilling confusion, a sense of denial, betrayed trust, and a lingering feeling that her own feeling—the pleasure, or the lack of pleasure, or the embarrassment, or the "not liking it"— just *don't count* in the face of the overpowering imperative of the half-wit's "inconsequential pleasure." Monroe recalls:

> It is all so complex and I distrust, I guess, my own accounting of it. For instance, I have often maintained that I was not very hurt by the experience. . . . As an adult I've been very happy sexually. Somehow I got an affirmative sense of my own personal sexual power from my father. . . . [But m]ake no mistake about this. I DID NOT ENJOY IT![55]

Just as it is not yet time for feminists to quit talking of power in negative terms, so also it is not yet time to focus on discourse rather than silence as the primary product of patriarchy, if for no other reason than that to do so would be to break faith with the "alert children" who for so long have been unable to break the silence that surrounds their sexual violation. Of course, we need to do other things as well. Most important, we need to *tell* stories, and give voice to the stories of others. We need to give them; we need to recategorize the world, we need to invent new vocabularies, we need to make up new legal categories, we need to find new poetic metaphors and new literary allusions. When we do these things, it may *become* true that we have created a world—a reality—out of our social experience. But as long as it is true, to paraphrase Adrienne Rich, that naming is power and silence is oppression, and as long as women and children remain overwhelmingly silent in the presence of overpowering violence, if we want to understand the contours of our oppression, we will have to come to grips with our forced, coerced, or collaborative silence, and not (only) with their developed and contradictory and oppressive discursive practices. And when we understand women's silence we will have a better understanding not only of patriarchy, but of men's

[275]

discourse, of men's discursive practices, and of masculine subjectivity as well.

MORALITY

The third tenet of postmodern social theory influencing legal studies is that since "all is politics," the moral or political transformative goal of the politically committed theorist can only be a society marked by a greater democratization of power than presently exists. As our social constraints—entrenched hierarchies and social roles—are comprised of the unrecognized, falsely assumed to be necessary, gellings of political institutions and imaginations, so our freedom consists in our capacity first to recognize those constraints as contingent rather than necessary, and then to break them. The critic's utopia, then, is a world in which the power to break free of the false necessity created by institutional and imaginative constructs is as widely distributed as possible. For the postmodern social theorist, power and its distributions exhaust the moral universe just as they exhaust the story of our past. Roberto Unger's moral vision is in this regard representative of critical legal scholarship and of postmodern social thought generally:

> The guiding theme of the program of social reconstruction is the attempt to imagine institutional arrangements and social practices that can advance the radical project beyond the point to which contemporary forms of governmental and economic organization have carried it. By the . . . project of the modernist visionary I mean the attempt to realize the many forms of individual or collective empowerment that result from our relative success in disengaging our practical and passionate dealings from the restrictive influence of entrenched social roles and hierarchies. . . . The program suggests how our contemporary formative contexts might be disentrenched, . . . how they might be more fully opened to challenge in the midst of our routine conflicts and therefore also how they might undermine or prevent rigid forms of social division and hierarchy. . . . The weakening of the influence of this prewritten social script is to be valued not only negatively, as an occasion for a broader range of choice, but affirmatively for the forms of empowerment it makes possible.[56]

Unger also urges the "denaturalization" of society, which is synonymous with the emancipation of society from social roles girded by false claims of necessity:

[D]ifferent institutional arrangements reflect varying degrees of advance in the denaturalization of society. Society becomes denaturalized to the extent that its formative practices and preconceptions are open to effective challenge in the midst of ordinary social activity. . . . The concept of denaturalization or of emancipation from false necessity includes the idea of a weakening of rigid roles and hierarchies. It therefore also refers to the development of forms of production, exchange, and passionate attachment that are less marked by such rankings and division. . . . I use the term negative capability to suggest the variety of forms of empowerment that denaturalization makes possible.[57]

There are three problems with this vision from a feminist point of view. First, it is simply not true—it is *emphatically* not true—as many women know and as some feminists have distinctively theorized,[58] that oppressive "power" in *any* of its manifestations is the necessary consequence of inequality and hierarchy, and that the end of hierarchy is therefore the necessary root of morality. Women of *all* cultures routinely, although not always, respond to their utterly unequal and hierarchic relationships with their infants and children with nurturance, care, and love rather than power, narcissism, and the imposition for the sake of ego gratification of the stronger's will upon the weaker's fate. The nurturant response the infant engenders in the mother seeks the fulfillment response of the needs of the weaker party; it does not seek to re-create or reinvent the weak in the image desired by the strong.[59] From a truly woman- and child-centered perspective, the bare fact of physical inequality takes on an entirely different hue from that projected by modern social theory. The physically unequal mother *in all cultures* typically breast-feeds and protects, rather than bullies or browbeats, the vulnerable infant and child. The powerful mother nurtures so as to give life and create growth in the weak. She does not impose so as to inscribe her will.

These simple, utterly unremarkable physical facts of life are of tremendous (and tremendously neglected) import not only to feminist legal theory, but to legal theory generally. For it is these straightforward but overlooked experiences—experiences of breast-feeding, nurturing, caring for, and loving the weak so as to make the weak healthy—that could ultimately form the foundation of a feminist, maternalist (and humanist) moral theory[60]—and therefore a legal theory[61]—which is grounded neither in the Enlightenment ideals of rationality and objectivity, nor in a post-Enlightenment glorification

[277]

FEMINISM, POSTMODERNISM, AND LAW

of power, but instead in an intersubjective sensitivity to the needs of others. If feminists are right to theorize and women are right to experience a respectful, nurturant, caring response that aims to promote rather then dominate the interest and well-being of the weaker "other" as one possible product of hierarchical relations, then the Ungerian descriptive claim that a dominating, positing, and delimiting power is the only product of hierarchy, and the moral claim that the destruction of hierarchy is the only intelligible political goal, are simply wrong. If we are right to trust our nurturant response within the natural inequality of the mother-infant relationship, then we are also right to suspect that hierarchic relationships such as parent-child, teacher-student, judge-litigant, and legislator-constituent could and should be infused *neither* with false claims of equality, objectivity, or a distanced and alienating respect, nor with levers by which the hierarchy can be smashed. Rather, those relationships can be infused, simply, with care.

The experience of nurturance—the experience of caring for and being cared for—and the possibility of a morality of care premised on those experiences are as precluded by Unger's utopia of democratized power as by the liberal legalist's utopia of principled reason or the economic legalist's utopia of egotistic rationality. To put the point starkly, the Ungerian ideal is a world in which contexts are there to be shattered—not understood, appreciated, interpenetrated, or infused with an ethic of care.[62] It is a world in which "nature" is there to be denigrated, conquered, transcended, and exploited, and it is a world in which passion creates not the basis of moral life but hierarchical ties to be broken. We should be extremely wary of any utopian strategies, including Ungerian and leftist ones, that definitionally exclude the emotional and subjective root of many women's and more than a few men's aspirational and moral lives.

The second and related problem with Unger's view of political morality, from a feminist perspective, is its relentless focus on discourse. According to Unger as well as most other critical social theorists, our ideals are not only reflected in but *embodied* in our uttered imaginings.[63] There is no transcendent or natural ideal state toward which we ought to work. There are, rather, only competing discursive formulae of where we ought to go. If women are to contribute to progress toward a better world, then the way to do so is clear: we must contribute to the dialogue.

[278]

In one sense, this admonition is clearly right: of course women must break their silence and contribute to the dialogue. In another sense, however, the imperative to limit our sense of the ideal to that which is expressed or expressive runs the risk of simply flatly denying the reality of many women's distinctive experiences of moral life. For many women, moral inclinations are neither reflected nor embodied in our modern discursive practices—any of them. We feel them instead to be rooted in our earliest, preverbal experiences of being loved and nurtured. If, as a culture, we were to centralize *this* natural experience we might develop a radically different picture of public moral life. We might conclude that morality is grounded in the experience of being cared for in symbiosis with a protective and nurturant other rather than in our later experiences of disciplined, disciplining, and verbose authority. We might conclude that moral ideals and moral inclinations derive from the quiet love of the mother rather than from the discursive guidance of the father. We might conclude that the root of moral life and moral experience is profoundly non- and preverbal. We might then decide that when we utter our idealized imaginings we ought to be acutely aware of their non- and preverbal origins. In other words, we need to understand the possibility that our moral inclinations are rooted not in our uttered "principles" of any sort, but rather in distinctively life-giving and entirely nonverbal feelings and actions. We will not do so if we acquiesce in the Ungerian insistence that we focus our idealistic and historical gaze on the verbal spheres of our "denaturalized" existence.

There is one final problem. Feminists and feminist legal theorists must be the first to object to false claims of natural necessity. However, we should also be extremely wary of the profound devaluation of nature, the denial of the significance of the natural realm, and the disregard and contempt for natural constraints and natural truths that play such a dominant role in Unger's critique of traditional morality, just as we should be wary of his glorification of cultural and societal empowerment. The social and critical legal scholar's renunciation of the "natural"—particularly in the moral sphere—sounds far more like a continuation than a repudiation of the profoundly destructive urge to banish, control, and deny the existence of a natural world. That urge is hardly distinctively postmodern, or even modern. It characterizes the history of patriarchal culture, at least from the Renaissance to the present. The oppression of women and the exploi-

[279]

tation of nature have been constant companions in the story of patriarchy; by correlation, as numerous feminists have insisted, respect for
nature and respect for women must play convergent roles in the story
of our mutual liberation.[64]

If feminist legal theorists are to share in healing the world, we will
have to do two things that will distinguish our work sharply from the
postmodern and post-structuralist work of critical legal scholars. First,
we will have to encounter patriarchy willingly, even aggressively, in
its most violent, negative, denying, oppressive, censorial mode. Second, we will have to remember, remain true to, and draw upon the
naturalism and quietness that have always been central to what has
been and is still most admirable about women's moral lives. There is
surely no way to know with any certainty whether women have privileged access to a way of life that is more nurturant, more connected,
more natural, more loving, and thereby more moral than the principled lives which both men and women presently pursue in the public
sphere, including the legal sphere of legal practice, theory, and pedagogy. But it does seem that whether by reason of sociological role,
psychological upbringing, or biology, women are *closer* to such a life:
if it is but a memory, then for women it is a more vivid memory; if it
is a utopian dream, then for women it is a dream we have never fully
denied and from which we routinely draw sustenance and guidance.
For those of us (men and women) for whom principled, reasoned
morality has come to seem but a thinly veiled excuse for cruelty,
and for whom the Ungerian glorification of democratized power is
depressingly more of the same, the suggestion that women—and
therefore the human community—can and should respond in a more
nurturant, caring, and natural way to the needs of those who are
weaker, is both more and less than a "contestable, empirical claim": it
is, rather, in the nature of a promise. It is one promise, among others,
that the human community can be reconstituted in a way that will
salvage the planet as well as save the species. We should explore it,
and test it against our hearts' challenges. We should not allow it to be
censored. Least of all should we self-censor it because it runs afoul of
a Nietzschean power-ideology now fashionable among postmodern
and critical legal scholars. That ideology not only threatens to silence
once again what is most distinctive in our voice but it is also itself
steeped, far more than the liberal theory against which it defines itself,
in a covert and overt contempt for women, feminism, nature, the

natural realm, and the feminine. We should be wary of it; we should not embrace it.

THE SELF

The last area of significance for feminist legal theory concerns the postmodern social theorist's distinctive critique of the self. The social-theoretic view of the self breaks down into two separate claims. The first and relatively modest claim of the postmodern social theorist is that the particular "self" familiar to modern, liberal society—arbitrarily desirous, sated by pleasure, sovereign over one's own subjectivity, knowledgeable of the objective world through reason and of the subjective world through introspection and confession—is the recent particular and contingent invention of the institutions and ideologies of liberal society.[65] The postmodern social theorist argues that this purportedly universal "liberal self" is in fact the invention of a particular set of powers that have dominated a relatively modern era. This claim has played a large and entirely healthy role in the critical legal studies movement, particularly in critical deconstructions of economic legalism—the branch of liberalism itself most heavily dependent upon a liberal conception of the self and its relations to the objects of its knowledge, acquisition, and discourse.[66]

The structure if not the substance of the social theorist's attack on the liberal self has also played a role in feminist legal theory, which has developed a critique parallel to that of the social theorists. According to the feminist critique, the "self" of economic and liberal legalism not only reflects a particular society, place, and time, but is also particular in yet another way: it reflects the particular experiences of the male gender. The experience of "selfhood" for women is very different from the experience of the desiring, rational, egotistic self relied upon by economic and liberal legal analysts. This is true even of women in that same culture, time, and place. The liberal self, then, is a gendered as well as cultural construct.

Feminists have explored several explanations for the difference between women and men's experience of self in liberal societies, only three of which I'll mention here. First, as Catharine MacKinnon insists in many different contexts,[67] and as I have argued elsewhere, it may be the case that a deep and thoroughly justified fear of acquisitive, violent male sexuality mars a woman's self-possession early in her development, rendering her what I have called a "giving self,"[68] ready to give, and to identify herself as one who gives, rather than endure the pain and fear of being one from whom her self is taken. If so, consensuality—the lodestar of value for the liberal legalist—is a very different experience for men than it is for women. Second, Nancy Chodorow[69] has argued that a young girl's early and distinctively uninterrupted identification with her mother may leave in women an indelible sense of "connectedness" that is itself at odds with the atomism and egotism assumed by the liberal self. As a result, women may experience the self as more continuous with others than do men. Third, as Nel Noddings suggests and as I have explored elsewhere, women may have a different experience of selfhood in part because of their distinctive role in the reproductive process.[70] All these otherwise different arguments point in the same direction, and it is a direction that should be endorsed by social theory: the liberal self at best reflects the male experience of selfhood within the liberal tradition. It is not an accurate account of women's experience.

The social and legal scholar's critique of the liberal self and the feminist critique of selfhood thus run on parallel tracks: they both aim to reveal the particular and the contingent behind the falsely claimed universal in the modern liberal's description of the desirous, rational, egotistic self. But this structural similarity, I think, obscures what may be far more significant differences between them. The feminist critique aims to show that the "liberal self" is an invention *not* of a particular societal power matrix, but instead of a very general power matrix—patriarchy—which exists across time and culture. According to the feminist critique, the masculine self, of which the liberal self is an instance, is the invention of a patriarchal power which both transcends and predates particular cultures. Thus, the liberal self may indeed be a social construct—the product of a particular society— but it is also an instance of a "masculine self" which is at root not a social construct at all but a patriarchal construct, the origin of which transcends and predates particular societal forms.

In spite of their shared logic, there are, consequently, striking differences between the feminist critique of the liberal self on the one hand and the critical scholar's critique of the liberal self on the other. The feminist argument assumes at least a "thin" universal gendered oppression across cultures that the critical theorist denies, while the critical theorist assumes a sameness across gender that the feminist critique denies. Both aim to show that a claimed natural universal essence—the "liberal self"—is in fact a particular construct of power, but they each purport to expose a different matrix of power. Briefly, critical social theory emphasizes that the "self" is a social construct, defined and produced by a liberal-cultural understanding, while feminism stresses that the same "self" is a gendered construct, both bound and produced by masculine, patriarchal and, to some degree, misogynist experience. Both seek to reveal the particular behind the purported universal, yet the "particular" being revealed by each is quite different, and it is not at all clear that both explanations can be right in any sort of simple way.

Thus, while there are surface similarities, there are also deep tensions between the critical and the feminist critique of the liberal self. That tension, though, is not what I want to focus on here. For there is an even deeper tension between what I will call the postmodernist social theorists' universalist claim regarding the self, and feminist interpretations of women's experiences. By the universalist claim I mean to refer to the social theorist's claim that not just the *particular* liberal self, but virtually *every* possible description of the nature of the self is a social construct. Although critical legal scholars occasionally equivocate on this point,[71] the postmodern social theorists generally do not. The postmodern theorist's claim is decidedly *not* that the liberal self is a *false* description that oppresses, censors, or denies the "true" nature of the self. Rather, the liberal self, like any description of the self, is an invention not a falsification. As such, it is subject not to claims of truth or falsity but rather to political modification. To use Foucault's formulation, the relation between the components of selfhood—pleasure, desire, and action—may vary across time and across culture, but in every case the experience of the nexus between pleasure, desire, and action has been societally invented; it is not the experience of something which is naturally there. Thus, the self is inevitably the invention of societal powers—there is no "natural self" with a "true inner nature" for society either to liberate or oppress, or for a particular description such as the liberal self to either mirror faithfully or misdescribe inartfully. There simply is no "true self." Society inevitably constructs, rather than represses, the true inner self.

Put affirmatively rather than skeptically, the critical postmodernist theorist's claim is that *whatever* is experienced as selfhood is a socially constructed self—there is no selfhood that pre-exists society. If we think of postmodern theory as a kind of consciousness-raising, we might put the insight as a two-step phenomenological process. What one experiences on a daily basis as "selfhood" is in fact a socially constructed web of subjectivity. What one comes to realize after having seen the social light, so to speak, is not only the constructivity of one's prior experience of the everyday "self," but also both the negativity and the potentiality of what remains: the potential for change, and the jolt of suppressed power that inevitably accompanies a sudden awakening to the contingency and malleability of one's life and world.

Now the question I want to pose is whether this universal claim that *any* description of a concrete, given, natural, precultural self is delusional, and that our only true inner nature is one of instability, potentiality, negative capability, and susceptibility to change—that our inessentialism is our essence—is an accurate account of women's inner lives. It may, of course, be true of men but not true of women. At least one strand of feminist writing beginning with de Beauvoir[72] and continuing through the object-psychologic tradition of Chodorow[73] suggests very strongly that something like the universalist claim may indeed be true *of men*; there may inevitably be, in both the experience as well as ideal of masculine subjectivity, a hard but fragile "knot" of "self." This knot of self, regardless of its particular societal description, has not only been invariably "socially constructed," but precisely because of its vulnerability and contingency requires near-constant reaffirmation and reconstruction both by the bolstering efforts of others (such as women), and the very existence of the other (again, women). The existence, the fragility, the social and psychological contingency, and the artificiality of this inner masculine knot of selfhood are also confirmed, less formally, from women's reports of their own experiences of masculinity: women's folklore, consciousness-raising sessions, and conversations are replete with recountings of the sheer time and energy expended in the never-ending and enormous female task of maintaining the male's masculine sense of self.

Whether or not the universal claim is a valid description of men, the question still remains: is it a true account of the sense of self experienced by modern women? The Herculean efforts of post-structuralist feminists notwithstanding, there are enormous problems aligning the universalist claim with modern women's experiences.

[284]

Rather, many women's experiences, recounted in feminist discourse, *reverse* the phenomenological description of awareness given above in two ways. First, on a very literal level, the modern description of the daily experienced "socially constructed" self is simply wrong: what women experience on a daily basis is not a socially constructed *selfhood,* but rather a socially constructed *lack* of self, a sense of selflessness. Put another way, women distinctively bear the mark of patriarchal power by denying rather than acting upon (even if that action takes the form of renouncing) their pleasures, and internalizing and identifying with rather than avoiding their pains.[74] While the affirmative, nonjuridical powers in varying societies may construct women in many different ways, *patriarchy,* by contrast, has not been constructive or inventive in the way claimed by postmodern social theory. Modern patriarchy does much for and to women, but one thing it does not do is create on her behalf anything that even re- motely resembles a subjective "self." Indeed, if patriarchy has affirm- atively created a social existence for women, it is one of objecthood or otherhood, but most assuredly not selfhood—this is one of the central insights of the feminist movement, and one of the essential moments of consciousness-raising.

Of course, even this cross-cultural feminist critique—that patriar- chy denies women not only the liberal's egotistic, desiring self, but virtually every description of the self—is not literally incompatible with the social theorist's claim that the experience of selfhood is a social construct. It denies only the universality of the construction. But to limit feminism to this narrow focus on the constitutive con- structs of patriarchy is to truncate feminism needlessly. The point of so much contemporary feminist writing, particularly nonacademic feminist writing, is not simply that patriarchy denies women one form of being—selfhood—and constructs for them another form of being— objecthood. Rather, the point is that patriarchy, and more particularly patriarchal violence, is blindly destructive, not constructive, of all that is of value within us.

As we become more aware of the presence of patriarchal power, we become more aware of that which is within us—whether or not we decide to call it a "self"—and of that which is vulnerable to patriar- chy's terrible destructivity. "Feminism" construed most broadly, his- torically has aimed to reclaim that which is destroyed, not just to identify that which is constructed by patriarchy. The narrative of at least some forms of feminist consciousness-raising, then, is precisely the reverse of the social-theoretical description given above: while the postmodern theorist experiences a daily but constructed self, and comes, through critical enlightenment, to experience a negative capability or selflessness, women experience a daily but false sense of selflessness—which is experienced not as negative potentiality but as an exceedingly still incapacity. Through consciousness-raising, women come to reclaim a self that is within. This "reclamation of that which is within" is utterly incompatible with the critical theorist's understanding of the self.

Let me mention four aspects of our internality that modern feminists persuasively argue are threatened by the destructivity, rather than constructivity, of patriarchal power. First, Adrienne Rich eloquently maintains that a young girl's natural, early, fierce, loving, erotic, and caring identification with women and girls is shattered by the pervasive patriarchal institution of compulsory heterosexuality.[75] All these institutions, which include marriage, romance, and the censorship in almost all cultures of the rich history of women bonding with women, redirect the young girl's affective identification toward men. This destruction of the woman-to-woman bond is pervasive, universal, sometimes subtle and psychological and sometimes overt and violent, but it is no less criminal for its boring and banal typicality. It stunts our emotional lives and it perverts our wholeness. It eats away first at our self-affection and then at our self-esteem; it teaches us to deny our desires, our instincts, and our pleasures, and to distrust and distance ourselves from those from whom we have received that which has best sustained us. Adrienne Rich calls this aspect of our destroyed internality the "Lesbian in Us,"[76] and she describes the destruction of this part of herself thus:

I was born in 1929. In that year, Virginia Woolf was writing of the necessity for a literature that would reveal "that vast chamber where nobody has been"—the realm of relationships between women. . . . Two women, one white, one black, were the first persons I loved and who I knew loved me. Both of them sang me my first songs, told me my first stories, became my first knowledge of tenderness, passion, and finally, rejection. Each of them, over time, surrendered me to the judgment and disposition of my father and my father's culture: white and male. My love for the white woman and the black woman became blurred with anger, contempt, and guilt. I did not know which of them had injured me; they became merged together in my inarticulate fury. I did not know that neither of them had had a choice.[77]

On the subject of "woman-to-woman relationships," Rich continues, quoting Emily Dickinson, "My Classics veiled their faces." She then discusses her own reclamation of her internality:

Reading . . . [an essay by Bertha Harris on the silence surrounding the lesbian] I found she had described to me for the first time my own searches through literature in the past, in pursuit of a flickering, often disguised reality which came and went throughout women's books. That reality was nothing so simple and dismissible as the fact that two women might go to bed together. *It was a sense of desiring oneself; above all, of choosing oneself; it was also a primary intensity between women, an intensity which in the world at large was trivialized, caricatured, or invested with evil.*

Even before I knew I was a lesbian, it was the lesbian in me who pursued that elusive configuration. And I believe it is the lesbian in every woman who is compelled by female energy, who gravitates toward strong women, who seeks a literature that will express that energy and strength. It is the lesbian in us who drives us to feel imaginatively, render in language, grasp, the full connection between woman and woman. It is the lesbian in us who is creative, for the dutiful daughter of the fathers in us is only a hack.[78]

Ellen Bass discusses a somewhat different aspect of our threatened internality. She argues that our pornographic, incestuous, and sexually abusive culture shatters women's natural, playful and affective eroticism—to use Ellen Bass's language, "a basic and vital impulse—the desire to be seen, to be known, naked, in sexual sharing."[79] This abusive culture identifies sexuality with female degradation, helplessness, mutilation, and, in the extreme, with injury and death. Bass relates the shattering of her own eroticism in this way:

I would be distracted by an image of myself as a stripper, gyrating in a dark theater in front of ogling men. This picture disgusted me. I didn't understand it. I hated that it was a part of my mind. Then I remembered: When I was a small child, my mother took me to the doctor. In the examining room I took off my clothes. I don't know whether I misunderstood the directions about what clothes to remove, whether I seemed cheerful about disrobing, or whether the doctor . . . said something that elicited this response from my mother, but she laughed and joked, "She's going to be a striptease artist when she grows up."

[287]

I was horribly embarrassed. Although . . . I had never seen a stripper . . . I was enough of a child of our culture to feel degradation and shame. . . . And way back, the calendar in the candy store . . . The picture: a woman holding groceries in both arms, her back to me, but she looked over her shoulder right at me, her mouth a surprised red O, her underpants having slipped down to her ankles, wind blowing up her skirt, her rosy buttocks exposed. . . . The woman is helpless, her arms are full. She cannot pull up her pants, push down her skirt, walk or run. The viewer, presumably, is chuckling, enjoying his view of her, enjoying her "appealing" dismay as well as her nakedness. . . . How many little girls and boys sat looking at that calendar? . . . Notice, next time you are shopping, the covers of magazines at children's eye level.[80]

Bass describes first the mutilation and then the reclamation of that "which should be a birthright" in this way:

I was not sexually abused. Yet I was sexually abused. We were all sexually abused. The images and attitudes, the reality we breathe in like air, it reaches us all. It shapes and distorts us, prunes some of our most tender, trusting, lovely and loving branches. We learn that this is who a woman is. . . .

We all, women and men, live our lives in an environment that fouls one of the magnificent, holy aspects of our natural world. Creation, love, fertility, and union of two becoming one, joining in body and in ecstasy—this possibility, which should be our birthright, has been fouled. . . . Recently I have recognized that the image of the stripper is a perverted travesty of a basic and vital impulse—the desire to be seen, to be known, naked, in sexual sharing. . . . When I realized this, I was overwhelmed with feelings: anger and sadness at the insidiousness of our culture's effect on our lives; relief in finally understanding why such ugliness was a part of me; and exhilaration at reclaiming the erotic strength and vigor of the original desire, that of sharing who I truly am with my lover, both as a gift and as an affirmation of my self.[81]

Third, Tillie Olsen, argues that patriarchy shatters our will to create. It shatters the belief in the validity, strength, vitality, and beauty of that which can be molded from one's own life experiences. Olsen describes this aspect of women's expropriated internality:

How much it takes to become a writer . . . how much conviction as to the importance of what one has to say, one's right to say it. And the will, the measureless store of belief in oneself to be able to come to, cleave to, find the form for one's own life comprehensions. Difficult for any male not born into a class that breeds such confidence. Almost impossible for a girl, a woman. . . . Sparse indeed is the literature on the way of denial to small girl children of the development of their endowment as born human: active vigorous bodies; exercise of the power to do, to make, to investigate, to invent, to conquer obstacles, to resist violations of the self; to think, create, choose; to attain community, confidence in self. Little has been written on the harms of instilling constant concern with appearance; the need to please, to support; the training in acceptance, deferring. But it is there if one knows how to read for it, and indelibly there in the resulting damage. One—out of twelve.[82]

Lastly, and most controversially, the French feminist Luce Irigaray contends[83] that patriarchal society destroys, excludes, negates, and renders fantastic women's internal, prelingual, and even presymbolic sense of ourselves as witness to the truth that the violence done upon the world by discursive categorization—this breaking into subjects, objects, principles, rights, and wrongs—is false, is wrong, and is not all. Irigaray explained in an interview:

What a feminine syntax might be is not simple nor easy to state, because in that "syntax" there would no longer be either subject or object, "oneness" would no longer be privileged, there would no longer be proper meanings, proper names, "proper" attributes. . . . Instead, that "syntax" would involve nearness, proximity, but in such an extreme form that it would preclude any distinction of identities, any establishment of ownership, thus any form of appropriation. . . .

I think the place where it could best be deciphered is in the gestural code of women's bodies. But, since their gestures are often paralyzed, or part of the masquerade, in effect, they are often difficult to "read." Except for what resists or subsists "beyond." In suffering, but also in women's laughter. And again: in what they "dare"—do or say—when they are among themselves. There are also more and more texts written by women in which another writing is beginning to assert itself, even if it is still often repressed by the dominant discourse.[84]

Affirmatively, this voice within speaks sometimes by not speaking. It speaks in silent, sometimes laughing collaboration with particular women and with all women for an affirmative recognition of the "self within." It speaks as a source of fulfilled need, pleasure, desire, communion, intersubjectivity, and *jouissance:*

If you/I hesitate to speak, isn't it because we are afraid of not speaking well? But what is "well" or "badly"? . . . What claim to raise ourselves up in a worthier discourse? Erection is no business of ours: we are at home on the flatlands. We have so much space to share . . . we have so many voices to invent in order to express all of us everywhere. . . . Stretching upward, reaching higher, you pull yourself away from the limitless realm of your body. Don't make yourself erect, you'll leave us. The sky isn't up there: it's between us.

And don't worry about the "right" word. There isn't any. No truth between our lips. There is room enough for everything to exist. Everything is worth exchanging, nothing is privileged, nothing is refused. . . . Between us, there are no proprietors, no purchasers. . . . Our bodies are nourished by our mutual pleasure . . . our exchanges are without terms, without end. How can I say it? The language we know is so limited. . . .

Let's leave definitiveness to the undecided; we don't need it. Our body, right here, right now, gives us a very different certainty. Truth is necessary for those who are so distanced from their body that they have forgotten it. But their "truth" immobilizes us, turns us into statues, if we can't loose its hold on us.[85]

Negatively, the voice within criticizes, intuits, witnesses and insists that this broken discourse we call culture is not ultimately human.

How can I say it? . . . that their history, their stories, constitute the locus of our displacement. It's not that we have a territory of our own; but their fatherland, family, home, discourse, imprison us in enclosed spaces where we cannot keep on moving, living, as ourselves. Their properties are our exile. Their enclosures, the death of our love. Their words, the gag upon our lips.

How can we speak so as to escape from . . . their distinctions and opposition: virginal/deflowered, pure/impure, innocent/experienced. . . . How can we shake off the chain of these terms. . . ? Disengage ourselves, *alive*, from their concepts? . . . You know that we are never completed, but that we only embrace ourselves whole. That one after another, parts—of the body, of space, of time—interrupt the flow of our blood. Paralyze, petrify, immobilize us. Make us paler. Almost frigid.[86]

The critical female self knows herself as a fantastic, unlived, unspeakable, unspoken alternative which cannot render itself more concrete, and which is known in large part through its absence from cultured life. It is, for example, that part of themselves which the silent and silenced female Yale law students know to be absent from law, legal culture, law school, and legal discourse. This anti-symbolic, uncultured, natural, loving, female self knows herself raped, abused,

[290]

and killed by the vicious side of patriarchy. She knows herself even more often as that which is trivialized, fantasized, and rendered unreal, untrustworthy, irrational, and ultimately nonexistent by the cultured side of patriarchy. It is no wonder that she hates and disowns herself. But paradoxically she also knows herself, at times, as exceedingly, painfully, achingly real. She knows herself as joyful, living, loving, and real, even as she knows herself as only dimly perceived because she is so universally denied. She knows herself, miraculously if only on occasion, not as the hated, feared, denied, trivialized, and trampled upon, but as worthy and beautiful, and as one who must be reclaimed from denial, fear, oppression, and loathing.[87]

What of *this* "self"—this woman-bonded, creative, playfully erotic, loving, unspeakable, and negative self? In a sense, of course, the social theorist is right to deny her existence. The social theorist is concerned with discursive truths, and the truth of this female self is by definition that which is unspeakable. But I believe feminists should not conclude from this discursive exclusion of the female self that we have discovered yet another socially constructed and ultimately nonexistent self which should be banished from all thought, dreams, and histories. We should conclude that we have discovered the logical limits of the discursive object of social theoretic understanding.

Feminist legal theories in particular should stay true to these glimpsed and occasional experiences of the self within. If we want an ideal to guide a critique of law that is total, if we want a source of light to guide legal reforms that are truly progressive, if we want to understand how we should begin to remake and reclaim the world in a way that is more loving and more holistic, then we should be extremely wary of the postmodern, post-structuralist, and social-theoretic claim that this nondiscursive, woman-bonded, creative, erotic, and quietly rebellious self within is but another product of a political, patriarchal, liberal, and societal discourse. Rather, we should attend to that most tentative, intuitive, unschooled, and above all else undisciplined female self that lies within. For it is that self who will show us truly new ways to judge, new ways to legislate, and new ways to order. It is that self who can show us how to create a safe world without killing the spontaneous, the physical, the natural, the unpredictable, and the pleasurable. And of course it is that self that has yet to make its presence felt in most of our hypothetical constructs or utopian dreams, much less in our societal and legal discursive reality.

[291]

CONCLUSION

What is of value in postmodern social theory for feminists? My suspicion is that what attracts many feminists to postmodernism is not its anti-essentialism but more simply its skepticism: its refusal to accept any particular account of truth or morality as the essential true, moral, or human viewpoint. This skepticism is entirely healthy and is something we should treasure. The anti-essentialism of the postmodernist vision, by contrast, is something we should reject. Surely we can have this both ways. A skepticism toward particular claims of objective truth, a particular account of the self, and any particular account of gender, sexuality, biology, or what is and is not natural, is absolutely necessary to a healthy and modern feminism. But that skepticism need not require an unwillingness to entertain descriptions of subjective and intersubjective authenticity, claims of a pervasive and cross-cultural patriarchy, various accounts of the female self, promises of a nurturant or caring morality, or remembrances of a feminine and feminist closeness to nature. These descriptions, claims, accounts, promises, and remembrances, considered so problematic by postmodern social and legal theory, are precisely what have animated feminist legal theory and practice. All I have argued here is that we should not forsake them out of a misguided attempt to remain true to a philosophical vision which, like the Enlightenment vision it seeks to replace, has not been of our own making.

Notes

Notes to the Introduction

1. MacKinnon, *From Practice to Theory, Or What is a White Woman Anyway?* 4 YALE J. L. & FEMINISM 13 (1991).
2. Carol Gilligan, *Reply to Critics,* 207 in AN ETHIC OF CARE: FEMINIST AND INTERDISCIPLINARY PERSPECTIVES (M. Larrabee, ed. 1993).
3. J. TRONTO, MORAL BOUNDARIES: A POLITICAL ARGUMENT FOR AN ETHIC OF CARE (1993).

Notes to Chapter 1

1. R. DWORKIN, LAW'S EMPIRE (1986).
2. R. POSNER, THE ECONOMICS OF JUSTICE (1981).
3. R. DWORKIN, A MATTER OF PRINCIPLE (1985); R. DWORKIN, LAW'S EMPIRE.
4. J.B. WHITE, JUSTICE AS TRANSLATION: AN ESSAY IN CULTURAL AND LEGAL CRITICISM (1990).
5. C. GILLIGAN, IN A DIFFERENT VOICE: PSYCHOLOGICAL THEORY AND WOMEN'S DEVELOPMENT (1982).
6. *See, e.g.,* C. GILLIGAN, IN A DIFFERENT VOICE; N. NODDINGS, CARING: A FEMINIST APPROACH TO ETHICS AND MORAL EDUCATION (1984); V. HELD, FEMINIST MORALITY: TRANSFORMING CULTURE, SOCIETY AND POLITICS (1993); Baier, *Caring About Caring,* 53 SYNTHESE 291 (1982); Baier, *What Do Women Want in a Moral Theory?* 19 NOUS 53 (1985); N. CHODOROW, THE REPRODUCTION OF MOTHERING: PSYCHOANALYSIS AND THE SOCIOLOGY OF GENDER (1978).
7. *See* Saffle v. Parks, 191 S. Ct. 1257 (1990).
8. W. BYRON, QUADRANGLE CONSIDERATIONS (1989).

9. *Id.* at 108–9.
10. R. BOLT, A MAN FOR ALL SEASONS: A PLAY IN TWO ACTS (1962).
11. *Id.* at 140.
12. W. BYRON, QUADRANGLE CONSIDERATIONS, at 109.
13. *Id.* at 109–10.
14. R. DWORKIN, LAW'S EMPIRE.
15. *See, e.g.*, Karl Vick, *MD Judge Taking Heat in Cuckolded Killer Case,* WASHINGTON POST, October 30, 1994, at A1.
16. *Id.*
17. *Id.*
18. Editorial, *Judge Cahill's Grievous Failure,* BALTIMORE SUN, October 19, 1994, at 16A; Editorial, *She Strays, He Shoots, Judge Winks,* NEW YORK TIMES, October 22, 1994, at 22; Tamar Lewin, *What Penalty for a Killing in Passion,* NEW YORK TIMES, October 21, 1994, at 18.
19. Oath of Justices and Judges, 28 U.S.C. Section 453 (1988).
20. Code of Judicial Conduct for United States Judges, 69 F.R.D. 273 (1975). *See generally,* Resnik, *On The Bias: Feminist Reconsiderations of the Aspirations of Our Judges,* 61 S. CAL. L. REV. 1877–1944 (1988).
21. PROSSER & KEETON, LAW OF TORTS 5th ed. 263–355 (1984).
22. *Id.* at 356–85.
23. *See generally* Sunstein, *Incompletely Theorized Arguments,* 108 HARV. L. REV. 1733 (1995).
24. To mention only three prominent examples from liberal jurisprudence, Dworkin's liberal writings on justice extol the centrality of the virtue of institutional *consistency* to adjudication; Immanuel Kant famously placed the virtue of integrity, and more specifically of promise keeping, at the heart of the categorical imperative; and Rawls' writings are readily recognizable as an eloquent and immensely successful attempt to work out the institutional implications of the demands of the blindfold—of impartiality and universality—for social justice. *See* R. DWORKIN, LAW'S EMPIRE; I. KANT, THE GROUNDING OF THE METAPHYSICS OF MORALS (1981 ed.); and J. RAWLS, A THEORY OF JUSTICE (1971).
25. J.B. WHITE, THE LEGAL IMAGINATION: STUDIES IN THE NATURE OF LEGAL THOUGHT AND EXPRESSION (1985).
26. *Aliens* (1986).
27. H. MELVILLE, BILLY BUDD, SAILOR (AN INSIDER NARRATIVE) (1962 ed.).
28. *But see* R. WEISBERG, THE FAILURE OF THE WORD: THE PROTAGONIST AS LAWYER IN MODERN FICTION 139 (1984), for a convincing argument to the effect that Budd is not in fact guilty of the only crime for which he could legitimately be charged, and that Vere dishonestly manipulates legal doctrine to convince his drumhead court that he is.
29. H. MELVILLE, BILLY BUDD, SAILOR, at 111.
30. *Quoted in* Howarth, *Deciding to Kill: Revealing the Gender in the Task Handed to Capitol Jurors,* 1994 WISC. L. REV. 1345, 1353 (1994).
31. *Id.* at 1354.

32. In philosophy, *see, e.g.*, V. HELD, FEMINIST MORALITY; M. FRIED-MAN, WHAT ARE FRIENDS FOR? FEMINIST PERSPECTIVES ON PERSONAL RELATIONSHIPS AND MORAL THEORY (1993); AN ETHIC OF CARE: FEMI-NIST AND INTERDISCIPLINARY PERSPECTIVES (M. Larrabee, ed. 1993); J. TRONTO, MORAL BOUNDARIES: A POLITICAL ARGUMENT FOR AN ETHIC OF CARE (1993). In psychology, *see, e.g.*, C. GILLIGAN, IN A DIFFERENT VOICE, and J. MILLER, TOWARD A NEW PSYCHOLOGY OF WOMEN (1976). In education, *see* N. NODDINGS, CARING; and M. BELENKY et al., WOMEN'S WAYS OF KNOWING: THE DEVELOPMENT OF SELF, VOICE AND MIND (1986). For an excellent general review of this literature, *see* Menkel-Meadow, *What's Gender Got to Do with It? The Politics and Morality of an Ethic of Care,* 22 N.Y.U. REV. L. & SOC. CHANGE 265 (1996).

33. C. GILLIGAN, IN A DIFFERENT VOICE.

34. V. HELD, FEMINIST MORALITY.

35. M. NUSSBAUM, LOVE'S KNOWLEDGE: ESSAYS ON PHILOSOPHY AND LITERATURE (1990).

36. A. BAIER, MORAL PREJUDICES: ESSAYS ON ETHICS (1994); Baier, *Trust and Antitrust,* 96 ETHICS 231 (1986).

37. For an excellent discussion and review of the literature, *see* Wallace, *Reconstructing Judgment: Emotion and Moral Judgment,* 8 HYPATIA 61 (1993).

38. *See* Nelson, *Thinking About Gender,* 7 HYPATIA 138 (1992). *See generally* BEYOND ECONOMIC MAN: FEMINIST THEORY AND ECONOMICS (M. Ferber & J. Nelson, eds. 1993).

39. England, *The Separative Self: Androcentric Bias in Neoclassical Assumptions,* in BEYOND ECONOMIC MAN (M. Ferber & J. Nelson, eds.), at 41–43.

40. J. TRONTO, MORAL BOUNDARIES. *See generally* Menkel-Meadow, *What's Gender Got to Do with It?* at 265.

41. C. GILLIGAN, IN A DIFFERENT VOICE, at 73, 167.

42. N. NODDINGS, CARING.

43. S. RUDDICK, MATERNAL THINKING: TOWARDS A POLITICS OF PEACE (1989).

44. Only a few of the moral philosophers who have studied the ethic of care take up explicitly the issue of its relationship to justice, and of those only a few regard the relationship as other than oppositional. Exceptions include Marilyn Friedman and Virginia Held, both of whom argue that an ethic of care is not *incompatible* with an ethic of justice: that caring *can be* just, and that justice can be caring. V. HELD, FEMINIST MORALITY, at 227–28, and Friedman, *Beyond Caring: The Demoralization of Gender,* in AN ETHIC OF CARE, at 263–67 (M. Larrabee, ed.).

45. *See, e.g.*, Williams, *Deconstructing Gender,* 87 MICH. L. REV. 797 (1989). Marilyn Friedman suggests that Gilligan has located a *symbolic* difference between men and women's moral voices, which is entirely explained by stereotyping of the sexes and the divisions of labor between them. Friedman, *Beyond Caring,* at 259–63.

46. *See* L. FISHER, THE LIFE OF MAHATMA GANDHI (1950). *See also* E. ERIKSON, GANDHI'S TRUTH ON THE ORIGINS OF THE MILITANT NONVIOLENCE 29, 382 (1969); and J. BROWN, GANDHI: PRISONER OF HOPE 41 (1989).

47. L. FISHER, THE LIFE OF MAHATMA GANDHI, at 158–62.

48. *Id.*

49. *Id.* at 205–14.

50. *Id.*

51. W. C. DIMOCK, RESIDUES OF JUSTICE: LAW, LITERATURE AND PHILOSOPHY (1996).

52. *Id.* at 112–13.

53. 489 U.S. 189, 212 (1989).

54. *See* Saffle v. Parks, 110 S. Ct. 1257 (1990). *See generally* West, *Foreword: Taking Freedom Seriously,* 104 HARV. L. REV. 43, 86 (1990).

55. O. HOLMES, THE COMMON LAW (1881).

56. *Id.* at 96.

57. *See generally* R. WEISBERG, THE FAILURE OF THE WORD, at 141–59.

58. *Id.*

59. O'Connor, *The Lame Shall Enter First,* in F. O'CONNOR, THE COMPLETE SHORT STORIES 445 (1982).

60. M. TWAIN, THE ADVENTURES OF HUCKLEBERRY FINN (1988 ed.).

61. *Id.* at 87–89.

62. *See* Wallace, *Reconstructing Judgment,* for a discussion of Finn suggesting as much.

63. R. WEISBERG, VICHY LAW AND THE HOLOCAUST IN FRANCE (1996).

64. R. COVER, JUSTICE ACCUSED (1975).

65. J. NOONAN, PERSONS AND MASKS OF THE LAW (1976).

66. For a general discussion, *see* West, *Foreword,* at 43, 85–93. *See also* Nussbaum, *Equity and Mercy,* 22 PHIL. & PUB. AFF. 83 (1993).

67. *But see* Resnik, *On the Bias,* at 1877, for a critique of the virtue of objectivity. The *Yale Journal of Law and Feminism* has on its cover the drawing of a blindfolded female judge peeking out from behind the blindfold.

68. Vonnegut, *All the King's Horses,* collected in K. VONNEGUT, WELCOME TO THE MONKEY HOUSE 84 (1986).

69. 84 N.H. 114 (1929).

70. 382 P. 109 (Okla. 1962).

71. 382 P. 109 (1962).

72. *See, e.g.,* In the Matter of Baby M, 217 N.J.Super. 313 (1987); In the Matter of Baby M, 109 N.J. 396 (1988).

73. In the Matter of Baby M, 217 N.J.Super. 313 (1987).

74. Epstein, *Unconscionability: A Critical Reappraisal,* 18 J. LAW & ECON. 293 (1973).

75. *See* Epstein, *Surrogacy: The Case for Full Contractual Enforcement,* 81 VA. L. REV. 2305 (1995).

76. 350 F. 2d 445 (D.C. 1965)

77. *Contrast* Duncan Kennedy's essay on Walker Thomas, in *Distributive and Paternalist Motives in Contract and Tort Law, with Special Reference to Compulsory Terms and Unequal Bargaining Power,* 41 MD. L. REV. 563 (1982) with Epstein, *Unconscionality,* at 293. *See generally* West, *Taking Preferences Seriously,* in R. WEST, NARRATIVE, AUTHORITY AND LAW 299 (1993).

78. J. RAWLS, A THEORY OF JUSTICE 12, 15, 72.

79. R. NOZICK, ANARCHY, STATE AND UTOPIA 224–27 (1974).

80. M. SANDEL, LIBERALISM AND THE LIMITS OF JUSTICE (1982).

81. Vonnegut, *Harrison Bergeron,* collected in K. VONNEGUT, WEL-COME TO THE MONKEY HOUSE 7.

82. For the seminal argument along these lines, *see* Thompson, *A Defense of Abortion,* 1 PHIL. & PUB. AFF. 47 (1971). Thompson famously argued for the morality of some abortions by analogizing the pregnant woman to a genderless individual involuntarily hooked up to an ailing famous violinist for nine months, who is told that she must remain so because her interest in mobility could not possibly outweigh his right to life. She concludes from the thought experiment that at least some involuntary pregnancies impose duties of good samaritanism on women which have no correlate in men's lives, and that for that reason women are justified in terminating them regardless of whether or not the fetus is construed as a person. Don Regan makes a comparable constitutional argument in *Re-Writing Roe v. Wade,* 77 MICH. L. REV. 1569 (1979). *See also* Amicus Brief of 274 Organizations in Support of Roe v. Wade in Turnock v. Ragsdale, nos. 88–790 and 88–805 (1989). For an excellent discussion of the strengths and weaknesses of these sorts of arguments, *see* R. COLKER, PREGNANT MEN: PRACTICE, THEORY AND LAW (1994).

83. S. RUDDICK, MATERNAL THINKING.

84. *See* C. GILLIGAN, IN A DIFFERENT VOICE, at 71–108.

85. *Id. See also* the Brief of Amici Curiae National Abortion Rights Action League, colloquially known as the "voices brief," chronicling the reasons and reasoning of women seeking abortions, filed in Thornburgh v. Am. College of Obstetricians and Gynecologists, 476 U.S. 747 (1985), and Torres & Forrest, *Why Do Women Have Abortions?* 20 FAMILY PLANNING PERSPECTIVE 169 (July-Aug. 1988). *See generally* West, *Foreword,* at 43, 81–85, and authorities cited and discussed therein.

86. For a liberal argument to this effect, *see, e.g.,* R. DWORKIN, LIFE'S DOMINION: AN ARGUMENT ABOUT ABORTION, EUTHANASIA, AND INDI-VIDUAL FREEDOM (1993). Marcy Wilder, legal director for the National Abortion Rights Action League, also suggests the increasing need of the reproductive rights movement to engage moral arguments for and against abortion, in *The Rule of Law, the Rise of Violence and the Role of Morality: Reframing America's Abortion Debate* (unpublished manuscript, on file with author).

Catharine MacKinnon suggests that acknowledgment of the fetus's interests is not fatal to radical arguments for abortion, particularly if we understand the decision as rooted in a woman's "deep responsibility as a mother. MacKinnon, *Reflections on Sex Equality Under Law,* 100 YALE L. J. 1281, 1318 (1991). From a postmodern perspective, Joan Williams has made a similar claim, although she couches it in strategic terms. Williams, *Gender Wars: Selfless Women in the Republic of Choice,* 66 N.Y.U. L. REV. 1559, 1589–94 (1991). *See also* Davis, *Neglected Stories and the Lawfulness of Roe v. Wade,* 28 HARV. C.R.-C.L. L. REV. 299 (1993); and Hanigsberg, *Homologizing Pregnancy and Motherhood: A Consideration of Abortion,* 94 MICH. L. REV. 371, 373 (1995).

Linda McClain has argued in a number of pieces that this argument and the literature expounding it pose serious threats to reproductive freedom. *See* McClain, *The Poverty of Privacy,* 3 COLUM. J. GENDER & L. 119, 139–40 (1992); and *Atomistic Man Revisited: Liberalism, Connection, and Feminist Jurisprudence,* 65 S. CAL. L. REV. 1171 (1992). For a useful and provocative analysis of this and related issues, *see* McClain, *Irresponsible Reproduction,* 47 HASTINGS L. REV. 339 (1996).

87. The best defense of this position is Ronald Dworkin's. *See* Dworkin, *Liberalism,* in R. DWORKIN, A MATTER OF PRINCIPLE, at 181.

88. For a recent attempt to argue for wealth redistribution along these lines, *see* C. SUNSTEIN, THE PARTIAL CONSTITUTION 338–45 (1993).

89. For an extended argument to this effect, *see* S. RUDDICK, MATERNAL THINKING.

90. *See, e.g.,* Brief for the Amici Curiae Women Who Have Had Abortions and Friend of Amici Curiae in Support of Appellees, Webster v. Reproductive Health Services, 109 S. Ct. 3040 (1989) (No. 88–605), and Brief of Amici Curiae National Abortion Rights Action League, Thornburgh v. Am. College of Obstetricians and Gynecologists, 476 U.S. 747 (1985) (Nos. 84–495 and 84–1379). *See also* the authorities cited in notes 85 and 86 *supra.*

91. *See* R. WEST, PROGRESSIVE CONSTITUTIONALISM: RECONSTRUCTING THE FOURTEENTH AMENDMENT (1994).

92. For a searing memoir that seeks to describe the extraordinary damage done to minority children by the proliferation, violence, intensity, and social acceptability of this racist hate speech in Little Rock, Arkansas at the end of the 1950s, *see* M. BEALS, WARRIORS DON'T CRY (1994).

93. 163 U.S. 537 (1896).

94. *Id.* at 559.

95. 60 U.S. 393 (1857).

96. P. WILLIAMS, THE ALCHEMY OF RACE AND RIGHTS: DIARY OF A LAW PROFESSOR (1991).

97. Tom Keyser, *Shunned: An Outcast's Lonely Mission,* BALTIMORE SUN, August 22, 1994, at 1.

98. For journalistic reports on the Peacock case, see Karl Vick, *MD Judge Taking Heat in Cuckolded Killer Case,* WASHINGTON POST, October 30, 1994, at A1.

99. For general discussions of the cultural defense, *see* Renteln, *A Justifi-*

cation of the Cultural Defense as a Partial Excuse, 2 S. CAL. REV. OF L. & WOMEN'S STUD. 488 (1993); and Note, *The Cultural Defense in the Criminal Law,* 99 HARV. L. REV. 1274 (1986).

100. *See* notes 15–18, *supra.*

101. *See* Grillo, *The Mediation Alternative: Process Dangers for Women,* 100 YALE L. J. 1545 (1991).

102. *See* West, *The Difference in Women's Hedonic Lives: A Phenomenological Critique of Feminist Legal Theory,* 3 WISC. WOMEN'S L. J. 81 (1987).

103. *See* ch. 2.

104. C. GILLIGAN, IN A DIFFERENT VOICE.

105. *Id.* at 164.

106. *Id.*

107. *Id.*

108. S. SILVERSTEIN, THE GIVING TREE (1964).

109. *See* N. CHODOROW, THE REPRODUCTION OF MOTHERING; M. FINEMAN, THE NEUTERED MOTHER: THE SEXUAL FAMILY AND OTHER TWENTIETH CENTURY TRAGEDIES (1995); A. HOCHSCHILD, THE SECOND SHIFT: WORKING PARENTS AND THE REVOLUTION AT HOME (1989).

110. *See* Russell, *Husbands Who Rape Their Wives,* in D. RUSSELL, RAPE IN MARRIAGE (1990); Estrich, *Rape,* 95 YALE L. J. 1087 (1986); D. RUSSELL, THE SECRET TRAUMA: INCEST IN THE LIVES OF GIRLS AND WOMEN (1986); D. RUSSELL, SEXUAL EXPLOITATION: RAPE, CHILD SEXUAL ABUSE, AND WORKPLACE HARASSMENT (1984).

111. On family law, *see, e.g.,* Weitzman, *The Economics of Divorce: Social and Economic Consequences of Property, Alimony and Child Support Awards,* 28 U.C.L.A. L. REV. 1181 (1981); and Becker, *Prince Charming: Abstract Equality,* 1987 SUP. CT. REV. 201 (1987); on criminal law, *see* Estrich, *Rape,* 95 YALE L. J. 1087 (1986); and MacKinnon, *Rape: On Coercion and Consent,* in TOWARD A FEMINIST THEORY OF THE STATE 171, 175 (1989); on Torts, see Larson, *"Women Understand So Little, They Call My Good Nature 'Deceit' ": A Feminist Rethinking of Seduction,* 93 COLUM. L. REV. 374 (1993). For a general bibliography of feminist writing on all legal topics, *see* FEMINIST JURISPRUDENCE, WOMEN AND THE LAW BIBLIOGRAPHY (R. Munro, ed. 1997).

112. West, *Equality Theory, Marital Rape, and the Promise of the Fourteenth Amendment,* 42 FLA. L. REV. 45 (1990).

113. 438 U.S. 265 (1978)

114. 488 U.S. 469 (1989).

115. 115 S. Ct. 2097 (1995).

116. W. BYRON, QUADRANGLE CONSIDERATIONS.

117. M. TUSHNET, THE AMERICAN LAW OF SLAVERY 69 (1981).

118. S. OKIN, JUSTICE, GENDER AND THE FAMILY (1989).

119. 347 U.S. 483 (1954).

120. *Id.*

NOTES TO CHAPTER 2

1. In AN INTRODUCTION TO THE PRINCIPLES OF MORALS AND LEG-ISLATION, ch. 1, 791–95 (1967 ed.), Jeremy Bentham postulated that the goal of law should be the minimization of pains and the maximization of pleasures, calculated hedonically. This utilitarian approach to law and legislation eventually coalesced in Instrumentalism, the Anglo-American movement which received its clearest exposition in R. SUMMERS, INSTRUMENTALISM AND AMERICAN LEGAL THEORY (1982). Most important for modern thinkers, in *The Problem of Social Cost,* 3 J. LAW & ECON. 1 (1960), Robert Coase asserts with no argument that the goal of legal rules should be to minimize the greatest harm in situations of conflict.

2. Mill, *On Liberty,* in J.S. MILL, UTILITARIANISM, ON LIBERTY, AND CONSIDERATIONS ON REPRESENTATIVE GOVERNMENT 65 (1972 ed.).

3. *See* Coase, *The Problem of Social Cost;* M. POLINSKY, AN INTRODUCTION TO LAW AND ECONOMICS (1983).

4. Coase, *The Problem of Social Cost.*

5. For further elaboration of this critique of formal equality, *see* Becker, *Prince Charming: Abstract Equality,* 1987 SUP. CT. REV. 201 (1987); and Littleton, *Reconstructing Sexual Equality,* 75 CAL. L. REV. 1279 (1987).

6. The literature is voluminous. *See* M. GORDON & S. RIGER, THE FEMALE FEAR (1989); S. BROWNMILLER, AGAINST OUR WILL: MEN, WOMEN, AND RAPE (1975); S. ESTRICH, REAL RAPE: HOW THE LEGAL SYSTEM VICTIMIZES WOMEN WHO SAY NO (1987); Henderson, *Real Rape* (Book Review), 3 BERK. WOMEN'S L. J. 193 (1987); Bumiller, *Rape as a Legal Symbol: An Essay on Sexual Violence and Racism,* 42 MIAMI L. REV. 75 (1987); Roberts, *Is the Law Male? Rape, Violence, and Women's Autonomy,* 69 CHI.-KENT L. REV. 359 (1993); MacKinnon, *Rape: On Coercion and Consent,* in C. MACKINNON, TOWARD A FEMINIST THEORY OF THE STATE 172 (1989).

7. MacKinnon discusses and criticizes this strategy in *Rape: On Coercion and Consent,* at 173–74.

8. *See, e.g.,* Schulhofer, *The Feminist Challenge in Criminal Law,* 143 PA. L. REV. 2151 (1995); Roberts, *Is the Law Male?* 359; Dripps, *Beyond Rape: An Essay on the Difference Between the Presence of Force and the Absence of Consent,* 92 COLUM. L. REV. 1780 (1992).

9. M. GORDON & S. RIGER, THE FEMALE FEAR.

10. *See* West, *Legitimating the Illegitimate: A Comment on "Beyond Rape,"* 93 COLUM. L. REV. 1442 (1993); Henderson, *Rape and Responsibility,* 11 LAW & PHIL. 127 (1992).

11. According to FBI statistics, in 1990 30% of women killed were murdered by their husbands or boyfriends while only 4% of men were murdered by their wives or girlfriends. B. Miller, *Thou Shalt Not Stalk,* CHICAGO TRIBUNE, Apr. 18, 1993, Sec. 10, at 16. *See generally* Mahoney, *Legal Images of Battered Women: Redefining the Issue of Separation,* 90 MICH. L. REV. 1

(1991); and Littleton, *Women's Experience and the Problem of Transition: Perspectives on Male Battering of Women*, 1989 U. CHI. LEG. F. 23 (1989).

12. Dripps et al., *Men, Women and Rape*, 63 FORDHAM L. REV. 125 (1994); Ingram, *Date Rape: It's Time for "No" to Really Mean "No,"* 21 AM. J. CRIM. L. 3 (1993); Rothschild, *Recognizing Another Face of Hate Crime: Rape as a Gender-Bias Crime*, 4 MD. J. CONT. LEG. ISS. 231 (1993); West, *Equality Theory, Marital Rape, and the Promise of the Fourteenth Amendment*, 42 FLA. L. REV. 45 (1990).

13. Stefan, *The Cloak of Benevolence* (Paper presented at Center for Advanced Feminist Studies (Oct. 1989); Beck & Van der Kolk, *Reports of Childhood Incest and Current Behavior of Chronically Hospitalized Psychotic Women*, 144 AM. J. PSYCHIATRY 1474 (1987).

14. Mantese et al., *Medical and Legal Aspects of Rape and Resistance*, 12 J. LEG. MED. 59 (1991).

15. *See* Bowman, *Street Harassment and the Informal Ghettoization of Women*, 106 HARV. L. REV. 517 (1993).

16. *Id.*

17. *See* J. BENTHAM, AN INTRODUCTION TO THE PRINCIPLES OF MORALS AND LEGISLATION, ch. 1, and Richard Posner's partial endorsement and partial critique of the Benthamic position in R. POSNER, THE ECONOMICS OF JUSTICE 41–42 (1981).

18. This is the damage done by even consensual heterosexuality which Andrea Dworkin has tried to articulate in her book INTERCOURSE (1988). I address these harms briefly in *The Harm of Consensual Sex*, 94 AM. PHIL. ASSOC. NEWSLETTER 52 (1995).

19. Lenore Walker, of course, famously identified this harm as a "syndrome." The "battered wife syndrome" can in some circumstances be used to explain to a jury the passivity, and then the sudden lethal violence, of a battered woman who eventually kills or severely injures her batterer, and can accordingly excuse the retaliatory act. See L. WALKER, THE BATTERED WOMAN (1979). Feminists are ambivalent over the ultimate value of the battered wife syndrome. Although it has obvious short-term political appeal, it also arguably disserves women by characterizing the battered woman as primarily burdened by a psychological "syndrome" rather than by an abusive, violent spouse: it focuses too much attention (and, implicitly, blame) on the battered woman rather than the batterer. *See* Littleton, *Women's Experience and the Problem of Transition*. It is also an oddly apposite characterization of many of the women in whose behalf the syndrome is invoked: the woman who *retaliates* is not, by definition, suffering from an excess of passivity. But whatever the political downside of identifying a "syndrome," those risks should not deter us from the work of properly describing the psychic harms occasioned by domestic violence. Most battered wives and girlfriends do not kill their batterers, and many make no attempt to leave. We need to explore why this might be so. One explanation is simply that their will is overborne, which is loosely the phenomenon I have tried to explicate in the text.

20. Relatedly, it is also true that a battered wife may well not leave her husband for the simple reason that she loves him, and has the strength and courage to forgive him.

21. For a full discussion of the problems facing battered women who seek to leave violent domestic relationships, *see* Mahoney, *Exit: Power and the Idea of Leaving in Love, Work, and the Confirmation Hearings,* 65 CAL. L. REV. 1283 (1992).

22. Those harms are well documented in Regan, *Re-Writing Roe v. Wade,* 77 MICH. L. REV. 1569 (1979).

23. For a moving account of this and related harms, *see* Paltrow, *National Abortion Rights Action League Amicus Brief for Richard Thornburgh v. Am. College of Obstetricians and Gynecologists,* 9 WOMEN'S RTS. L. REPORTER 3 (1986).

24. J. BENTHAM, AN INTRODUCTION TO THE PRINCIPLES OF MORALS AND LEGISLATION, at ch. 1.

25. I. KANT, THE GROUNDING OF THE METAPHYSICS OF MORALS (1981 ed.).

26. C. PAGLIA, SEXUAL PERSONAE: ART AND DECADENCE FROM NEFERTITI TO EMILY DICKINSON (1990).

27. Paglia argues this forcefully in SEXUAL PERSONAE, at 1–40. Simone de Beauvoir suggests something of this sort in THE SECOND SEX 386 (1952).

28. J. BENTHAM, AN INTRODUCTION TO THE PRINCIPLES OF MORALS AND LEGISLATION.

29. D. DINNERSTEIN, THE MERMAID AND THE MINOTAUR: SEXUAL ARRANGEMENTS AND HUMAN MALAISE (1976); N. CHODOROW, THE REPRODUCTION OF MOTHERING: PSYCHOANALYSIS AND THE SOCIOLOGY OF GENDER (1978); C. GILLIGAN, IN A DIFFERENT VOICE: PSYCHOLOGICAL THEORY AND WOMEN'S DEVELOPMENT (1982), at 24–63, (1982).

30. Louise Erdrich provides a moving account in THE BLUEJAY'S DANCE: A BIRTH YEAR (1995).

31. *See* the debate between MacKinnon and Gilligan in MacKinnon, Gilligan, Menkel-Meadow, *Feminist Discourse, Moral Values, and the Law: A Conversation,* 34 BUFF. L. REV. 11 (1985).

32. A. HOCHSCHILD, THE SECOND SHIFT: WORKING PARENTS AND THE REVOLUTION AT HOME (1989).

33. *See* Hadfield, *Households at Work: Beyond Labor Market Policies to Remedy the Gender Gap,* 82 GEO. L. J. 89 (1993).

34. T. OLSEN, SILENCES (1978).

35. *Quoted in* T. OLSEN, SILENCES, at 203–6.

36. Try to imagine a congresswoman breast-feeding a baby while conducting a house subcommittee hearing on defense appropriations.

37. For communitarian critiques of individualism, *see, e.g.,* R. BELLAH et al., HABITS OF THE HEART: INDIVIDUALISM AND COMMITMENT IN AMERICAN LIFE (1985); and M. REGAN, FAMILY LAW AND THE PURSUIT OF INTIMACY (1993).

38. N. NODDINGS, CARING: A FEMINIST APPROACH TO ETHICS AND MORAL EDUCATION (1984); C. GILLIGAN, IN A DIFFERENT VOICE; S. RUDDICK, MATERNAL THINKING: TOWARDS A POLITICS OF PEACE (1989); Resnik, *On the Bias: Feminist Reconsiderations of the Aspirations for Our Judges,* 61 S. CAL. L. REV. 1877 (1988); Menkel-Meadow, *Portia Redux: Another Look at Gender, Feminism, and Legal Ethics,* 2 VA. J. SOC. POL'Y & L. 75 (1994); R. WEST, NARRATIVE, AUTHORITY AND LAW (1993).

39. M. GORDON & S. RIGER, THE FEMALE FEAR.

40. *See* West, *The Difference in Women's Hedonic Lives: A Phenomenological Critique of Feminist Legal Theory,* 3 WISC. WOMEN'S L. J. 81 (1987).

41. C. PAGLIA, VAMPS AND TRAMPS: NEW ESSAYS 264 (1994).

42. Nedelsky, *Reconceiving Autonomy: Sources, Thoughts, and Possibilities,* 1 YALE J. L. & FEM. 7 (1989).

43. *Little Big Man* (1970).

44. N. NODDINGS, CARING; S. RUDDICK, MATERNAL THINKING.

45. PAGLIA, SEXUAL PERSONAE. *See also* R. POSNER, SEX AND REASON (1992).

46. C. GILLIGAN, IN A DIFFERENT VOICE, at 164–65; A. RICH, ON LIES, SECRETS, AND SILENCE: SELECTED PROSE, 1966–78, 185–94 (1979).

47. Unger, *The Critical Legal Studies Movement,* 96 HARV. L. REV. 561 (1983); R. BELLAH et al., HABITS OF THE HEART.

48. Hadfield, *Households at Work.*

49. M. REGAN, FAMILY LAW AND THE PURSUIT OF INTIMACY.

50. Becker & Murphy, *The Family and the State,* 31 J. LAW & ECON. 1 (1988).

51. S. RUDDICK, MATERNAL THINKING; V. HELD, FEMINIST MORALITY: TRANSFORMING CULTURE, SOCIETY AND POLITICS (1993).

52. *See generally* Kennedy, *Distributive and Paternalist Motives in Contract and Tort Law, with Special Reference to Compulsory Terms and Unequal Bargaining Power,* 41 MD. L. REV. 563 (1982).

53. Deborah Tannen has explored the more benign implications of this in her work on the differences in speech patterns between women and men in the workplace. *See* D. TANNEN, TALKING FROM NINE TO FIVE: HOW WOMEN'S AND MEN'S CONVERSATIONAL STYLES AFFECT WHO GETS HEARD, WHO GETS CREDIT, AND WHAT GETS DONE AT WORK (1994).

54. For some empirical support, *see* Ayres, *Further Evidence of Discrimination in New Car Negotiations and Estimates of Its Cause,* 94 MICH. L. REV. 109 (1995).

55. *See* Becker, *Politics, Differences, and Economic Rights,* 1989 U. CHI. L. REV. 169, 183–88 (1989).

56. Rose, *Bargaining and Gender,* 18 HARV. J. L. & PUB. POL. 547 (1995).

57. *Id.*

58. *See* A. HOCHSCHILD, THE SECOND SHIFT; Hadfield, *Households at Work. See generally* BEYOND ECONOMIC MAN: FEMINIST THEORY AND ECONOMICS (M. Ferber & J. Nelson, eds. 1993).

59. C. GILLIGAN, IN A DIFFERENT VOICE, at 5–24.

60. S. FIRESTONE, THE DIALECTIC OF SEX: THE CASE FOR FEMINIST REVOLUTION 232 (1970). *See generally* Regan, *Re-Writing Roe v. Wade.*

61. At least, the adoption reform movement aimed toward open adoptions, and largely fueled by the desires of adoptees and birth mothers, would seem to indicate as much. *See* Sanger, *Separating from Children,* 96 COLUM. L. REV. 375, 489–94 (1976). *See generally,* Becker, *Maternal Feelings: Myth, Taboo, and Child Custody,* 1 S. CAL. REV. L. & WOMEN'S STUD. 133 (1992).

62. Indeed, Carol Sanger argues provocatively that separations from children are quite routine in the lives of many mothers, and that law should recognize that fact. *See* Sanger, *Separating from Children.*

63. *See generally* C. GILLIGAN, IN A DIFFERENT VOICE, 151–74.

64. A report from economist June O'Neill, of the Congressional Budget Office, suggests that the wage gap between full-time male and female employees is virtually entirely attributable to either short- or long-term departures from the workforce for child raising. *See* D. Crittenden, *Yes, Motherhood Lowers Pay,* NEW YORK TIMES, Aug. 22, 1995, at 15.

65. *See* B. Lonsdorf, *The Role of Coercion in Affecting Women's Inferior Outcomes in Divorce: Implications for Researchers and Therapists,* in THE CONSEQUENCES OF DIVORCE: ECONOMIC AND CUSTODIAL IMPACT ON CHILDREN AND ADULTS 69 (C. Everett, ed. 1991). *See generally* Becker, *Strength in Diversity: Feminist Theoretical Approaches to Child Custody and Same-Sex Relationships,* 23 STETSON L. REV. 701, 720–21 (1994); Singer, *The Privatization of Family Law,* 1992 WISC. L. REV. 1443 (1992); Fineman, *Dominant Discourse, Professional Language, and Legal Change in Child Custody Decisionmaking,* 101 HARV. L. REV. 727 (1988).

66. *See* Dowd, *Work and Family: The Gender Paradox and the Limitations of Discrimination Analysis in Restructuring the Workplace,* 24 HARV. C.R.-C.L. L. REV. 79 (1989). *See also* Brinig, *Comment on Jana Singer's "Alimony and Efficiency,"* 82 GEO. L. J. 2423 (1994).

67. Whether women choose such work or whether the employees structure pay scales in a way that penalizes such women is a contested interpretive issue. The question arose most clearly in EEOC v. Sears, 628 F. Supp. 1264 (N.Dt. Ill. 1986), in which Sears successfully argued as a defense to a Title VII discrimination case that its female employees voluntarily "chose" low-paying, noncommissioned sales jobs so as to facilitate child-raising responsibilities. For discussions of the Sears case, *see* Schultz, *Telling Stories About Women and Work: Judicial Interpretations of Sex Segregation in the Workplace in Title VII Cases Raising the Lack of Interest Argument,* 103 HARV. L. REV. 1749, 1840–41 (1990); Milkman, *Women's History and the Sears Case,* 12 FEMINIST STUD. 375 (1986); and Finley, *Choice and Freedom: Elusive Issues in the Search for Gender Justice,* 96 YALE L. J. 914 (1987).

68. Estimates suggest that women with small children spend as much as

70 to 80 hours a week minimum child rearing. Polatnick, *Why Men Don't Rear Children: A Power Analysis,* in MOTHERING: ESSAYS IN FEMINIST THEORY (J. Trebilcot, ed. 1984). *See also* Komter, *Hidden Power in Marriage,* 3 GENDER & SOCIETY 187 (1989).

69. C. GILLIGAN, IN A DIFFERENT VOICE, at 171.

70. *See* N. CHODOROW, THE REPRODUCTION OF MOTHERING, at 134.

71. C. GILLIGAN, IN A DIFFERENT VOICE, at 171; N. CHODOROW, THE REPRODUCTION OF MOTHERING, at 134.

72. Aafke Komter found, after interviewing 60 couples in the Netherlands, that the women interviewed were significantly more dissatisfied in their marriages than the men, particularly with respect to leisure time, sexuality, and domestic labor. Generally, women wanted more emotional connection than men, and reported, in greater numbers than did men, having sacrificed friendships of which their husbands did not approve and doing substantially more household labor. *See* Komter, *Hidden Power in Marriage.*

Hope Landrine concludes from a study of depression in women that women suffer from depression at twice the rate as men, and that married women are more at risk than single women or married men. *See* Landrine, *Depression and Stereotypes of Women: Preliminary Empirical Analyses of the Gender-Role Hypothesis,* 19 SEX ROLES 527 (1988).

73. Glaspell, *A Jury of Her Peers,* in LAW IN LITERATURE: LEGAL THEMES IN SHORT STORIES 124 (E. Gemmette, ed. 1992).

74. N. CHODOROW, THE REPRODUCTION OF MOTHERING, at 168.

75. Nel Noddings suggests as much. N. NODDINGS, CARING, at 128.

76. J.C. SMITH & C. FERSTMAN, THE CASTRATION OF OEDIPUS: PSYCHOANALYSIS, POSTMODERNISM, AND FEMINISM (1996).

77. *Id.* at 207–55.

78. For a full discussion of the legal implications of this sociobiological insight, *see* R. POSNER, SEX AND REASON.

79. Rich, *Compulsory Heterosexuality and Lesbian Existence,* 5 SIGNS 631 (1980).

80. A. HOCHSCHILD, THE SECOND SHIFT.

81. Schulhofer, *The Feminist Challenge in Criminal Law,* 143 PA. L. REV. 2151 (1995); Dripps, *Beyond Rape: An Essay on the Difference Between the Presence of Force and the Absence of Consent,* 92 COLUM. L. REV. 1780 (1992); Henderson, *Rape and Responsibility,* 11 LAW & PHIL. 127 (1992).

82. West, *Equality Theory, Marital Rape, and the Promise of the Fourteenth Amendment.*

83. S. ESTRICH, REAL RAPE; Henderson, *Real Rape,* (Book Review).

84. *See generally,* S. ESTRICH, REAL RAPE.

85. 410 U.S. 113 (1973).

86. *Id.*

87. 381 U.S. 479 (1965).

88. For an exhaustive history of Roe v. Wade which seems, perhaps unwittingly, to support this interpretation, *see* D. GARROW, LIBERTY AND SEXUALITY: A RIGHT TO PRIVACY AND THE MAKING OF ROE V. WADE (1994).

I comment in more length on this history in my book review of Garrow's work, in 13 LAW & HISTORY 433 (1995).

89. *See* MacKinnon, *Reflections on Sex Equality under Law,* 100 YALE L. J. 1281 (1991); MacKinnon, *Abortion: On Public and Private,* in C. MACKIN-NON, TOWARD A FEMINIST THEORY OF THE STATE 184 (1989); MacKin-non, *Privacy v. Equality: Beyond Roe v. Wade,* in C. MACKINNON, FEMINISM UNMODIFIED: DISCOURSES ON LIFE AND LAW 93 (1987).

90. In a recent piece on abortion, Judith Jarvis Thomson notes that while the "literature on abortion typically refers to pregnant women, . . . thirteen year old girls are not women, they are children. . . . [I]t is an outrageous idea that a child, pregnant due to rape or seduction, is morally required to carry the fetus to term." Thomson, *Abortion,* 20(3) BOSTON REVIEW, Summer 1995.

91. This aspect of abortion rights is emphasized by Feminists for Life. *See* Amicus Brief of Feminists for Life, No. 90–985, in Bray v. Alexandria Women's Health Clinic, 113. S. Ct. 753 (1993). For general discussions, *see* K. LUKER, ABORTION AND THE POLITICS OF MOTHERHOOD (1984); M. FRYE, THE POLITICS OF REALITY: ESSAYS IN FEMINIST THEORY 100–101 (1983); and E. FOX-GENOVESE, FEMINISM WITHOUT ILLUSIONS: A CRITIQUE OF INDIVIDUALISM (1991).

92. C. MACKINNON, FEMINISM UNMODIFIED; Sunstein, *Feminism and Legal Theory: Feminism Unmodified,* 101 HARV. L. REV. 826 (1988).

93. *See generally* C. WILLIAMS, BLACK TEENAGE MOTHERS: PREG-NANCY AND CHILD REARING FROM THEIR PERSPECTIVE (1991).

94. *See* J. TENBROEK, EQUAL UNDER LAW (1965). I discuss this in detail in *Toward an Abolitionist Interpretation of the Fourteenth Amend-ment,* 94 W.VA. L. REV. 111 (1991).

95. West, *Equality Theory, Marital Rape, and the Promise of the Four-teenth Amendment*; Note, *To Have and to Hold: The Marital Rape Exemption and the Fourteenth Amendment,* 42 FLA. L. REV. 45 (1990).

96. *See* West, *Equality Theory.*

97. *Id.* at 45–48.

98. *Id.*

99. Bowman, *Street Harassment and the Informal Ghettoization of Women.*

100. L. WEITZMAN, THE DIVORCE REVOLUTION: THE UNEXPECTED SOCIAL AND ECONOMIC CONSEQUENCES FOR WOMEN AND CHILDREN IN AMERICA (1985); Singer, *Divorce Reform and Gender Justice,* 67 N.C. L. REV. 1103 (1989).

101. Singer, *The Privatization of Family Law,* 1992 WISC. L. REV. 1443 (1992).

102. Becker, *Maternal Feelings: Myth, Taboo, and Child Custody,* 1 S. CAL. REV. L. & WOMEN'S STUD. 133 (1992).

103. For a collection of the law on the status of interspousal tort immunity in all jurisdictions, *see* Siegal, *The Rule of Love: Wife Beating as Prerogative and Privacy,* 105 YALE L. J. 2117, 2162–63 (1996).

104. Woodhouse, *Sex, Lies and Dissipation: The Discourses of Fault in a No-Fault Era,* 82 GEO. L. J. 2525 (1994).

105. *Id.*

106. *See generally* Singer, *The Privatization of Family Law.*

107. *See* Fineman, *The Neutered Mother,* 46 MIAMI L. REV. 653 (1992); M. FINEMAN, THE NEUTERED MOTHER: THE SEXUAL FAMILY AND OTHER TWENTIETH CENTURY TRAGEDIES (1995).

108. Becker, *Maternal Feelings.*

109. Field, *Surrogacy Contracts: Gestational and Traditional: The Argument for Nonenforcement,* 31 WASHBURN L. J. 1, 5–13, 17 (1991).

110. Carol Sanger argues that the traditional refusal of the law to consider the preferences of birth mothers for some continuing contact with adopted children stemmed from its insistence on motherhood as an "all or nothing proposition." Sanger, *Separating from Children,* at 489–94.

111. Becker, *Maternal Feelings,* at 172–73.

112. M. FINEMAN, THE NEUTERED MOTHER.

113. *See generally* THE POLITICS OF LAW: A PROGRESSIVE CRITIQUE (D. Kairys, ed. 1990).

114. *See* Beermann & Singer, *Baseline Questions in Legal Reasoning: The Example of Property in Jobs,* 23 GA. L. REV. 911 (1989).

115. *See* Kennedy, *Distributive and Paternalist Motives in Contract and Tort Law with Special Reference to Compulsory Terms and Unequal Bargaining Power*; and Kennedy, *Form and Substance in Private Law Adjudication,* 89 HARV. L. REV. 1685 (1976).

116. R. POSNER, THE ECONOMICS OF JUSTICE, at 7.

117. These two examples are explored in more detail in Gordon, *Unfreezing Legal Reality: Critical Approaches to Law,* 15 FLA. ST. L. REV. 195 (1987); and Beermann & Singer, *Baseline Questions in Legal Reasoning: The Example of Property in Jobs,* 23 GA. L. REV. 911 (1989).

118. For critiques, *see, e.g.*, West, *Submission, Choice, and Ethics: A Rejoinder to Judge Posner,* 99 HARV. L. REV. 1449 (1986); Ehrenreich, *The Colonization of the Womb,* 43 DUKE L. J. 492 (1993).

119. *See* Reed v. Reed, 404 U.S. 71 (1971); Frontiero v. Richardson, 411 U.S. 677 (1973); Craig v. Boren, 429 U.S. 190 (1976).

120. This objection to formal equality is explored in Becker, *Prince Charming: Abstract Equality.*

121. *See* Olsen, *The Family and the Market: A Study of Ideology and Legal Reform,* 96 HARV. L. REV. 1497 (1983).

122. G. BECKER, A TREATISE ON THE FAMILY (1981); Posner, *The Radical Feminist Critique of Sex and Reason,* 25 CONN. L. REV. 515 (1993).

123. *See* Williams, *Equality's Riddle: Pregnancy and the Equal Treatment/Special Treatment Debate,* 13 REV. L. & SOC. CHANGE 325 (1984); W. KAMINER, A FEARFUL FREEDOM (1990).

124. *See* Siegal, *The Rule of Love,* at 2117.

125. *See* Regan, *Spouses and Strangers: Divorce Obligations and Property Rhetoric,* 82 GEO. L. J. 2303 (1994).

126. *See* American Booksellers Ass'n, Inc. v. Hudnut, 771 F.2d 323 (7th Cir. 1985), aff'd, 475 U.S. 1001 (1986); Bowman, *Street Harassment and the Informal Ghettoization of Women*; C. MACKINNON, SEXUAL HARASSMENT OF WORKING WOMEN (1979); C. MACKINNON, ONLY WORDS (1993).

127. 477 U.S. 57 (1986).

128. MacKinnon, *Frances Biddle's Sister: Pornography, Civil Rights, and Speech,* in C. MACKINNON, FEMINISM UNMODIFIED 163; MacKinnon, *Pornography, Civil Rights, and Speech,* 20 HARV. C.R.-C.L. L. REV. 1 (1985).

129. Bowman, *Street Harassment and the Informal Ghettoization of Women.*

130. American Booksellers Ass'n, Inc. v. Hudnut, 791 F.2d 323 (7th Cir. 1985), aff'd, 475 U.S. 1001 (1986).

131. 477 U.S. 57 (1986).

132. RAV v. City of St. Paul, 505 U.S. 377 (1992).

133. *Id.* at 410.

134. Bowman, *Street Harassment and the Informal Ghettoization of Women,* at 546.

135. American Booksellers Ass'n, Inc. v. Hudnut, 791 F.2d 323 (7th Cir. 1985), aff'd, 475 U.S. 1001 (1986). *See also* Emerson, *Pornography and the First Amendment: A Reply to Professor MacKinnon,* 3 YALE J. L. & POL. REV. 130 (1984).

136. *See* C. SUNSTEIN, DEMOCRACY AND THE PROBLEM OF FREE SPEECH (1993).

137. West, *Constitutional Skepticism,* 72 B. U. L. REV. 765 (1992).

138. C. SUNSTEIN, THE PARTIAL CONSTITUTION (1993).

139. Unger, *The Critical Legal Studies Movement,* 96 HARV. L. REV. 561 (1983).

140. *See* Nedelsky, *Reconceiving Autonomy: Sources, Thoughts, and Possibilities,* 1 YALE J. L. & FEM. 7 (1989).

141. *See generally* C. SUNSTEIN, THE PARTIAL CONSTITUTION.

142. Most persuasively, C. SUNSTEIN, THE PARTIAL CONSTITUTION.

143. For an argument to this effect, *see* Cole & Eskridge, *From Hand-Holding to Sodomy: First Amendment Protection of Homosexual (Expressive) Conduct,* 29 HARV. C.R.-C.L. L. REV. 319 (1994).

144. *Id.*

145. *See* Bowers v. Hardwick, 478 U.S. 186 (1986).

146. *See* Eskridge, *A History of Same-Sex Marriage,* 79 VA. L. REV. 1419 (1993).

147. Bottoms v. Bottoms, 249 Va. 410, 457 S.E.2d 102 (1995); Alison D. v. Virginia M., 77 N.Y.2d 651, 572 N.E.2d 27 (1991); S.E.G. v. R.A.G., 735 S.W.2d 164 (Mo.App. 1987).

148. *See* Ehrenreich, *The Colonization of the Womb.*

149. Karen Czapanskiy discusses this asymmetry in *Volunteers and Draftees: The Struggle for Parental Equality,* 38 U.C.L.A. L. REV. 1415 (1991).

150. Bottoms v. Bottoms, 249 Va. 410, 457 S.E.2d 102 (1995).

151. For discussions of the studies documenting varying rates of abuse as

well as differences in sentencing of male and female abusers, *see* Raeder, *Gender and Sentencing: Single Moms, Battered Women, and Other Sex-Based Anomalies in the Gender-Free World of the Federal Sentencing Guidelines,* 20 PEPP. L. REV. 905, 908 (1993); Raeder, *"Gender Neutral" Sentencing Wreaks Havoc in the Lives of Women Offenders and their Children,* 8 A.B.A. CRIM. JUST. 21, 23 (1993); and Ashe & Cahn, *Child Abuse: A Problem for Feminist Theory,* 2 TEX. J. WOMEN & L. 75, 86–90 (1993). For discussions of the disproportionate prosecution of minority, poor, single mothers for child abuse, *see* Abrams, *Complex Claimants and Reductive Moral Judgments: New Patterns in the Search for Equality,* 57 PITT. L. REV. 337, 340–41 (1996); and Roberts, *Punishing Drug Addicts Who Have Babies: Women of Color, Equality, and the Right of Privacy,* 104 HARV. L. REV. 1419 (1991).

152. Hyde Amendment, upheld in Harris v. McRae, 448 U.S. 297 (1980).

153. It is worth noting that the concept of harm plays an even smaller role in the jurisprudential movements that compete with instrumentalism for mainstream dominance: liberal, conservative, and radical legalism. Each of these three jurisprudential movements disputes the central instrumentalist claim that the minimization of harm is the point of law. First, for liberal legalists, law is "driven" not so much by a collective urge to use monopolized state force so as to minimize social harms, as by a collective desire to systematically put into practice a set of norms derived from consistent moral, social, and political *principle. See, e.g.,* R. DWORKIN, LAW'S EMPIRE (1986), A MATTER OF PRINCIPLE (1985), and TAKING RIGHTS SERIOUSLY (1977). What we aim to do with law, quite generally, is not so much minimize harms, as embody in the state a set of political principles—such as equal liberty, or representative governance—upon which we can build a morally justifiable community of free individuals. Whether or not someone is entitled to legal redress, then, depends upon whether a principle has been violated. The infliction of unnecessary harm upon one citizen by another may or may not figure as one such principle. If it does, harm has a role to play but it is by no means central.

For conservative legalists, by contrast, law is properly driven by neither an urge to minimize harms nor to systematize and put into practice social and moral principles, but rather by the need to preserve social traditions against the precipitous winds of change. *See, e.g.,* Kronman, *Precedent and Tradition,* 99 YALE L. J. 1029 (1990). Law creates, in essence, a wall of resistance against attacks on the citadel of established, and in some sense "prelegal" social and cultural artifacts, such as the family, property entitlements, high culture, or a tradition of civility. Those traditions themselves, presumably, might or might not bear some loose relationship to the ideal of minimizing harm, and if they do, minimizing harm will have a role to play in conservative understandings of law. But here as well that role is peripheral, it is not central. Law exists so as to preserve the civility of the past against the tumult, or chaos, or unpredictability, of future change. This is in essence what it is to be civilized, and law is the guardian of that ideal.

Harm plays a relatively minor role within the critical legal studies movement as well. For critical scholars, law is for the most part neither principled, nor traditional, but hierarchical: what it "aims" to do, to use Ronald Dworkin's phrase, is to perpetuate social and economic hierarchies. See THE POLITICS OF LAW: A PROGRESSIVE CRITIQUE (D. Kairys, ed.). At best, what it can do, more or less in spite of itself, only on occasion, and only because of the central indeterminacy of its language, is to become a tool—an instrument— for the *inversion*, rather than the perpetuation of hierarchies. *See* Unger, *The Critical Legal Studies Movement,* for the strongest statement of this faith. The actual ideal of law, most of the time, is maintenance of privilege, while the normative ideal of legal criticism, and on occasion of law itself, is substantive *equality*, not freedom from harm, or for that matter any other articulable moral ideal. Any other goal—such as freedom from harm—is compromised, given critical premises, by the degree to which our understanding of the goal itself is constituted by hierarchies of power which are themselves largely unjust. It follows that our conception of what harms us is not sufficiently independent of the hierarchies within which we live to be a trustworthy moral guide to reform. As an ideal, freedom from harm, no less than principled individualism or protection of social tradition, is too vulnerable to co-optation to be serviceable as a political or moral goal.

Finally, even within feminist jurisprudence, the concept of harm plays a de minimis role. Liberal and libertarian feminists tend to assume that women's well-being will be enhanced not so much by using law so as to minimize harms, as by using law to open up to women a greater panoply of choices, and then guaranteeing equal treatment by the state. Radical feminists, by contrast, view women's well-being as enhanced only through an expansion of their power. As I have argued at length elsewhere, both then attempt to improve women's well-being and to minimize the harms they suffer only indirectly— the first by maximizing choices, and the second by enhancing power. Following the liberal and radical legal theory on which they are largely modeled, neither liberal nor radical feminism aim directly at harm as the proper target of law, or well-being as the proper goal. As a consequence, legal reforms pursued by liberal feminists—such as reproductive freedom—tend to employ the language and ideals of liberalism—thus, the pro-*choice* movement. Legal reforms pursued by radical feminists—such as the anti-pornography move- ment—tend to speak the language and employ the egalitarian ideals of radi- calism. Thus, pornography is held to be a subordinating impediment to wom- en's power, and an anti-pornography ordinance an enhancement of women's equality—rather than the former simply being a harm, and the latter an enhancement of well-being. This reluctance to cast reform in the language of women's well-being and the harms women suffer in part reflects legal neces- sity: reproductive rights, if they are to be constitutionalized, must be cast in a language that resonates with the constitutional culture. If freedom from pornography is to be guaranteed as a civil right, it must be cast in the anti- discriminatory, egalitarian language of the civil rights acts. But these strategic alliances reflect—or perhaps have helped forge—a deeper intellectual con- gruence: even theoretical feminist legal scholarship reflects the anti-instrumentalist bias of the liberal and radical legal scholarship movements with which it has been closely allied. Feminist scholars tend to eschew direct reliance on harms as sufficient justification for reform, for the most part because liberal legalism and radical legalism themselves have tended to do so.

154. *See* R. SUMMERS, INSTRUMENTALISM AND AMERICAN LEGAL THEORY (1982).

155. R. POSNER, THE ECONOMICS OF JUSTICE, at 42.

156. R. POSNER, AN ECONOMIC ANALYSIS OF LAW (1992).

157. West, *Economic Man and Literary Woman: One Contrast,* 39 MERCER L. REV. 867 (1988).

158. Kelman, *Choice and Utility,* 1979 WISC. L. REV. 769, 778 (1979).

159. *Id.*

160. The slippage into libertarian distrust of the state is done most explicitly in Posner, *The Ethical Significance of Free Choice: A Reply to Professor West,* 99 Harv. L. Rev. 1431 (1986). For a discussion, *see* M. KELMAN, A GUIDE TO CRITICAL LEGAL STUDIES, at 283 (1987).

161. Coase, *The Problem of Social Cost,* at 1,6.

162. *Id.*

163. For a general discussion of the ethics of this worldview, *see* M. SAGOFF, THE ECONOMY OF THE EARTH (1988).

164. *See generally* Kelman, *Spitzer and Hoffman on Coase: A Brief Rejoinder,* 53 S. CAL. L. REV. 1215 (1980); Kennedy & Michelman, *Are Property and Contract Efficient?* 8 HOFSTRA L. REV. 711 (1980).

165. This richer, more objective form of instrumentalism owes much to J.S. Mill's famous formulation of an "ideal utilitarianism," in his essay *On Utilitarianism,* in J.S. MILL, UTILITARIANISM, ON LIBERTY, AND CONSIDERATIONS ON REPRESENTATIVE GOVERNMENT 1. Modern thinkers often express this notion in terms of human flourishing. I discuss this in West, *Disciplines, Subjectivity, and Law,* in R. WEST, NARRATIVE, AUTHORITY AND LAW 265 (1993). For closely related approaches, *see* M. NUSSBAUM, THE FRAGILITY OF GOODNESS (1986); and Radin, *Market Inalienability,* 100 Harv. L. Rev. 1849 (1987).

166. M. SAGOFF, THE ECONOMY OF THE EARTH.

167. *See* Sunstein, *Naked Preferences and the Constitution,* 84 COLUM. L. REV. 1689 (1984).

168. *See* West, *Women's Hedonic Lives,* in R. WEST, NARRATIVE, AUTHORITY AND LAW 179; West, *Submission, Choice, and Ethics: A Reply to Judge Posner.*

169. I discuss this in more detail in West, *Economic Man and Literary Woman: One Contrast,* in NARRATIVE, AUTHORITY AND LAW 251.

170. MacKinnon, *Reflections on Sex Equality under Law,* 100 YALE L. J. 1281 (1991).

171. *See, e.g.,* Okin, *Sexual Difference, Feminism, and the Law,* 16 LAW & SOC. INQUIRY 553 (1991); S. OKIN & J. MANSBRIDGE, FEMINISM (1994); J. MANSBRIDGE, BEYOND SELF-INTEREST (1990); S. OKIN, JUSTICE, GENDER AND THE FAMILY (1989).

172. For example, consider Justice White's declaration in Bowers v. Hardwick regarding rape and sodomy. 478 U.S. 186, 195 (1986).

173. *See* L. WEITZMAN, THE DIVORCE REVOLUTION; Singer, *Alimony and Efficiency: The Gendered Costs and Benefits of the Economic Justification for Alimony,* 82 GEO. L. J. 2423 (1994); Singer, *Divorce Reform and Gender Justice,* 67 N.C. L. REV. 1103 (1989). On child custody, see Becker, *Judicial Discretion in Child Custody: The Wisdom of Solomon?* 81 ILL. BAR J. 650 (1993).

174. C. MACKINNON, ONLY WORDS; Dworkin, *Pornography Is a Civil Rights Issue for Women,* 21 U. MICH. J. L. REFORM 55 (1987); Dworkin, *Against the Male Flood: Censorship, Pornography, and Equality,* 8 HARV. WOMEN'S L. J. 1 (1985); A. DWORKIN, PORNOGRAPHY: MEN POSSESSING WOMEN (1979). *See also* Thomas I. Emerson, *Pornography and the First Amendment: A Reply to Professor MacKinnon,* 3 YALE L. & POL'Y REV. 130 (1984); Strossen, *A Feminist Critique of the Feminist Critique of Pornography,* 79 VA. L. REV. 1099 (1993).

175. *See* Fiss, *The Death of Law,* 72 CORNELL L. REV. 1 (1986).
Feminists who doubt the efficacy of legal reform tend to adopt one or more of three arguments. First, following Audre Lorde's dictum that "you cannot dismantle the master's house with the master's tools," a number of feminists simply eschew legal reforms as too compromised by the sexism of the legal institutions within which law must operate to be effective in achieving real improvements in women's lives. Others have argued that the best hope for achieving meaningful improvement in women's lives is by expanding the sphere of nonintrusion by the state, and then advocating educational and cultural changes to improve women's well-being within those spheres. Still others, following current trends in cultural and literary studies, view language and culture as of far greater causal weight than law, and accordingly view efforts to change women's circumstances through legal means, rather than more fundamentally changing ways of speaking and thinking, as well-meaning but simply misguided. The case against legal reform that stems from critical legal studies is primarily that the harms done, through the process of legitimation, outweigh whatever benefits might be obtained. Thus, legal reforms that appear to benefit a subordinated group must be weighed against the harms done all subordinated persons by the very real risk that those reforms further legitimate, in the minds of the subordinate as well as the dominant, the unjust hierarchies which the legal system, in its entirety, overwhelmingly promotes.

176. I. BERLIN, TWO CONCEPTS OF LIBERTY (1958).

177. M. SAGOFF, THE ECONOMY OF THE EARTH.

NOTES TO CHAPTER 3

1. Holmes, *The Path of the Law,* 10 HARV. L. REV. 457, at 460 (1897).

2. *See generally* Gemmette, *Law and Literature: Joining the Class Action,* 29 VAL. L. REV. 665, at 671–72 (1995).

3. My own course evaluations and student surveys in law and literature seminars, at least, consistently repeat this theme.

4. *Id.*

5. J.B. WHITE, THE LEGAL IMAGINATION: STUDIES IN THE NATURE OF LEGAL THOUGHT AND EXPRESSION (1985); J.B. WHITE, HERACLES' BOW: ESSAYS ON THE RHETORIC AND POETICS OF THE LAW (1985); J.B. WHITE, JUSTICE AS TRANSLATION: AN ESSAY IN CULTURAL AND LEGAL CRITICISM (1990); J.B. WHITE, ACTS OF HOPE: CREATING AUTHORITY IN LITERATURE, LAW AND POLITICS (1994). *See also* White, *Is Cultural Criticism Possible?* 84 MICH. L. REV. 1373 (1986).

6. J.B. WHITE, ACTS OF HOPE.

7. White, THE LEGAL IMAGINATION, at xiv; White, *Economics and Law: Two Cultures in Tension,* 54 TENN. L. REV. 161, 202 (1987).

8. J.B. WHITE, THE LEGAL IMAGINATION, at xxiv-xxv.

9. R. FERGUSON, LAW AND LETTERS IN AMERICAN CULTURE (1984).

10. *See, e.g.*, White's discussion of Huck Finn in THE LEGAL IMAGINA-TION, at 19, and his discussion of Lincoln's Second Inaugural Address in ACTS OF HOPE, at 275. Compare his reading of Mandela's Speech from the Dock in ACTS OF HOPE, at 275. It is no coincidence that White's area of legal specialization is the law of slavery, and race relations more generally. The institution of slavery, and the laws that constructed it, strike at the heart of the ethical and aesthetic sensibility he aims to instill in the lawyering process: a deep and equal respect for the uniqueness of each individual, and a willing-ness to attend to the "stories" of all.

11. *See* White, *Economics and Law.*

12. J.B. WHITE, ACTS OF HOPE, at 182–83.

13. For his clearest statement of this claim, *see* White, *Is Cultural Criti-cism Possible?*

14. J.B. WHITE, THE LEGAL IMAGINATION.

15. J.B. WHITE, WHEN WORDS LOSE THEIR MEANING 240 (1984).

16. Harris, *Race and Essentialism in Feminist Legal Theory,* 42 STAN. L. REV. 581 (1990).

In a similar vein, Taunya Banks, who teaches constitutional law at Univer-sity of Maryland Law School, has her entire class come to the front of the room on the first day. Then she tells all the women and people of color to sit down. Then she tells everyone who doesn't own any real property to sit down. Then she informs the class that the two or three students still standing will write a constitution for the class beginning with the ringing declaration, "We the People."

17. Resnik & Heilbrun, *Convergences: Law, Literature and Feminism,* 99 YALE L. J. 1913 (1990).

18. Mann, *The Universe and the Library: A Critique of James Boyd White as Writer and Reader,* 41 STAN. L. REV. 959 (1989).

19. Delgado & Stefancic, *Norms and Narratives: Can Judges Avoid Seri-ous Moral Error?* 69 TEX. L. REV. 1929 (1991).

20. Milner Ball examines this quality of legal prose in THE WORD AND THE LAW (1993).

21. *See* White, *The Rhythms of Hope and Disappointment in the Language of Judging,* 70 ST. JOHN'S LAW REV. 101 (1996).

22. J.B. WHITE, ACTS OF HOPE, at ix-xii.

23. For attempts to answer the question, *see* Karst, *A Woman's Constitution,* 1984 DUKE L. J. 447 (1984); MacKinnon, *Reflections on Sex Equality Under Law,* 100 YALE L. J. 1281 (1991); Becker, *The Politics of Women's Wrongs and the Bill of "Rights": A Bicentennial Perspective,* 59 CHI. L. REV. 453 (1992).

24. The point was classically made by Robert Cover in his essay *Violence and the Word,* 95 YALE L. J. 1601 (1986).

25. For criticism of White on this score, *see* Cover, *Violence and the Word;* West, *Communities, Texts and Law: Reflections on the Law and Literature Movement,* 1 YALE J. L. & HUM. 129 (1988); Kennedy, *The Turn to Interpretation,* 58 S. CAL. L. REV. 251 (1985); Weisberg, *The Law-Literature Enterprise,* 1 YALE J. L. & HUM. 1 (1988). White summarizes the criticism, and responds in ACTS OF HOPE, at 182.

26. White argues that justice is largely aesthetic in a number of works, but most persuasively in JUSTICE AS TRANSLATION.

27. This is a recurrent theme in defenses of legal positivism. *See, e.g.,* Hart, *The Demystification of the Law,* in H.L.A. HART, ESSAYS ON BENTHAM 21 (1982); Hart, *Law and Morals,* in H.L.A. HART, THE CONCEPT OF LAW 181 (1972).

28. Nussbaum, *Equity and Mercy,* 22 PHIL. & PUB. AFF. 83 (1993); Nussbaum, *Skepticism about Practical Reason,* 107 HARV. L. REV. 714 (1994).

29. M. NUSSBAUM, LOVE'S KNOWLEDGE: ESSAYS ON PHILOSOPHY AND LITERATURE (1990).

30. *See* Nussbaum, *Skepticism about Practical Reason.*

31. *Id.*

32. *Id.*

33. *Id.*

34. *See* Brooke Thomas's work on the law and literature of the antebellum era for what may be the best example to date of an attempt to criticize the law and ideology of a particular historical era through the medium of literary interpretation. B. THOMAS, CROSS EXAMINATIONS OF LAW AND LITERATURE: COOPER, HAWTHORNE, STOWE, AND MELVILLE (1987).

35. I make this argument at greater length in my introduction in NARRATIVE, AUTHORITY AND LAW (1993). *See also* B. THOMAS, CROSS EXAMINATIONS, at 1-18.

36. B. THOMAS, CROSS EXAMINATIONS.

37. R. WEISBERG, THE FAILURE OF THE WORD: THE PROTAGONIST AS LAWYER IN MODERN FICTION (1984).

38. *Id.*

39. *Id.* at 1-19.

40. *Id.* at 131–77.
41. *Id.* at 114–30.
42. *Id.* at 65–83.
43. French feminism emphasizes this theme more than Anglo-American. *See, e.g.*, L. IRIGARAY, THIS SEX WHICH IS NOT ONE (1985 ed.). For a good discussion and critique, *see* Butler, *Variations on Sex and Gender: Beauvoir, Wittig and Foucault,* in FEMINISM AS CRITIQUE: ESSAYS ON THE POLITICS OF GENDER (Benhabib and D. Cornell, eds. 1987).
44. J.C. SMITH & C. FERSTMAN, THE CASTRATION OF OEDIPUS: PSYCHOANALYSIS, POSTMODERNISM, AND FEMINISM (1996).
45. D. LUBAN, LEGAL MODERNISM (1994).
46. *Id.* at 299–321.
47. *Id.* at 318, note 135.
48. For a treatment of *The Oresteia* that explicates these themes for a legal audience, *see* Gewirtz, *Aeschylus' Law,* 101 HARV. L. REV. 1043 (1988).
49. D. LUBAN, LEGAL MODERNISM 306–21.
50. Nussbaum, *Equity and Mercy.*
51. Nussbaum, *Skepticism about Practical Reason.*
52. Allen, *The Jurisprudence of Jane Eyre,* 15 HARV. WOMEN'S L. J. 173 (1992).
53. Weil, *Virginia Woolf's To the Lighthouse: Toward an Integrated Jurisprudence,* 6 YALE J. L. & FEM. 1 (1994).
54. Menkel-Meadow, *Portia in a Different Voice: Speculations on a Woman's Lawyering Process,* 1 BERK. WOMEN'S L. J. 39 (1985); Menkel-Meadow, *Portia Redux: Another Look at Gender, Feminism, and Legal Ethics,* 2 VA. J. L. & SOC. POL'Y 75 (1994); R. WEISBERG, POETHICS AND OTHER STRATEGIES OF LAW AND LITERATURE (1992).
55. Koffler, *Posner in Paradise,* 10 CARDOZO L. REV. 2099 (1989).
56. Koffler, *The Feminine Presence in Billy Budd,* 1 CARDOZO STUD. L. & LIT. 1 (1989).
57. West, *Authority, Autonomy and Choice,* in R. WEST, NARRATIVE, AUTHORITY AND LAW 27–88.
58. *See* Resnik & Heilbrun, *Convergences: Law, Literature, and Feminisms*; Mann, *The Universe and Library*; Delgado & Stefancic, *Norms and Narratives.*
59. M. TWAIN, THE ADVENTURES OF HUCKLEBERRY FINN (1888).
60. *See* J.B. WHITE, THE LEGAL IMAGINATION; West, *Communities, Texts, and Law.*
61. A. BLOOM, THE CLOSING OF THE AMERICAN MIND (1987).
62. T. MORRISON, BELOVED: A NOVEL (1987).
63. I discuss this at length in *Communities, Texts, and Law.*
64. T. MORRISON, BELOVED, at 239–75.
65. Glaspell, *A Jury of Her Peers,* in LAW IN LITERATURE: LEGAL THEMES IN SHORT STORIES 124 (E. Gemmette, ed. 1992).
66. *Id.*
67. Cover, *Violence and the Word.*

68. Fiss, *Objectivity and Interpretation,* 34 STAN. L. REV. 739 (1982).

69. Dworkin, *How Law Is Like Literature,* in R. DWORKIN, A MATTER OF PRINCIPLE 119 (1985).

70. S. FISH, DOING WHAT COMES NATURALLY (1989); S. FISH, IS THERE A TEXT IN THIS CLASS: THE AUTHORITY OF INTERPRETIVE COMMUNITIES (1980); S. FISH, THERE'S NO SUCH THING AS FREE SPEECH (AND ITS A GOOD THING TOO) (1994).

71. Michaels, *Against Formalism: Chickens and Rocks,* in INTERPRETING LAW AND LITERATURE: A HERMENEUTIC READER 215 (S. Levinson & S. Mailloux, eds. 1988).

72. Balkin, *Deconstructive Practice and Legal Theory,* 96 YALE L. J. 743 (1987); Balkin, *Tradition, Betrayal, and the Politics of Deconstruction,* 11 CARDOZO L. REV. 1613 (1990).

73. *See generally* R. POSNER, LAW AND LITERATURE: A MISUNDERSTOOD RELATION 220–47 (1988).

74. *Id.*

75. *See generally,* F. LENTRICCHIA, AFTER THE NEW CRITICISM (1980); T. EAGLETON, LITERARY THEORY: AN INTRODUCTION, at 128 (1983); J. CULLER, ON DECONSTRUCTION: THEORY AND CRITICISM AFTER STRUCTURALISM, at 94 (1982).

76. The Warren Court in *Brown* famously eschewed reliance on the original meaning of the constitution, perhaps prompting the turn to more contemporary and less intentionalist theories of interpretation. Brown v. Board of Education, 347 U.S. 483 (1954).

77. *See generally* INTERPRETING LAW AND LITERATURE (S. Levinson & S. Mailloux, eds.).

78. Grey, *The Constitution as Scripture,* 37 STAN. L. REV. 1–25 (1984).

79. West, *Adjudication Is Not Interpretation,* in R. WEST, NARRATIVE, AUTHORITY AND LAW 89.

80. *See* Sherry, *Civic Virtue and the Feminine Voice in Constitutional Adjudication,* 72 VA. L. REV. 543 (1986); Sherry, *The Founders' Unwritten Constitution,* 54 CHI. L. REV. 1127 (1987). *See also* Henderson, *Authoritarianism and the Rule of Law,* 66 IND. L. J. 379 (1991).

81. Dalton, *An Essay in the Deconstruction of Contract Doctrine,* 94 YALE L. J. 997 (1985).

82. Cornell, *Toward a Modern/Postmodern Reconstruction of Ethics,* 133 PA. L. REV. 291 (1985).

83. C. MACKINNON, TOWARD A FEMINIST THEORY OF THE STATE 123 (1989).

84. Luban, *Fish v. Fish or, Some Realism about Idealism,* 7 CARDOZO L. REV. 693 (1986); West, *Adjudication Is Not Interpretation;* Cornell, *"Convention" and Critique,* 7 CARDOZO L. REV. 679 (1986).

85. West, *Adjudication Is Not Interpretation.*

86. C. GILLIGAN, IN A DIFFERENT VOICE: PSYCHOLOGICAL THEORY AND WOMEN'S DEVELOPMENT (1982).

87. *Id.* at 24–63.

88. Henderson, *Legality and Empathy,* 85 MICH. L. REV. 1574 (1987); Henderson, *The Dialogue of Heart and Head,* 10 CARDOZO L. REV. 123 (1988).

89. *See, e.g.*, M. MINOW, MAKING ALL THE DIFFERENCE: INCLUSION, EXCLUSION AND AMERICAN LAW (1990); Minow & Spelman, *In Context,* 63 S. CAL. L. REV. 1597 (1990).

90. M. NUSSBAUM, LOVE'S KNOWLEDGE.

91. Nussbaum, *Equity and Mercy*; Nussbaum, *Skepticism about Practical Reason.*

92. Sherry, *The Gender of Judges,* 4 J. L. & INEQUALITY 159 (1986).

93. Resnik, *On the Bias: Feminist Reconsiderations of the Aspirations of Our Judges,* 61 S. CAL. L. REV. 1877 (1988).

94. M. NUSSBAUM, LOVE'S KNOWLEDGE.

95. W. C. DIMOCK, RESIDUES OF JUSTICE: LAW, LITERATURE AND PHILOSOPHY (1996).

96. J.B. WHITE, THE LEGAL IMAGINATION; White, *Economics and Law.*

97. R. WEISBERG, POETHICS AND OTHER STRATEGIES OF LAW AND LITERATURE.

98. Critical essays attacking the new "narrative jurisprudence" are a cottage industry. *See* Farber & Sherry, *Telling Stories Out of School: An Essay on Legal Narratives,* 45 STAN. L. REV. 807 (1993); Tushnet, *The Degradation of Constitutional Discourse,* 81 GEO. L. J. 251 (1992). For a more balanced appraisal, *see* Abrams, *On Hearing the Call of Stories,* 79 CAL. L. REV. 971 (1991).

99. The scholarship is by this point far too vast to survey in a single note. For an excellent critical guide, *see* Abrams, *On Hearing the Call of Stories.*

100. By "feminist scholarship" I mean to include African American feminist scholarship. There are, however, sometimes overlapping and sometimes different reasons for the inclusion of narrativity in critical race scholarship, and as African American feminist scholarship obviously participates in both genres, with respect to that growing genre the explanation or story told here will only be partial.

101. Carter, *Men Aren't Angry, Just Confused,* 1 NEW YORK TIMES BOOK REVIEW, June 25, 1995, Section 7.

102. E. COSE, A MAN'S WORLD: HOW REAL IS MALE PRIVILEGE—AND HOW HIGH IS ITS PRICE? (1995).

103. Carter, *Men Aren't Angry, Just Confused* (quoting Cose).

104. *See, e.g.*, S. ESTRICH, REAL RAPE: HOW THE LEGAL SYSTEM VICTIMIZES WOMEN WHO SAY NO (1987).

105. Mahoney, *Legal Images of Battered Women: Redefining the Issue of Separation,* 90 MICH. L. REV. 1 (1991); West, *The Difference in Women's Hedonic Lives: A Phenomenological Critique of Feminist Legal Theory,* 3 WISC. WOMEN'S L. J. 81 (1987).

106. Paltrow, *National Abortion Rights Action League Amicus Brief, for Richard Thornburgh v. Am. College of Obstetricians and Gynecologists,* 9 WOMEN'S RTS. L. REPORTER 3 (1986).

107. Ashe, *Zig-zag Stitching, and the Seamless Web: Thoughts on Reproduction and the Law,* 13 NOVA L. REV. 355 (1989).

108. C. MACKINNON, SEXUAL HARASSMENT OF WORKING WOMEN (1979).

109. Bowman, *Street Harassment and the Informal Ghettoization of Women,* 106 HARV. L. REV. 517 (1993).

110. *See* Henderson, *Without Narrative* (unpublished manuscript on file with author).

111. Littleton, *Women's Experience and the Problem of Transition: Perspectives on Male Battering of Women,* 1989 U. CHI. LEG. F. 23 (1989); MacKinnon, *Sex Equality: On Difference and Dominance,* in C. MACKINNON, TOWARD A FEMINIST THEORY OF THE STATE, at 215 (1989).

112. Mahoney, *Legal Images of Battered Women;* Littleton, *Women's Experience and the Problem of Transition. See also* Schneider, *Describing and Changing: Women's Self-Defense Work and the Problem of Expert Testimony on Battery,* 14 WOMEN'S RTS. L. REPORTER 213 (1992); Schneider, *Equal Rights to Trial for Women: Sex Bias in the Law of Self-Defense,* 15 HARV. C.R.-C.L. L. REV. 623 (1986).

113. Coughlin, *Excusing Women,* 82 CAL. L. REV. 1 (1994).

114. *See* Crenshaw, *Demarginalizing the Intersection of Race and Sex: A Black Feminist Critique of Antidiscrimination Doctrine, Feminist Theory, and Antiracist Politics,* 1989 U. CHI. LEG. F. 139 (1989).

115. Crenshaw, *Mapping the Margins: Intersectionality, Identity Politics, and Violence Against Women of Color,* 43 STAN. L. REV. 1241 (1991).

116. Crenshaw, *Demarginalizing the Intersection of Race and Sex.*

117. Roberts, *Punishing Drug Addicts Who Have Babies: Women of Color, Equality, and the Right of Privacy,* 104 HARV. L. REV. 1419 (1991).

118. *See generally* Harris, *Race and Essentialism.*

119. Banks, *Two Life Stories: Reflections of One Black Woman Law Professor,* 6 BERK. WOMEN'S L. J. 46 (1990).

120. P. WILLIAMS, THE ALCHEMY OF RACE AND RIGHTS: DIARY OF A LAW PROFESSOR (1991); Minow, *Justice Engendered,* 101 HARV. L. REV. 10 (1987); M. MINOW, MAKING ALL THE DIFFERENCE; Harris, *Race and Essentialism.*

121. *See* M. BALL, THE WORD AND THE LAW.

122. Ashe, *Zig-zag Stitching, and the Seamless Web.*

123. Farber & Sherry, *Telling Stories Out of School.*

124. *See* Weisberg, *The Law-Literature Enterprise;* Kennedy, *The Turn to Interpretation;* Mann, *The Universe and the Library.*

125. B. THOMAS, CROSS EXAMINATIONS.

126. J.B. WHITE, JUSTICE AS TRANSLATION.

127. R. WEISBERG, THE FAILURE OF THE WORD.

128. M. MINOW, MAKING ALL THE DIFFERENCE.

129. C. MACKINNON, TOWARD A FEMINIST THEORY OF THE STATE; C. MACKINNON, ONLY WORDS (1993).

130. C. GILLIGAN, IN A DIFFERENT VOICE.

NOTES TO CHAPTER 4

1. For a general introduction, *see* THE POLITICS OF LAW: A PROGRESSIVE CRITIQUE (D. Kairys, ed. 1990).

2. B. THOMAS, CROSS EXAMINATIONS OF LAW AND LITERATURE: COOPER, HAWTHORNE, STOWE, AND MELVILLE (1987).

3. Page numbers will be to Melville, *Bartleby the Scrivener,* in H. MELVILLE, THE SHORTER NOVELS OF HERMAN MELVILLE 114 (1956 ed.)

4. B. THOMAS, CROSS EXAMINATIONS, at 164–82.

5. Glaspell, *A Jury of Her Peers,* in LAW IN LITERATURE: LEGAL THEMES IN SHORT STORIES 124 (E. Gemmette, ed. 1992).

6. Melville, *Bartleby,* at 120–21.

7. *Id.* at 114.

8. *Id.* at 118.

9. *Id.* at 118.

10. *Id.* at 114.

11. *Id.* at 121.

12. *Id.* at 147.

13. *Id.* at 120.

14. *Id.*

15. *Id.* at 122.

16. *Id.* at 134.

17. *Id.* at 135.

18. *Id.* at 129, 132, 136, 146.

19. *Id.* at 143.

20. B. THOMAS, CROSS EXAMINATIONS, at 177.

21. Melville, *Bartleby,* at 132.

22. B. THOMAS, CROSS EXAMINATIONS, at 165.

23. *Id.* at 165, and 173.

24. *Id.* at 177.

25. *Id.* at 167–69.

26. *Id.* at 169–72.

27. *Id.* at 172–73.

28. *See* Page, *The Ideology of Law and Literature,* 68 B. U. L. REV. 805, 811 (1988); B. THOMAS, CROSS EXAMINATIONS, at 169.

29. B. THOMAS, CROSS EXAMINATIONS, at 173.

30. Melville, *Bartleby,* at 117–18.

31. *Id.* at 133.

32. *Id.* at 115.

33. *Id.* at 120.

34. *Id.* at 144.

35. *Id.* at 137.

36. *Id.* at 124–25.
37. *Id.* at 137–38.
38. *Id.* at 114.
39. *Id.* at 138–39.
40. *Id.* at 130.
41. *Id.* at 139.
42. *Id.* at 139–40.
43. R. WEISBERG, THE FAILURE OF THE WORD: THE PROTAGONIST AS LAWYER IN MODERN FICTION, at 134 (1984).
44. *Id.* at 133–76.
45. B. THOMAS, CROSS EXAMINATIONS, at 179–80.
46. *See* Page, *The Ideology of Law and Literature,* at 811–12.
47. Glaspell, *A Jury of Her Peers,* at 125.
48. *Id.* at 131.
49. *Id.* at 132.
50. *Id.* at 135.
51. *Id.*
52. *Id.* at 137.
53. Angel, *Criminal Law and Women: Giving the Abused Woman Who Kills "A Jury of Her Peers" Who Appreciate Trifles,* 33 AM. CRIM. L. REV. 229, 235 (1996).
54. *Id.* at 241–46.
55. Glaspell, *A Jury of Her Peers,* at 128–29.
56. *Id.* at 125.
57. *Id.* at 129.
58. *Id.* at 134–35.
59. *Id.* at 137.
60. *Id.* at 130.
61. *Id.* at 138.
62. *Id.* at 133.
63. *Id.* at 134.
64. *Id.* at 136.
65. *Id.* at 139.
66. *Id.*
67. Melville, *Bartleby,* at 129.
68. For a full discussion and critique of this literature, *see* Abrams, *Sex Wars Redux: Agency and Coercion in Feminist Legal Theory,* 95 COLUM. L. REV. 304 (1995).

NOTES TO CHAPTER 5

1. M. FOUCAULT, DISCIPLINE AND PUNISH (A. Sheridan, trans. 1979).
2. *Id.*
3. *Id.* at 194 (emphasis added).
4. Thus critical legal scholars reject the liberal and mainstream view of law as the product of a competition of "social interests," as well as the

Marxists' contention that law is the necessary consequence of class struggle situated at a particular moment in a determined history. *See,* for example, Gordon, *Critical Legal Histories,* 36 STAN. L. REV. 57, 71–116 (1984); Gordon, *Historicism in Legal Scholarship,* 90 YALE L. J. 1017, 1024–36 (1981); THE POLITICS OF LAW: A PROGRESSIVE CRITIQUE (D. Kairys, ed. 1992); M. KELMAN, A GUIDE TO CRITICAL LEGAL STUDIES (1987).

5. Foucault's studies of power have focused on the disciplines instilled by such institutions as hospitals, penal systems, and schools. The critical legal scholars have, in a roughly parallel manner, focused on the disciplines instilled by legal institutions, ideology, and doctrine.

6. *See* C. MACKINNON, FEMINISM UNMODIFIED: DISCOURSES ON LIFE AND LAW (1987); S. BROWNMILLER, AGAINST OUR WILL: MEN, WOMEN, AND RAPE 1–5 (1975); D. RUSSELL, RAPE IN MARRIAGE (1990).

7. For an introduction to the postmodern feminist literature, *see* DISCOVERING REALITY: FEMINIST PERSPECTIVES ON EPISTEMOLOGY, METAPHYSICS, METHODOLOGY, AND PHILOSOPHY OF SCIENCE (S. Harding & Merill B. Hintikka, eds. 1983); Harding, *The Instability of the Analytical Categories of Feminist Theory,* 11 SIGNS 645 (1986); Flax, *Postmodernism and Gender Relations in Feminist Theory,* 12 SIGNS 621 (1987).

8. *See* Olsen, *Feminism, Post-Modernism and Critical Legal Studies,* unpublished manuscript on file with author; Olsen, *The Family and the Market: A Study of Ideology and Legal Reform,* 96 HARV. L. REV. 1497 (1983).

9. Olsen describes the contradictions very well, and from a feminist perspective, in *Feminism, Post-Modernism and Critical Legal Studies.*

10. The danger of sexual violence renders women vulnerable and more likely to accede to the pressures of relatively "safe" men. This is what is meant by the phrase "male protection racket." For a further exploration of this, *see* West, *The Difference in Women's Hedonic Lives: A Phenomenological Critique of Feminist Legal Theory,* 3 WISC. WOMEN'S L. J. 81 (1987).

11. For an example of the power of law as a weapon against the power of patriarchy, *see* C. MACKINNON, SEXUAL HARASSMENT OF WORKING WOMEN (1979). For a contrary view of law's ability to address sexual violence adequately, *see* the critique of feminist legal reform in S. ESTRICH, REAL RAPE: HOW THE LEGAL SYSTEM VICTIMIZES WOMEN WHO SAY NO (1987).

12. Patriarchal power is protected by the constitutional guarantee of free speech and, to a lesser extent, constitutional guarantees of privacy. *See generally* C. MACKINNON, FEMINISM UNMODIFIED.

13. We have a great deal of feminist legal scholarship concerning the former, but very little concerning the latter. The noteworthy exception is D. RUSSELL, RAPE IN MARRIAGE.

14. *See* C. MACKINNON, FEMINISM UNMODIFIED, at 127–213, 221–26.

15. This is the central claim that unifies Foucault's work. *See, e.g.,* M. FOUCAULT, THE ORDER OF THINGS (1970); M. FOUCAULT, DISCIPLINE AND PUNISH; M. FOUCAULT, THE HISTORY OF SEXUALITY, vol. 1 (R. Hurley, trans. 1980).

16. *See, e.g.*, F. RUSH, BEST KEPT SECRET: SEXUAL ABUSE OF CHILDREN (1981); I NEVER TOLD ANYONE (E. Bass & L. Thornton, eds. 1983); E. PIZZEY, SCREAM QUIETLY OR THE NEIGHBORS WILL HEAR (1977).

17. A. RICH, ON LIES, SECRETS, AND SILENCE: SELECTED PROSE, 1966–78 (1979).

18. A. DWORKIN, INTERCOURSE (1987).

19. I NEVER TOLD ANYONE (E. Bass & L. Thornton, eds.).

20. *Id.*

21. F. RUSH, BEST KEPT SECRET.

22. The titles of these works alone speak volumes: Florence Rush writes of the silence around child sexual abuse in BEST KEPT SECRET; Ellen Bass and Louise Thornton treat the same subject in I NEVER TOLD ANYONE, and an early and important study on domestic violence is Erin Pizzey's SCREAM QUIETLY OR THE NEIGHBORS WILL HEAR.

23. L. SANFORD & M. DONOVAN, WOMEN AND SELF ESTEEM (1984).

24. T. OLSEN, SILENCES (1978).

25. *Id.*

26. *Id.*

27. *Id.*

28. *Id.* at 25–27 (emphasis in original).

29. M. BELENKY et al., WOMEN'S WAYS OF KNOWING: THE DEVELOPMENT OF SELF, VOICE AND MIND (1986).

30. *Id.* at 23–24.

31. *Id.* at 32–34.

32. *Id.* at 30.

33. *Id.* at 23.

34. Weiss & Melling, *The Legal Education of Twenty Women,* 40 STAN. L. REV. 1299, 1333 (1988).

35. M. FOUCAULT, THE HISTORY OF SEXUALITY, vol. 1, at 45–49, 53–73.

36. Rush, *Foreword,* in I NEVER TOLD ANYONE 13 (E. Bass and L. Thornton, eds.).

37. T. OLSEN, SILENCES, at 204–5.

38. *Id.* at 205–6.

39. Payton, *Releasing Excellence: Erasing Gender Zoning from the Legal Mind,* 18 IND. L. REV. 629, 641 (1985).

40. M. FOUCAULT, THE HISTORY OF SEXUALITY, vol. 1.

41. *Id.* at 31–36.

42. *Id.* at 31–32.

43. *Id.* at 53–73.

44. *Id.* at 32–35 (emphasis in original).

45. Foucault has noticed and analyzed the silence of others, particularly the silence produced by the break in discourse between modernity and the madman. *See* M. FOUCAULT, MADNESS AND CIVILIZATION, at x–xi (1982). I am indebted to Jennifer Goldstein (Chicago, class of 1989) for this insight.

46. M. FOUCAULT, THE HISTORY OF SEXUALITY, vol. 1, at 33.

47. *Id.* at 31.

48. *Id.* at 31.

49. *Id.* at 32.

50. *Id.* at 32.

51. *Id.* at 159.

52. I NEVER TOLD ANYONE (E. Bass & L Thornton, eds.), at 108.

53. *Id.* at 107.

54. *Id.* at 93–96.

55. *Id.* at 90.

56. R. UNGER, FALSE NECESSITY 9 (1987).

57. *Id.* at 164.

58. *See* Ruddick, *Maternal Thinking,* 6 FEM. STUD. 342 (1980); Resnik, *On the Bias: Feminist Reconsiderations of the Aspirations of Our Judges,* 61 S. CAL. L. REV. 1877 (1988).

59. *See* N. NODDINGS, CARING: A FEMINIST APPROACH TO ETHICS AND MORAL EDUCATION 59–78 (1984).

60. *See* Ruddick, *Maternal Thinking*; Resnik, *On the Bias*; WOMEN AND MORAL THEORY (E. Kittay & D. Meyers, eds. 1987); C. GILLIGAN, IN A DIFFERENT VOICE: PSYCHOLOGICAL THEORY AND WOMEN'S DEVELOPMENT (1982); N. CHODOROW, THE REPRODUCTION OF MOTHERING: PSYCHOANALYSIS AND THE SOCIOLOGY OF GENDER (1978).

61. *See* Menkel-Meadow, *Portia in a Different Voice: Speculations on a Woman's Lawyering Process,* 1 BERK. WOMEN'S L. J. 39 (1985); Resnik, *On the Bias;* West, *Jurisprudence and Gender,* 55 U. CHI. L. REV. 1 (1988).

62. This commitment is starkly made in R. UNGER, FALSE NECESSITY.

63. *Id.*

64. *See* I NEVER TOLD ANYONE (E. Bass & L Thornton, eds.), at 42–43; E. KELLER, REFLECTIONS ON GENDER AND SCIENCE (1985).

65. *See* M. FOUCAULT, DISCIPLINE AND PUNISH; M. FOUCAULT, THE HISTORY OF SEXUALITY, vol. 1.

66. *See* M. KELMAN, A GUIDE TO CRITICAL LEGAL STUDIES, at 112–13.

67. *See* C. MACKINNON, FEMINISM UNMODIFIED.

68. *See* West, *The Difference in Women's Hedonic Lives,* 3 WISC. WOMEN'S L. J. 81 (1987).

69. N. CHODOROW, THE REPRODUCTION OF MOTHERING, at 211–12.

70. N. NODDINGS, CARING, at 128–31; West, *Jurisprudence and Gender,* 55 U. CHI. L. REV. 1 (1988).

71. Stanley Fish explores their equivocation in Fish, *Anti-Professionalism,* 7 CARDOZO L. REV. 645 (1986). *See also* M. KELMAN, A GUIDE TO CRITICAL LEGAL STUDIES, at 112–13.

72. S. DE BEAUVOIR, THE SECOND SEX (H. Parshley, trans. 1952).

73. *See* N. CHODOROW, THE REPRODUCTION OF MOTHERING.

74. I discuss this in West, *The Difference in Women's Hedonic Lives.*

75. A. RICH, ON LIES, SECRETS, AND SILENCE, at 199–201, 223–30.

76. *Id.* at 199.

77. *Id.* at 199–200.

78. *Id.* at 200–201 (emphasis added).

79. I NEVER TOLD ANYONE (E. Bass & L. Thornton, eds.).

80. *Id.* at 51.

81. *Id.* at 53.

82. T. OLSEN, SILENCES, at 27–28.

83. *See* L. IRIGARAY, THIS SEX WHICH IS NOT ONE (C. Porter, trans. 1985); L. IRIGARAY, SPECULUM OF THE OTHER WOMAN (G. Gill, trans. 1985).

84. L. IRIGARAY, THIS SEX WHICH IS NOT ONE, at 134.

85. *Id.* at 213–14.

86. *Id.* at 212.

87. For a general introduction to French feminism, *see* C. DUCHEN, FEMINISM IN FRANCE (1986). For a critique of the essentialism I have defended here and elsewhere, and a comparison of it to French feminist thought, *see* D. CORNELL, BEYOND ACCOMMODATION: ETHICAL FEMINISM, DECONSTRUCTION AND THE LAW 22–64 (1991).

Bibliography

Abrams, *On Hearing the Call of Stories*, 79 CAL. L. REV. 971 (1991).

Abrams, *Sex Wars Redux: Agency and Coercion in Feminist Legal Theory*, 95 COLUM. L. REV. 304 (1995).

Abrams, *Complex Claimants and Reductive Moral Judgment: New Patterns in the Search for Equality*, 57 PITT. L. REV. 337 (1996).

Allen, *The Jurisprudence of Jane Eyre*, 15 HARV. WOMEN'S L. J. 173 (1992).

Angel, *Criminal Law and Women: Giving the Abused Woman Who Kills "A Jury of Her Peers" Who Appreciate Trifles*, 33 AM. CRIM. L. REV. 229 (1996).

Ashe, *Zig-zag Stitching, and the Seamless Web: Thoughts on Reproduction and the Law*, 13 NOVA L. REV. 355 (1989).

Ashe & Cahn, *Child Abuse: A Problem for Feminist Theory*, 2 TEX. J. WOMEN & L. 75, 86–90 (1993).

Ayres, *Further Evidence of Discrimination in New Car Negotiations and Estimates of Its Cause*, 94 MICH. L. REV. 109 (1995).

Baier, *Caring About Caring*, 53 SYNTHESE 291 (1982).

Baier, *What Do Women Want in a Moral Theory?* 19 NOUS 53 (1985).

Baier, *Trust and Antitrust*, 96 ETHICS 231 (1986).

BAIER, A., MORAL PREJUDICES: ESSAYS ON ETHICS (1994).

Balkin, *Deconstructive Practice and Legal Theory*, 96 YALE L. J. 743 (1987).

Balkin, *Tradition, Betrayal, and the Politics of Deconstruction*, 11 CARDOZO L. REV. 1613 (1990).

BALL, M., THE WORD AND THE LAW (1993).

Banks, *Two Life Stories: Reflections of One Black Woman Law Professor* 6 BERK. WOMEN'S L. J. 46 (1990).

BASS, E., & L. THORNTON (eds.), I NEVER TOLD ANYONE (1983).

BEALS, M., WARRIORS DON'T CRY (1994).

Beck & Van der Kolk, *Reports of Childhood Incest and Current Behavior of Chronically Hospitalized Psychotic Women*, 144 AM. J. PSYCHIATRY 1474 (1987).

BECKER, G., A TREATISE ON THE FAMILY (1981).

Becker, *Prince Charming: Abstract Equality*, 1987 SUP. CT. REV. 201 (1987).

Becker, *Politics, Differences, and Economic Rights*, 1989 U. CHI. L. REV. 169 (1989).

Becker, *Maternal Feelings: Myth, Taboo, and Child Custody*, 1 S. CAL. REV. L. & WOMEN'S STUD. 133 (1992).

Becker, *The Politics of Women's Wrongs and the Bill of "Rights": A Bicentennial Perspective*, 59 CHI. L. REV. 453 (1992).

Becker, *Four Feminist Theoretical Approaches and the Double Bind of Surrogacy*, 69 CHI-KENT L. REV. 303 (1993).

Becker, *Judicial Discretion in Child Custody: The Wisdom of Solomon?* 81 ILL. BAR J. 650 (1993).

Becker, *Strength in Diversity: Feminist Theoretical Approaches to Child Custody and Same-Sex Relationships*, 23 STETSON L. REV. 701 (1994).

Becker & Murphy, *The Family and the State*, 31 J. LAW & ECON. 1 (1988).

Beermann & Singer, *Baseline Questions in Legal Reasoning: The Example of Property in Jobs*, 23 GA. L. REV. 911 (1989).

BELENKY, M., B. CLINCHY, N. GOLDBERGER, & J. TARULE, WOMEN'S WAYS OF KNOWING: THE DEVELOPMENT OF SELF, VOICE AND MIND (1986).

BELLAH, R., R. MADSEN, W. SULLIVAN, A. SWIDLER, & S. TIPTON, HABITS OF THE HEART: INDIVIDUALISM AND COMMITMENT IN AMERICAN LIFE (1985).

BENTHAM, J., AN INTRODUCTION TO THE PRINCIPLES OF MORALS AND LEGISLATION (1967 ed.).

BERLIN, I., TWO CONCEPTS OF LIBERTY (1958).

BLOOM, A., THE CLOSING OF THE AMERICAN MIND (1987).

BOLT, R., A MAN FOR ALL SEASONS: A PLAY IN TWO ACTS (1962).

Bowman, *Street Harassment and the Informal Ghettoization of Women*, 106 HARV. L. REV. 517 (1993).

Brinig, *Comment on Jana Singer's "Alimony and Efficiency,"* 82 GEO. L. J. 2423 (1994).

BROWN, J., GANDHI: PRISONER OF HOPE (1989).

BROWNMILLER, S., AGAINST OUR WILL: MEN, WOMEN, AND RAPE (1975).

Bumiller, *Rape as a Legal Symbol: An Essay on Sexual Violence and Racism*, 42 MIAMI L. REV. 75 (1987).

BURKE, E., REFLECTIONS ON THE FRENCH REVOLUTION AND OTHER ESSAYS (1910 ed.).

Butler, *Variations on Sex and Gender: Beauvoir, Wittig and Foucault*, in FEMINISM AS CRITIQUE: ESSAYS ON THE POLITICS OF GENDER (Benhabib & D. Cornell, eds., 1987).

BYRON, W., QUADRANGLE CONSIDERATIONS (1989).

Carter, *Men Aren't Angry, Just Confused*, 1 NEW YORK TIMES BOOK RE-VIEW, section 7 (June 25, 1995).

CHODOROW, N., THE REPRODUCTION OF MOTHERING: PSYCHOANALY-SIS AND THE SOCIOLOGY OF GENDER (1978).

Coase, *The Problem of Social Cost*, 3 J. LAW & ECON. 1 (1960).

Cole & Eskridge, *From Hand-Holding to Sodomy: The First Amendment Protection of Homosexual (Expressive) Conduct*, 29 HARV. C.R.-C.L. L. REV. 319 (1994).

COLKER, R., PREGNANT MEN: PRACTICE, THEORY AND LAW (1994).

Cornell, *Toward a Modern/Postmodern Reconstruction of Ethics*, 133 PA. L. REV. 291 (1985).

Cornell, *"Convention" and Critique*, 7 CARDOZO L. REV. 679 (1986).

COSE, E., A MAN'S WORLD: HOW REAL IS MALE PRIVILEGE—AND HOW HIGH IS ITS PRICE? (1995).

Coughlin, *Excusing Women*, 82 CAL. L. REV. 1 (1994).

COVER, R., JUSTICE ACCUSED (1975).

Cover, *Violence and the Word*, 95 YALE L. J. 1601 (1986).

Crenshaw, *Demarginalizing the Intersection of Race and Sex: A Black Feminist Critique of Antidiscrimination Doctrine, Feminist Theory, and Antiracist Politics*, 1989 U. CHI. LEG. F. 139 (1989).

Crenshaw, *Mapping the Margins: Intersectionality, Identity Politics, and Violence Against Women of Color*, 43 STAN. L. REV. 1241 (1991).

CULLER, J., ON DECONSTRUCTION: THEORY AND CRITICISM AFTER STRUCTURALISM (1982).

Czapanskiy, *Volunteers and Draftees: The Struggle for Parental Equality*, 38 U.C.L.A. L. REV. 1415 (1991).

Dalton, *An Essay in the Deconstruction of Contract Doctrine*, 94 YALE L. J. 997 (1985).

Davis, *Neglected Stories and the Lawfulness of Roe v. Wade*, 28 HARV. C.R.-C.L. L. REV. 299 (1993).

DE BEAUVOIR, S., THE SECOND SEX (H. Parshley, trans. 1952).

Delgado & Stefancic, *Norms and Narratives: Can Judges Avoid Serious Moral Error?* 69 TEX. L. REV. 1929 (1991).

DIMOCK, W.C., RESIDUES OF JUSTICE: LAW, LITERATURE AND PHILOSO-PHY (1996).

DINNERSTEIN, D., THE MERMAID AND THE MINOTAUR: SEXUAL AR-RANGEMENTS AND HUMAN MALAISE (1976).

Dowd, *Work and Family: The Gender Paradox and the Limitations of Discrimination Analysis in Restructuring the Workplace*, 24 HARV. C.R.-C.L. L. REV. 79 (1989).

Dripps, *Beyond Rape: An Essay on the Difference Between the Presence of Force and the Absence of the Consent*, 92 COLUM. L. REV. 1780 (1992).

Dripps et al., *Men, Women and Rape*, 63 FORDHAM L. REV. 125 (1994).

DUCHEN, C., FEMINISM IN FRANCE (1986).

DWORKIN, A., PORNOGRAPHY: MEN POSSESSING WOMEN (1979).

Dworkin, *Against the Male Flood: Censorship, Pornography, and Equality,* 8 HARV. WOMEN'S L. J. 1 (1985).

DWORKIN, A., INTERCOURSE (1987).

Dworkin, *Pornography Is a Civil Rights Issue for Women,* 21 U. MICH. J. L. REFORM 55 (1987).

DWORKIN, R., TAKING RIGHTS SERIOUSLY (1977).

DWORKIN, R., A MATTER OF PRINCIPLE (1985).

DWORKIN, R., LAW'S EMPIRE (1986).

DWORKIN, R., LIFE'S DOMINION: AN ARGUMENT ABOUT ABORTION, EU-THANASIA, AND INDIVIDUAL FREEDOM (1993).

EAGLETON, T., LITERARY THEORY: AN INTRODUCTION (1983).

Ehrenreich, *The Colonization of the Womb,* 43 DUKE L. J. 492 (1993).

Emerson, *Pornography and the First Amendment: A Reply to Professor MacKinnon* 3 YALE J. L. & POL'Y REV. 130 (1984).

Epstein, *Unconscionability: A Critical Reappraisal,* 18 J. LAW & ECON. 293 (1973).

EPSTEIN, R., CASES AND MATERIALS ON TORTS, 4th ed. (1984).

Epstein, *Surrogacy: The Case for Full Contractual Enforcement,* 81 VA. L. REV. 2305 (1995).

ERDRICH, L., THE BLUEJAY'S DANCE: A BIRTH YEAR (1995).

ERIKSON, E., GANDHI'S TRUTH ON THE ORIGINS OF MILITANT NONVIO-LENCE (1969).

Eskridge, *A History of Same-Sex Marriage,* 79 VA. L. REV. 1419 (1993).

Estrich, *Rape,* 95 YALE L. J. 1087 (1986).

ESTRICH, S., REAL RAPE: HOW THE LEGAL SYSTEM VICTIMIZES WOMEN WHO SAY NO (1987).

EVERETT, C. (ed.), THE CONSEQUENCES OF DIVORCE: ECONOMIC AND CUSTODIAL IMPACT ON CHILDREN AND ADULTS (1991).

FARBER, D., & S. SHERRY, A HISTORY OF THE AMERICAN CONSTITUTION (1990).

Farber & Sherry, *Telling Stories Out of School: An Essay on Legal Narratives,* 45 STAN. L. REV. 807 (1993).

FERBER, M., & J. NELSON (eds.), BEYOND ECONOMIC MAN: FEMINIST THEORY AND ECONOMICS (1993).

FERGUSON, R., LAW AND LETTERS IN AMERICAN CULTURE (1984).

Field, *Surrogacy Contracts: Gestational and Traditional: The Argument for Nonenforcement,* 31 WASHBURN L. J. 1 (1991).

Fineman, *Dominant Discourse, Professional Language, and Legal Change in Child Custody Decisionmaking,* 101 HARV. L. REV. 727 (1988).

Fineman, *The Neutered Mother,* 46 MIAMI L. REV. 653 (1992).

FINEMAN, M., THE NEUTERED MOTHER: THE SEXUAL FAMILY AND OTHER TWENTIETH CENTURY TRAGEDIES (1995).

Finley, *Choice and Freedom: Elusive Issues in the Search for Gender Justice,* 96 YALE L. J. 914 (1987).

FIRESTONE, S., THE DIALECTIC OF SEX: THE CASE FOR FEMINIST REVO-LUTION (1970).

FISH, S., IS THERE A TEXT IN THIS CLASS: THE AUTHORITY OF INTER-PRETIVE COMMUNITIES (1980).

Fish, *Antiprofessionalism,* 7 CARDOZO L. REV. 645 (1986).

FISH, S., DOING WHAT COMES NATURALLY (1989).

FISH, S., THERE'S NO SUCH THING AS FREE SPEECH (AND ITS A GOOD THING TOO) (1994).

FISHER, L., THE LIFE OF MAHATMA GANDHI (1950).

Fiss, *Objectivity and Interpretation,* 34 STAN. L. REV. 739 (1982).

Fiss, *The Death of Law,* 72 CORNELL L. REV. 1 (1986).

Flax, *Postmodernism and Gender Relations in Feminist Theory,* 12 SIGNS 621 (1987).

FOUCAULT, M., THE ORDER OF THINGS (1970).

FOUCAULT, M., THE ARCHAEOLOGY OF KNOWLEDGE (1972).

FOUCAULT, M., DISCIPLINE AND PUNISH (A. Sheridan, trans. 1979).

FOUCAULT, M., THE HISTORY OF SEXUALITY, vol. 1 (R. Hurley, trans. 1980).

FOUCAULT, M., MADNESS AND CIVILIZATION (1982).

FOX-GENOVESE, E., FEMINISM WITHOUT ILLUSIONS: A CRITIQUE OF INDIVIDUALISM (1991).

FRASER, N., & S. BARTKY (eds.), REVALUING FRENCH FEMINISM: CRITI-CAL ESSAYS ON DIFFERENCE, AGENCY AND CULTURE (1992).

FRIEDMAN, M., WHAT ARE FRIENDS FOR? FEMINIST PERSPECTIVES ON PERSONAL RELATIONSHIPS AND MORAL THEORY (1993).

FRYE, M., THE POLITICS OF REALITY: ESSAYS IN FEMINIST THEORY (1983).

GARROW, D., LIBERTY AND SEXUALITY: A RIGHT TO PRIVACY AD THE MAKING OF ROE V. WADE (1994).

Gemmette, *Law and Literature: Joining the Class Action,* 29 VAL. L. REV. 665 (1995).

Gewirtz, *Aeschylus' Law,* 101 HARV. L. REV. 1043 (1988).

GILLIGAN, C., IN A DIFFERENT VOICE: PSYCHOLOGICAL THEORY AND WOMEN'S DEVELOPMENT (1982).

Gilligan, *Reply to Critics,* in AN ETHIC OF CARE: FEMINIST AND INTERDIS-CIPLINARY PERSPECTIVES (M. Larrabee, ed. 1993).

Glaspell, *A Jury of Her Peers,* in LAW IN LITERATURE: LEGAL THEMES IN SHORT STORIES 124 (E. Gemmette, ed. 1992).

Gordon, *Historicism in Legal Scholarship,* 90 YALE L. J. 1017 (1981).

Gordon, *Unfreezing Legal Reality: Critical Approaches to Law,* 15 FLA. S. L. REV. 195 (1987).

Gordon, *Critical Legal Histories,* 36 STAN. L. REV. 57 (1984).

GORDON, M., & S. RIGER, THE FEMALE FEAR (1989).

Grey, *The Constitution as Scripture,* 37 STAN. L. REV. 1 (1984).

Grillo, *The Mediation Alternative: Process Dangers for Women,* 100 YALE L. J. 1545 (1991).

Hadfield, *Households at Work: Beyond Labor Market Policies to Remedy the Gender Gap,* 82 GEO. L. J. 89 (1993).

[329]

Hanigsberg, *Homologizing Pregnancy and Motherhood: A Consideration of Abortion,* 94 MICH. L. REV. 371 (1995).

Harding, *The Instability of the Analytical Categories of Feminist Theory,* 11 SIGNS 645 (1986).

HARDING, S., & M. HINTIKKA (eds.), DISCOVERING REALITY: FEMINIST PERSECTIVES ON EPISTEMOLOGY, METAPHYSICS, METHODOLOGY, AND PHILOSOPHY OF SCIENCE (1983).

Harris, *Race and Essentialism in Feminist Legal Theory,* 42 STAN. L. REV. 581 (1990).

HART, H.L.A., THE CONCEPT OF LAW (1972).

HART, H.L.A., ESSAYS ON BENTHAM (1982).

HELD, V., FEMINIST MORALITY: TRANSFORMING CULTURE, SOCIETY AND POLITICS (1993).

Henderson, *Legality and Empathy,* 85 MICH. L. REV. 1574 (1987).

Henderson, *Real Rape,* 3 BERK. WOMEN'S L. J. 193 (1987).

Henderson, *The Dialogue of Heart and Head,* 10 CARDOZO L. REV. 123 (1988).

Henderson, *Authoritarianism and the Rule of Law,* 66 IND. L. J. 379 (1991).

Henderson, *Rape and Responsibility,* 11 LAW & PHIL. 127 (1992).

Henderson, *Without Narrative* (unpublished manuscript on file with author).

HOCHSCHILD, A., THE SECOND SHIFT: WORKING PARENTS AND THE REVOLUTION AT HOME (1989).

Hodges, *Writing in a Different Voice,* 66 TEXAS L. REV. 629 (1988).

HOLMES, O., THE COMMON LAW (1881).

Holmes, *The Path of the Law,* 10 HARV. L. REV. 457 (1897).

Howarth, *Deciding to Kill: Revealing the Gender in the Task Handed to Capitol Jurors,* 1994 WISC. L. REV. 1345 (1994).

Ingram, *Date Rape: It's Time for "No" to Really Mean "No",* 21 AM. J. CRIM. L. 3 (1993).

IRIGARAY, L., SPECULUM OF THE OTHER WOMAN (G. GIll, trans. 1985).

IRIGARAY, L., THIS SEX WHICH IS NOT ONE (C. Porter, trans. 1985).

KAIRYS, D. (ed.), THE POLITICS OF LAW: A PROGRESSIVE CRITIQUE (1990).

KAMINER, W., A FEARFUL FREEDOM (1990).

KANT, I., THE GROUNDING OF THE METAPHYSICS OF MORALS (1981 ed.).

Karst, *A Woman's Constitution,* 1984 DUKE L. J. 447 (1984).

KELLER, E., REFLECTIONS ON GENDER AND SCIENCE (1985).

Kelman, *Choice and Utility,* 1979 WISC. L. REV. 769 (1979).

Kelman, *Spitzer and Hoffman on Coase: A Brief Rejoinder,* 53 S. CAL. L. REV. 1215 (1980).

KELMAN, M., A GUIDE TO CRITICAL LEGAL STUDIES (1987).

Kennedy, *Form and Substance in Private Law Adjudication,* 89 HARV. L. REV. 1685 (1976).

Kennedy, *Distributive and Paternalist Motives in Contract and Tort Law, with Special Reference to Compulsory Terms and Unequal Bargaining Power,* 41 MD. L. REV. 563 (1982).

Kennedy, *The Turn to Interpretation,* 58 S. CAL. L. REV. 251 (1985).

Kennedy & Michelman, *Are Property and Contract Efficient?* 8 HOFSTRA L. REV. 711 (1980).

KITTAY, E., & D. MEYERS (eds.), WOMEN AND MORAL THEORY (1987).

Koffler, *The Feminine Presence in Billy Budd,* 1 CARDOZO STUD. L. & LIT. 1 (1989).

Koffler, *Posner in Paradise,* 10 CARDOZO L. REV. 2099 (1989).

Kolk, *Reports of Childhood Incest and Current Behavior of Chronically Hospitalized Psychotic Women,* 144 AM. J. PSYCHIATRY 1474 (1987).

Komter, *Hidden Power in Marriage,* 3 GENDER & SOCIETY 187 (1989).

Kronman, *Precedent and Tradition,* 99 YALE L. J. 1029 (1990).

Landrine, *Depression and Stereotypes of Women: Preliminary Empirical Analyses of the Gender-Role Hypothesis,* 19 SEX ROLES 527 (1988).

LARRABEE, M. (ed.), AN ETHIC OF CARE: FEMINIST AND INTERDISCIPLINARY PERSPECTIVES (1993).

Larson, *"Women Understand So Little, They Call My Good Nature 'Deceit' ": A Feminist Rethinking of Seduction,* 93 COLUM. L. REV. 374 (1993).

LENTRICCHIA, F., AFTER THE NEW CRITICISM (1980).

LEVINSON S., & S. MAILLOUX (eds.), INTERPRETING LAW AND LITERATURE: A HERMENEUTIC READER (1988).

Littleton, *Reconstructing Sexual Equality,* 75 CAL. L. REV. 1279 (1987).

Littleton, *Women's Experience and the Problem of Transition: Perspectives on Male Battering of Women,* 1989 CHI. LEG. F. 23 (1989).

Lonsdorf, *The Role of Coercion in Affecting Women's Inferior Outcomes in Divorce: Implications for Researchers and Therapists,* in THE CONSEQUENCES OF DIVORCE: ECONOMIC AND CUSTODIAL IMPACT ON CHILDREN AND ADULTS (C. EVERETT, ed. 1991).

Luban, *Fish v. Fish or, Some Realism about Idealism,* 7 CARDOZO L. REV. 693 (1986).

LUBAN, D., LEGAL MODERNISM (1994).

LUKER, K., ABORTION AND THE POLITICS OF MOTHERHOOD (1984).

MACKINNON, C., SEXUAL HARASSMENT OF WORKING WOMEN (1979).

MacKinnon, *Pornography, Civil Rights, and Speech,* 20 HARV. C.R.-C.L. L. REV. 1 (1985).

MACKINNON, C., FEMINISM UNMODIFIED: DISCOURSES ON LIFE AND LAW (1987).

MACKINNON, C., TOWARD A FEMINIST THEORY OF THE STATE (1989).

MacKinnon, *From Practice to Theory, or What Is a White Woman Anyway?* 4 YALE J. L. & FEMINISM 13 (1991).

MacKinnon, *Reflections on Sex Equality Under Law,* 100 YALE L. J. 1281 (1991).

MACKINNON, C., ONLY WORDS (1993).

MacKinnon, Gilligan, & Menkel-Meadow, *Feminist Discourse, Moral Values, and the Law: A Conversation,* 34 BUFF. L. REV. 11 (1985).

Mahoney, *Legal Images of Battered Women: Redefining the Issue of Separation,* 90 MICH. L. REV. 1 (1991).

Mahoney, *Exit: Power and the Idea of Leaving in Love, Work, and the Confirmation Hearings,* 65 CAL. L. REV. 1283 (1992).

Mann, *The Universe and the Library: A Critique of James Boyd White as Writer and Reader,* 41 STAN. L. REV. 959 (1989).

MANSBRIDGE, J., BEYOND SELF-INTEREST (1990).

Mantese et al., *Medical and Legal Aspects of Rape and Resistance,* 12 J. LEG. MED. 59 (1991).

McClain, *The Poverty of Privacy,* 3 COLUM. J. GENDER & L. 119 (1992).

McClain, *Irresponsible Reproduction,* 47 HASTINGS L. REV. 339 (1996).

MELVILLE, H., THE SHORTER NOVELS OF HERMAN MELVILLE (1956 ed.).

MELVILLE, H., BILLY BUDD, SAILOR (AN INSIDER NARRATIVE) (1962 ed.).

Menkel-Meadow, *Portia in a Different Voice: Speculations on a Woman's Lawyering Process,* 1 BERK. WOMEN'S L. J. 39 (1985).

Menkel-Meadow, *Portia Redux: Another Look at Gender, Feminism, and Legal Ethics,* 2 VA. J. SOC. POL'Y & L. 75 (1994).

Menkel-Meadow, *What's Gender Got to Do with It? The Politics and Morality of an Ethic of Care,* 22 N.Y.U. REV. L. & SOCIAL CHANGE 265 (1996).

Michaels, *Against Formalism: Chickens and Rocks,* in INTERPRETING LAW AND LITERATURE: A HERMENEUTIC READER (S. Levinson & S. Mailloux, eds. 1988).

Milkman, *Women's History and the Sears Case,* 12 FEMINIST STUD. 375 (1986).

MILL, J.S., UTILITARIANISM, ON LIBERTY, AND CONSIDERATIONS ON REPRESENTATIVE GOVERNMENT (1972 ed.).

MILLER, J., TOWARD A NEW PSYCHOLOGY OF WOMEN (1976).

Minow, *Justice Engendered,* 101 HARV. L. REV. 10 (1987).

MINOW, M., MAKING ALL THE DIFFERENCE: INCLUSION, EXCLUSION AND AMERICAN LAW (1990).

Minow & Spelman, *In Context,* 63 S. CAL. L. REV. 1597 (1990).

MORRISON, T., BELOVED: A NOVEL (1987).

MUNRO, R., ed., FEMINIST JURISPRUDENCE, WOMEN AND THE LAW BIBLIOGRAPHY (1997).

Nedelsky, *Reconceiving Autonomy: Sources, Thoughts, and Possibilities,* 1 YALE J. L. & FEM. 7 (1989).

Nelson, *Thinking about Gender,* 7 HYPATIA 138 (1992).

NODDINGS, N., CARING: A FEMININE APPROACH TO ETHICS AND MORAL EDUCATION (1984).

NOONAN, J., PERSONS AND MASKS OF THE LAW (1976).

Note, *The Cultural Defense in the Criminal Law,* 99 HARV. L. REV. 1274 (1986).

Note, *To Have and to Hold: The Marital Rape Exemption and the Fourteenth Amendment,* 42 FLA. L. REV. 45 (1990).

NOZICK, R., ANARCHY, STATE AND UTOPIA (1974).

NUSSBAUM, M., THE FRAGILITY OF GOODNESS (1986).

NUSSBAUM, M., LOVE'S KNOWLEDGE: ESSAYS ON PHILOSOPHY AND LITERATURE (1990).

Nussbaum, *Equity and Mercy*, 22 PHIL. & PUB. AFF. 83 (1993).

Nussbaum, *Skepticism about Practical Reason*, 107 HARV. L. REV. 714 (1994).

O'CONNOR, F., THE COMPLETE SHORT STORIES (1971).

OKIN, S., JUSTICE, GENDER AND THE FAMILY (1989).

Okin, *Sexual Difference, Feminism, and the Law*, 16 LAW & SOC. INQUIRY 553 (1991).

OKIN, S., & J. MANSBRIDGE, FEMINISM (1994).

OLSEN, T., SILENCES (1978).

Olsen, *The Family and the Market: A Study of Ideology and Legal Reform*, 96 HARV. L. REV. 1497 (1983).

Olsen, *Feminism, Post-Modernism and Critical Legal Studies*. (unpublished manuscript).

Page, *The Ideology of Law and Literature*, 68 B. U. L. REV. 805 (1988).

PAGLIA, C., SEXUAL PERSONAE: ART AND DECADENCE FROM NEFERTITI TO EMILY DICKENSON (1990).

PAGLIA, C., VAMPS AND TRAMPS: NEW ESSAYS (1994).

Paltrow, *National Abortion Rights Action League Amicus Brief for Richard Thornburgh v. Am. College of Obstetricians and Gynecologists*, 9 WOMEN'S RTS. L. REPORTER 3 (1986).

Payton, *Releasing Excellence: Erasing Gender Zoning from the Legal Mind*, 18 IND. L. REV. 629 (1985).

Phelps, *The Story of the Law in Huckleberry Finn*, 39 MERCER L. REV. 889 (1988).

PIZZEY, E., SCREAM QUIETLY OR THE NEIGHBORS WILL HEAR (1977).

Polatnick, *Why Men Don't Rear Children: A Power Analysis*, in MOTHERING: ESSAYS IN FEMINIST THEORY (J. Trebilcot, ed. 1984).

POLINSKY, M., AN INTRODUCTION TO LAW AND ECONOMICS (1983).

POSNER, R., THE ECONOMICS OF JUSTICE (1981).

Posner, *The Ethical Significance of Free Choice: A Reply to Professor West*, 99 HARV. L. REV. 1431 (1986).

POSNER, R., LAW AND LITERATURE: A MISUNDERSTOOD RELATION (1988).

POSNER, R., AN ECONOMIC ANALYSIS OF LAW (1992).

POSNER, R., SEX AND REASON (1992).

Posner, *The Radical Feminist Critique of Sex and Reason*, 25 CONN. L. REV. 515 (1993).

PROSSER & KEETON, LAW OF TORTS 5th ed. (1984).

Radin, *Market Inalienability*, 100 HARV. L. REV. 1849 (1987).

Raeder, *"Gender Neutral" Sentencing Wreaks Havoc in the Lives of Women Offenders and Their Children*, 8 A.B.A. CRIM. JUST. 21, 23 (1993).

Raeder, *Gender and Sentencing: Single Moms, Battered Women, and Other*

Sex Based Anomalies in the Gender-Free World of the Sentencing Guidelines, 20 PEPP. L. REV. 905 (1993).

RAWLS, J., A THEORY OF JUSTICE (1971).

Regan, *Re-Writing Roe v. Wade,* 77 MICH. L. REV. 1569 (1979).

REGAN, M., FAMILY LAW AND THE PURSUIT OF INTIMACY (1993).

Regan, *Spouses and Strangers: Divorce Obligations and Property Rhetoric,* 82 GEO. L. J. 2303 (1994).

Renteln, *A Justification of the Cultural Defense as a Partial Excuse,* 2 S. CAL. REV. OF L. & WOMEN'S STUD. 488 (1993).

Resnik, *On the Bias: Feminist Reconsiderations of the Aspirations of Our Judges,* 61 S. CAL. L. REV. 1877 (1988).

Resnik, *Complex Feminist Conversations,* 1989 U. CHI. LEG. F. 1 (1989).

Resnik & Heilbrun, *Convergences: Law, Literature and Feminism,* 99 YALE L. J. 1913 (1990).

RICH, A., ON LIES, SECRETS, AND SILENCE: SELECTED PROSE, 1966–78 (1979).

Rich, *Compulsory Heterosexuality and Lesbian Existence,* 5 SIGNS 631 (1980).

Roberts, *Punishing Drug Addicts Who Have Babies: Women of Color, Equality, and the Right of Privacy,* 104 HARV. L. REV. 1419 (1991).

Roberts, *Is the Law Male? Rape, Violence, and Women's Autonomy,* 69 CHI.-KENT L. REV. 359 (1993).

Rose, *Bargaining and Gender,* 18 HARV. J. L. & PUB. POL. 547 (1995).

Rothschild, *Recognizing Another Face of Hate Crime: Rape as a Gender-Bias Crime,* 4 MD. J. CONT. LEG. ISS. 231 (1993).

Ruddick, *Maternal Thinking,* 6 FEM. STUD. 342 (1980).

RUDDICK, S., MATERNAL THINKING: TOWARDS A POLITICS OF PEACE (1989).

RUSH, F., BEST KEPT SECRET: SEXUAL ABUSE OF CHILDREN (1980).

RUSSELL, D., SEXUAL EXPLOITATION: RAPE, CHILD SEXUAL ABUSE, AND WORKPLACE HARASSMENT (1984).

RUSSELL, D., THE SECRET TRAUMA: INCEST IN THE LIVES OF GIRLS AND WOMEN (1986).

RUSSELL, D., RAPE IN MARRIAGE (1990).

SAGOFF, M., THE ECONOMY OF THE EARTH (1988).

SANDEL, M., LIBERALISM AND THE LIMITS OF JUSTICE (1982).

SANFORD, L., & M. DONOVAN, WOMEN AND SELF ESTEEM (1984).

Sanger, *Separating from Children,* 96 COLUM. L. REV. 375 (1976).

Schneider, *Equal Rights to Trial for Women: Sex Bias in the Law of Self-Defense,* 15 HARV. C.R.-C.L. L. REV. 623 (1986).

Schneider, *Describing and Changing: Women's Self-Defense Work and the Problem of Expert Testimony on Battery,* 14 WOMEN'S RTS. L. REPORTER 213 (1992).

Schulhofer, *The Feminist Challenge in Criminal Law,* 143 PA. L. REV. 2151 (1995).

Schultz, *Telling Stories About Women and Work: Judicial Interpretations of*

Sex Segregation in the Workplace in Title VII Cases Raising the Lack of Interest Argument, 103 HARV. L. REV. 1749 (1990).

Sherry, *Civic Virtue and the Feminine Voice in Constitutional Adjudication,* 72 VA. L. REV. 543 (1986).

Sherry, *The Gender of Judges,* 4 J. L. & INEQUALITY 159 (1986).

Sherry, *The Founders' Unwritten Constitution,* 54 CHI. L. REV. 1127 (1987).

Siegal, *The Rule of Love: Wife Beating as Prerogative and Privacy,* 105 YALE L. J. 2117 (1996).

SILVERSTEIN, S., THE GIVING TREE (1964).

Singer, *Divorce Reform and Gender Justice,* 67 N.C. L. REV. 1103 (1989).

Singer, *The Privatization of Family Law,* 1992 WISC. L. REV. 1443 (1992).

Singer, *Alimony and Efficiency: The Gendered Costs and Benefits of the Economic Justification for Alimony,* 82 GEO. L. J. 2423 (1994).

SMITH, J., & C. FERSTMAN, THE CASTRATION OF OEDIPUS: PSYCHO-ANALYSIS, POSTMODERNISM, AND FEMINISM (1996).

Strossen, *A Feminist Critique of the Feminist Critique of Pornography,* 79 VA. L. REV. 1099 (1993).

STROSSEN, N., DEFENDING PORNOGRAPHY (1995).

SUMMERS, R., INSTRUMENTALISM AND AMERICAN LEGAL THEORY (1982).

Sunstein, *Naked Preferences and the Constitution,* 84 COLUM. L. REV. 1689 (1984).

Sunstein, *Feminism and Legal Theory: Feminism Unmodified,* 101 HARV. L. REV. 826 (1988).

C. SUNSTEIN, DEMOCRACY AND THE PROBLEM OF FREE SPEECH (1993).

C. SUNSTEIN, THE PARTIAL CONSTITUTION (1993).

Sunstein, *Incompletely Theorized Arguments,* 108 HARV. L. REV. 1733 (1995).

TANNEN, D., TALKING FROM NINE TO FIVE: HOW WOMEN'S AND MEN'S CONVERSATIONAL STYLES AFFECT WHO GETS HEARD, WHO GETS CREDIT AND WHAT GETS DONE AT WORK (1994).

TENBROEK, J., EQUAL UNDER LAW (1965).

THOMAS, B., CROSS EXAMINATIONS OF LAW AND LITERATURE: COO-PER, HAWTHORNE, STOWE, AND MELVILLE (1987).

Thompson, *A Defense of Abortion,* 1 PHIL. & PUB. AFF. 47 (1971).

Thomson, *Abortion,* 20(3) BOSTON REVIEW (Summer 1995).

TRONTO, J., MORAL BOUNDARIES: A POLITICAL ARGUMENT FOR AN ETHIC OF CARE (1993).

TUSHNET, M., THE AMERICAN LAW OF SLAVERY (1981).

Tushnet, *The Degradation of Constitutional Discourse,* 81 GEO. L. J. 251 (1992).

TWAIN, M., THE ADVENTURES OF HUCKLEBERRY FINN (1988 ed.).

Unger, *The Critical Legal Studies Movement,* 96 HARV. L. REV. 561 (1983).

UNGER, R., FALSE NECESSITY (1987).

VONNEGUT, K., WELCOME TO THE MONKEY HOUSE (1986).

WALKER, L., THE BATTERED WOMAN (1979).

Wallace, *Reconstructing Judgment: Emotion and Moral Judgment,* 8 HY-PATIA 61 (1993).

Weil, *Virginia Woolf's To the Lighthouse: Toward an Integrated Jurisprudence,* 6 YALE J. L. & FEM. 1 (1994).

WEISBERG, R., THE FAILURE OF THE WORD: THE PROTAGONIST AS LAWYER IN MODERN FICTION (1984).

Weisberg, *The Law-Literature Enterprise,* 1 YALE J. L. & HUM. 1 (1988).

WEISBERG, R., POETHICS AND OTHER STRATEGIES OF LAW AND LITERATURE (1992).

R. WEISBERG, VICHY LAW AND THE HOLOCAUST IN FRANCE (1996)

Weiss & Melling, *The Legal Education of Twenty Women,* 40 STAN. L. REV. 1299 (1988).

Weitzman, *The Economics of Divorce: Social and Economic Consequences of Property, Alimony and Child Support Awards,* 28 U.C.L.A. L. REV. 1181 (1981).

WEITZMAN, L., THE DIVORCE REVOLUTION: THE UNEXPECTED SOCIAL AND ECONOMIC CONSEQUENCES FOR WOMEN AND CHILDREN IN AMERICA (1985).

West, *Submission, Choice, and Ethics: A Rejoinder to Judge Posner,* 99 HARV. L. REV. 1449 (1986).

West, *The Difference in Women's Hedonic Lives: A Phenomenological Critique of Feminist Legal Theory,* 3 WISC. WOMEN'S L. J. 81 (1987).

West, *Communities, Texts and Law: Reflections on the Law and Literature Movement,* 1 YALE J. L. & HUM. 129 (1988).

West, *Economic Man and Literary Woman: One Contrast,* 39 MERCER L. REV. 867 (1988).

West, *Jurisprudence and Gender,* 55 U. CHI. L. REV. 1 (1988).

West, *Equality Theory, Marital Rape, and the Promise of the Fourteenth Amendment,* 42 FLA. L. REV. 45 (1990).

West, *Foreword: Taking Freedom Seriously,* 104 HARV. L. REV. 43, 85–93 (1990).

West, *Toward an Abolitionist Interpretation of the Fourteenth Amendment,* 94 W. VA. L. REV. 111 (1991).

West, *Constitutional Skepticism,* 72 B.U. L. REV. 765 (1992).

West, *Legitimating the Illegitimate: A Comment on "Beyond Rape,"* 93 COLUM. L. REV. 1442 (1993).

WEST, R., NARRATIVE, AUTHORITY AND LAW (1993).

WEST, R., PROGRESSIVE CONSTITUTIONALISM: RECONSTRUCTING THE FOURTEENTH AMENDMENT (1994).

West, *The Harm of Consensual Sex,* 94 AM. PHIL. ASSOC. NEWSLETTER 52 (1995).

WHITE, J.B., WHEN WORDS LOSE THEIR MEANING (1984).

WHITE, J.B., HERACLES' BOW: ESSAYS ON THE RHETORIC AND POETICS OF THE LAW (1985).

WHITE, J.B., THE LEGAL IMAGINATION: STUDIES IN THE NATURE OF LEGAL THOUGHT AND EXPRESSION (1985).

White, *Is Cultural Criticism Possible?* 84 MICH. L. REV. 1373 (1986).

White, *Economics and Law: Two Cultures in Tension,* 54 TENN. L. REV. 161 (1987).

White, *Law and Literature: "No Manifesto,"* 39 MERCER L. REV. 739 (1988).

WHITE, J.B., JUSTICE AS TRANSLATION: AN ESSAY IN CULTURAL AND LEGAL CRITICISM (1990).

WHITE, J.B., ACTS OF HOPE: CREATING AUTHORITY IN LITERATURE, LAW AND POLITICS (1994).

White, *The Rhythms of Hope and Disappointment in the Language of Judging,* 70 ST. JOHN'S L. REV. 101 (1996).

Wilder, Marcy. *The Rule of Law, the Rise of Violence and the Role of Morality: Reframing America's Abortion Debate* (unpublished manuscript).

Williams, *Equality's Riddle: Pregnancy and the Equal Treatment/Special Treatment Debate,* 13 REV. L. & SOC. CHANGE 325 (1984).

Williams, *On Being the Object of Property,* 14 SIGNS 5 (1988).

Williams, *Deconstructing Gender,* 87 MICH. L. REV. 797 (1989).

WILLIAMS, P., THE ALCHEMY OF RACE AND RIGHTS: DIARY OF A LAW PROFESSOR (1991).

Williams, *Gender Wars: Selfless Women in the Republic of Choice,* 66 N.Y.U. L. REV. 1559 (1991).

WILLIAMS, C., BLACK TEENAGE MOTHERS: PREGNANCY AND CHILD REARING FROM THEIR PERSPECTIVE (1991).

Woodhouse, *Sex, Lies and Dissipation: The Discourses of Fault in a No-Fault Era,* 82 GEO. L. J. 2525 (1994).

Yudof, *Tea at the Palaz of Noon: The Human Voice in Legal Rules,* 66 TEXAS L. REV. 589 (1988).

Index

Abandonment
  of children, 162–63
  women's fear of, 119, 123
Abortion
  funding for, 164
  morality of, 297–98
  as separation, 127–28
Abortion rights. *See also* Reproductive
    freedom
  arguments for, 297–98, 306
  equality and, 66–68, 90, 297
  ethic of care and, 70–71
  gender-specific impact of, 141–42
  negative social consequences of, 66–67
  nurturance and, 72–74, 90–91
  as positive liberty, 73–74
Action(s)
  desire and, 103. *See also* Hedonic con-
    nections
  morality and, 106
  versus speech, in literature, 197–99
Adarand Constructors Inc v. *Pena,* 85
Adoption, legal inadequacies in treating,
    149, 307
Aeschylus, 193–94
Aesthetic integrity, justice and, 22, 188
Affirmative action jurisprudence, failures
    of, 85–87
African Americans. *See* Black women
Aliens (movie), 31–32
Allen, Anita, 194
"All the King's Horses" (Vonnegut), 50–51
Alternative Dispute Resolution move-
    ment, 78

Altruism. *See also* Giving self; Selfless-
    ness
  assumptions about, 111–13
  choice and, 114, 120–21
  community, 113, 123
  cultural enforcement of, 136–37
  fear and, 82–83, 114, 116–20, 122–23
  harms of, 113–27, 139, 154
  healthy, 122
  ideal environment for, 123
  individual, 105
  intimate, 109–27
  as moral voice, 110, 113
  public, 123–25
  sexual, 114–17
  women and, 109–27
Amendment(s)
  first, 139, 157–58
  fourteenth, 27, 74
Amish, shunning practice of, 76–77
Angel, Marina, 246–49, 258
Anglo-American law, historic gender-bias
    of, 97–98
Anti-abortion laws, harms of, 141
Anti-discrimination law, and legitimation
    of harms, 153–55
Anti-essentialism, postmodernism and,
    292
Anti-Semitism, French constitutional law-
    yers and, 46–47
Art, law as, 181–83, 188
Ashe, Marie, 215
Attribute(s), as political outcome, 11–
    12

Autonomous individual. *See also* Individualism
  altruism in, 105
  versus giving self, 121
  hedonic connections and, 103
  inability to develop, 123–24
  liberal legalism and, 4–5
  pregnancy undermining, 105–7
  sexual threats to, 101, 104–5

Baier, Annette, 34
Balance. *See* Scale of balance image
Ball, Milner, 215
Banks, Taunya, 313
Bartleby the Scrivener (Melville), 219–42, 256–58
Bass, Ellen, 266, 287–88
Battered spouse syndrome
  feminist view of, 301
  and self-defense law, 212, 301
Belenky, M., 267
Belief(s)
  and legitimation of harms, 219
  in patriarchal culture, 137–38
Beloved (Morrison), 197–98
Bentham, Jeremy, 167, 300
Billy Budd, Sailor (Melville), 32–33, 43–44, 192, 294
  comparison with *Bartleby,* 238, 240–41
Biological differences between sexes, 13–14
  in connection to fetus, 127
  in connection to newborn, 117–18
  in separation, 127, 131
Birth, as separation, 127, 131
Birth control right, gender-specific impact of, 141
Blackmun, Justice, 48
Black women
  narrative voice of, 213
  subordination of, 12, 14–16
Blindfolded judge image, 26, 29–30
  implications of, 30
  limitations of, 50, 54, 56
Bloom, A., 196
Body(ies), women's
  alienation from, 137
  destruction of security of, 102, 109
  invasion of, 100–105
  men's need of, 133–35

Bolt, Robert, 26
Bowman, Cynthia, 156
Boy(s). *See also* Men
  connection to mothers, 129, 131
  maturation and self-concept of, 146–47
Breast-feeding
  constraints of, 117–18
  natural inequality in, 277
  separation following, 129
Brontë, Charlotte, 194
Brothers Karamazov, The (Dostoyevsky), 192
Brown v. *Board of Education,* 93
Brownmiller, Susan, 14
Byron, Father William J., 25–26

Camus, Albert, 192
Cardozo, Judge, 47
Care. *See also* Ethic of care
  common perception of, 23
  as goal of judging, 24–25
  hierarchical relationships of, 277–78
  images of, 30–33
  and justice
    interdependence of, 24, 38–88
    opposition of, 9, 23, 35–36
    philosophical study of, 295
    synthesis of, 88–93
  justice without, 39–74
  without justice, 74–88
  and morality, 278–80
Caregiving
  as moral work, 7, 23
  implications of, 33–34
  objections to, 10–12
  in relational feminists' view, 33–37
Caring (Noddings), 35
Carrol, Hattie, 28
Carter, Stephen, 208–10
Case law
  exemplars of injustice in, 46–47
  exemplars of justice in, 93
  impartiality without relationship in, 52–55, 59–60
  nurturance without consistency in, 75–76
  particularity without impartiality in, 85
Causation, limiting doctrine of, 29

Particularity. *See also* Relationship(s)
impartiality without, 50–61
without impartiality, 84–88
Passivity, female, 107
cultural enforcement of, 133–34, 136–
37
Paternalism, displacement by laissez-faire
capitalism, 229, 239
Paternity, knowledge of, 135
Patriarchy
constitutional basis of, 157–61
definition of, 132
discourse in, 262–63, 265
feminist approaches to, 261–64
free speech and, 157–58, 160, 321
harms done by, 132–38
illegal nature of, 263
and law, 132–33, 138–39, 263–64
legal protection of, 164
and natural world, destruction of, 279–
80
Nietzschean analysis of, 134
postmodern social theory and, 259
power in, 261–64, 285
and self
deconstruction of, 285–86, 288–89
liberal, 282–83
silence as product of, 265, 275
social enforcement of, 132–33
verbosity of, 193
Payton, Sallyanne, 270
Peacock v. *Maryland,* 78
Peevyhouse v. *Garland Coal and Mining
Co.,* 53–54
Personal integrity. *See* Integrity
Persons and Masks of the Law (Noonan),
47
Philosophy
caregiving and, 34
duty versus compassion in, 41–43
Plain meaning, in legal interpretation, 202
Pleasure
female sacrifice of, 114–16
in hedonic connections, 103
Plessey v. *Ferguson,* 75
Plumb-line test
failure to meet, 27–28
image of, 26
implications of, 30
limitations of, 49

Political justice
impact on legal justice, 62
Rawlsian theory of, 62–64
Politics
caregiving and, 34
and connections to others, 3
and gender-specific harms, 164–65
household labor and, 112
law as product of, 187, 260, 309
Pollution, and cost-benefit analysis, 169–
70
Pornography
and harms to women, 155–56
message of, 134
proposed ordinances against, 156–57
radical feminist movement against, 310
Posner, Richard, 167
Postmodern feminism, 11–12. *See also*
Feminism/feminist jurisprudence
critique of, 16–17
versus relational feminism, 36–37, 295
Postmodern legalism, 5–6
Postmodern social theory, 259–92
Post-structuralism, in legal scholarship,
201–2
Power
democratization of, 276–77
as discourse, 263, 265
law as, 186–87, 260, 263–64. *See also*
Legal power
liberal self and, 283
and morality, 276–77, 280
patriarchal, 261–64, 285
postmodern idea of, 259–64, 276–77,
321
productivity of, 260, 265
verbal forms of, 192–93
as violence, 261–64
Precedential logic, limitations of, 61–62
Preference(s)
individual freedom and, 226–27
satisfaction of, and harm minimization,
166–70
Pregnancy
harms of, 105–7, 141–42
involuntary nurturance in, 105–7
and self, 108
unwanted, harms of, 105–7, 141
Principle, versus context, in jurisprudence, 205